The industrial archaeology of North-west England

Overleaf The North West: relief, rivers and county boundaries

Owen Ashmore

The
industrial
archaeology
of
North-west
England

MANCHESTER UNIVERSITY PRESS

Contents

Copyright © Owen Ashmore 1982

Published by
MANCHESTER UNIVERSITY PRESS
Oxford Road, Manchester M13 9PL

British Library cataloguing in publication data

Ashmore, Owen
    The industrial archaeology of
    North-west England.
    1. Industrial archaeology – England,
    Northern I. Title
    609.427   T26.G7

    ISBN 0 7190 0820 4

Typeset by
Bookworm Typesetting, Manchester

Printed in Great Britain
by Unwin Brothers Limited,
The Gresham Press, Old Woking

Preface

This survey of sites of industrial archaeological interest in north-west England is largely the direct result of fieldwork carried out in 1978–79, though based on work over a much longer period of time. Each site recorded in the four counties has been personally visited by the author. Inevitably, however, demolition and change are constantly taking place, and a proportion of the sites recorded will have been affected by the time the book is published. The author would always be glad to hear details of changes from anyone who may have particular knowledge of individual sites or local areas.

The sites have been selected with a number of considerations in mind: firstly, to illustrate the wide range and different types of industrial sites of historical interest within the region, drawing attention to particularly good examples of their kind; secondly, to give a good geographical distribution so as to bring out the characteristic features of different parts of the region; thirdly, to convey the particular character of the sites and surviving buildings of individual towns or villages, e.g. the cotton-spinning mills of Oldham, the silk mills and weavers' garrets in Congleton and Macclesfield, the docks and warehouses of Liverpool and Birkenhead, the weaving sheds of Burnley, Nelson and Colne; fourthly, to illustrate the historical development in time of different types of buildings or structure, e.g. by recording cotton mills of different periods in Stockport or Preston.

It should be possible for the reader to use the book as a guide to the sites of particular interest over the full range of the subject, as a guide to buildings or works of a particular kind, e.g. canal structures, corn mills, railway stations, or as a guide to individual places or local areas, both in terms of the main surviving sites and of the effects of industrial development on the landscape. Some sites may be included for historical rather than strictly archaeological reasons. For example, the ICI chemical works at Winnington consists mainly of recent buildings but it is so important in the industrial history of the region that it is an automatic choice for inclusion.

Acknowledgements

As indicated in the preface, this book is the result of twenty years' interest in a growing field of study and owes much to the help of a great many individuals. A special word of mention is due to Mr. W. J. Smith, who drew the maps and line drawings and whose local knowledge of vernacular architecture and domestic workshops have been of the greatest assistance. I would also like to pay tribute to the help and advice received over a considerable period of time from Professor W. H. Chaloner, Dr Richard Hills, Dr. J. D. Marshall, Mr J. Harold Norris, Mr. Frank Mullineux, Dr W. N. Slatcher and Dr J. H. Smith.

Much is also owed to public libraries, record offices and museums throughout the region. Particular mention should be made of the North Western Museum of Science and Industry in Manchester, but all the museums referred to in the text under the appropriate places have contributed to the final result. A great deal has also come from contacts over the years with local historical and archaeological societies and with regional societies, including the Lancashire and Cheshire Antiquarian Society, the Manchester Region Industrial Archaeological Society and the North Western Society for Industrial Archaeology and Industry. As a university extra-mural tutor of long standing, I have inevitably heard much from classes and individual members in centres including Ashton under Lyne, Blackburn, Macclesfield, Marple, Oldham, Saddleworth and Wigan.

Industrial firms and public bodies have invariably been helpful in terms of access to sites and buildings, as well as to records and photographic material. I would like in particular to thank the staff of: Abbey Corn Mills, Whalley; Ashton Bros & Co. Ltd, Hyde; Associated British Hat Manufacturers Ltd, Stockport; W. & A. Bradley Ltd, Crowton; Bridgewater Transport Services Ltd; British Rail; British Salt Ltd, Middlewich; British Waterways Board, Runcorn; Carrington Vyella Ltd; Courtaulds Ltd; Crossley-Premier Engines Ltd, Manchester; Ferranti Ltd, Hollinwood; Fodens Ltd, Sandbach; GEC Power Engineering Ltd, Trafford Park; Greater Manchester Transport; Green Bros (Whalley) Ltd, Billington; R. Greg & Co. Ltd, Stockport; E. & H. Hibbert Ltd, Park Bridge; Joshua Hoyle (Bacup) Ltd; Hydraulic Engineering Co. Ltd, Chester; Imperial Chemical Industries Ltd, Organics Division, Blackley, and Mond Division, Winnington; Ingram Thompson & Sons Ltd, Lion Salt Works, Marston; Kay-Metzeler Ltd, Marple; Lappet Manufacturing Co. Ltd and John Lean & Son Ltd, Calder Vale; Mather & Platt Ltd, Newton Heath; Melland & Coward Ltd, Stockport; Mersey Docks & Harbour Co. Ltd; Mirlees Blackstone Ltd, Hazel Grove; John Myers & Co. Ltd, Stockport; National Coal Board; National Trust; William Nelstrop & Co. Ltd, Stockport; North Western Electricity Board; North West Water Authority; J. Nutter & Sons Ltd, Barnoldswick; Pilkington Bros Ltd, St Helens; Platt Saco Lowell Ltd; Port of Manchester; Queen Street Manufacturing Co. Ltd, Briercliffe; Ribblesdale Cement Ltd, Clitheroe; Rochdale Canal Co., Manchester; Rylands-Whitecross Ltd, Warrington; Ernest Scragg & Co. Ltd, Macclesfield; Sutcliffe & Clarkson Ltd, Burnley; Sykes & Co. Ltd, Stockport; TBA Industrial Products Ltd, Rochdale; Tootal Ltd.

Finally I would like to thank my wife, Sheila, for her work in typing the manuscript and helping with proof reading and correction, as well as for her encouragement throughout the period of fieldwork and writing.

Introduction

THE REGION

The area covered comprises the old counties of Cheshire and Lancashire except Furness and Cartmel, the new counties of Cheshire, Lancashire, Greater Manchester and Merseyside. The total population is 6½ million, with the main concentrations in the conurbations of Merseyside and Greater Manchester and in the old north-east Lancashire. The metropolitan boroughs of the Greater Manchester County are to a large extent based on the nineteenth-century industrial towns – Bolton, Bury, Oldham, Rochdale, Salford, Stockport, Wigan and Manchester itself. It is one of the classic areas of industrial growth in the eighteenth and nineteenth centuries, particularly in textiles and engineering, and has one of the greatest concentrations of industrial monuments in the British Isles.

Geographically the area is bounded by the Lake District hills in the north, the Pennines in the east, and the Irish Sea in the west. The contrast of eastern hills and western plain has been significant. The gritstone moors of the Pennines, with a high rainfall and relatively difficult farming conditions, provided ideal conditions for the early growth of an indigenous textile industry based on the combination of farming and domestic manufacture. The plentiful streams running down from the moors provided both water power for the early mills and pure processing water for textile finishing and paper-making. The gritstone rocks provided the stone out of which many of the industrial towns were built. The western plain, including the Fylde, the area between Southport and Liverpool and a large part of west and central Cheshire, has by contrast been an area of agricultural production, with Cheshire particularly famous for its dairy industry and its cheeses. North of the Mersey much of the plain was occupied by mosses and meres which were drained only in the nineteenth century, producing the characteristic landscape of rectangular fields, dykes, and roads following the dykes. The plain extends east into the Manchester area, providing routes through to the Midlands and making Manchester an important centre of communications from the time of the Roman occupation.

Coal and salt have been major factors in industrial growth. The coalfield includes within its boundaries most of the industrial towns of east Lancashire as well as the 'new' glass and chemical towns of Widnes and St Helens. When steam began to take over as the main source of power for the local industries the coal was readily available near by. Cheshire salt, exploited from at least Roman times for food purposes, became in the nineteenth century an important raw material for the chemical and indirectly for the soap and glass industries. The links between the saltfield, the river Mersey, Liverpool and the south-west Lancashire coalfield were the main factor in the industrialisation of that part of the region.

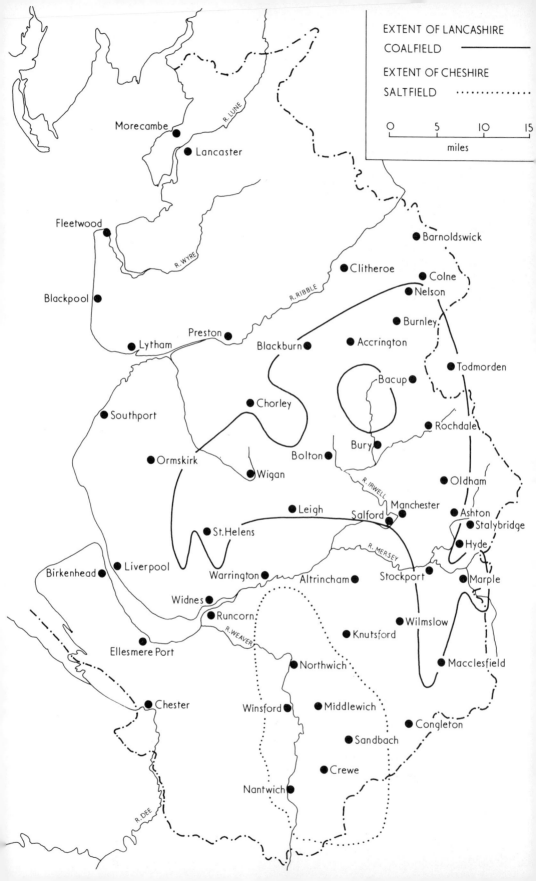

EXTENT OF LANCASHIRE
COALFIELD ———

EXTENT OF CHESHIRE
SALTFIELD ·········

0   5   10   15
miles

Morecambe
Lancaster
R. LUNE

Fleetwood
R. WYRE

Barnoldswick
Clitheroe
Colne
Nelson
Burnley
R. RIBBLE
Blackpool
Lytham
Preston
Blackburn
Accrington
Todmorden
Bacup

Southport
Chorley
Rochdale

Ormskirk
Bury
Bolton
Wigan
Oldham
R. IRWELL

Leigh
Manchester
Salford
Ashton
Stalybridge
Hyde
St.Helens
R. MERSEY

Liverpool
Birkenhead
Warrington
Altrincham
Stockport
Marple

Widnes
Runcorn
R. WEAVER
Wilmslow
Knutsford

Ellesmere Port
Macclesfield

Chester
Northwich

Winsford
Middlewich
Congleton

Sandbach

Crewe

Nantwich

R. DEE

The outlet to the Irish Sea and the estuaries of the main rivers – Dee, Mersey, Wyre and Lune – stimulated the growth of overseas trade at an early period, certainly by the sixteenth century. The overseas trade in turn stimulated much of the industrial development, for example in textiles, and in the eighteenth century both Lancaster and Liverpool extended their commercial activities across the Atlantic. In the nineteenth century new ports developed and both the canals and the railways helped to link the ports more effectively with the areas of industrial production.

TEXTILES

The origins of the North West's major historical industry go back at least to the early thirteenth century, when an indigenous woollen industry was developing in the Pennine area. By the time of Queen Elizabeth I there were sizable woollen and linen industries, based on domestic production of yarn and cloth, with finishing processes such as fulling, dyeing and shearing in the hands of specialised workers and sometimes carried out on the premises of the merchants. These merchants – clothiers and linen drapers – who sold the finished cloth operated from the market towns, with the bigger dealers in Manchester and Salford exporting cloth, mainly through London, to many parts of Europe.

In the seventeenth century, the new raw material, cotton, was introduced from the eastern Mediterranean and used in the production of mixed cloths, often with linen warp and cotton weft, commonly known as fustians. Fustian manufacture predominated particularly around Manchester and Oldham and to the north in Bolton and Blackburn. The emphasis was on woollens to the east around Rochdale, Rossendale and Burnley, and on linens in west Lancashire and the Fylde. At this stage the use of water power was confined to the fulling of woollen cloth. The great revolution in textiles began in the eighteenth century, with the first developments in silk, when the Lombe brothers erected a water-powered factory on the river Derwent in Derby using Italian-style throwing machines to make silk yarn. Following the expiry of their patent in 1732, silk-throwing mills were built in Stockport, Macclesfield and Congleton. In the longer term Stockport went over to cotton but Macclesfield and Congleton continued as important centres of silk production.

From about 1750 John Kay's flying shuttle was being adopted and increased productivity on the weaving side of the textile industry, thus further stimulating the attempts to mechanise spinning. James Hargreaves's spinning jenny, first used about 1764, was a hand-operated machine spinning several threads at once (eventually up to 120) and was widely used in small workshops in the cotton industry until the 1820s, considerably later in woollens. The big step towards factory production came with the patenting of Arkwright's water frame in 1769 and the subsequent development of Samuel Crompton's mule, to which water power was applied from about 1790. Water-powered cotton-spinning mills were built along the banks of the streams in east Lancashire and east Cheshire wherever a suitable fall was available, sometimes in urban sites such as Stockport, sometimes in remote moorland valleys. Mechanisation was slower in woollens, but water-powered scribbling and carding mills for preparing the raw material for spinning were being built in Saddleworth, the Rochdale area and Rossendale before 1800. At the same time there was a trend towards the introduction of cotton-spinning into the traditional wool-

Facing The North West: main towns, coalfield and saltfield

len areas, and Rossendale and Burnley had both become predominantly cotton centres by 1840. The siting of the mills to take advantage of water power meant that factory owners had to provide housing and social institutions, and there are a number of good surviving examples of industrial communities of the period.

The revolution in spinning was not accompanied by a parallel revolution in weaving, which remained a hand-loom and, to a large extent, a domestic process, leading to a period of boom on this side of the industry and to the construction and conversion of many domestic workshops of varying styles and arrangements. Characteristic of the Pennine woollen area are the three-storey stone-built structures with top-floor workshops and long, mullioned windows: there are some fine examples in Saddleworth, some on the scale of weaving communities. Three storeys tend also to be the general rule for the silk-weaving workshops of Macclesfield and Congleton. In cotton, by contrast, it is common to find workshops at ground-floor or basement level, with evidence of former usage now provided by double or triple windows, maybe blocked.

The change to power-loom weaving in cotton came in the 1820s, starting in the south and south-east around Manchester, Stockport, Ashton, Hyde and Stalybridge, and spreading rather later to north-east Lancashire. Although Edmund Cartwright patented his first power looms in 1785–86 it was some thirty years before they had been improved to a point where they were really satisfactory and productive enough to become an economic alternative to putting out to hand-loom weavers. Gradually more and more owners of spinning mills installed power looms in the lower floors, and later built the single-storey weaving sheds with north-light roofs which are so characteristic of this side of

production. The change to the power loom came later in woollens than in cotton, later still in silk. The period of change-over to power-loom weaving also saw the change-over from water power to steam power. At first beam engines were used to pump water to the top of a wheel, but from the 1780s rotative engines came into use to drive machinery direct, though often as a supplement to water power. As the engines became more powerful, more reliable and smoother-running many mills were built for the use of steam power from the start and by 1840 steam engines outnumbered water wheels in the industry by three to two. This in turn affected location: mills were built on the coalfield in the growing cotton towns and, where available, along the banks of the canals which provided not only transport but water for the boilers.

The peak of the cotton industry came just before the first world war, when 85 per cent of the cloth produced in Lancashire was exported, following the opening up of markets in the Far East. The characteristic buildings of the period are the large spinning mills of south-east Lancashire, with 100,000 spindles or more, steel and concrete structures allowing a much larger window area, with often elaborate decoration and ornamental water towers, driven by large, powerful horizontal and vertical steam engines in separate engine houses with rope drive through a rope race to the different floors. As south-east Lancashire specialised more in spinning, north-east Lancashire specialised in weaving, creating the typical landcape of Burnley, Nelson, Colne or Darwen, with large single-storey weaving sheds, two or three-storey preparation blocks, separate engine houses, boilers and chimneys.

A late survivor of domestic production into this period was fustian or velvet cutting, where the cloth was woven with loops, which were then cut through manually to give a vertical pile, using a sharp knife with long handle and rest, with the cloth stretched tightly over a table. The process was carried out in domestic workshops or in specially built workshops in the rural or semi-rural area on both sides of the Mersey between Manchester and Warrington, for example in Cadishead, Culceth, Lymm, Knutsford, Wilmslow, Poynton.

The finishing end of the textile industry went through two revolutions – mechanical and chemical. The introduction of chlorine bleaching at the end of the eighteenth century led to a change from open-air bleaching grounds to the bleachworks with its internal bleachcroft and bleaching tanks. Sulphuric acid and, later, chemically made alkalis replaced natural materials such as buttermilk or alkalis made from plant ashes. Waterwheels and steam engines were used to drive mangles, washing machines, calenders and, later, drying and finishing machines.

Lancashire played a major role in the development of calico printing, with early experiments in the use of wooden hand blocks, on which the pattern was cut, in the 1760s at Mosney Works in Walton le Dale, at Bamber Bridge, and by Robert Peel at Brookside, Oswaldtwistle. The printing machine with the pattern engraved on copper rollers was introduced in the 1780s and gradually superseded hand-block methods during the first half of the nineteenth century. Printworks were built in a number of areas where suitable processing water was available – in north-east Lancashire, in the valleys of the Irwell, Irk and Medlock, along the tributaries of the Mersey – the Goyt, Tame and Etherow – south-east of Manchester. On the colour and dyeing side in the later nineteenth century the natural dyes were gradually replaced by artificial dyestuffs made from aniline pro-

ducts, arising from the distillation of coal tar. Firms in the Manchester area played a pioneering role – the Clayton Aniline Co., for example, and Levinstein's at Blackley, the forerunners of the present ICI Dyestuffs Division.

METALS

Iron ore was mined and smelted in bloomeries with charcoal in the northern part of the region, particularly in Furness, now part of Cumbria, from the thirteenth century, with a leading role played by the monks of Furness Abbey. There is evidence at the same period of bloomeries and forges at work in the forest areas of Bleasdale, Trawden, Rossendale and Tottington. Following the introduction of the blast furnace with water-powered bellows, the peak of the charcoal iron industry came in the late seventeenth and eighteenth centuries, when a number of new furnaces and forges were started in north Lancashire, as well as farther south in the Wigan area, and in Cheshire. Burdett's map of Cheshire in 1777 shows seven forges, two furnaces, and three slitting mills, including the one of which there are still remains at Lymm, supplying local nailmakers. The change-over to coke smelting in the late eighteenth century led to a new phase of the industry in the north, and the introduction of the Bessemer process for making steel from the late 1850s also led to the development of a number of new works, including the Kirklees works of the Wigan Coal & Iron Co. and the Carnforth ironworks.

Copper was mined in both the northern and southern parts of the region from at least the late seventeenth century. There are still traces of the copper workings on Warton Crag, north of Lancaster. Mining has taken place on two of the sandstone hills of Cheshire: Alderley Edge, where there may have been activity in Roman times and where the main peaks of production came in the mid-eighteenth and mid-nineteenth centuries, and Bickerton Hill. Alderley Edge copper was used in processing works in Macclesfield and Bosley. The copper works built at Warrington and St Helens in the eighteenth century were supplied with ore mainly from Parys Mountain on Anglesey. Lead mining has taken place in Rossendale and in Cliviger, east of Burnley, and there are still considerable traces of the Anglezarke mines, east of Chorley, which were at their most active in the late eighteenth century. Lead for the nineteenth-century works with its shot tower at Chester came originally from the Flintshire mines.

The coalfield area around Wigan, Warrington and Liverpool was a major centre of small metal trades. Wigan itself was well known for pewter-making, brassfounding and bell-making in the seventeenth century, supplying tableware and utensils to the households of the region. Inventories of the period indicate some tradesmen of substantial means, and marketing over quite a wide area. Nail-making was a small workshop industry in the seventeenth, eighteenth and early nineteenth centuries in Atherton, Tyldesley, Westhoughton, Hindley, Abram, Orrell and Winstanley, with documentary evidence of forges with water-powered bellows or hammers. Warrington was a major centre of trade in bar iron and there were a number of slitting mills in the vicinity. To the west, the manufacture of files and tools, often on a putting-put basis, was a major occupation: there is the well known business conducted in the late eighteenth century by Peter Stubs in Warrington itself. Files were cut by hand on steel blanks with chisels in numerous small workshops.

Perhaps the most interesting of all these small-workshop trades is the manufacture of watch parts and tools, centred particularly in Prescot from the late seventeenth century. By the early nineteenth the trade was highly specialised, with separate makers of watch files, broaches for reaming out holes in watch parts, springs, balances, wheels, pinions, verges, movements, hands, cases. In the later nineteenth century treadle-operated machine tools were introduced into some of the workshops. The industry supplied watchmakers in London and, in the nineteenth century, overseas, and only declined with the growth of Swiss and American competition. Quite a number of workshop buildings survive in Prescot.

In the same area, and associated with other metal trades, was the craft of wire drawing. The modern industry, concentrated in Warrington, dates from the late eighteenth century. The method was to draw rolled iron rod through steel 'wortle plates' with a series of holes of a size and cross-section appropriate to particular types of wire. It has now been replaced by continuous drawing through tungsten carbide dies.

ENGINEERING

In the early Victorian period the Manchester region became one of the greatest engineering centres in the world. With the development of production in cast and wrought iron and with the new demand for machinery, most of the growing towns in the area had iron foundries and forges making a wide variety of products, including castings for machine parts, steam engines, cylinders, boilers, waterwheels, shafting and gear wheels for mill drives, and constructional ironwork for bridges and for factory buildings.

The growing textile industry created its own engineering trade, supplying the new machines and machine parts, including rollers for drawing, roving and spinning frames. Specialised manufacturers, including Hannah Lees & Sons at Park Bridge in Ashton under Lyne (roller manufacturers), Platt Bros and Asa Lees & Co. in Oldham, Dobson & Barlow in Bolton (mule makers), started in the late eighteenth century, supplying the new spinning factories, and evenutally expanded into major concerns often with a world-wide market in the later nineteenth century. Other firms specialised in making power looms or finishing machinery. Mather & Platt of Salford Iron Works were major suppliers of bleaching, dyeing and calico-printing equipment from the 1830s. Specialisation was often affected by the local industrial pattern: Walker Bros and the Worsley Mesnes Ironworks in Wigan supplied coal-mining equipment, Robert Daglish of St Helens Foundry glass-making machinery. In Bury there were several firms producing paper-making machinery in the later nineteenth century. The machine age in turn created a demand for machine tools, machines to make machines, to carry out the processes of turning, planing, shaping, drilling and slotting which earlier had to be done by hand. Sharp Roberts & Co. in Manchester were producing a variety of machine tools from 1816 and played an important part in the development of the self-acting spinning mule. One of the greatest pioneers was James Nasmyth, whose works at Patricroft, near Eccles, was one of the first 'mass-production' style engineering shops in the world, making a wide variety of machine tools for stock, with printed catalogues, and using semi-skilled labour. Joseph Whitworth, who had a machine-tool works in Chorlton Street, Manchester, from 1833 and later moved to Openshaw, was a pioneer in accurate measurement and in the development of standardisation, particularly of screw threads.

In the early railway days locomotives were often supplied by general engineering firms in the area, but as the system expanded specialised works were started, like the Vulcan Works at Newton le Willows, opened in 1830, or Beyer Peacock & Co. at Gorton, Manchester, started in 1854. Both firms exported locomotives to all parts of the world in the later nineteenth century. The railway companies themselves also went into locomotive and rolling stock production: there were three major company works – at Crewe, Earlestown and Horwich.

The later nineteenth century saw both more specialisation and the introduction of new types of engineering. Crossley Bros of Openshaw, Manchester, who started business in 1867, became pioneers in Britain of the internal combustion gas engine, based on the Otto cycle, and later went into the manufacture of diesel engines. The National Gas Engine Co. in Ashton under Lyne produced a different type of engine and there was also a 'Stockport gas engine' made by a firm in Reddish. Foden's at Sandbach in Cheshire progressed from the making of steam traction engines and portable engines to steam lorries and eventually to diesel lorries. The first Ford motor-car works in Britain was started in Trafford Park in 1911–12, and there were a number of other, lesser-known, car manufacturers in the area. Leyland Motors developed from a firm making steam vans and steam lorries from 1897. From about 1880 electrical engineering was introduced. Mather & Platt diversified from the textile-finishing business into the production of dynamos at their new Newton Heath works. Ferranti's were great pioneers in the supply of electric-power equipment, with a works at Hollinwood, Oldham. In the same field the American firm of George Westinghouse & Co. moved into the new industrial estate at Trafford Park, where Glover's cable works was also located. Cable works were also started in Prescot and Helsby. On the side of battery and accumulator production, the Chloride company started at the

Clifton Junction Works in the Irwell valley in 1893. In another field altogether, that of hydraulic power supply, very important in warehouses, docks and harbours, the Hydraulic Engineering Co. of Chester, developed from a local iron foundry, became major suppliers from about 1870.

In more recent years the older, heavy engineering, firms have declined and even machine-tool production has dwindled to a very small-scale contribution. New lines have developed, particularly in electronics, chemical engineering, nuclear-power engineering and computer manufacture, in line with the constant process of adaptation to world markets and general economic change.

COAL MINING

The Lancashire coalfield has been a decisive factor in the whole industrial expansion of the region. It covers some 500 square miles and includes the cotton area of east Lancashire, the manufacturing area around Wigan and the south-western industrial area around St Helens and Prescot, where coal was the basis for the location of new industries – copper, glass, soap and chemicals. The seams occur at three levels and the lower measures go down to over 3,500 ft (1,060 m) so that there were some of the deepest mines in Britain at the end of the nineteenth century. There is a southern extension of the field south of Manchester with the important collieries at Poynton in Cheshire.

Mining goes back to the Middle Ages and there is plenty of evidence in the sixteenth and seventeenth centuries of activity in all parts of the coalfield, with landowners often playing a major role in the exploitation of the resources, for example the Bradshaighs at Haigh, near Wigan, where the workings were on a sufficient scale to warrant the construction of a major drainage sough, the Bankes in Billinge and Winstanley, the

Warrens in Poynton. Pits were relatively shallow, and were worked along galleries as far as ventilation permitted before a new pit was sunk, hence the large number of pit sites and spoil heaps some of which still survive.

The industrial demands of the eighteenth century led to growth on a much larger scale, assisted by the development first of river transport, then of canals, helping to open up new mining areas. Both the Sankey Canal from St Helens to the Mersey and the Bridgewater Canal from Worsley to Manchester were promoted almost entirely with coal supplies in mind, and the Ashton Canal was built largely to open up coal resources in the area east of Manchester. In the later eighteenth century the construction of horse-drawn tramroads greatly facilitated the movement of the coal: there was a major network in the Wigan area terminating at various points on the river Douglas or the Leeds & Liverpool Canal, including the famous Wigan Pier. Some of the methods of engineering on these early lines – the mounting of the rails on stone blocks, the use of inclines to overcome gradients – were carried over into the early days of main-line railway construction. Drainage of mines was greatly assisted by the use of Newcomen steam pumping engines, though winding was still largely carried out by horse gins.

The nineteenth century saw an enormous increase in demand, both for household coal with a growing population, and for industrial use in steam-powered factories of all kinds, for locomotives and steamships. There were well over 300 pits at work in the Wigan coalfield alone by 1850, while the late nineteenth century saw the development both of larger pits and of larger colliery companies in different parts of the field operating several collieries, each with several shafts. The peak of production was reached just before the first world war – 26½ million tons a year.

While the coal industry contributed so much to the mechanisation of other industries, it was itself increasingly mechanised. Winding and haulage were steam-powered, and a few of the later steam winding engines still survive, usually made by local firms. More powerful pumping engines, particularly Cornish engines, came into use. In the later nineteenth century the system of furnace ventilation, using the heat to create a flow of air through the workings by convection, was replaced by mechanical fans, driven by steam engines and made by local colliery engineering firms. The biggest fans could circulate up to 250,000 cu. ft of air a minute. Compressed air, produced by steam-powered compressors, was used for some haulage systems, and later for coal-cutting machinery, introduced into some collieries in the 1870s, but not becoming general until after the first world war. Mechanisation also developed at the pithead. Coal was sorted on mechanically driven movable-bar screens, on to which the coal was tipped by mechanical tipplers. Conveyor belts were introduced for picking out stone and other waste, a job often undertaken by the 'pit ladies', who were employed in considerable numbers in the later period. By the end of the century mechanical washeries to separate the smaller sizes of coal and slack were in general use. The pithead installations of large collieries were like factories in themselves, with winding houses, compressor houses, sorting areas, washeries and workshops, including carpenters' shops, smithies, fitting shops and wagon repair shops. Many of the collieries also had coke ovens, in the earlier nineteenth century of the old 'beehive' type, by 1900 often the new by-product ovens, which enabled the recovery of a number of chemicals. Banks of coke ovens are often found at sites along canals.

The twentieth century has seen a dramatic decline in coal production, especially since the second world war. By 1956 output was running at about half of the pre-first world war peak. Nearly 300 pits were closed between 1914 and 1954, when some seventy collieries were still at work. Now there are seven. As pits are closed the buildings are soon demolished and increasingly the spoil heaps are landscaped, so that all traces of the old colliery scene tend to disappear. A stranger visiting Wigan might even not be aware from the landscape alone that it had been a major mining area.

There are some interesting examples of colliery communities, though usually not as isolated as those in east Derbyshire or Nottinghamshire, and a number of surviving groups of colliers' houses. Poynton is perhaps the best example, an estate village with remains of the collieries, colliery railways and miners' houses surviving amidst twentieth-century suburbia.

STONE QUARRYING

Sandstone and gritstone for building purposes have been quarried from the north-western hills for centuries: there are invariably many sites of small-scale workings near the towns and villages. In the nineteenth century, with the growth of population, the increasing urbanisation of the region and the development of rail transport, stone resources were exploited on a much larger scale, providing building materials not only for the local towns, streets, mills and public buildings but also for towns in other parts of the country. There were some major operations in the Pennines and the outlying hills to the west: for example, around Blackburn and Darwen, in Whitworth and Bacup, where the Britannia quarries were among the biggest, in Longridge, east of Preston, in the hills around Dalton, Up Holland and Billinge to the west and south-west of Wigan. The red sandstones of Cheshire were also exploited and are well represented in buildings of the area, particularly in Merseyside. There are examples of major workings at Runcorn and in the Storeton quarries on Wirral, with a tramroad link to Bromborough Pool.

Limestone has provided the basis of a sizable industry in two areas: in north Lancashire around Carnforth, and in Clitheroe and Chatburn north of Pendle Hill. The origins of the industry go back to the seventeenth century, when lime was used for land improvement, and there are many surviving examples of small farm or individual kilns, loaded from the top, with a grate at the bottom from which the lime could be extracted. In the nineteenth century the increasing demand for limestone for building and as a raw material for the new chemical industry led to much bigger quarrying operations and to the construction of banks of kilns, often with tramroad links to the quarries. At Clitheroe in recent times the quarries have become the basis of cement manufacture. Kilns are also found in the areas of Cheshire within reach of the Derbyshire limestone quarries north of Buxton – for example, on the Peak Forest Canal at Disley and Marple.

SALT

Salt was produced by evaporation from sea water in salterns or saltcotes along the Lancashire coast from the Ribble estuary northwards from the thirteenth to the seventeenth century. The process was carried out in lead pans, using peat from the local turbaries as the fuel. There are many references to saltcotes, turbaries, salt carts and other equipment in seventeenth-century inventories in the area around Pilling and Cockerham. At a much later date the salt marshes at the mouth of the river Wyre provided a basis for

chemical works in Preesall and Fleetwood.

The main centre of the industry, however, and indeed the main centre of the industry in Britain, was the Cheshire saltfield, an area about twelve miles (19·3 km) north–south, two miles (3·2 km) east–west, in the basins of the river Weaver and the river Dane, from Anderton in the north to Betchton and Wheelock in the south. There are natural brine springs and rock salt occurs at two different levels. These became a major industrial resource in the nineteenth century, particularly in relation to the chemical, soap and glass industries. There is evidence of salt production at Middlewich (Salinae) in Roman times, mostly in the form of briquetage from the furnaces, and some possibility also of production at Northwich in the same period. The industry was certainly well established in Nantwich, Middlewich and Northwich before the Norman Conquest, as is confirmed by evidence from Domesday Book. In the Middle Ages the method of production was to lift the brine in buckets from wells or pits 20 ft to 30 ft (6 m to 9 m) deep and convey it in troughs to the salt works, which usually had four, six or eight lead pans in which the evaporation took place. The salt was raked out into wicker baskets for drying. There is evidence that at least some of the lead pans were made locally. Salt was carried for sale over a wide area, and there are a number of place names – Saltersford, Saltersgate, Saltersway – which refer to the old routes used by the carriers. Nantwich remained the biggest centre until the late seventeenth century: there were 300 salt works there according to Leland, writing in the mid-sixteenth century. In 1670, however, the discovery of rock salt at Marbury, near Northwich, led to the development of mines in that area and to the growing importance of Northwich, described by Celia Fiennes as a '. . . town . . . full of smoke from salterns on all sides'. Other changes were taking place: iron pans replaced the lead pans for boiling, coal increasingly replaced charcoal or wood as a fuel.

The improvement of the river Weaver in the early eighteenth century further stimulated production and confirmed the growing supremacy of Northwich, and later of Winsford, as against Nantwich, to where the navigation was never extended. Shipments of rock salt down the Weaver quadrupled between 1747 and 1777, and salt works were established on the river Mersey close to the coalfield. In the late eighteenth century mining was extended to the lower rock-salt beds at a depth of over 300 ft (91 m) and work on the upper beds gradually diminished. The method was to sink two shafts to aid ventilation and to work on a pillar-and-stall system, leaving pillars of salt to support the roof. Increasingly steam engines took over for brine pumping and rock-salt winding, replacing the earlier horse gins, waterwheels and even windmills. Pumping as well as mining took place at a greater depth.

The peak of the industry came in the nineteenth century, when it was the basis of new soap, glass and chemical industries located either close to the south-west Lancashire coalfield or on the Cheshire side. Sodium chloride was a basic raw material in the Leblanc process for alkali manufacture, and alkalis in turn were raw materials in the glass and soap industries. The links between Cheshire salt, Lancashire coal, the river Weaver, the river Mersey, the Sankey Canal and the port of Liverpool created a whole Merseyside industrial area. Salt production rose from about 300,000 tons in 1823 to 1 million tons in 1850 and 1¾ million tons in 1876, by which time over 75 per cent of British salt production came from Cheshire. Winsford became the main production

centre, with works along both banks of the Weaver, having about two-thirds of all Cheshire salt pans by 1888. Flats, often owned by the salt proprietors, carried the salt down the river to Liverpool, Birkenhead and Runcorn and later to the Weaver docks at Weston Point.

The traditional method of evaporation in large open iron pans continued throughout the century. Salt was pumped from the brine pits into storage cisterns and thence to the pans. Pans were about 24 ft (7·3 m) wide, between 30 ft and 80 ft (9 m and 24 m) long, and 12 in. to 16 in. (30 to 40 cm) deep. The larger pans were used for coarse salts, and there were usually three or four furnaces to each pan. Boiling took pace at 226°F and as the salt evaporated it was raked to the sides and put into conical baskets for drying in stoves beyond the salt-pan area. The pans were separated by walkways to facilitate removal of the salt. The pan houses were simple sheds with louvred roofs to enable the steam to escape. Only one works, the Lion Works at Marston, still uses the open-pan process. There are items of equipment generally related to the process – rakes, chipping paddles, skimmers, baskets, barrows – in the Salt Museum in Northwich. Firms were generally small, with some employment of boys from the age of nine or ten, often helping their fathers.

There was increasing concern during the century about competition and falling prices, and from about 1815 there were several attempts at forming combines or price-fixing arrangements, culminating in the Cheshire Salt Union, started by H. E. Falk of the Meadowbank Works in Winsford, and involving sixty-four firms. Rock-salt production declined in the later nineteenth century: Calvert in 1881 listed nineteen mines open, of which nine were in production, mainly in Marston, Wincham and Witton.

As mining and brine bumping were extended there was a growing problem of subsidence, particularly in the Northwich area, with dramatic effects on the local buildings, and even involving the collapse of whole salt works. The flashes resulting from subsidence are a characteristic feature of the landscape. The Brine Subsidence Compensation Act of 1891 introduced a system of levies to provide a fund to compensate property owners, but the long-term solution lay in controlled pumping, developed from 1928. This involved pumping water down and pumping brine up, with limits on the amount taken out, leaving behind saline solution in the cavity.

In the twentieth century the historic open-pan process was gradually replaced by the vacuum process, first introduced at Winsford in 1905. It involved boiling at much lower temperatures in closed containers using steam to create the necessary vacuum as well as to heat the brine solution. There are usually three containers, with the highest temperature and lowest vacuum in the first. The salt falls to the bottom for extraction and drying. Another development was the building of long-distance pipelines from the brine sources to supply the salt works, which developed at Winnington and Runcorn. At the time of writing there are six salt works operating in the area, all except one of the vacuum type.

CHEMICALS AND SOAP

The oldest chemical industry in the area was the production of alum, used as a mordant in textile dyeing. There were mines in Pleasington near Blackburn, which were visited by James I in 1617 and which were being worked in the late eighteenth century. The textile industry also had a market for sulphuric acid, used for example as a souring agent in bleaching. In the late eighteenth and early nineteenth centuries some acid was produced from copperas, ferrous sulphate or green vitriol, made from iron pyrites which occurred in coal-mining areas: there are references to copperas works in Wigan, Aspull, Blackrod and Bardsley, near Oldham. The lead-chamber process for making sulphuric acid by burning sulphur with nitre and dissolving the vapours (sulphur dioxide) in water inside the chambers was introduced in the late eighteenth century: there was a works with eight chambers at Pilsworth Moor, near Bury, in 1783. Bealey's at Radcliffe, who had six chambers in 1799, were also bleachers and among the pioneers of chlorine bleaching in the area.

The later heavy chemical industry, concentrated in the Merseyside area, was based on the invention of the Leblanc process for making soda (sodium carbonate) from salt, readily available in Cheshire. Salt was treated with sulphuric acid to form saltcake (sodium sulphate), which was roasted with limestone and coal to form black ash, from which soda was evaporated by soaking in water. The first works in the North West was started by Muspratt & Gamble in Liverpool in 1822. The concentration was in St Helens and Widnes, where coal was readily available and salt and limestone could easily be transported. Seven works were built at Widnes between 1847 and 1855 and there were thirty-six alkali works in Lancashire in 1864.

A further stage came with the replacement of the Leblanc process by the soda-ammonia process, developed by a Belgian, Ernest Solvay, in 1863. It was based on the carbonisation of a solution of common salt saturated with ammonia, carried out in Solvay towers by blowing carbon dioxide up as the solution passed down. The resultant sodium bicarbonate was heated in furnaces to produce soda. A two-year option on the British rights of the process was acquired by Ludwig Mond, who had been working in the chemical industry in Widnes. Mond formed a partnership with J. T. Brunner, who had worked at Hutchinson's alkali plant in Widnes, and they purchased a site at Winnington Hall, near Northwich, where they were producing over 200,000 tons a year by 1900. Three years earlier, in 1897, the Castner-Kellner Co. began production at Runcorn, using the process for making soda by electrolysis developed by the American, Hamilton Young Castner. The works was taken over by Brunner Mond & Co. in 1920.

The region also played a major part in the development of artificial dyestuffs, based on the by-products of gasworks, and the coal-tar industry. The first aniline dye – mauveine – was produced by William Henry Perkins in 1856, followed by a series of colours in the 1860s, some of German origin. One of the first manufacturers in the Manchester area was Ivan Levinstein, who had been educated at Berlin University and started a works at Blackley in 1864, the forerunner of ICI Dyestuffs Division. In 1876 Charles Dreyfus from Alsace started the Clayton Aniline Co., later taken over by the Swiss firm Ciba. There was another works in Clayton, established by Claus and Ree in 1891 and taken over by Levinstein's in 1916. By then German competition was strong, and in 1919 Levinstein's amalgamated with British Dyes, which had developed from another pioneer firm, Read Halliday's, in Huddersfield.

Merseyside also provided a natural setting for the soap industry which grew up in the late eighteenth and early nineteenth centuries. There were local supplies of salt and coal, while tallow, palm and coconut oils, kelp and barilla could be imported through Liverpool, where there were eleven soap-boilers in 1814–15. From the 1830s local chemical works could supply cheaper synthetic soda. By 1835 the area was producing more soap than London, and Liverpool

was a main exporter. The old method was to boil tallow or other animal fats and vegetable oils with alkalis made from plant ashes in coppers. The soap was then poured into wooden frames to solidify and was cut by wires into bars. Production was on a relatively small scale. The growing demand from a rising population, from exports and from the developing textile industry led to the establishment of larger firms looking to mass markets. Mechanisation was introduced: steam power was used for pumping and driving agitators, cutting machines, boring and packing machinery.

Joseph Crosfield, son of a grocer, started a new works at Bank Quay, Warrington, in 1815, which later expanded into chemical production. Hazelhurst's were making soap in Runcorn by the 1820s. Johnson's in Runcorn had their own soda works. William Lever started at Warrington in 1885, but moved to a new site in the Wirral near Bromborough Pool in 1888. He was one of the great pioneers of tablet-soap production and of large-scale advertising.

The later nineteenth century saw a general trend towards the production of toilet soap made by shredding the soap base, milling it through rollers and extruding it into bars in plodding machines. Proprietary names such as Erasmic, made by Crosfield's, and Sunlight, made by Lever's, became increasingly well known. In the twentieth century soap powders were introduced: Persil, based on a German invention, by Crosfield's, Rinso by Lever's. Both firms also started making scouring powders, Glitto and Vim, and soap flakes, Feather Flakes and Lux ('the Ladies' soap').

GLASS

There are references to glass-making at Haughton Green near Denton in the seventeenth century, where excavations in 1970 provided evidence of the production of domestic glass between 1600 and 1643. A list of glasshouses in 1696 includes one near Liverpool and one in Warrington: by that date the Leaf family may have started their works at Thatto Heath, near the later town of St Helens. In the 18th century a considerable number of glassworks were established: two in Liverpool, one in Atherton, at least one in Salford. Many of these would be producing window glass by the crown method. In this a quantity of glass was gathered from the furnace, blown into a pear shape and flattened against an iron plate, then transferred to an iron rod or 'punty' and rotated quickly to transform it into a flat circular sheet, from which the window panes could be cut.

A big step forward came at the end of the century with the introduction of plate-glass casting, first pioneered in France in the Picardy area. Early experiments in England failed, but in 1773, with French technical help, the British Plate Glass Co. established a works at Ravenhead, St Helens, which succeeded after some early difficulties. In this process molten glass from the furnace was ladled on to an iron casting table and rolled into a plate, followed by grinding and polishing. Two other works were started in St Helens, which by the 1860s was the main centre of plate-glass manufacture in the country: there were several factors in the location – coal supply, alkalis from the chemical works, good supplies of suitable sand. Grinding and polishing were mechanised at an early stage and in the 1890s disc grinding on large circular steel tables was introduced from Belgium. The old furnaces in which the glass was melted in pots were replaced by tank furnaces with regenerative systems using exhaust gases to store heat.

Many works continued to make crown glass throughout the nineteenth century, and the cones that housed the furnaces were a distinctive feature of the landscape. Window glass was also made by the cylinder process, in which a sizable quantity of glass was swung mechanically in a trench to form a cylinder, which was cut along its length, removed and flattened. Pressed glass formed in moulds for tableware came into use during the century and the process was at least partly mechanised before 1900. In the late nineteenth century mechanised moulding using compressed air for blowing bottles was introduced into the bottle-making side of the industry.

It would be wrong to think that glassworks were confined to St Helens at this period. There were crown glassworks in Warrington and Newton le Willows and numerous flint-glass works making tableware in Manchester and Salford, for example. The twentieth century has seen even greater technical development. In the 1920s the production of plate glass became a continuous in-line process from the tank furnaces, through the rolling, grinding and polishing stages. The drawn-sheet process, developed in Belgium and the United States, gradually replaced the crown and cylinder processes for making window glass. In this process glass from the furnace was drawn through a slot in a fireclay boat floating on the molten glass and pulled up between asbestos covered rollers in a vertical annealing tower, then cut to size as required. Safety glass using laminated layers was introduced by the Triplex company in France in 1909, and by the English Triplex Co. at St Helens in 1912. In recent years the casting of plate glass has been replaced by the floatglass process, in which the sheets are formed on a bath of molten tin.

PAPER-MAKING

There is evidence of paper-making at a number of places in the region in the late seventeenth century: at Cark in

Cartmel (as early as 1617), at Pincock Mill, Euxton (first reference 1651), at Farnworth by 1674, at Chester near the old Dee Bridge. During the eighteenth century there was considerable expansion as the population grew and there was an increase in the volume of correspondence and in the publication of books, newspapers and journals. By 1700 there were some twenty-five mills in the North West, with particular concentrations in the Irwell valley around Bury and Radcliffe and in the Manchester area. Locational factors that were important were the availability of good water for processing and a supply of rags as raw material, hence a link with the textile industry. It is not unusual to find textile finishing and paper-making as alternative trades carried on at different dates in the same premises.

The method of making paper at this period was by hand, using vats for the pulp and a mould of brass wire for forming the sheets. Mills were small, usually one or two vats, though there were some larger ones by the end of the century – four vats, for example, at Throstle Nest, near Manchester. The rags were sorted, then cut by hand, often by women and children, and beaten into pulp by heavy wooden stamps operated by water power, hence the common use of existing water-power sites. The pulp was transferred to the vat, the sheet formed by the vatman and turned off the mould on to felt for pressing by the coucher. The sheets were dried by hanging on ropes in lofts, then sized and polished. One technical improvement introduced in the later eighteenth century was the mechanical *hollander* or *beater*, in which the rags were beaten by a roll fitted with iron knives acting against a bed plate, as the material circulated in an oblong tub, rounded at the ends.

A great change came over the industry with the introduction of the paper-making machine invented by Nicolas-Louis Robert in 1799 and developed in England by the Fourdrinier brothers, London stationers, and Bryan Donkin, an engineer. The change-over to machine production was further accelerated by the introduction of the continuous drying process, using steam-heated iron cylinders, for which T. B. Crompton of the Farnworth paper mills was mainly responsible. By 1830 half the paper made in Great Britain was made by machine, by 1860 about 95 per cent. The essential feature of the machine was the formation of the paper on an endless moving wire sieve from which it was taken off to pressing rollers and thence to the drying stage.

As a result of the introduction of the machine, a considerable number of new works were started. Ten mills opened in the Bury–Radcliffe area between 1835 and 1880, mostly upstream of the eighteenth-century sites, along the valleys of the Irwell and Roch and their tributaries, while some of the older mills closed. New engineering firms making machinery for the paper industry were started: Bentley & Jackson and Walmsley's in Bury in the 1860s, for example. New raw materials replaced rags: wood pulp from about 1850, esparto grass from 1860. Some new works have been started in the twentieth century, and paper-making remains a significant industry in the region.

One specialised development was that of paper staining and printing, very much associated with calico-printing and with the town of Darwen, which had a paper mill in the early nineteenth century with a Fourdrinier machine. The pioneer work on paper was done by Charles and Harold Potter, whose family had a calico-printing works in Darwen, using an adaptation of the calico-printing machine. Potter's became a large industrial concern and eventually in 1899 part of Wallpaper Manufacturers Ltd. They contributed much to the interior decoration of the houses of the Victorian period.

HAT-MAKING

Felt-hat making was introduced into England in the sixteenth century and concentrated in London, where the trade was controlled by the Feltmakers' Company. In the seventeenth century it developed in a number of provincial centres, which in the North West included Chester, Manchester, Oldham, Warrington and Preston. Fur was collected by local farmers and made into felt in small workshops. The trade expanded considerably in the eighteenth century, still very much based on small-workshop production. The main firms, for example in Denton and Stockport, worked on a commission basis, giving out the raw materials and often equipment to the small masters. London firms, like Christy's of Bermondsey, employed agents in the North West in Stockport, Macclesfield and Oldham. Hats were made from fur or a mixture of wool and fur. The wool was cleaned and carded, and the fur (usually rabbit or beaver) cut from the skins. The next stage was bowing, where piles of wool and fur were put on a wooden bench and vibrated by means of the string of a hatters' bow suspended from the ceiling to form an even layer. The material was then formed into a rough conical hood and *planked*, that is, dipped repeatedly into a kettle of nearly boiling water with a very small amount of sulphuric acid, and pressed and worked on sloping planks around the kettle, resulting in shrinking and felting. The felt was then shaped and blocked into hat form on wooden blocks of appropriate design, then dyed, stiffened, trimmed and finished. Bowing and planking would usually take place in different workshops from the finishing stages.

In the early nineteenth century a number of London firms established factories in the provinces: Christy's, for example, took over the works of T. & J. Worsley in Stockport in 1826. By that date the industry was becoming more concentrated in certain centres: Baines's *Lancashire Directory* of 1825 lists fifty-eight hat manufacturers in Manchester, thirty-one in Stockport, twenty-five in Denton, nineteen in Oldham, eleven in Audenshaw and Hooley Hill. More work was done indoors in the factories, though outwork remained important and a number of small planking and finishing workshops were still operating in Stockport in the 1840s.

Mechnisation was slow. Cutting machines for removing the fur from the skin were introduced before 1840, as were blowing machines to separate the finer from the coarser fur. There was a setback in the 1840s and 1850s with the increasing scarcity of beaver fur and the widespread introduction of the silk hat: a revival came in the later nineteenth century with the new fashions for bowler hats in the 1860s, homburgs and trilbies in the 1890s. Planking and forming machines were introduced from the United States, and by 1900 there were a number of factories at work in both the main centres, Stockport and Denton.

The peak was reached at the beginning of the twentieth century: in the 1920s the industry still employed half Denton's working population. The depression of the 1930s hastened decline, and after the second world war as people simply stopped wearing hats most of the factories closed. At the present time there is one major firm operating in Stockport, one in Denton.

CORN MILLING

Windmills were a prominent feature of the North West landscape, especially in the Fylde, the western plain between the Ribble and the Mersey and the Wirral. Yates's map of Lancashire in 1786 shows seventy-nine windmills, seventy of them in the Fylde and the West Lancashire plain. Burdett's map of Cheshire in 1777 shows sixteen windmills, twelve of which are in the Wirral: there are some forty-three marked on the several maps of the county published at about this period. Windmills were not of course confined to these western areas; there is evidence of mills working in Preston, Blackburn, Royton, Denton, Manchester, Stockport, Bollington and Macclesfield, among other places. But in the west the prevailing winds and the nature of the topography provided good conditions for the exploitation of wind power.

Little remains of the earlier timber post mills, where the whole body of the mill revolved on a substantial wooden post to turn the sails into the wind. About the only survival is at Warton, near Lytham, in the Fylde. They were generally replaced in the eighteenth or nineteenth century by tower mills usually of brick, with a movable wooden cap on which the sails were mounted. The cap was turned into the wind either by a fantail, mounted at right angles to and at the opposite end of the cap from the sails, or by a tail wheel operated by a long rope or chain and moved by means of a rack and curb between the tower and the cap. Many of these tower mills continued to work throughout the nineteenth century, though affected by the increasing use of steam power for milling in the towns. Most closed between the wars as the National Grid gradually made electric power much more widely available.

A considerable number of the towers survive, a few of them with cap, or even sails. Many have been converted to residences, some stand empty and ruined as a reminder of an older industrial period. Two mills have been preserved with machinery: Bidston in the Wirral and Marsh Mill at Thornton Cleveleys, near Blackpool.

Water-powered mills were much more numerous. Burdett's map of Cheshire in 1777, for example, shows 140 water mills, the majority of which were used for corn milling. J. H. Norris's 1964–65 survey of water-powered corn mills in Cheshire lists 187 sites with some physical remains, and more would be added by the use of aerial photography and documentary evidence. In the urban areas of what is now Greater Manchester and east Lancashire many of the mills were demolished or changed their use as the towns developed. In many of the towns steam-powered mills with beam engines driving several sets of stones were built and tended to replace the old uneconomical and more local mills. There were three in Stockport, for example, one in Warrington, three in Chester. North of the Ribble there are still a considerable number of mill sites along the streams which feed the Ribble itself, the Wyre and the Lune.

Only a handful of mills are still working, though not always with the original water-power system. The interest in conservation has led to the restoration into working order of three mills in Cheshire: Stretton, Bunbury and Trafford, while the mill at Nether Alderley, restored at an earlier stage, survives as a major industrial monument. Waterwheels of various types survive at a number of mill sites, and very often considerable traces of the water supply system – mill ponds, races, sluices, weirs. Mill buildings, usually related to the local vernacular tradition of building, are also numerous and in recent years a number have been converted to private residences. In a few cases there are drying kilns, with floors of square perforated tiles on which the grain was spread: more often, perhaps, remnants of the tiles are the main evidence of a former kiln.

There were a number of examples of tidemills along the coast: one at Bromborough Pool in the Wirral, one in the

Liverpool dock area, one at Freckleton in the Fylde, one at Pilling, where there was also a windmill. In these the millpond was filled with water by the incoming tide and then used to drive the mill for a number of hours, so that working had to be adjusted to a degree to the changing time of high tides.

In the late nineteenth century roller milling, introduced into this country by Henry Simon, began to take over from the old method of grinding with a bedstone and runner stone. Simon's built a works at Cheadle Heath near Stockport in the early 1920s for the production of milling machinery. The new method was used not only in the steam-powered mills in the North West towns but in the new, much larger-scale mills built to process imported grain, particularly from North America, at the ports – Liverpool, Birkenhead, Wallasey, Ellesmere Port, for example.

ROAD TRANSPORT

The roads of the North West must have carried a considerable volume of traffic from at least the later sixteenth century, with the carriage of textile raw materials and finished goods, which by then were being distributed widely within the country and exported overseas through London, Hull, Chester and other ports. In the Pennine areas there are many examples of old pack-horse roads which cross the moors between the market towns or between Lancashire and Yorkshire. Some of them, for example in Rossendale, in the Rochdale area and in Saddleworth, show considerable evidence of engineering, with management of gradients, embankments, partial paving and the construction of bridges. Well known, too, are the old salt roads by which Cheshire salt was distributed to many parts of the region.

The first turnpike roads were related to the trunk route between London and Manchester (Manchester & Buxton Trust, 1725) and to the links between Liverpool and the south-west Lancashire coalfield (Liverpool–Prescot Trust, 1725, later extended to St Helens). The main road north from Warrington to Preston followed in 1726. Two routes linking Manchester across the Pennines with Yorkshire, via Oldham and Rochdale, were turnpiked in the 1730s. As industrial traffic grew there was greater activity in promoting trusts. By 1755 seven of the main roads out of Manchester had been turnpiked. Between 1750 and 1772 twenty-seven new trusts were created in Lancashire, twelve in Cheshire. There was another period of great activity in the 1790s and early 1800s, and again in the 1820s, when some twelve new trusts were started. The last turnpikes to be established were Nantwich–Congleton and Chester–Sandbach–Congleton in Cheshire, Radcliffe–Bolton–Bury in Lancashire.

Trusts were relatively small concerns, mostly operating comparatively short stretches of road: there were sixty-five separate trusts in Lancashire, with the roads heavily concentrated in the industrial area in the east. In the earlier period methods of road construction followed on from some of those used by the parishes or townships, which continued to bear responsibility for the lesser roads. Causeways for horse-drawn traffic were built using local stone, flags or even copper slag. In the late eighteenth and early nineteenth centuries the 'new' road engineering pioneered by Metcalfe, MacAdam and Telford was increasingly used, with better foundations, surfaces and drainage. Metcalfe worked on the Stockport–Ashton and Stockport–Mottram roads and on part of the Bury–Haslingden–Whalley road. Some of the later roads were new or improved routes, supplementing the previously turnpiked routes – the Blackburn–Preston new road via Samlesbury, the Bury

New Road and Ashton New Road out of Manchester, the 1826 Wellington Road section of the Manchester–Buxton turnpike through Stockport from Heaton Chapel to Bramhall Lane.

Inevitably, much of the evidence for the construction of these roads is buried below modern surfaces, and will only occasionally be revealed. But in many places it is possible to see the lines of earlier roads, with new sections made by the turnpike trustees.

There are surviving examples of the single or two-storey tollhouses erected at the tollbars for the toll collectors, usually positioned to give good visibility along the road in each direction and often along side roads. Yates's map of Lancashire shows forty toll bars, and a study of the first edition of the six-inch Ordnance Survey maps of the 1840s reveals a total of well over 200. The trustees also built many bridges, of which there are some excellent examples, and provided milestones along the route, some of stone, some of cast iron. In Cheshire, for example, there are numerous surviving examples of the cast iron variety, erected by the county council in the 1880s and 1890s.

Ferries were another feature of the region: there were a very large number across the Mersey from Liverpool right up to Manchester. The turnpike trustees of the Wilmslow road, for example, built a bridge to replace the old ferry across the Mersey between Manchester and Cheadle in the 1750s. Similarly there was a series of ferries across the Ribble between Preston and Clitheroe, and across the Wyre, where two of them were later replaced by Shard Bridge and Cartford Bridge.

There was a rapid increase in coaching and carrying services on the roads between 1780 and 1835, linking the towns of the region and connecting them in turn with London, Yorkshire and the Midlands. The impact of the railways was felt quickly as the network

was built: surviving records show a rapid fall in revenue from tolls in the 1840s and 1850s. On the other hand there was some increase in internal traffic in the towns, as either the local authorities or private operators provided horse buses (from the 1820s) and horse trams, first introduced in Birkenhead in 1860. Manchester had sixty-six miles of horse-tram tracks in 1900. Some towns in the area – Accrington, Blackburn, Burnley, St Helens, Wigan, for example – operated steam trams. With the development of the electricity supply industry and the building of local power stations there was quite a rapid change-over to electric trams from about 1900. A number of the tram depots built at this period survive, often extended at a later date when motor buses were introduced. There were even experiments with gas trams, using Otto-type engines, in Trafford Park and for a limited period between Blackpool and Lytham.

Since the 1930s motor transport has taken over, and the trunk roads which developed from the turnpikes (the A6, for example) have been superseded for long-distance traffic by the motorways of the post-second world war period, again altering the constantly changing pattern of roads on the ground, which has always been a feature of their history.

RIVERS AND CANALS

Three river improvement schemes authorised by Acts of Parliament between 1719 and 1721, and coming into effective use in the 1740s, contributed a great deal to the industrial development of the region. The Mersey & Irwell Navigation made the river navigable from Warrington up to Manchester and provided an important route between Manchester and Liverpool which was cheaper than road transport and which continued to flourish long after the opening of the Bridgewater Canal. The

Douglas Navigation further opened up the resources of the Wigan coalfield by providing a link with the Ribble estuary, and was eventually taken over by the Leeds & Liverpool Canal Co. The Weaver Navigation from Winsford to the Mersey was a vital factor in the development of the saltfield in the eighteenth and nineteenth century. The link with the Mersey and Liverpool, and later via the Sankey Canal with the St Helens coalfield, was the basis for much of the new industrial growth of Merseyside. The Irwell was used until the late nineteenth century; the Weaver continues in use for some traffic between Anderton and Weston Point, Runcorn.

The improvement schemes involved the making of new cuts to obviate the twists and turns of the older river course, and the building of locks to enable vessels to pass the weirs which provided power for mills of all kinds along the route. There were eight sets of locks on the river Irwell between Manchester and Warrington, of which little trace now remains. Originally there were twelve sets of locks, with timber sides, on the Weaver, rebuilt in stone before 1800, and later doubled and lengthened as the size of the boats increased. In more recent times the number of locks has been reduced to four. Wharves and warehouses were built along the route, at Bank Quay and Howley Quay, in Warrington on the Mersey and Irwell, for example, at Northwich on the Weaver, while the wharf in Manchester is commemorated in the name of Quay Street.

Two of the river navigation companies built what were in effect canals or artificial cuts. The Mersey & Irwell Co. built the Runcorn & Latchford Canal, opened in 1804, to provide a more direct route and to compete more effectively with the Bridgewater Canal. The Weaver Trustees built the Weaver Canal from Frodsham to Weston Point,

Runcorn, where they gradually developed their own dock system during the nineteenth century.

The first canals were largely related to coal transport and sprang to some extent from river improvement schemes. The Sankey Canal from the Mersey west of Warrington to St Helens was promoted by Liverpool merchants, salt proprietors and colliery owners, planned as an 'improvement' of the Sankey brook, but built as a separate cut, opened in part in 1759. The Bridgewater Canal scheme followed an earlier proposal for the improvement of Worsley brook. The line from the Duke of Bridgewater's Worsley collieries to Manchester was built between 1759 and 1761. The success of these early canals led to other schemes. The idea for the longest canal in the region (146 miles, 240 km), the Leeds & Liverpool, was first mooted in 1765, and the Act of Parliament passed in 1770. By 1779 the line was open from Liverpool to Wigan, and from Leeds to Gargrave. There was then a long delay before work was resumed in the 1790s, and the line was finally completed in 1816. Also during the 1770s the extension of the Bridgewater Canal through Cheshire from Stretford to Runcorn was completed, linking at Preston Brook with the Trent & Mersey Canal from the Potteries, opened in 1775. The Chester Canal from Chester to Nantwich was opened in 1775 but was not a financial success and fell into disuse at an early stage, later becoming part of the Shropshire Union system.

The 1790s were the period of the 'canal mania', and five or six new schemes were promoted in Lancashire. Two new routes were built over the Pennines: the Ashton Canal, promoted to link Manchester with the coal-mining areas around Oldham and Ashton under Lyne, was joined to the Huddersfield Narrow Canal; the Rochdale Canal connected Manchester with the Aire &

Calder Navigation in Yorkshire. Manchester's industrial links were further strengthened by the building of the Manchester Bolton & Bury Canal, with its two main branches, dividing at Prestolee. The Lancaster Canal, promoted in 1792, was not completed until 1819; it provided a route between the industrial areas south of Preston and the agricultural and limestone areas of north Lancashire up to Kendal. It had the novel feature of a central section in the form of a tramroad across the Ribble at Preston. On the Cheshire side the Ellesmere Canal was promoted in 1789 with the idea of linking the river Mersey with Shrewsbury (never in fact fully carried out) and the industrial area around Ruabon and Wrexham. The Wirral section between Chester and what later became Ellesmere Port was opened in 1795 and led to a restoration and revival of activity on the Chester Canal to Nantwich, from 1797. This linked in turn with the Birmingham & Liverpool Junction Canal from Wolverhampton, and all eventually became part of the Shropshire Union system, which was connected with the Trent & Mersey at Middlewich in 1833.

By the early nineteenth century Manchester was the hub of a considerable canal system and the industrial areas of the North West were linked with the Potteries, the Midlands (and thence with London) and with Yorkshire and the east coast. The last major schemes were the Macclesfield Canal, completed in 1831, providing another route between the Potteries and the industrial area east of Manchester and connected at Marple with the Peak Forest Canal, built in the 1790s to open up the Derbyshire limestone quarries; and the Birmingham & Liverpool Junction, opened in 1835.

The canals have many engineering features, described in more detail in the gazetteer. There are major flights of locks at Wigan, Marple, Bosley and Audlem; major stone aqueducts at Lancaster, Garstang, Failsworth and Marple, as well as a number of iron aqueducts on the Cheshire canals at Congleton, Macclesfield and Nantwich; the longest tunnel on the canal system at Standedge on the Huddersfield Narrow Canal. Along the routes in the main towns as well as the smaller places are numerous wharves and warehouses, once centres of great commercial activity. Two canal ports developed on the Mersey estuary at Ellesmere Port and Runcorn, and Glasson Dock at the mouth of the Lune was linked with the Lancaster Canal by a specially constructed branch.

The Manchester Ship Canal was an engineering venture on a much larger scale. The idea goes back in origin to the 1820s or earlier, but it was revived in the late 1870s, when Manchester businessmen feared a permanent trade recession and were concerned about the cost of trading through Liverpool docks. Following the passing of the Act in 1885, the thirty-five-and-a-half-mile (57 km) canal was built between 1887 and 1894, enabling seagoing vessels to come up from Eastham to the new docks in Salford and making Manchester into a major port. Apart from the work on the main cut and the locks, the construction involved the building of major railway deviation bridges and swing bridges on the main road crossings.

RAILWAYS

The origins of railway transport in the North West, as elsewhere, are to be found in the numerous tramroads of the late eighteenth century, linking coal mines and quarries with the nearest river, canal or road distribution point. The first public railway was the Bolton & Leigh, engineered by George Stephenson and opened throughout in 1829, using locomotive haulage. It has inevitably been overshadowed by the

Liverpool & Manchester Railway, opened a year later, whose success in passenger carrying provided the stimulus for rapid railway growth of the succeeding years.

The main lines of the system were created between 1830 and 1850. Liverpool and Manchester were linked with Birmingham (and thence with London) by the Grand Junction Railway, opened in 1837 to Warrington and joined to the Liverpool–Manchester tracks at Newton le Willows. The direct Manchester–Birmingham route followed in 1843, with Crewe becoming a major junction as well as the site of the Grand Junction's engineering works. It was out of these various companies that the London & North Western Railway was created in 1848. The main line north from Warrington through Wigan and Preston to Carlisle was the work of four different companies, reaching Carlisle in 1846.

Manchester was linked with the cotton areas of east Lancashire and with the West Riding of Yorkshire by what later became the Lancashire & Yorkshire system. The Manchester & Leeds Railway, with a tunnel through the Pennines between Littleborough and Todmorden, was opened in 1841. Clifton Junction on the Salford–Bolton line (opened in 1838) was the starting point for the East Lancashire Railway's routes to Bury and Rossendale and to Accrington, Blackburn, Burnley and Colne, built in 1846–48. By 1850 the line from Bolton through Darwen and Blackburn to Clitheroe had been completed, as had the Blackburn & Preston Railway. The East Lancashire system was connected to Liverpool by the line from Preston through Ormskirk, and by the Liverpool & Bury Railway through Bolton and Wigan. Lines were built to the coast. The Preston & Wyre's line to Fleetwood, associated with the development of the new town and port, was opened in 1840, and branches were built to Blackpool and Lytham in 1846. Southport was reached by the Liverpool Crosby & Southport Railway in 1850 and by the Lancashire & Yorkshire line from Wigan in 1855. The new seaside resort of Morecambe began to develop with the building of the 'little' North Western Railway from Lancaster in 1848, linked through the Lune valley with the Midland system at Skipton. Two other lines were built across the Pennines. The Sheffield Ashton under Lyne & Manchester Railway (later the Manchester Sheffield & Lincolnshire), with a long tunnel at Woodhead, was opened in 1845. Four years later the LNWR route from Manchester to Huddersfield was completed, with an even longer tunnel at Standedge.

In Cheshire, Chester as well as Crewe became an important junction, where the line from Crewe, the Chester & Birkenhead line through the Wirral, the Lancashire & Cheshire Junction Railway from Warrington, the Chester & Holyhead Railway and the GWR line from Shrewsbury met. These routes were important in the growth of traffic to North Wales and to Ireland via Holyhead as well as providing a route between Birkenhead and London.

In the later nineteenth century many more branches were built and some connections were duplicated by different companies. One major new venture, the Cheshire Lines Committee, formed in 1865 by the Manchester Sheffield & Lincolnshire, the Great Northern and the Midland, built routes across the county from the area around Hyde and Marple, through Stockport, Altrincham, Knutsford and Northwich to Chester. It also provided an alternative route from Manchester to Liverpool south of the LNWR and passing through Warrington and Widnes. The Midland Railway through Derbyshire reached Manchester in 1867, via the Manchester Sheffield & Lincolnshire tracks from New Mills: the direct line through Disley tunnel to Manchester Central was not opened until 1902.

The route mileage has shrunk considerably since the second world war, and many stations have been closed. There are surviving examples of many of the original engineering works: on the Liverpool & Manchester Railway, for example, the cutting at Edge Hill, the Olive Mount cutting, the Sankey viaduct, the original terminus at Liverpool Road in Manchester, as well as a number of smaller bridges. There are some fine surviving brick-built viaducts – at Stockport, Whalley, Holmes Chapel, Acton, for example – as well as later ones of wrought iron and steel, and a number of arched cast iron bridges. Apart from Liverpool Road, there are some fine terminal or major junction stations: Manchester Central, Liverpool Lime Street, Chester General, for example. The intermediate stations show a great variety of styles, related sometimes to local building materials, sometimes to the standard designs of a particular company. Another feature of the railway scene, especially in the towns, is the multi-storey warehouses built by the companies, which played an important role in the movement of goods in the Victorian period. They range from traditional structures of brick and timber, like the old warehouse at Liverpool Road, Manchester, through cast iron structures similar to the cotton mills of the period, to more developed structures using wrought iron and steel at the end of the century.

The first electrified line was the Liverpool Overhead Railway (electric from the start), built in 1893–96, with a power station at Bramley-Moore Dock. The Mersey Railway under the river was converted from steam to electric power in 1903. The Lancashire & Yorkshire Railway carried out a number of electrification projects, including the Liverpool–Southport line in 1904, the Manchester–Bury line and the Bury–Holcombe Brook line in 1916. All these were third-rail schemes, while the Midland's Lancaster–Morecambe–Heysham electrification of 1908 was based on an overhead system. Also overhead was the LMS's Manchester–Altrincham electrification in the 1930s, which has now been altered to conform to the voltage of the main inter-city network.

The North West has three railway towns created largely by railway engineering works: Crewe on the Grand Junction; Earlestown, developed by the LNWR from a local foundry in the 1850s; Horwich, a late venture of the 1880s by the Lancashire & Yorkshire Railway.

PORTS AND HARBOURS

Chester is the ancient port of the region, with remains of a Roman quay by the Roodee, just outside the walls of the fortress of Deva, and evidence of likely use in prehistoric times. It was a major port in the later Middle Ages, with much traffic to and from Ireland and Europe and a wide range of imports and exports. Liverpool had been created as a port by King John in 1207, with a royal charter, but it remained comparatively small.

Because of silting in the river Dee Chester was in some difficulties in the sixteenth century, and a new quay was built at Neston in 1541 which continued in use for about a century. Indeed, there was a tendency for the 'port of Chester' to extend along the Dee shore of the Wirral, with landing places at Shotwick, at Parkgate from the late seventeenth century, and at Caldy. Liverpool was still a creek of Chester and paid only £15 in Ship Money under Charles I, compared with £100 paid by the mother port. Much farther north, two creeks were in use at the mouth of the Wyre, Skippool and Wardleys. Wardleys had a sizable trade with the

Baltic, continued through the eighteenth century, importing timber, tar, tallow and flax, the last of which was connected with the growth of the linen industry around Kirkham. Ships also came up the Ribble as far as Preston, anchoring below Penwortham. Liverpool first began to develop as a major port after the Restoration, and was reckoned to be the third port in England by 1699. Apart from trade with Ireland and northern Europe there was a growing business with Africa and with Virginia and the West Indies.

In the eighteenth century there were particularly striking developments in Lancaster and Liverpool. In the early part of the century there was a much used anchorage and warehouses on the north side of the Lune estuary at Sunderland Point. The great period at Lancaster itself was between 1750 and 1800 when the local merchants built up trade not only along the coast, north and south, and with Ireland but also across the Atlantic with the West Indies and the American colonies, with sugar and tobacco and later cotton as the main imports. It was ranked as the fourth port in the country in 1787 and was slightly involved in the slave trade. As on the Dee, there were problems of silting up of the channel, and a new dock was built by the Dock Commissioners at Glasson on the south side of the Lune estuary at the end of the century. In the same period Liverpool's trade grew on a much larger scale and the port had over 60 per cent of the country's African trade by 1795, with a much greater involvement in the slave trade. As at Lancaster, ancillary industries such as shipbuilding, rope-making and sugar refining developed. The population rose from about 5,000 in 1700 to 77,000 in 1801. By the later date six of the docks had been built.

Freckleton on the north side of the Ribble, west of Preston, operated as a small port in the eighteenth century, and there was also some traffic to Tarleton on the opposite shore. Parkgate enjoyed its heyday as a port for travel to Ireland in the early part of the century, and a new cut was made for the Dee channel from 1735, which did something for a time to restore Chester's fortunes as a port.

In the nineteenth century rapid industrial expansion, growth of population and improvement in communications led to the starting of a number of new ports as well as the further expansion of existing ones. Some of the new ventures were directly related to canal-building and river improvement. Ellesmere Port, at the Mersey end of the canal from Chester, became particularly important in the mid-nineteenth century when the Shropshire Union system was complete and a big iron ore trade with the Midlands developed. Runcorn had three sets of docks associated with inland navigations: the Bridgewater Docks from c. 1785, a new wharf built by the Mersey & Irwell Navigation at the end of their Runcorn & Latchford Canal in 1803, and the Weaver Trustees' Weston Point Docks at the end of the Weston Canal, opened in 1810. The first and last are still in use. On the opposite side of the Mersey, Widnes was both a canal and a railway port, with a new dock built at the end of the extension of the Sankey Canal from Fiddlers Ferry in 1833, and at the same time a new rail link from the coalfield at St Helens. Tarleton on the river Douglas had a considerable coastal trade following the new cut made by the Leeds & Liverpool Canal Co. in 1805. The late eighteenth-century dock at Glasson at the mouth of the Lune was joined to the Lancaster Canal by a new branch in 1826 and became an important point of interchange.

Widnes has been mentioned as a railway port: in 1853 the line was extended along the coast to Garston, south of Liverpool, where eventually three docks were built. The new town of Fleetwood, built on sandhills at the mouth of the Wyre by the local landowner, was part of a scheme for London–Scotland traffic, involving the building of the railway from Preston. Later in the century another railway company, the Lancashire & Yorkshire, built the new dock and timber pool, as well as the new passenger terminus. For a time from 1853 Morecambe was a significant port, with steamer services to Scotland and Ireland, following the building of the little North Western Railway from Skipton. It was later eclipsed by Barrow and concentrated on becoming a seaside resort, but the Midland Railway returned to the area in the early twentieth century when it built a new harbour down the coast at Heysham. The new quay and warehouse at Preston, built in the 1840s along with improvements in the Ribble navigation, was linked with the mainline railway by a branch line. The corporation of the town itself built the big new dock, opened in 1892, whose future is now in doubt.

The expansion at Liverpool was on a larger scale altogether, as is witnessed by the five-mile-long stretch of docks which were in use by the early years of this century. Traffic was greater than at London in c. 1860, though less by the end of the century. Cotton was a major import: over half the nation's cotton came in through Liverpool in 1850, and an important business in cotton broking was one result, bringing the east Lancashire manufacturers regularly to the port. Steamer traffic began in the 1820s, or earlier in the case of one or two ferries, and the big shipping lines, with their services across the Atlantic, to Africa and to the Far East – Alfred Holt, Cunard, White Star – provided much of the dock traffic. Liverpool is above all the place to study dock installations, hydraulic power systems and warehouses. The great passenger ships have gone, with the growth of air traffic, but there is still plenty of activity in the north docks and a growing container trade. Across the Mersey, Birkenhead Docks were a new venture, planned in the 1820s, but only coming to fruition from the late 1840s when the first docks were built at the mouth of Wallasey Pool.

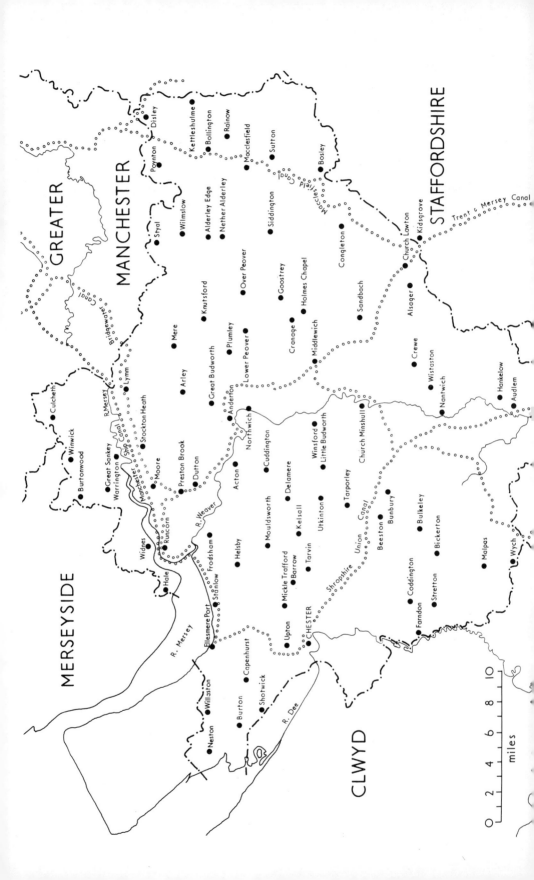

Cheshire

The new county of Cheshire excludes the former cotton area of Stockport, Hyde, Stalybridge and Dukinfield as well as the northern part of the Wirral peninsula. It includes Warrington and Widnes with the adjoining townships, which were formerly in Lancashire. The principal industries have been salt (in the Weaver basin around Northwich, Winsford, Middlewich and Nantwich), silk (especially in Congleton and Macclesfield) and, more recently, chemicals. Much of the plain is largely agricultural and there are numerous surviving sites of water-powered corn mills. The county is crossed by four canal systems: the Macclesfield, Trent & Mersey, Bridgewater and Shropshire Union.

ACTON BRIDGE

Acton Corn Mill SJ 578747. Four-storey brick-built mill converted to residence, with windows in place of loading openings on east front. Wooden upright shaft, great spur wheel and pair of millstones preserved inside house. Large pond to east, sluice with rack-and-pinion gear. Formerly had two waterwheels and two sets of machinery.

Acton bridge SJ 601761. Electrically operated swing bridge of 1932 carrying A49 over Weaver Navigation. Near site of former Acton Bridge locks, originally built 1732, rebuilt 1778, doubled by 1857, now removed.

ADLINGTON

Wood Lane SJ 935820. Pit bank of former colliery with embankment of tramroad (now footpath) running south-east to Macclesfield Canal. Miners' Arms near the wharf was a typical local pub but has been modernised almost out of recognition.

ALDERLEY EDGE

Copper mines. Remains of shafts, adits and workings of numerous mines for copper, lead and cobalt ores found in Bunter and Keuper sandstones. Finds of stone hammers suggest working in prehistoric times, though there is no certain evidence of activity in the Roman period. Working again from 1690s. Charles Roe, who had copper works in Macclesfield, Eaton and Bosley, operated on the Edge 1755 to 1771, when he transferred his interest to Parys mountain, Anglesey. Very active period 1857–78, James Mitchell and Alderley Edge Mining Co., with peak of 13,000 to 15,000 tons per annum, developing Wood and West Mines. Further working in early 20C, mining finally ceased 1919. Principal sites are at West Mine, SJ 849775, where there was an opencast working, now filled in, and an ore-treatment works connected to the mine entrance by tramroad; Wood Mine to east; east of Macclesfield Road,

Engine Vein Mine, SJ 861775, with three shafts and two adit entrances; Pillar Mine and Doc Mine near Stormy Point, SJ 861778. There is an excellent account of the geology, history and workings in Chris J. Carlon, *The Alderley Edge Mines*, 1979. It must be emphasised that unauthorised exploration of the mines is extremely dangerous.

ANDERTON

Township north of Northwich crossed by Trent & Mersey Canal and, on southern boundary, by river Weaver. Formerly had several salt works: at least five in 1860.

Anderton Lift SJ 647753. One of the most important canal monuments in the North West. Built 1872–75 by Weaver Trustees to link navigation with canal. Idea of Leader Williams, designed by Edwin Clark of Clark Stansfield & Clark, Westminster. Operated hydraulically with two wrought-iron caissons working side by side in an iron framework, lifting boats 50 ft (15·2 m). Caissons, weighing 240 tons with water, supported by iron rams moving vertically in hydraulic presses, connected by pipe. Lift worked by removing water from lower caisson. Converted to electric drive 1903–08, rams removed, new framework, pulleys and counterweights. Survives as rebuilt and is in use. Connected to main line of Trent & Mersey Canal by wrought iron aqueduct 162 ft (50 m) long supported on 30 iron piers. Before building of lift two navigations were connected by tramroad and by chutes down which salt was tipped into Weaver flats.

AUDLEM

Audlem locks. On Birmingham & Liverpool Junction Canal (later Shropshire Union), opened 1835. Flight of 15 locks in a mile-and-a-half (2·4 km) between Kinsell Farm, SJ 659416, and Moss Hall bridges, SJ 654440. Brick

sides, masonry coping, double lower gates with gate paddles, single upper gates with ground paddles. Cast iron mileposts at two locks, iron rubbing posts to prevent ropes fraying on five bridges. Locks south of Audlem bridge closer together. At Audlem Wharf, SJ 658435, two-storey brick-built lock keeper's house, cranes and 'Shroppie Fly' inn, which appears to be converted from a warehouse. At **Moss Hall Basin** SJ 654441 Old Stables on west bank, two-storey brick-built, outside staircase at east end. **Weaver aqueduct** SJ 653443 below locks, single-arch, brick, built into long steep embankment. The disused GWR Nantwich–Market Drayton line (opened 1863, closed 1964) runs along the western side of the township.

BARNTON

Weaver Navigation. The southern boundary of the township follows the old course of the Weaver. To north is Barnton Cut, constructed 1832–35 from Winnington, SJ 637744, to Saltersford, SJ 623752. Saltersford locks, SJ 627752, were doubled in 1850s and rebuilt in later 19C.

Trent & Mersey Canal. Two tunnels without towpaths: **Barnton tunnel**, 572 yd (523 m) long, **Saltersford tunnel**, 424 yd (387 m) long. Opened 1777.

BARROW

Great Barrow Corn Mill SJ 475684. Remains of brick-built mill, with pond to north-east, weir 60 yd (50 m) above mill. Traces of wheel pit.

Barrow railway station SJ 469701. Typical CLC station building, two-storey brick-built, two gables on platform front, verandah with cast-iron pillars, ornamental woodwork on gables, ornamental slates. On Mouldsworth–Chester line, opened 1874–75. Station closed 1953.

BEESTON

Beeston locks on Shropshire Union

Canal (Chester & Ellesmere Canal). No. 33 with lock cottage at SJ 556596. No. 34 east of A49 is **Beeston iron lock** SJ 554599. Constructed by Telford 1827–28. Sides of cast iron plates, double iron gates at upper end. Old line of canal visible north of lock: masonry blocks, site of overflow weir. Beeston Wharf west of A49 with two-storey brick-built warehouse.

BETCHTON

Formerly three big salt works between Trent & Mersey Canal and North Staffordshire Railway at Malkins Bank, including Brunner Mond's works, SJ 764590. Now almost no trace, area landscaped. Two photographs of Brunner Mond works in Calvert, *Salt in Cheshire*, pp. 767–8.

Trent & Mersey Canal. A series of **double locks** between Hassall, SJ 777584, and Malkins Bank, SJ 761592. Double gates with gate paddles at lower end, single gates with ground paddles at upper end. Brick sides, masonry coping. Footbridges on cast iron brackets at lower end. Brick, humped, double-arched bridge at Malkins Bank, SJ 763592. **Chellshill aqueduct** SJ 796579. Single arch, brick, curved in plan, stone quoins at sides of arch.

BICKERTON

Bickerton Hill copper mines SJ 517543. North of A534 are shafts and workings of copper mines started in 1697. Worked spasmodically in 18C and 19C: last attempt by Edmund Spargo & Sons of Liverpool, 1906. Rectangular sandstone chimney for flue from boilers of pumping engine.

BOLLINGTON

A visually striking cotton town, with earlier silk and woollen manufacture in the hills north of Macclesfield. Water-powered sites on Harrop brook and

Double locks, Trent & Mersey Canal, Malkins Bank, Betchton, 1979

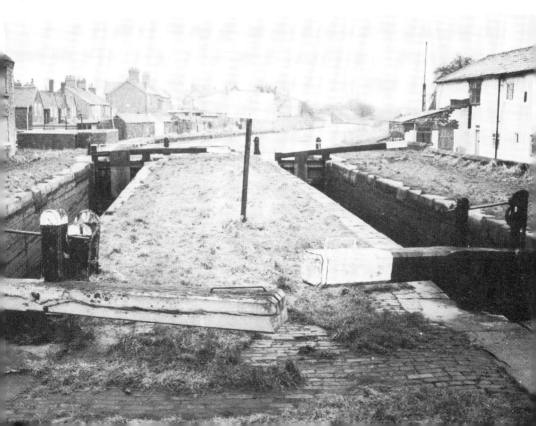

river Dean, later steam-powered mills on Macclesfield Canal, opened 1831. Provided yarn for Nottingham lace industry. Prominent in cotton trade was the Swindells family, whose papers are in the Cheshire Record Office. See Wilmslow Historical Society, *Cotton Town: Bollington and the Swindells Family in the Nineteenth Century*, 1973.

Bollington Higher and Lower Mills SJ 939776/938777. Two former water-powered mills on river Dean worked at one time by Swindells family. Millpond east of Higher Mill, which was used as hat works in late 19C, brewery in early 20C. Now occupied by Shrigley Dyers. Lower Mill taken over in 1875 by Henry & Leigh Slater, paper stainers, still working.

Adelphi Mill SJ 930773. Built in 1850s by George Swindells on west bank of Macclesfield Canal. Six storeys, stone-built, nineteen bays with six-bay extension at south. Internal structure of cast-iron pillars and timber beams (cast iron beams and brick arches on ground floor). Engine house, boiler house and octagonal brick chimney on stone plinth at north. Now occupied by Cheshire Group of Companies.

Clarence Mill SJ 934782. Fine example of mid–19C cotton mill, originally built in 1830s by Martin Swindells. Buildings of three periods, all five-storey, stone-built. Oldest is in centre with internal structure of cast iron pillars and beams, brick arches, twenty bays. On north-west, building of 1854 also with cast iron pillars and beams, brick arches. At south-eastern end late 19C/early 20C block, brick decoration in window arches and below parapet, ornamental staircase and water tower, engine house and tall circular brick chimney. **Rock Bank House** south-east of mill was occupied by members of the Swindells family. Mill is now used by a number of firms.

Lowerhouse Mill SJ 922777. Important textile community on river Dean west of Bollington. Started as water-powered cotton mill by George Antrobus, 1811. Taken over 1832 by Samuel Greg of Quarry Bank Mill, Styal, who further developed the associated community. Main mill building four storeys, stone-built, engine house and boiler house at south end, former water-wheel house at north end. Internally two rows of cast iron pillars, cast iron beams, brick arches, stone-flag floors. Staircase turret projects on east front with clock face at top. Two ponds east of mill, weir on river Dean. Later three-storey building to west, single-storey weaving shed on east. Now occupied by Slater Harrison (from 1933).

Community was built south and west of mill. South of Albert Road is **Long Row**, twenty-four two-storey four-room stone-built cottages, stone-flag roofs, small gardens in front, yards at the back, privies with pitched roofs, one between two cottages. In **Moss Brow** five similar cottages to Long Row on east side, eight later cottages to south. On west side, five two-storey brick-built cottages with stone-flag roofs, continued into Moss Lane. North-west of Moss Lane is **Lowerhouse Library** of 1862 and **Abbots Close**, six two-storey stone-built cottages with overhanging gables, similar in style to library. Samuel Greg formerly lived at the **Mount** SJ 916775.

Stone quarrying. A very important industry in the town in the 19C, supplying stone for public buildings, churches, monuments, setts, kerb-stones, flags. The main quarries were along Kerridge ridge on south side of the township, SJ 9376. There are traces of the former tramroad built 1830–34 between the site of the windmill at SJ 937767 and a wharf on the Macclesfield Canal at SJ 931768.

Macclesfield Canal. Two good examples of aqueducts, single-arched, stone, curved in plan, built into high embankments. One crosses **Wellington Road** just west of town centre, SJ 933779, the other **Grimshaw Lane** SJ 930774.

Bollington viaduct SJ 930779. The Macclesfield Bollington & Marple Railway, opened 1869, now closed, is carried across the valley of the river Dean on a stone viaduct of 22 arches.

BOSLEY

Bosley Old Mill SJ 923648. Former corn mill on tributary of river Dane, three and four storeys, brick-built. Waterwheel was replaced by turbine, latterly used in garage business.

Dane Mills. Higher Works or Danewood Mills SJ 914648. Extensive corn-mill site used by Charles Roe for copper rolling in 18C. In 19C two corn mills, joinery and, at one time, cotton mill and silk throwing. Corn milling until *c.* 1933. Now occupied by Wood Treatment. Mostly recent buildings, but some older, including workers' cottages: one row of six two-storey stone-built, one row of four three-storey brick-built. **Lower Works or Bridge Mills** SJ 913651. In middle of modern buildings four-storey brick-built corn mill, pond on south, clear traces of mill race from Higher Mill.

Bosley locks, Macclesfield Canal. Flight of twelve locks in one mile between Bullgate Lodge, SJ 905670, and Pecker Pool, SJ 908655: fall of 118 ft (36 m), masonry walls, double gates each end, gate paddles on lower ground paddles at upper gates. Iron footbridges at lower end. Rectangular, stone-built, side ponds on west side at each lock linked with overflow weir. **Bosley Reservoir** was built by canal company with feeder from dam to top of locks.

Bosley Station SJ 914647. The North Staffordshire Railway's North Rode–Uttoxeter line, opened 1849, is closed and track removed. Station house survives, but the section at High-er Works has gone. Station was closed 1960–64.

BRERETON

Brereton Corn Mill SJ 774659. On river Croco, three-storey, brick-built, early 19C mill, six bays long, pitched slate roof. Rectangular brick chimney at north-eastern end. Iron window frames with Gothic tracery in top storey. High-breast tension water wheel at north-east end. Foden steam engine of c. 1890. Pond (Brereton Pool) south-east of mill silted up.

BUERTON

Buerton Windmill SJ 685440. Four-storey brick tower with remains of timber cap.

BUNBURY

Bunbury Corn Mill SJ 574581. Restored by North West Water Authority and opened to public 1977. Three storeys, brick, built into dam, c. 1850. Loading opening on to dam road. Pool on south. At ground-floor level overshot water wheel 12 ft 6 in. (3·8 m) diameter, iron shaft and hub, wooden spokes and buckets. Penstock with paddles operated by roller and chains. Iron pit wheel driving wallower wheel on timber main shaft, great spur wheel with drive (underdrift) from stone nuts to two pairs of stones. Separate drive to sack hoist. Twin roller mill by V. J. Booth, Park Works, Congleton. Drying kiln east of wheel pit: hearth at ground-floor level, drying floor above with iron bars supporting perforated floor tiles (partially restored for demonstration purposes). Open to public at weekends.

Bunbury locks SJ 578590. On Shropshire Union Canal (Ellesmere & Chester). Two locks in staircase, brick side walls, masonry coping. Gate paddles on middle and lower gates, ground paddles on upper gates, two-storey brick-built lock cottage on north side. On south

Chester lead works and shot tower, 1978

side stables along towpath, single-storey, brick-built, seven stable doors on canal side with small windows each side. Occupied by firm of boat builders and repairers. Two-storey brick-built warehouse west of stables. Overflow weir north side above upper lock.

BURTON
Burton windmill SJ 313745. Remains of sandstone roundhouse of former post mill, largely destroyed by gale in 1879.

CHESTER
One of the great historic towns of the North West, noted for its Roman and medieval remains, which is also of interest to the industrial archaeologist and historian. Industries have included lead manufacture, engineering, paper-making, leather, glove-making, tobacco-pipe manufacture, flour milling and brewing. Until 19C and silting up of river Dee, Chester was an important

port. The sites are listed in a generally east–west direction.

Chester Water Works SJ 419666. The water works at Boughton go back in origin to 16C but were developed as modern works with steam pumping engines from 1853. On south bank of Chester Canal is circular, brick-built, four-storey water tower with large cast iron tank on top and four-bay brick-built pumping-engine house adjoining.

Hoole Bridge lock. SJ 417666. On Chester Canal, opened to Nantwich 1779. Brick side walls, masonry coping, double gates each end. Lock keeper's cottage on north side.

Chester Lead Works SJ 415667. On north bank of Chester Canal. Started early 19C by Walker Parker & Co., smelting lead and making lead pipes and shot. Prominent feature is circular brick-built shot tower with semi-circular arched windows. Molten lead was poured through a circular tray at the top and the pellets hardened as they fell down the tower into a tank of cold water at the bottom.

Chester Steam Mills SJ 413666. Range of three, five and six-storey brick buildings on south side of canal, with older buildings west of Steam Mill Street, which have iron-framed windows with small panes. Late 19C water tower with ornamental brickwork and name 'Milns Seeds' in white letters.

Chester General Station SJ 413669. One of the finest stations in the North West, built by Francis Thompson 1847–48 for Chester & Crewe, Chester & Birkenhead, Chester & Holyhead Railways. Main Italianate front over 1,000 ft (305 m) long, originally with single platform, 750 ft (228 m) long. Opposite is magnificent **Queen Hotel** of 1859–60, three and four storeys, brick with elaborate stone detailing. To north, **Goods Station** with three-aisle, brick-built warehouse, now occupied by National Carriers.

LNWR wagon works SJ 412669. Off Crewe Street. Two sides survive of single-storey brick workshops built round square. Started by Chester & Crewe Railway.

Hydraulic Engineering Co. SJ 410668. Range of late 19C and early 20C workshops between Charles Street and Egerton Street. Started by Cole Whittle & Co. in early 19C and carried on by John Johnson and his sons from 1832. Joined by Edward B. Ellington, one of the pioneers of hydraulic power, in 1869 and became Hydraulic Engineering Co. in 1874. One of the major firms in the development of the use of hydraulic power and machinery in late 19C and early 20C. Installed power stations and public supply systems in Hull, London, Birmingham, Manchester and Glasgow, supplied dock machinery in Liverpool, London, Portsmouth, Chatham, Devonport,

Chester General station, south front, 1978

Gibraltar, Malta, Hong Kong; machinery for numerous railway goods depots. Special development of processing machinery for East African sisal industry from 1926. In early 20C foundry, cupola, brass foundry, three erecting and machine shops, turning and fitting shops, pattern shops. Supplied set of hydraulic engines for Barton aqueduct on Manchester Ship Canal (see *Eccles*, under *Greater Manchester*). Now make hydraulic presses and pumps.

Albion Corn Mill SJ 410666. On north bank of canal west of Seller Street bridge. Handsome five-storey, brick-built steam mill, seven by three bays, loading openings on canal and road fronts. Flour mill in 1870: J. Wiseman, corn dealer, 1894. Occupied as furniture showrooms.

Canalside Corn Mill SJ 409666. Partly derelict remains of steam corn mill of Griffiths Bros on south side of canal. Range of two, three and five-storey buildings with loading openings on canal front. Steam mill on OS map of 1875: Griffiths Bros in 1893–94 directory.

Queens Park bridge SJ 410660. Suspension bridge built before 1860 to link Chester with the growing suburb of Queen's Park. Rebuilt by Chester Corporation 1923 with two steel ropes each side anchored to rock.

Old Dee bridge SJ 407657. Late 14C sandstone bridge, widened in 1826. Mixture of pointed and segmental arches. Triangular openings in parapet wall from footpath on east side. Footpath on west side corbelled out in 1826.

Dee Mills. Immediately east of old bridge is weir which supplied the former corn mills on the north side of the river, dating back in origin to the Norman period. Rebuilt after fires in 1789, 1819, 1847 and 1895. Had three external waterwheels. Became small hydro-electric power station established by city, 1913. Two arched openings to turbines with grilles and sluice controls.

Grosvenor bridge SJ 403656. Magnificent single segmental stone arch with 200 ft (61 m) span, built by Harrison 1827–32. Described in White's *Cheshire Directory*, 1860, as '. . . unrivalled as a work of art in the history of bridge building'.

Northgate locks SJ 402666. Chester Canal. Approached from east by 500 yd (457 m)-long cutting in sandstone below city wall. Three-rise staircase, double gates, ground paddles except at bottom gates. Sandstone side walls, partly cut in natural rock. Iron footbridge at lower end of each lock. At top lock two-storey, three-bay, brick-built lock cottage with pyramidical roof.

Tower Wharf SJ 401667. Just south of junction of Chester Canal and Dee Basin arm. Georgian office building: former headquarters of Shropshire Union Canal Co. Three-storey, brick-built warehouse with central loading opening on canal front. North of wharf in angle between two arms is **dry dock** SJ 399667, built 1798, single dock, stone stepped sides, double wooden gates at north end, covered by hipped slate roof on cast iron pillars. To north is Ellesmere Canal, opened to Ellesmere Port 1795; to south, arm runs through two locks to **Dee Basin** SJ 399666, partly filled in on north side. At west end is recently rebuilt lock into river Dee.

Dee viaduct SJ 397658. Three steel lattice-girder spans over river on line to Holyhead. First built with three 100 ft (30·5 m) cast iron spans, which partially collapsed in 1847, wrecking a train and killing five people. Accident was one of major factors in abandonment of long cast iron spans. On north-east side, long 48–arch brick approach viaduct across Roodee.

CHURCH LAWTON
Canals. The junction of the Hall Green branch of the Trent & Mersey Canal with the main line is in the adjoining township of Kidsgrove at SJ

835546. The main line was opened in 1777, the Hall Green branch in 1831 to join the Macclesfield Canal. The two run parallel for half-a-mile, then the Hall Green branch crosses the main line on **Pool Locks aqueduct** SJ 830549: mainly brick, with stone arch and coping, single segmental arch, curved in plan. Stone tablet each side inscribed 'Pool Locks Aqueduct MDCCCXXVIIII'. East of aqueduct on main line is a set of double locks. At south end of aqueduct Hall Green branch is crossed by iron footbridge with brick abutments and side walls, and there is a small boatyard off the canal. On main line west of A34 is **Red Bull Wharf** SJ 828551, with three-storey, brick-built warehouse, crane and water tank. West of Red Bull Wharf are further sets of locks in pairs at Townfield, Church locks, and east of Snape's aqueduct. On Hall Green branch north of Pool Locks aqueduct is Telford's single-arch aqueduct over the A50, SJ 831551.

CHURCH MINSHULL

Church Minshull Corn Mill SJ 667608. Long four-storey brick mill being converted to residence. Two undershot water wheels remain, side by side, fed by same head race from river Weaver, now dried up. Worked until *c.* 1954. There were two sets of machinery and stones, one east, one west of waterwheels.

CONGLETON

Congleton developed as a centre of the silk industry from the middle of 18C, the first mill being erected near Dane bridge in 1752–55. Apart from silk throwing and spinning Congleton specialised also in ribbon weaving: there were twelve firms in this branch in 1860. The peak of the industry was reached in the mid-19C: there were over 50 silk mills in 1850 and about a third of the population were employed. With growing French competition the industry declined in the later 19C: 22 mills in 1886, seven in 1910. Cotton spinning was also introduced but never on the scale of silk.

CENTRAL AREA

Domestic workshops. There were many silk hand-loom workshops in 19C: examples of three-storey buildings with workshops with long windows on top storey and living accommodation below in Mill Street, SJ 858632, just south of Dane bridge, and at corner of Rood Hill and Ryle Street, SJ 857634.

Old Mill SJ 859632. A modern works stands on the site of the silk-throwing mill at Mill Green on the north bank of the river Dane. Built by John Clayton and William Pattison 1752–55 and driven by 20 ft (6·1 m) diameter water wheel. Samuel Pearson & Son, silk throwsters, in later 19C.

Salford Mill SJ 857634. On north bank of Dane, east of Mill Street. Good example of 'Georgian' mill style: three storeys and basement, brick-built, twelve bays long with three-bay pediment on south front.

Brookside Mill SJ 858632. South of river Dane and west of Mill Street. Five storeys plus basement and attic, brick-built, eight by six bays, projecting latrine turret at east end. Older four-storey building to west: windows with stone sills and lintels. Occupied by silk throwsters in 1860.

Meadow Mill SJ 860631. In Park Road, good example of mid-Victorian silk mill. Three storeys, brick-built, rectangular windows with stone sills and lintels, 14 by 3 bays, pitched slate roof, stone plaque on south front with date 1860. Occupied by two firms of silk throwsters in 1874. To west is another and later mill, three storeys, 16 bays long, windows with blue-brick arched lintels, 19-bay building at right angles in Hall Street.

Worrall Street Mill SJ 861631. Impressive four-storey, 24-bay brick-built mill, occupied by manufacturer of shirts and pyjamas.

Park Street Mill SJ 862629. Four-storey mill of similar date to Worrall Street Mill, sixteen bays long. George Kent, silk throwster, in 1874. Occupied by engineering firm.

Foundry Mill SJ 862630. Silk mill between river Dane and Willow Street, taken over by Berisford's, ribbon manufacturers, in 1858. Four-storey spinning/throwing mill with single-storey north-light weaving shed to east. East again is site of **Victoria Mill**, where Isaac Berisford started in business. The firm has a modern factory in Brook Street to north.

Canal Street SJ 863628. There are two three-storey brick-built mills on south side of street, which runs south-east from town centre. William Toad, silk throster, Canal Street Mill, appears in White's *Cheshire Directory*, 1860. Silk throwster and silk manufacturer in 1874.

EAST AND SOUTH-EAST

Congleton Wharf SJ 866622. On Macclesfield Canal, opened 1831. **Aqueduct** over Canal Road, cast iron arch in six sections, iron trough and railings, five iron plates on each side of trough. Curved stone side walls. Very good example. To west is **wharf** with three-storey, brick-built warehouse, rectangular windows with stone sills and lintels, pitched slate roof, loading openings on canal front. **Wharf Inn** at entrance from Canal Road.

Congleton Railway. Former tram-road, built *c.* 1807, which ran from coal yard on Moss Road, SJ 865612, across ridge of Mow Cop to Stonetrough Colliery in Wolstanton, Staffs. Stone blocks, on which rails were fixed, and fragments of rail have been found along route. Line visible near Fairfields, SJ 867604, and where it crosses Mow Cop Road, SJ 866584.

Dane in Shaw viaduct SJ 877627. Ten-arch brick viaduct on North Staf-fordshire Railway's Congleton–Macclesfield line, opened 1849.

Dane in Shaw Mill SJ 883620. On Dane in Shaw brook north of Reades Lane, perhaps the best surviving example of a silk mill in Congleton. Three storeys and basement, brick-built, rectangular windows with stone sills and lintels, 18 bays long, two-bay centre pediment with clock, hipped roof. Fine setting facing on to mill pond on south. Richard Grinder, silk throwster, in 1860.

Timbersbrook Mill SJ 896627. Pond only survives of former water-powered silk-throwing mill. On Timbers brook to north-east is **Pool Bank Mill** SJ 891629, two storeys, stone-built, with brick and timber additions, silted-up pond to east. Marked as silk mill on OS six-inch map of 1882.

NORTH-EAST

Buglawton, north of Buxton Road, had a number of silk mills. There are 19C buildings each side of **Havannah Street** SJ 867637, and at **Dane Row** SJ 865636 an earlier mill by the river, four and five storeys with basement, brick-built but with older stone-built section in middle of range. South-west of this is site of **Washford Mill**.

Bath Vale Mill SJ 873633. Former cotton mill, three storeys, brick-built, stone-faced on main front. At south-east row of five cottages, three storeys at front, two at back. Only weir survives of nearby **Primrose Vale Silk Mill**. Peter Hunt was silk throwster there in 1860.

Congleton viaduct SJ 896657. Twenty-arch brick-built viaduct over Dane valley on Congleton–Macclesfield line, 1849. 110 ft (33·5 m) above river bed.

WEST

Dane Mill SJ 849636. Another good example of originally water-powered silk mill, just south of river. Four storeys, brick-built, 24 bays long with four-bay central pediment on south-eastern front, square brick chimney.

Hargreaves Wharf iron aqueduct, Macclesfield Canal, Congleton, 1978

Dane in Shaw silk mill, Congleton, south front, 1978

Weir to east. Occupied by Henry Barton, silk throwster, and James Pearson & Co. ribbon manufacturers, in 1874. Pearson's also in 1896.

CRANAGE

Cranage Corn Mill SJ 757677. On river Dane south of Cranage bridge. Modern buildings around part of older brick-built mill, occupied by animal-food manufacturers. Fine curved sandstone weir, iron paddle gear at entrance to mill race by Ames Crosta Mills & Co. of Heywood. 90 h.p. water turbine.

CREWE

One of the great railway towns, developed from rural townships of Church Coppenhall and Monks Coppenhall after the Grand Junction Railway opened its engineering works in 1840–43. Meeting point of Grand Junction Railway, Manchester & Birmingham Railway and Chester & Crewe Railway, all of which were absorbed into LNWR in 1846. The history of the town and railway community is fully discussed in W. H. Chaloner, *Social and Economic Development of Crewe, 1780–1923*, 1950, reprinted 1971.

Crewe Station SJ 712547. Perhaps the most famous of all railway junctions. Started as small station on Grand Junction 1837–40, rebuilt 1845–46, 1867, 1895–1901, enlarged 1903–06. Recent entrance on Nantwich Road. Station buildings of late 19C/early 20C survive with alterations. Two-storey buildings on platforms 1 and 2, 5 and 6, single-storey buildings on platforms 3 and 4. Yellow brick with stone detailing and red-brick decoration above windows and doors and below parapet on upper storeys. Moulded heads in keystones of arches on platforms 3, 4 and 5. Some iron window frames with semi-circular arched heads. Fine bow windows on platforms 4 (Paddock Buffet) and 5. Arcaded yellow-brick walling between platforms 2 and 3, platforms 3

and 4 and east of platform 6: looks earlier than buildings.

Crewe Arms Hotel SJ 711549. Opposite station entrance, three storeys with six gables on Nantwich Road front. In Gresty Road south of station is Rail House, recent 13-storey office block, beyond it is **Cattle Market** developed by Crewe Cattle Market & Abattoir Co. from 1883. South again are single-storey brick buildings erected for Electric Signal and Telephone Department, 1903–04. A particularly interesting survival is one of the **enginemens' barracks**, built 1897 to accommodate train crews while waiting for their duties, three storeys, brick-built, fifteen bays long, gables each end, now empty. South of Gresty bridge are the wagon repair works and the goods station.

Marmion Clothing Works SJ 706548. In Camm Street, north of Nantwich Road. One of a number of clothing factories started in later 19C. Opened on site of former printing works after 1887. Bought by CWS 1917, extended 1937–38. Long two-storey yellow and red brick building on Camm Street, seven-aisled building with north-light roof to north. Another surviving clothing factory is **Buxton Works** SJ 714556 in Buxton Avenue, opened 1894. Two storeys, six bays, very much like a fustian-cutting workshop. Worked by Heap's, who took over in 1912.

Old Works SJ 708554. Site of railway works built by GJR 1840–43, now closed. Became main locomotive works of LNWR. Superintendents included Francis Trevethick, 1841–57, John Ramsbottom, 1857–71, F. W. Webb, 1871–1903. Over 10,000 employed at peak in 1920. Almost nothing survives of the adjoining community built up by GJR and LNWR, planned by Joseph Locke, with John Cunningham as architect. There were over seven hundred houses in 1858, of four different

Enginemen's barracks, Gresty Road, Crewe, 1979

types according to the status of the occupiers. Now there is one pair of houses in **Prince Albert Street** SJ 706556, partly used by BR Veterans' Insitute, partly derelict. Even Christ Church, opened 1845 and built with financial help from GJR, has been largely demolished: tower and later chancel survive. LNWR were patrons of the living. There were also a National School, baths, mechanics' institute and savings bank. Later 19C housing north of Victoria Street is also being cleared: good row survives in Victoria Street, south side, Nos. 76–90, SJ 704560.

Deviation Works SJ 703555. Built from 1867 inside loop when Chester & Holyhead line was diverted from Old Works. Long ranges of brick-built workshops along line, empty and becoming derelict. Tall octagonal brick chimney makes prominent landmark at east end. At west end in Flag Lane is a fine cast iron water tank on tall red and blue-brick arches.

LNWR Steel Works SJ 695558. Opened 1864 for making steel by the new Bessemer process: the first Bessemer-steel rails in the world had been laid at Crewe Station, 1861. Made rails and later locomotive boilers. Three-high rail-rolling mill in 1892. Bessemer process superseded from 1901. Steel works and rail mill closed down 1932. Now BR engineering works. To west is **Rolls Royce works**, established 1938 for manufacture of aeroplane engines as part of rearmament programme.

CROWTON
Crowton Corn Mill SJ 578747. On Crowton brook, occupied by W. & A. Bradley. Modern buildings east of road, old mill west of road: three storeys, brick-built, wooden loading doors on each floor. Site of wheel pit on ground

floor inside mill. Millpond and Mill House to west.

CUDDINGTON
Cuddington Mills There were three water-powered corn mills on Cuddington Brook. Old Mill SJ 594715, corn and saw mill, long leat along valley. **Higher Mill** SJ 595720: millpond survives, foundations of stone and brick in valley below. **Lower Mill** SJ 597724, converted to residence and entirely modernised; pond remains. In 18C and early 19C one of sites was used as paper mill.

DARNHALL
Darnhall Corn Mill SJ 635633. On Ash brook, tributary of Weaver. Four storeys, brick-built, whitewashed. Iron frames with small panes in many of windows. Two loading doors on west front: inscription 'WTC 1829' between doors. Two waterwheels: south wheel, overshot, 12 ft 6 in. (3·8m) diameter, wooden main shaft, great spur wheel, stone nuts driving three sets of stones, overdrift. Two sets of stones at north end. Attractive pool to west, sluice with rack-and-pinion paddle gear, stone weir. Working when Norris reported in 1969, now empty.

DAVENHAM/HARTFORD
Vale Royal locks SJ 640704. On Weaver Navigation. Site of original timber lock, 1732. Rebuilt *c.* 1778, doubled in late 19C. 220 ft (67·05 m) long.

DELAMERE
Tollhouse SJ 541687. On Chester–Northwich road east of Kelsall. Single-storey, three bays, Gothic windows, hipped slate roof, two chimney stacks.

DISLEY
Disley tunnel SJ 978852/944862. 3,800 yd (3,474 m) long tunnel on Midland Railway: direct line from New Mills to Manchester Central opened 1902. Series of air shafts along line, including two on Disley golf course.

DUTTON
River Weaver. Pickerings Cut SJ 574763/582764, 850 yd (777 m) long. Remains of **Pickerings lock** at west end: masonry walls, anchors and recess for gate pivots. Handsome lock house and toll house on north side. Locks removed after 1945. **Dutton locks** SJ 587769: one of original timber-lock sites, doubled in 1830s, rebuilt late 19C.

Dutton viaduct SJ 582765. Sandstone railway viaduct of 20 arches each of 63 ft (19·2 m) span carrying Crewe–Warrington line across Weaver. Built by George Stephenson and Joseph Locke for Grand Junction Railway.

EATON
Havannah SJ 869647. Industrial community on the river Dane near Congleton, named in commemoration of British capture of Havannah, 1762. Copper works established by Charles Roe of Macclesfield, 1763, made brass wire and copper sheeting. Worked until early 19C. There was also a silk mill and an older corn mill. Only survivals are fine stone weir and a long row of brick-built workers' cottages with stone-flag roofs.

ELLESMERE PORT
New canal port on the Mersey at northern end of the Ellesmere Canal (later Shropshire Union), opened from Chester 1796. Series of docks and warehouses built in mid- and late 19C with particular period of development by Thomas Telford and William Cubitt 1830–43. Peak of traffic before Manchester Ship Canal was built through to Eastham in 1894. Goods from Midlands and Potteries, important iron-ore trade from Furness and Cumberland in opposite direction. Now site of **Boat Museum**, open to public Easter to

September, established by North West Museum of Inland Navigation. In 20C big development of new industries along Ship Canal, including Stanlow oil refineries, started 1924. For historical background see Adrian Jarvis, *Ellesmere Port – Canal Town, 1795–1921*, 1977.

Canal terminus and docks SJ 405772. Canal from south-east enters **Upper Basin**, where there are the **Upper Engine House** for the hydraulic power system, with wooden accumulator tower; **Island Grain Warehouse**, 1871, two storeys, brick-built, three aisles, 15 bays long, six loading openings on north-east front, main area of museum. Beyond Upper Basin are two sets of two locks side by side, replacing single pair of 1843, with three-storey **Canal Office** (now Museum headquarters), on west, remains of stables, pattern shop and work shop on east. Locks lead down to **Inner Dock**, 270 ft by 350 ft (82·3 m by 100·6 m) with remains of Victoria arm, Bone-Ash Warehouse and arm to Iron Shed of 1884. North of Inner Dock is **Lower Engine House** with another wooden accumulator tower, and single lock to **Tidal Basin** connected to Mersey. Through lock to south-west of Tidal Basin is large dock in use by 1834, 435 ft by 139 ft (133 m by 42 m): on north side, foundations of great E-plan General Warehouse and of China Clay and General Warehouse of *c.* 1890. Still standing is **China Clay Shed** of 1844, brick-built, single-storey, two aisles with pitched slate roofs. On the pier north of the entrance to the Tidal Basin is a slender octagonal brick-built **lighthouse** of *c.* 1800. North-west of the dock area is the remains of the flour-mill canal arm, built to service three roller mills of early 20C.

The Shropshire Union Canal Co. also built houses for employees. Adjoining the dock at **1–4 Lower Mersey Street** is a handsome terrace of four three-storey brick-built Georgian

houses for senior officials. South-west of the new by-pass is an interesting area of housing in Grace Road, Westminster Road, Wilkinson Street, Edward Street and George Street, much of it built round an open recreation area. Notable are some forty pairs of semi-detached houses with gables to the road and bay windows.

Manchester Ship Canal runs east–west along the south bank of the Mersey with an embankment 6,200 yd (5,670 m) long, two cast iron syphons 12 ft (3·7 m) diameter to take the river Gowy under the canal, and at **Mount Manisty** SJ 393789 an artificial hill formed from material excavated from rock cutting during the construction of the canal.

Railways. Two good examples of sandstone station buildings with ornamental gables and chimneys on the GWR/LNWR Helsby–Hooton line, opened 1863: **Ellesmere Port** SJ 403675 and **Little Sutton** SJ 372769. **Hooton Station** SJ 350783 is junction of line from Helsby with Chester & Birkenhead Railway, opened 1840, ᴗ 1 line to Parkgate and West Kirby, opened 1866 and 1886. Four platforms, three-arch sandstone bridge on north, disused platform on west for West Kirby line, with former waiting room, and station name, now part of Wirral Way.

FRODSHAM
Bradley Corn Mills SJ 532766. There were formerly two mills on the brook. At the **Higher Mill** is a dried-up pond, remains of sandstone and brick walling, site of wheel pit and slight traces of wheel. Pond for **Lower Mill** converted to garden: mill is now a residence.

River Weaver. Frodsham bridge SJ 530784, on A50, sandstone, three segmental arches. Formerly ship building yards, coal and slate wharf in area. **Frodsham Cut and locks** SJ 537783/ 544778: 900 yd (823 m) cut made by

1781, later by-passed by River Weaver Canal, closed 1955.

Frodsham Station SJ 518779. On Birkenhead Lancashire & Cheshire Junction Railway line from Warrington to Chester, opened 1850. Two-storey, brick station building with stone detail on north, single-storey brick goods shed on south.

GRAPPENHALL and THELWALL

Cliff Lane Tannery SJ 646863. Tanning was an important local industry in 19C. The building of the former CWS tannery survives in Cliff Lane, four storeys, brick-built, three loading doors on road front. Knutsford Road Tannery has been demolished.

Bridgewater Canal. Good example of humped, single-arch, brick bridge at Stanley Lunt, SJ 636864. **Halfacre Lane aqueduct** SJ 654871, stone, single-arch, brick inside arch, curved side walls, tunnel 24 yd (29·9 m) long.

Thelwall Station SJ 654871. On LNWR (Warrington & Stockport) line, opened 1853, station closed 1956. To west is interesting bridge over Halfacre Lane with six inverted T section iron beams.

GREAT SANKEY

Sankey Canal (St Helens Canal), opened 1757–59, extended to Fidlers Ferry 1771. **Sankey bridges** SJ 585876, where canal joined Sankey brook, developed boat building, lime kilns, coal wharves and a rope works. There are a number of swing bridges along the line of the canal. The electrically operated lift bridge on the A57 has been replaced by a fixed bridge.

Bewsey lock SJ 593897. Derelict, masonry sides, recesses and anchors for gate pivots, iron bollards, crossed by wooden swing bridge with iron bracing.

Sankey Station SJ568886. On CLC Manchester–Liverpool line, opened

1874. Typical CLC cottage station building.

HARTFORD

Vale Royal viaduct SJ 643706. Five-arch stone viaduct across Weaver, on Grand Junction Railway, opened 1837. 1,600 yd (1,463 m)-long cutting west to Hartford Station.

Vale Royal locks see **Davenham**.

HASLINGTON

Winterley Corn Mill SJ 747571. Three-storey brick mill, built against dam, loading opening on A534 road front. Large millpond east of road. On roadside is Cheshire County Council cast iron milestone of 1896.

HASSALL

Roughwood Lower Corn Mill SJ 775582. Four-storey brick-built late 19C mill replacing earlier building. Worked until 1939: overshot water wheel. Now residence.

HELSBY

Helsby Quarries on Helsby Hill supplied stone for public buildings (including Liverpool Customs House), churches and docks in Liverpool, Birkenhead and Wirral.

Helsby Station SJ 486757. At junction of Birkenhead Lancashire & Cheshire Junction Railway lines from Warrington to Chester, opened 1850, Helsby to Hooton, opened 1863, and CLC line from Northwich to Helsby, opened 1869. Disused station building on east side, two storeys, stone-built, Dutch-style gables with finials, single-storey building to north. Single-storey building of similar style on west platform. LNWR-type signalbox at north end.

BICC Cables SJ 484746. Late 19C and early 20C buildings and housing. Started by G. Crosland-Taylor as Telegraph & Trading Co., 1906, and later became part of British Insulated Callender's Cables.

HOLMES CHAPEL
Holmes Chapel railway viaduct SJ 773678. Viaduct across valley of river Dane on Manchester & Birmingham Railway, opened 1842. Engineer, G. W. Buck. Twenty-three arches each of 63 ft (18·2 m) span. Brick piers on stone plinths, brick arches, stone parapet.

HURLESTON
Hurleston Junction SJ 627553. Junction of main line of Shropshire Union Canal with Welsh Canal to Llangollen, opened 1805. Four locks in 200 yd (192·6 m) west of junction.

KETTLESHULME
Lumbhole Mill SJ 985804. Stone-built late 18C candlewick mill with 25 ft (7·6 m) diameter breast-shot water-wheel, coupled to simple steam beam engine by Sherratt's of Salford *c*. 1830. Now used as store and workshop for overhauling industrial machinery.

KINGSLEY
Kingsley Corn Mill SJ 563750. Former water-powered mill with older buildings on west, four storeys, brick-built, loading openings on west front, partly of early date (17C ?). Site of waterwheel inside: worked until 1957. Recent buildings on east. Pond raised above road. Occupied by manufacturers of animal foods.

KNUTSFORD
Knutsford Station SJ 754784. On CLC (Cheshire Midland) line from Altrincham to Northwich, opened 1862–63. On south side, three-storey and single-storey buildings, late 19C, blue-brick decoration, Gothic windows and door openings. Wooden canopy over platform on six cast-iron pillars. On north side, waiting area with timber back and side walls, canopy on cast iron pillars with ornamental brackets. CLC

wooden signal box east of station.

LITTLE BUDWORTH
Little Budworth Corn Mill SJ 600656. Two and three-storey brick building with stonework at lower level, loading openings on road side. No machinery. Pond (Budworth Pool) on west.
  Oulton Mill SJ 581651. Three-storey brick-built mill against dam of large pond across road on west. Central wooden loading doors on road front. Wing at right-angles to east. Iron plate on gable end with three crossed arrows and date 1781. Formerly had two water-wheels. Now used as store.

LYMM
Fustian cutting. The process of cutting through the loops of the various types of fustian and velvet was an important domestic and small-workshop industry in 19C Lymm. White's *Cheshire Directory* in 1860 lists 24 fustian cutters. There are two good surviving examples of domestic workshops: **11–19 Church Road** SJ 678871, row of five three-storey brick-built cottages with top-storey workshops with long windows, outside stone staircase to workshops at east; **Woodland Avenue** SJ 691886, row of four three-storey brick-built cottages, top-storey workshops with multi-light windows, partially modernised.
  Lymm Slitting Mill SJ 682875. Former water-powered mill for slitting wrought iron bars for nail-making, started in early 17C. In 18C made barrel hoops for gunpowder factory at Thelwall. Used by woollen manufacturer from *c*. 1800, pulled down *c*. 1835. Excavated 1968, 1971, 1973 by Lymm and District Historical Society and North Cheshire Archaeological Group. Remains preserved: millpond, stone dam, curved weir, wheel pit, foundations of forge, furnace and rolling shop, tunnels for tail race and by-pass.

Fustian-cutting domestic workshops, Church Road, Lymm, 1979

Foundations of cottage to east; see *CBA Group 5 Archaeological News Letter*, No. 23, March 1974, and *Lymm and District Local History Society Newsletter*, No. 70, January 1974, for accounts of the excavations.

Lymm Corn Mill SJ 684873. Buildings demolished 1935 but pond survives near village centre and sluice with rack-and-pinion paddle gear.

Bridgewater Canal. Good examples of single-arch brick and stone aqueducts at **Heatley** SJ 703873, **Lymm** SJ 682873, with tunnel 30 yd (27·4 m) long, and **Statham** SJ 673873. At **Heatley Wharf** SJ 705873 is a three-storey brick-built warehouse, five bays with semi-circular arched windows. **Lymm Wharf** SJ 683873 has a two-storey toll-house/office and a three-storey warehouse.

LNWR (Warrington & Stockport Railway), opened 1853. At **Lymm Lane crossing** SJ 698882 good example of brick-and-timber signal box. Crossing house and station buildings survive

at **Heatley & Warburton Station** SJ 704883, crossing house and brick-and-timber signal box at **Lymm Station** SJ 679876, both closed 1962.

MACCLESFIELD

One of Cheshire's two great silk towns. Cottage industry of silk button-making from time of Queen Elizabeth I. Silk throwing of yarn by water power introduced in mid-18C following ending of patent of Lombe brothers, who had mill in Derby. Hand-loom weaving of silk cloth from *c.* 1790. Seventy mills by 1825, 5,000 looms, over 600 weavers with looms in workshops at home. Power weaving gradually introduced in late 19C: 48 manufacturers, 24 throwsters in 1857/58. There are some thirty surviving mill buildings, mostly used for other processes, and numerous rows of three-storey brick-built domestic workshops. The mills are of brick, mostly three to five storeys, the earlier ones with traditional structure of timber beams, joists and floors, late ones with cast iron pillars, and occasionally cast iron beams.

CENTRAL AREA

Frosts Mill SJ 919732. Park Green. Built as water-powered silk-throwing mill on river Bollin in late 18C by Dainty & Ryle, later taken over by William Frost & Sons. Badly damaged by fire in 1976 and south-eastern block largely demolished. Main block fronting Park Green remains: five storeys, brick-built, 13 bays with three-bay central pediment with clock and bell turret, hipped stone-flag roof, internal structure of timber beams, joists and floors, rooms 84 ft by 18 ft (25·6 m by 5·5 m). Waterwheel pit on Mill Lane front for 16 ft (4·9 m) diameter wheel, scrapped 1906, fed by underground culvert and cast iron pipe.

Paradise Mills SJ 918732. Park Lane. Early 19C mills, four and five storeys, partly with timber structure, partly cast iron pillars and timber beams. Taken over by present occupiers, Cartwright & Sheldon, in 1920s and still used for silk weaving. Top floor used for hand-loom weaving until recently: one jacquard loom now in North Western Museum of Science and Industry, Manchester.

SOUTH

Pool Street SJ 921729. East of Mill Lane. Interesting early group of five three-storey cottages with workshops, four storeys at back, four-light windows in top (workshop) floor.

Copper works. In area of Windmill Street east of river Bollin, SJ 923729. Site of works run by Charles Roe from 1758 to c1801. Copper ore from Alderley Edge and Parys Mountain (Anglesey). Windmill used for grinding ore. Only survival is street names: Copper Street, Calamine Street. Roe also had works at Bosley and Eaton (Havannah).

St George's Street Mill SJ 919729. Impressive 32-bay-long mill, three storeys and basement, projecting latrine turret on east front, square brick chimney projecting through roof. Dendy & Beard, silk manufacturers, in late 19C. In this area west of Mill Lane there are good examples of three-storey domestic workshops in **Pitt Street**, Nos. 4–14, long four-light windows in top storey, windows in gable ends; **High Street**, two rows of three cottages; **Peel Street**, Nos. 56–70 with three and four-light windows on top floor.

Albion Mill SJ 921725, London Road. Four storeys and basement, windows with stone sills and lintels, hipped slate roof. Date 1845 on stone pediment above main front. Built in front of older mill along river Bollin.

Wilshaw Mill SJ 920724. Built originally 1840s, south of Albion Mill. Five storeys, 15 by 4 bays, moulded brickwork, ornamental wooden brackets below cornice, hipped slate roof, internal structure of timber beams and wooden plank floors. Staircase tower at east. Octagonal brick chimney, shortened. Macclesfield Silk Manufacturing Society, a co-operative venture, from 1888, jacquard power-loom weaving.

WEST

Hope Mill SJ 915733. Fine five-storey mill, 18 by three bays, six-bay central pediment with clock, hipped slate roof, water tower at Owen Street end, square tapering brick chimney projecting from roof at rear. Joshua Oldfield Nicholls, silk throwing and manufacturing, in later 19C.

Paradise Street SJ 914733. Probably best surviving examples of domestic workshops in the town, recently restored. Row of seventeen cottages on north, fifteen on south, built uphill in steps. Three-light windows with small panes on top (workshop) floors. Good examples also in **Crossall Street** and **Newton Street** near by.

Catherine Street SJ 913739. Row of seven three-storey domestic workshops with four-light windows on top floor, Nos. 27–39. At corner of **Primrose**

Silk weavers' domestic workshops, Paradise Street, Macclesfield, 1979

Street, three-storey mill building, ten by five bays, transitional between domestic workshops and power-driven mill.

Crompton Road SJ 911732. Nos. 142–56, row of eight three-storey cottages with workshops, with four-light windows. Nos. 183–9 **Crompton Mount**, dated 1877, four cottages with long top-storey windows with arched lintels. Further row at Nos. 196–200. Good examples also in **Bond Street**, row of thirteen cottages.

Crompton Road Mill SJ 911736. Early four-storey six-bay mill with stone-flag roof on south, latrine turret at south-east corner. Later weaving shed to south, and three-storey mill to north. Could have started as water-powered throwing mill. William Pownall & Sons, silk throwers and manufacturers, in later 19C. Occupied by engineering firm.

Oxford Road Mill SJ 909735. Good mid-19C example, five storeys and attic, 18 by 4 bays, pitched slate roof, latrine turret at north-east, four-storey wing on Oxford Road with name 'J. Dunkerly &

Son Ltd', who were silk manufacturers and throwsters in late 19C. Interesting early workshop behind house opposite mill.

Chester Road Mill (Card Factory) SJ 909736. Fine example, five storeys and attic, 17 by 5 bays, central five-bay pediment with clock, bell turret and weather vane, (cf. Frosts Mill). Square brick chimney at rear, latrine tower at east, water tower added at west. Built in 1820s as steam-powered mill with internal structure of cast iron pillars, lengthwise cast iron beams, crosswise timber beams, replaced by modern steel structure. John Birchenough & Sons in late 19C.

EAST

Union Flour Mill SJ 924734. Formerly steam-powered mill on east bank of Macclesfield Canal, south of Buxton Road, five storeys, brick-built, blue-and-white brick decoration below parapet, sixteen bays on canal front, stone-arched opening from canal, loading slots, iron railings along parapet. Engine house and circular brick chimney at north-east. Twentieth-century block on east. Fitton's, flour millers, in 1880s, taken over by Hovis: name 'Hovis Mills' on north end wall. Now industrial estate.

Hurdsfield Mills SJ 923740. Complex of buildings associated with Brocklehurst's for over 200 years, now Brocklehurst Whiston Amalgamated. John Brocklehurst joined Acton & Street, button makers, on site in 1745 and started silk throwing: two-storey Georgian cottage on Hurdsfield Road and four-storey mill developed from button works. Late 18C/early 19C three-storey buildings on east. Two mills built for steam power (beam engines) in 1820s and 1830s in Arbourhay Street/Fence Street area. Albert Mill, 1840s, with structure of cast iron pillars and beams, brick arches. Victoria Mill, 1887, five storeys. Single-storey weaving shed rebuilt in 1930s.

MARSTON

Township north of Northwich which formerly had a number of salt works and rock-salt mines, served for transport by Trent & Mersey Canal. White's *Cheshire Directory*, 1860, lists nine salt works and five rock-salt mine proprietors.

Lion Salt Works SJ 671755. The only surviving open-pan salt works in Cheshire. Started 1842, now Ingram Thompson & Co. Four shallow iron pans where brine, pumped from wells on site, is evaporated by heat from oil-fired furnaces. Drying room with eight flues, grinding mill, circular saws for cutting block salt. Store and bagging area. Principal market now in West Africa. Open to public in summer.

Adelaide Salt Works SJ 671757. Flash on site of mine and salt works which collapsed through subsidence in 1928. Two shafts 330 ft (101 m) deep in 1891. Neumann's Flashes, also the result of subsidence, some 600 yd by 500 yd (549 m by 457 m), now almost dry.

MERE

Mere Corn Mill SJ 737828. On

Hoisting rock salt tubs, salt mine, Marston, 1923. *Courtesy Cheshire County Museums*

Rostherne brook. Three storeys, brick-built, six bays long, becoming derelict. Four buttresses on north front, where there is a steep slope to stream. Pond filled in but mill race is traceable. Turbine installed c. 1920.

MICKLE TRAFFORD

Trafford Corn Mill SJ 451708. On river Gowy, one of most interesting Cheshire mills, being restored by North West Water Authority. Main 19C building three storeys, brick, pitched slate roof, nine bays, arched windows. Two-storey building to west: wagon shed (now forge), stable (now woodworking shop). Had two wheels and sets of machinery. At north end, 16 ft (14·9 m) diameter single-spoke undershot waterwheel, wooden axle, iron rims with sockets for starts on to which paddles were fixed, timber clasp-arm pit wheel with iron teeth, wooden upright shaft, iron wallower and great spur wheel. Not working at present. At south end, internal wheel pit with 18 ft 6 in (5·6 m) diameter undershot waterwheel, iron axle, hubs and rims, wooden spokes and paddles. Drive by pit wheel to wallower wheel on wooden

upright shaft mounted on cast iron arch. Great spur wheel with three stone nuts, wooden levers for adjustment. Three pairs of French burr stones in wooden casing, hoppers fed from floor above. Crown wheel driving sack hoist and auxiliary shafting to buildings on west. Former drying kiln projects east side of mill. Mill pond reduced in size.

MIDDLEWICH

One of the major salt towns of Cheshire, with Roman name 'Salinae'. Remains of Roman workings from excavations by Middlewich Archaeological Society in King Street and Kinderton Street are preserved in the county library in Lewis Street: clay supports and briquetage, fire bars, amphorae. There were 107 salt houses in 1605. Trade increased during 18C but in 19C Middlewich lost ground to Northwich and Winsford, partly as a result of development of Weaver Navigation.

British Salt SJ 714648. The only salt works still functioning in the town. Modern 6-effect vacuum evaporation plant opened 1969 on site of former Cerebos works. The vacuum process, boiling the brine under pressure, gra-

Undershot waterwheel (south wheel), Trafford corn mill, Mickle Trafford, 1978

dually replaced the open-pan process from the early 20C.

Canal junction SJ 707656. Junction of main line of Trent & Mersey Canal, opened 1777, and Shropshire Union Canal (Middlewich branch), opened from Barbridge in Wardle, 1833. South of junction is **Kings Lock**, with stone side walls, double gates at lower, single gate at upper end, Kings Lock Hotel on east side. To west, **Wardle lock**, with ornamental cottage-style lock keeper's house. Towpath of Trent & Mersey is carried over Wardle Canal by humped stone footbridge, dated 1829.

Brooks Lane Salt Works SJ 708661. Remains of Mid-Cheshire works, built 1890, closed 1970. Single-storey brick-built pan houses, brine pump in timber frame. To south-east is site of former Murgatroyd's works, now occupied by firm of diesel vehicle manufacturers.

Middlewich locks SJ 707666. Three locks on Trent & Mersey main line, curved flights of stone steps at lower end, wooden lock-end bridges on iron brackets. Dry dock at middle of three locks. Locks lead down to **Middlewich Wharf** SJ 705662, with three-storey brick-built warehouse, whitewashed, pitched roof, three-storey loading opening on east end wall, brick-built tollhouse. In 1860 there were five carrying companies operating from the wharf and boat building was carried on in the area.

Kinderton Corn Mill SJ 705663. Three-storey mill, brick and stone, stone quoins, buttresses, ball finials, mullioned windows: mainly 17C. Later building at north-east. Waterwheel removed 1963. Pond, fed from river Croco, almost dry. Occupied by firm of car repairers.

Big Lock SJ 702668. Trent & Mersey lock with lock keeper's cottage on east, late 19C. Big Lock Inn, west.

Newton aqueducts SJ 697658. On Shropshire Union Canal, west of town: single arch, blue brick, built into embankment, one over A530, one over river Wheelock.

MOORE

Bridgewater Canal. Moore bridge SJ 581844. Typical single elliptical arch, brick, stone course over arch, stone coping, curved in plan.

Manchester Ship Canal. Moore Lane bridge SJ 578853. Steel-girder swing bridge, with brick hydraulic-power engine house, control tower and ornamental accumulator tower.

Railway junction SJ 582847/585853. Complex railway site involving lines of Grand Junction Railway (later LNWR) and Birkenhead Railway (later joint GWR/LNWR). At Moore Lane on north-west is present double electrified track of Warrington–Crewe line. Immediately south-east is disused line of GJR with tunnel to north-east and early single-arch brick-and-stone bridge to south-west. South-east again is present double-track Warrington–Chester line; south-east of that, disused line of Birkenhead Lancashire & Cheshire Junction Railway, opened 1850. The changes were made in 1893 to provide the necessary clearance over the Manchester Ship Canal, and the embankments approaching the high-level Acton Grange viaduct can also be seen. The two lines were then linked by a connecting track, also visible.

NANTWICH

Country town which was important centre of salt production from Roman times until 17C, then declined as Winsford and Northwich rose in importance: only one works by 1860. Leather trades were also important in 19C: tanning, shoe-making and glove-making. White's *Cheshire Directory* of 1860 lists 37 boot and shoe makers, mostly producing for London and Manchester dealers. There was also a cotton mill started in late 18C, which worked until 1874: see W. H. Chaloner, *History of the*

Cotton Manufacture in Nantwich, 1785–1874, 1938.

Nantwich Corn Mill SJ 650523. Site only of four-storey mill which stood next to the cotton mill. Bridge over mill race at west end of Mill Street: sluice with rack-and-pinion paddle gear, traces of mill foundations. Near by is single-arch sandstone bridge with balustrade over river Weaver.

Shropshire Union Canal. Nantwich aqueduct, SJ 643526, 30 ft (9·1 m)-span iron aqueduct designed by Telford, completed 1835. Six cast iron arches, curved brick side walls, sandstone piers, iron railings. **Nantwich Basin** SJ 639528, opening on south side of canal, brick buildings including tollhouse, and Wharf Cottage. Single-arched humped, brick bridge with iron rubbing posts at entrance. In use by British Waterways Board.

Nantwich Station SJ 653519. On LNWR Crewe–Shrewsbury line, opened 1858, GWR Nantwich–Market Drayton line, opened 1863. Level crossing, wooden gates, hand-operated by wheel from wooden signal box with slate roof and ornamental ridge tiles. Late 19C blue-brick station buildings, two-storey with gables on north, seven-bay single storey on south.

NESTON CUM PARKGATE

Denhall Colliery SJ 289763. Spoil heaps, pit bank and shafts of colliery which operated from *c.* 1850 until 1928, latterly worked by Wirral Colliery Co., employing 200–250 men. Remains of Denhall Quay to south and of railway branch from Birkenhead Railway to north.

Neston Quay SJ 286767. Built by City of Chester in mid-16C as New Quay: became known as Old Quay or Neston Quay. Used until late 17C. Stone wall and steps.

Parkgate was developed as port and regular terminus of packet service to Dublin from early 18C until *c.* 1820.

Quay opposite George Hotel (now part of Mostyn Hall School). Later became fashionable seaside resort. Ferry services to Bagillt in Flintshire until late 19C: linked by coach service to Birkenhead and later horse bus to Hooton Station. Pier near Boathouse Restaurant (formerly site of Pengwern Arms or Ferry House Inn) at north end of Parade.

NETHER ALDERLEY

Nether Alderley Corn Mill SJ 844763. One of the best preserved mills in Cheshire, 16C, stone-built, stone-flag roof. Owned by National Trust and open to public. Worked until 1939. Restored to working condition by Dr Cyril Boucher. Built against dam of millpond, which is also moat of Alderley Old Hall. Two overshot wheels, one above the other, 13 ft and 12 ft (4 m and 3·7 m) diameter, iron axles and rims, wooden spokes and buckets. Both drive two pairs of stones on first floor, sack hoist and auxiliary drive. Fire box and arch of former drying kiln.

NEWBOLD ASTBURY

Watery Lane aqueduct SJ 853603. On Macclesfield Canal, single arch, sandstone, with curved side walls and tunnel 30 yd (27·4 m) long.

NORTHWICH

With Winsford, Northwich became the main centre of the Cheshire salt industry in 19C, with peak production in 1870s and 1880s. Brine pumped from springs at depth of approx. 90ft (27 m) to reservoirs near open-pan works by steam engines. In late 19C direct pumping by pipeline to chemical works at Winnington and Runcorn. Rock-salt mining from late 17C: four mines working in 1880s: Barons Quay, Penny Lane, Witton Bank and Witton Hall. Problem of subsidence in late 19C and early 20C: formation of flashes. Only surviving salt works is part of ICI plant at Winnington.

Hunts Lock SJ 656729. The river Weaver was improved from Frodsham bridge to Winsford bridge between 1721 and 1740 and played a major part in the development of Northwich as the commercial centre of the salt industry. Vessels of up to 160 tons could sail up to Northwich bridge. The locks, originally wooden, were deepened and widened after 1760, in mid-19C and again in late 19C. The river is still in use up to Anderton Wharf. Hunts Locks are the only surviving set in Northwich. Large double locks, approx. 280 ft (85 m) long, masonry side walls, capstans for operating wooden gates by chain drive, windlass for ground paddles. On east side, pair of lock cottages and tollhouse. Two semaphore signals at each end, two old gas lamps, iron bollards. Nearby is iron swing footbridge over old course of river.

Weaver viaduct SJ 663734/655730. Fifty-arch viaduct across valley of river Dane and river Weaver, 1,040 yd (950 m) long, stone with brick inside arches, iron spans over two rivers. On CLC Northwich–Helsby line, opened 1869.

Salt Museum, Weaver Hall SJ 658732. London Road, in former workhouse of 1837, two storeys, brick-built with pediment and clock turret. In process of development as museum by Cheshire County Council to illustrate geology, chemistry and history of salt-mining and salt-making, effects of subsidence, development of Weaver Navigation. Equipment on display includes briquetage from Middlewich, wicker drying baskets, wooden salt shovels, rakes and skimmers, iron chipping paddles, dodging hammers for breaking up scale in bottom of evaporation pans, lofters' spikes for throwing salt lumps into warehouse.

Northwich Wharf SJ 656735. Former Weaver dockyards and repair yards, now used by British Waterways Board. Two-storey brick building with wooden clock tower and cupola. Former Weaver Navigation offices in Navigation Road, two storeys, five bays, Georgian, with ornamental door-

Hunts Locks, lockkeeper's house and tollhouse, Weaver Navigation, Northwich, 1978

way and fanlight. Opposite is **Cephos Terrace**, 1857, three rows of two-storey brick cottages. There were formerly a number of shipyards along the river: seven shipbuilders were listed in 1860. At north is **Hayhurst bridge**, steel-girder swing bridge, 1899, designed by J. A. Saner, engineer to Weaver Trustees, built by Handyside's of Derby, electrically driven, turning on roller bearings, timber control house with slate roof, iron road gates. **Town Bridge** SJ 657737, to north, is of same design and structure.

Northwich Station SJ 669739. The CLC (Cheshire Midland) line from Knutsford reached Northwich in 1863 and was extended to Helsby in 1869. The LNWR line from Sandbach, which joins the CLC west of the station, was opened in 1868. Single-storey yellow-brick station building of 1897, Gothic windows, glass and iron canopy over platform on cast-iron pillars with decorated capitals and brackets. Iron footbridge on cast iron pillars at west, old-style semaphore signals between footbridge and road bridge. Goods station north-east with sixteen-bay single storey brick-built shed.

ICI Winnington Works SJ 642745. Chemical works for making soda by Solvay's soda-ammonia process started in 1873 by John Brunner and Ludwig Mond, when they bought Winnington Hall from Lord Stanley of Alderley. Limited company in 1881, became part of ICI in 1926. Brine pumped from Holford rock-salt deposits east of Northwich, limestone from Tunstead Quarry near Buxton, Derbyshire. **Two Solvay plants:** one at main works, the other at Wallerscote Works, making soda ash only. **Soda-crystal plant** at Island Works: four-aisle timber sheds, four rows of eight iron pans, 30 ft by 8 ft (9 m by 2·4 m), originally two rows of eight iron pans above. Soda liquor fed from Solvay plant into pans, allowed to crystallise, removed into iron tipping

waggons for crushing, screening, drying and packing as washing soda. Silicate furnaces used in manufacture of sodium silicate, developed in 1920s. Plants for production of sodium bicarbonate, one of early by-products of works, caustic soda, sodium sesquicarbonate (used in toilet preparations and detergents), sodium aluminate (used in water softening and paper-making).

Mond House. Original office of Brunner Mond & Co., two and three storeys. brick-built, date 1899 on clock. Timber-framed Recreation Club and Library, 1923, extended 1937. **Winnington Hall**, timber-framed house of 16C/17C, altered, with late 18C wing. Stable block to east: first offices were in this area. Brunner and Mond both lived in Hall until 1884. Members of Brunner family lived there until 1894: became club in 1897.

South of the works is the associated industrial community. **Winnington Park Primary School** SJ 648745, built by company in early 20C. Housing in **Solvay Road**: at north, two rows of 10 and 12 two-storey brick-built cottages with front gables and porches; at south, on east side, row of 52 two-storey four-roomed cottages; on west side, row of 39 two-storey cottages with ornamental brick-arch lintels and brickwork below parapets, projecting string course over doors and windows; **Bond Street:** on east, rows of six and ten two-storey cottages with five pairs of later semi-detached houses to north, on west similar rows of six and eight two-storey cottages; **Dyer Terrace:** at south end of Solvay Street, row of six substantial two-storey houses for managerial staff; **Henning Street**, west of Solvay Street, on east, row of 33 two-storey cottages with gardens in front, similar in design to houses on west side of Solvay Street. Larger houses on hill west of Henning Street. All the cottages have yards and privies at back, some have rear extensions.

NORTON
Halton tunnel SJ 555811/544799. 2,000 yd (1,830 m)-long tunnel under high ground between Norton and Halton on Birkenhead Lancashire & Cheshire Junction Railway (later GWR/LNWR joint) line from Warrington to Helsby, opened 1850. Norton Station at north end of tunnel was closed in 1952: two-storey brick building with gables and ornamental woodwork survives.

ODD RODE
Snape's aqueduct SJ 810565. Carries Trent & Mersey Canal over old road now by-passed by A50. Single arch, brick, stone quoins at sides of arch, curved in plan, battered outwards, brick buttresses on north side.

Rode Heath bridge SJ 807571. Typical single-arch, brick, humped Trent & Mersey Canal bridge. Near by are foundations of former **Lowton Salt Works**, started 1779, taken over by Salt Union 1888.

Rode Heath Corn Mill SJ 805573. Formerly steam-powered corn mill on north-east side of canal. Four storeys, brick-built, gable to canal, loading openings, blocked in south wall, four-storey projecting section over canal with arches at canal level, engine house at north.

Thurlwood locks SJ 801576/804574. Two sets of double locks, brick side walls, masonry coping, double gates at lower, single gates at upper end. At upper locks is a new steel lock replacing one of the old ones, steel tank with lift gates and pipes for transfer of water between chambers.

Rode Corn Mill SJ 822578. Three-storey brick-built mill, pitched slate roof, two-storey loading opening on east front. Square brick chimney for auxiliary steam engine at south end. Waterwheel and machinery removed: pond to east.

PENKETH
Former Lancashire township west of Warrington, now transferred to Cheshire. Crossed by four water navigations: the Sankey (St Helens) Canal, river Mersey, Runcorn & Latchford Canal and Manchester Ship Canal, and by St Helens & Runcorn Gap Railway.

Fiddlers Ferry SJ 563867. Fiddlers Ferry Inn survives at the site at one of the old ferries across the Mersey. The Sankey Canal was extended from Sankey bridges to Fiddlers Ferry in 1762 and to Runcorn Gap (Widnes) in 1833. There are still traces of the entrance locks connecting canal to Mersey, SJ 561804; and good examples of wooden swing bridges along canal line. **Fiddlers Ferry & Penketh Station** on the St Helens & Runcorn Gap Railway, extended to Warrington 1853, was closed to passengers in 1950 and is now derelict. The line runs along the north side of the canal.

Runcorn & Latchford Canal Built by Mersey & Irwell Navigation 1799–1804 to compete with Bridgewater Canal extension to Runcorn. The abandoned line is traceable south of the Mersey from Baxters Bridge, SJ 588863, to Bobs Bridge, SJ 568851. A good point at which to see the remains is **Moore Bridge** SJ 577858, accessible from Moore Lane, water in canal to west, overgrown to east, towpath.

PLUMLEY
Holford on west of township is major area for controlled brine pumping, supplying alkali works at Winnington and Lostock Gralam, salt works at Winsford and Weston Point, Castner-Kellner chemical works at Runcorn.

Holford Corn Mill SJ 707756. Remains of mill built across Peover Eye stream west of bridge in Long Lane leading to Holford Hall. Worked until at least 1935. Two wheel pits for undershot waterwheels with main mill building between. In south pit, wooden axle of wheel, iron pit wheel and bearing for upright main shaft. In north pit, wooden axle, iron hub with openings for six timber spokes, two of which survive, remains of iron rim with large slots for ends of spokes, twin holes to take starts on which paddles were fixed. By-pass for water on north, remains of sluice controls. In mill part of wooden main shaft with iron wallower wheel and remains of crown wheel with wooden arms mortised to shaft. North of north wheel pit is site of drying kiln: numerous square perforated tiles which formed floor.

PEOVER SUPERIOR

Bate Corn Mill SJ 801724. On Peover Eye at Peover–Chelford boundary. Two-storey mill built across stream, with twin-arched opening for feed to waterwheel and by-pass. 13 ft 6 in. (4 m) diameter undershot waterwheel, iron axle, hub and rim, wooden spokes and paddles, formerly drove two sets of stones. Later assisted by Crossley diesel engine and electric motor. Has not worked since about the end of 1977. Also on Peover Eye is site of former **Peover Superior Mill** SJ 757728, stone walls of wheel pits, remains of sluice gear.

Peover Eye viaduct SJ 797723. Tall ten-arch brick viaduct on Manchester & Birmingham Railway, opened 1842.

POTT SHRIGLEY

Hilly township between Bollington and Poynton where there has been a good deal of coal mining, including recent drift operations, and brickmaking. White's *Cheshire Directory* in 1860 speaks of 'collieries . . . producing an abundance of coal of superior quality'.

Pott Brickworks SJ 953796. Site of former firebrick works in Bakestonedale, along Kettleshulme Road: some buildings, square stone and brick chimneys, old shafts – ovens now demolished. Working by 1850, closed only a few years ago.

POULTON WITH FERNHEAD

Paddington lock SJ 628888. Filled-in site of lock at west end of Woolston New Cut on Mersey & Irwell Navigation, completed 1821. Line of side walls visible, iron bollards. Converted two-storey lock keeper's house on north, feeder for Runcorn & Latchford Canal on south: feeder aqueduct across Mersey removed.

Padgate Station SJ 631900. On CLC Liverpool–Manchester line, opened 1874. Typical CLC station buildings, brick-built, cottage style, two gables with ornamental woodwork and patterned roof slates, three-bay canopy between gables on cast iron pillars with ornamental brackets. Similar style waiting room on opposite platform. Cf. Urmston, Flixton, Glazebrook, Great Sankey, Widnes North, Hough Green

POYNTON

Now a growing residential township south of Stockport, but earlier a thriving coal-mining community, of which there are considerable traces under the suburban veneer. There was also some handloom silk weaving and fustian cutting in 19C.

Poynton Collieries. Developed from early 17C by local landowners, Warrens in 17C and 18C, Vernons in 19C. Main expansion in 19C after George Warren bought Worth in 1791. Directly managed by Vernons from 1831. In 1847 employed over 1,100 men and boys. In later 19C smaller pits closed. Production ceased in 1935, when there were 115 miners. The coal was originally distributed by road to Stockport and Macclesfield, after 1831 by the Macclesfield Canal to a wider market, and after 1845 by rail to depots from Manchester in the north to Crewe and Winsford in south. The collieries had their own internal railway transport, preceded by tramroads (see map). The development of the standard-gauge lines followed the opening of the Manchester & Birmingham Railway branch from Cheadle Hulme to the collieries in 1845 (extended to Macclesfield the same year). Originally horse and rope working, locomotives from 1876.

Poynton Station SJ 911838. 1887, buildings with yellow and blue-brick decoration, ornamental stonework round windows, Station House and Station Cottage near by. Replaced earlier station at **Midway** SJ 915827, where the old station house survives west of London Road. From the station the colliery railway ran east, crossing Poynton brook on wooden bridge, to **West Yard** SJ 920839, cobbled area with coal merchants' offices. Level crossing over A523, formerly with hand-operated double gates to **East Yard**, where there were weighing machines for carts and later raised coal staithes.

From East Yard **Princes incline** ran one mile (1·6 km) to **Princes Pit**, single track, worked by rope and counterbalance system with passing loop at Tower Yard. Well preserved both sides of **Black Road**, which is itself on line of

former tramroad from Lord and Lady Pits to a yard at North Lodge on A523, SJ 925851.

Tower Yard, SJ 930841, became main colliery and railway maintenance centre after 1846, with smithies, foundry and saw mill. Between the yard and Princes Pit is site of former **Lower Vernon Pit** SJ 933842. Near here are railway branch north to **Park and Lawrence Pits** SJ 935847, spoil heaps, pithead buildings, remains of brickworks, developed from 1846 onwards; south to Petre Bank and across Worth Clough on a timber bridge, of which abutments remain, to **Quarry Pit** SJ 937835. The Princes incline was extended east past **Horsepasture Pit** SJ 942844, to **Canal Pit** SJ 948839, workings both sides of canal, on west side remains of pit bank, foundations of pit-head gear, square brick chimney. Latterly used for ventilation and pumping. The distance from Poynton Station to Canal Pit is 2 miles 500 yd (3·7 km). **Lady's incline** preserved as footpath, single-track, self-acting, opened by 1857, ran south-east

Poynton: collieries and colliery railways

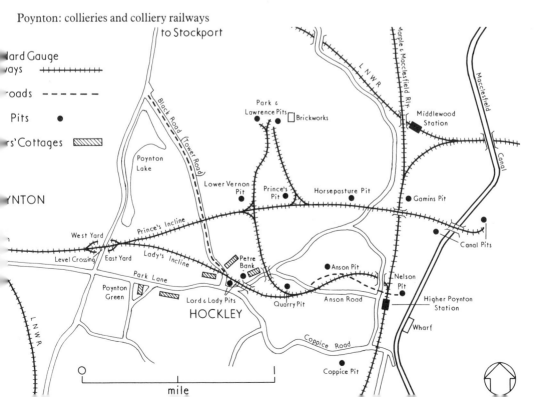

from East Yard 1,050 yd (960 m) to **Lord and Lady Pits** SJ 930834, at Hockley, closed early 20C. Lady Pit had Cornish beam pumping engine which worked until 1930s. By 1872 the incline was extended over Worth Clough by bridge, across Anson Road past Quarry Pit to **Anson Pit** SJ 940835, spoil heaps, to join branch from Marple & Macclesfield Railway (opened 1864) near **Higher Poynton Station** SJ 944834. Traces of cutting west of Green Lane. **Nelson Pit** SJ 945834, with spoil heaps between Marple & Macclesfield Railway and canal, had a basin on the canal and was connected by a narrow-gauge rope-worked railway driven by a donkey engine at Nelson Pit to Anson Pit. The line follows the pavement at the side of Anson Road. **Coppice Pit** SJ 940830, site still visible south of Coppice Road, was also connected to Nelson Pit by Tramroad.

All track was removed from the colliery railways in 1936, except for the section between Poynton Station and East Yard, where shunting continued until 1943.

The colliery community. The Vernons in 19C built rows of cottages for the workers and their families and the village developed along Park Lane from Poynton Green to Hockley. *The Report of the Royal Commission on the Employment of Children*, 1841, gives detailed information of the living conditions of six Poynton families, presenting a picture of good earnings, well furnished houses with gardens and vegetable plots, a satisfactory diet and provision for saving and sickness benefit.

Poynton Green SJ 924835. Row of six two-storey brick-built cottages, 1845, at junction of Chamber Road and Park Lane. Near by are **Lord Vernon Schools**, two schools, one for boys, one for girls, started 1841.

Long Row SJ 925834. 154–98 Park Lane, fine row of twenty-three two-storey cottages, date stone in centre: 'L1844V'.

Clayton Fold SJ 928824. Row of two-storey cottages north of Park Lane.

Dalehouse Fold SJ 930836. North of Lord and Lady Pits, row of twelve 2-storey cottages, built in 1840s.

Coppice Road SJ 933833. Four rows of ten two-storey stone-built estate cottages, later in date, slate roofs, gabled fronts on end houses, stone porches.

Petre Bank SJ 933836. The earliest surviving row, dated 1815 on central pediment. Sixteen two-storey brick-built cottages, windows with stone sills and lintels, stone lintels over doorways, yards and extensions at rear, gardens at front. Restored and re-roofed.

PRESTBURY

An attractive village, now largely residential. In 19C there was silk hand-loom weaving and a silk mill at **Butley** SJ 899774.

Prestbury Corn Mill SJ 902769. On river Bollin, south-east of parish church. Buildings recent. Pond filled in. Head race visible as ditch running south-east 800 yd (731 m) to weir. Occupied by Hamlyn & Co., corn millers.

PRESTON BROOK

Canal community at junction SJ 567810 of main line of Bridgewater Canal (Stretford to Runcorn), opened 1776, with branch to main line of Trent & Mersey Canal opened 1777. Near junction the Runcorn line crosses the LNWR (Grand Junction Railway) on a skew iron-trough aqueduct. To west is **Norton Cottages Wharf**, now being developed as canalside housing area with marina opposite. Arm off west side of canal with two side openings, single-storey brick-built goods shed on north-west, timber goods shed on south-east. Single-storey brick tollhouse.

Preston Brook tunnel SJ 574788 /570799. Trent & Mersey Canal, 1,240 yd (1,133 m) long, no towpath, partly brick-lined, partly cut in rock. North end is junction with Bridgewater Canal branch.

Preston Brook Wharf SJ 568807. North of A56 on west bank of canal. Row of two-storey brick-built cottages with three-storey Wharf House at north end. South of A56 on east bank of canal is **Old Number One Inn**, converted warehouse, two storeys and basement, brick-built, 15 by 3 bays, hipped slate roof, windows with stone sills and ornamental stone lintels, iron frames with small panes, projecting wooden loading bay supported on cast iron pillars on canal front.

RAINOW

Moorland township east of Bollington and Macclesfield which was formerly a considerable centre of cotton, silk and woollen manufacture. Water-powered mills built on river Dean and its tributaries. There were also a number of coal pits and stone quarries.

Gin Clough Mill SJ 958764. Earliest surviving former water-powered silk-throwing mill in Rainow, advertised for sale in 1822. Three storeys, stone-built, small-paned windows, stone-flag roof, square tapering chimney at south-east.

Tower Hill Mill SJ 946758. Pond and foundations of former silk-throwing mill which became bleach works after 1874.

Hough Hill Mill SJ 944766. Site of former water-powered cotton-spinning mill on river Dean, now garden of Wayside Cottage. Built at end of 18C by James Mellor. Millpond with race under road. Two rows of cottages. To east was Hough Hole engineering works, operated by William Miller in late 19C.

Ingersley Vale Works SJ 942774. On river Dean west of Ingersley Hall. Bleaching and calico-printing works started in early 19C, John Brier in 1850s and 1860s, A. J. King & Co. in late 19C and early 20C. Main building runs east–west, three storeys, stone, twelve bays long, stone-flag roof, date stone '1809 EC' (Edward Collier) on south front. At west, tall stone-built wheel house with long semi-circular arched windows, now blocked, iron feed trough across road from race. Housed water wheel 56 ft (17 m) diameter, 10 ft 6 in. (3·2 m) wide. Race runs 400 yd (383 m), partly embanked, along west side of valley to steep stone weir at south end of Clough Pool, 250 yd (229 m) long, becoming overgrown. Near by was former **Waulk Mill**, woollen fulling mill operating by 1716, with surviving cottages now bearing name. North of Ingersley Hall Mill is site of **Rainow Mill** SJ 941775, with weir as only trace of cotton mill started by Martin Swindells and John and Thomas Fernley in 1822 (see *Bollington* for Swindells family).

RIXTON WITH GLAZEBROOK

Another former Lancashire township east of Warrington transferred to Cheshire. Near **Hollins Green** SJ 698907 is the site of the former Hollin ferry across the Mersey. The community is described under the name **Moss Ferry** in Margaret Penn, *Manchester Fourteen Miles*, 1947.

Mersey & Irwell Navigation, Butchersfield Canal SJ 676891/681889. 360 yd (329 m)-long cut on Mersey & Irwell Navigation made after 1760 to eliminate large triple bend in river which extended to northern limits of Statham village. Entered through pair of locks. Later cut of 1820s to north.

Glazebrook Station SJ 695925. Good example of CLC station buildings.

RUNCORN

The outstanding feature is the development of the transport systems which led to the growth of a 'new' 19C town and port based on salt, soap, chemical and leather industries. The Bridgewater Canal line from Stretford through north Cheshire was opened in 1776, leading to the development of the Bridgewater Docks. The Mersey & Irwell Co.'s Runcorn & Latchford Canal from Warrington was built 1799–1804 with a terminus east of Runcorn and a tidal lock to the Mersey. The development of the Weaver Navigation's Weston Point Docks followed the building of the River Weaver Canal from Sutton Locks, opened 1810. The Manchester Ship Canal running along the Mersey shore was opened in 1894 and the canal company took over the Bridgewater Docks.

Bridgewater Canal. There is an interesting series of bridges along the line from east to west. **Bate's bridge** SJ 529829, typical Bridgewater, single arch, brick with stone coping and string course over the arch, humped, curved in plan. **Victoria Road bridge** SJ

519829, single arch with extension of three cast iron spans each side, Navigation Inn near by. **Doctor's bridge** SJ 511829, single arch of nine cast iron beams with brick and stone abutments. **Waterloo bridge** SJ 509829, three segmental sandstone arches, extensions east and west on cast iron arched beams, ornamental iron posts and railings. The canal now ends at this point and there is a former wharf to the east.

Old Quay bridge SJ 520833. Good example of steel-girder swing bridge across the Ship Canal with brick-built engine house, control tower and accumulator tower for hydraulic operation. Near by was the former terminal basin and wharf of the Runcorn & Latchford Canal, built in 1820s: name Old Quay Street survives. To west is **Old Quay lock**, connecting the Ship Canal with the river Mersey.

Runcorn Gap SJ 509835, between Runcorn and Widnes, where the Mersey estuary narrows to about 450 yd (410 m), has been an important crossing point. The Runcorn ferry was of early

LNWR Mersey viaduct of 1869 and modern road bridge, Runcorn, looking across to Widnes, 1978

Runcorn docks

RIVER MERSEY

MANCHESTER SHIP CANAL

Runcorn & Weston Canal

RUNCORN

L.N.W.R.

Modern Road Bridge

Old Quay Lock

Bridgewater House

Old Dock

Customs House

Tidal Basin

Old Basin

Waterloo Bridge

Doctors Bridge

New Locks

Coal Basin

BRIDGEWATER DOCKS

Wharf

Bridgewater Canal

Bridgewater Lock

Alfred Dock

Francis Dock

Fenton Dock

Delamere Dock

Tollemache Dock

Christ Church

Salt Works

WESTON POINT

School

Old Basin

ston ersey Lock

River Weaver Canal (Weston Canal)

Castner-Kellner Chemical Works

O   ¼   ½

MILE

WJS.

origin and there were six boats a day in 1860. A proposal by Telford in 1814 for a suspension bridge was never carried out. The famous transporter bridge, built 1901–05, was demolished in the early 1950s and replaced by the present single-steel-arch road bridge, completed 1961. Parallel to the road bridge on the west is the **LNWR railway viaduct** of 1868 with three wrought-iron spans, stone piers, and a long series of approach arches each side.

Runcorn locks. There were formerly two sets of locks on the Bridgewater Canal between Waterloo Bridge and the docks. **Old Locks**, built 1772–73, ran north-west, ten locks in staircase pairs, fall of 70 ft (21·3 m), last used 1939–40, now filled in. Entrance lock from river Mersey survives, sandstone walls, wooden gates, with traces of locks visible to south-east. **New Locks**, built 1825–27 to cope with increasing traffic, ran due west from Waterloo bridge to Tidal Dock, filled in, but entrance lock at west visible and traces of stone side walls along the line.

Bridgewater Docks SJ 503829 were developed from 1780 onwards. **Old Dock**, 400 ft by 120 ft (122 m by 37 m), with gate to Tidal Basin was in use by 1785, survives with masonry sides and traces of lock to **Coal Basin**, also in use by 1785, largely filled in but visible at north-eastern end. **Old Basin** to east is filled in but there are remains of warehouse walls. North-east of the older docks is **Bridgewater House** SJ 504831, three storeys, Georgian, occasionally used by Duke of Bridgewater when canal was under construction. To south-west are later docks: **Alfred Dock**, c. 1860, 600 ft by 130 ft (183 m by 40 m), Fenton Dock, 1875, 600 ft by 148 ft (183 m by 45 m) with lock connection to Runcorn & Weston Canal, both docks in use. The Arnold Dock and the north-eastern end of the canal have been filled in: the canal was built 1857–59 to connect the Bridgewater

Docks with the Weaver. West of Fenton Dock is the **Bridgewater lock** connecting the Manchester Ship Canal with the river Mersey.

Weston Point Docks SJ 494813. Developed from 1810 by the Weaver Navigation Co., now operated by British Waterways Board. **Old Basin** still in use, 900 ft (274 m) long, remains of entrance lock from Ship Canal (earlier river Mersey) at north, entrance lock from Weston Canal at south, electrically operated swing bridge. **New Basin** between Old Basin and Ship Canal, built 1850–56, filled in 1963–66, remains of entrances from Ship Canal at north, from Weston Canal at south still visible. West of New Basin is **Weston Mersey lock** connecting Ship Canal and the river. The two later docks to the north, **Delamere**, 1865–70, and **Tollemache**, 1885, have been made into one, known as **Delamache**. Lock to Ship Canal with double wooden gates operated by chains winding on iron rollers, now electrically driven, originally by capstan. Brick gateman's huts each side, single storey with pyramidical roofs. West of dock is **Christ Church**, built for watermen by Weaver Trustees in 1841. East of Old Basin was a community of houses and a school (closed 1963): the only survival is two brick cottages alongside the Runcorn & Weston Canal south of the Old Basin, near entrance lock from Weston Canal.

Weaver sluices SJ 499803. On west bank of Ship Canal south of Weston Docks, each 30 ft (9 m) wide, built by Ransome & Rapier of Ipswich to convey waters from river Weaver into Mersey estuary.

Weston Point Salt Works SJ 496815. ICI works on site of former Salt Union factory, where a vacuum evaporation plant was installed in 1911. To south is extensive works of ICI Mond Division's **Castner-Kellner Works**, started in 1896 to make caustic soda by electrolysis of brine.

Foden traction engine, 1883. *Courtesy Fodens Ltd*

SANDBACH

In 19C there were two or three silk mills in the town and a considerable salt manufacture in the area. Calvert in 1915 referred to salt-making as the 'principal industry': there were 69 evaporating pans at work in 1880. Now the principal occupation is engineering.

Foden's SJ 738612. At Elworth a mile and a quarter (2 km) east of Sandbach and near Sandbach Station is the famous works started by Plant & Hancock in 1850, joined by Edwin Foden as apprentice in 1856, partner in 1862. Manufactured agricultural machinery, threshing machines, traction engines and portable steam engines: pioneered development of compound traction engines in 1880s. Steam lorries from 1897: well known for 'overtype' with engine above boiler. Change-

over to diesel lorries from *c.* 1929 in association with Gardner's of Patricroft, Eccles. Also famous for works brass band, started in 1902. Modern assembly plant, foundry and forges in older buildings. Two-storey office building of 1913. North of Foden's is Prings' **Elworth Wire Works**, also an old-established firm.

Sandbach Corn Mill SJ 754598. Three-storey brick-built late 19C mill, large windows, loading openings at west end. Site of former overshot waterwheel at north. Millpond dried up. Had beam engine as well as wheel. Still occupied by firm of millers.

Wheelock Wharf SJ 751593. On Trent & Mersey Canal south of Sandbach. Three-storey brick-built warehouse east of road bridge. On west, warehouse now occupied by garden centre, three storeys, brick-built, whitewashed, semi-circular arched windows, loading doors on road front. East of wharf are two sets of double locks. To north is works of **Zan Enterprises**, manufacturers of shoe blacking and polishes: some of their early equipment is in Weaver Hall Museum, Northwich.

SAUGHALL

Gibbet Windmill SJ 363722. Three-storey, brick-built tower mill, whitewashed, built *c.* 1784, restored as residence 1971. Wirral-type wooden, boat-shaped cap, four common sails mounted on iron cross. Used until early 20C.

SIDDINGTON

Siddington Corn Mill SJ 844710. On Snape brook, west of A34. Four storeys, brick-built, pitched slate roof. Culvert under road to cast iron trough and site of former water wheel, later water turbine. Drying kiln. Still in use. East of A34 is stone-sided regulating pond, with main pool further up lane east of Siddington Church.

STANTHORNE

Stanthorne Mill SJ 694662. On river Wheelock just west of Middlewich: ancient mill site. Four-storey brick mill building still survives in derelict state. Norris in 1969 recorded two undershot waterwheels, machinery removed *c.* 1955. Weir above bridge to south.

STOCKTON HEATH

Township south of Warrrington crossed by Bridgewater Canal, formerly known for manufacture of spades, files and tools.

Lumb Brook aqueduct SJ 622861. Single arch, sandstone walls and abutments, brick arch and parapet.

Gibbet windmill, Great Saughall, 1979

Stockton Quay SJ 615857. By London Road bridge (rebuilt 1930), a formerly busy transit point on the Bridgewater Canal for goods and passenger traffic. On south bank, warehouse, four storeys and attic, brick-built, east half older than west, semicircular arched windows, loading openings on canal front. Later covered loading shed of timber and cast iron with roof extending over canal and half-way along front of warehouse. East of London Road bridge is flight of circular stone steps and remains of blacksmith's workshop. On north bank, timber buildings with arched roof on sandstone foundations west of bridge, crane by towpath east of bridge. This important site is fully described in *The Archaeology of Warrington's Past*, pp. 66–7.

STRETTON

Stretton Corn Mill SJ 454530. Restored 1975–78 by Cheshire County Council and open to public in summer months. Two storeys, stone and timber-framed with weatherboard covering, pitched slate roof replacing former thatched roof: 16C to 18C. Two waterwheels and sets of machinery, each driving two sets of stones. West wheel external, overshot, 10 ft (3 m) diameter, 6 ft 6 in. (2 m) wide, iron axle and rims, wooden spokes and buckets. East wheel internal, breast-shot, 14 ft (4·3 m) diameter, 5 ft 2 in. (1·6 m) wide, iron axle and rims, wooden spokes and buckets. Installed by W. Smith of Whitchurch Foundry 1852, worked until 1960. Millpond to south.

STYAL

Quarry Bank Mill SJ 834830. Famous cotton mill and community started by Samuel Greg of Belfast in 1784, presented to National Trust in 1939, and now being developed as textile museum and centre for study of cotton industry. Open to the public.

There is an excellent introduction in Mary B. Rose, *The Gregs of Styal* (National Trust), 1978.

The mill was built on the river Dean with substantial stone weir and mill race to south. The 1784 building is at north, five storeys, brick-built, 18 bays long, three-bay pediment with clock and bell turret, added circular brick chimney at north-east (the first steam engine was installed 1810). Internal structure of wooden beams and joists, plank floors, rooms 136 ft by 30 ft (41·5 m by 9·1 m). Adjoining to south is extension of 1819–22, five storeys and attic, mansard roof, rooms 60 ft by 45 ft (18·3 m by 13·7 m), central row of cast iron pillars, wooden beams, joists and floors. South again is two-storey office block of 1830s. On west are two and three-storey buildings, also 1830s, used for weaving: ten-bay section at south has central row of cast iron pillars, wooden beams, joists and floors. Inside mill is large wheel pit for 100 h.p. waterwheel, 32 ft (9·8 m) diameter, installed 1818, later replaced by 200 h.p. turbine. Immediately north of mill is **Quarry Bank House**, built by Samuel Greg 1797, occupied as residence.

The associated community was developed gradually, partly through purchase of existing farms and cottages, partly by new building. The **Apprentice House** SJ 837832 was used for about sixty years from 1790, up to 100 boys and girls, local at first, from farther afield later, run by master and mistress. Two storeys, brick-built, two aisles (one used by boys, one by girls). **Farm Fold Cottages** SJ 836835, opposite the Methodist chapel, were adapted from a barn in the 1790s. **Oak Cottages** SJ 835835, are the main new houses erected by the Gregs, 1819–22, when the mill was being extended. Two rows of brick-built cottages, two storeys and basement. Best cottages had four rooms with yard and privy at back. There was also a shop, still in use, which supplied foodstuffs and clothing, started by Gregs, later owned by Co-op. At south-western end of Oak Cottages is **School**, built in 1820s, where mill children spent four hours a day. **Norcliffe Chapel** SJ 834834 was built for workers 1823, first minister Baptist, Unitarian from 1833. Living conditions in the community are described in Frances Collier, *The Family Economy of the Working Classes in the Cotton Industry 1784–1833*, 1964, chapter 5.

SUTTON (near **Macclesfield**)

There were formerly a number of silk and finishing works, with Langley on the river Bollin as the main centre.

Langley Print Works SJ 941713. Important silk-printing works started in 1820s by William and John Smith and taken over by Whiston's. Closed 1964 and occupied by Scragg's, silk-machinery makers of Macclesfield. Ex-hibition Building, 1851, two storeys, brick-built, cast iron pillars, wooden beams, formerly used for hand-block printing. Reservoir to east.

Langley Village has interesting rows of workers' cottages in Main Road, including three three-storey buildings with long windows or double windows on top storey suggesting former domes-tic workshops.

Robin Lane tollhouse SJ 916707. Single-storey, brick-built, hexagonal tollhouse with extension, at junction of Robin Lane and A523 (Macclesfield–Leek road).

Brindley's house SJ 926717. East of Gurnett aqueduct on Macclesfield Can-al. Plaque on house where James Brind-ley, the famous engineer, lived when apprenticed to Abraham Bennett, 1733–40.

SUTTON (near **Runcorn**)

Sutton Corn Mill SJ 529785. On river Weaver east of Frodsham bridge. Long race from weir above Frodsham lock. Considerable demolition, but two-storey building with arched opening for tail race and three-storey building with loading openings direct to river survive. Described by White as 'extensive corn mill', by Norris in 1969 as 'largest of Cheshire mills'. Occupied for storage and warehousing.

Weaver viaduct SJ 528786. On Birkenhead Lancashire & Cheshire Junction Railway's (later GWR/LNWR joint) Warrington to Chester line, opened 1850. Twenty-one stone arches, two iron arches over river at south-western end. To north-east is high single-span iron-arch bridge over Weav-er Canal, with brick approach arches.

Sutton locks SJ 542785. On river Weaver, starting point of Weaver Canal (Weston Canal) to Weston Point, Run-corn, opened 1810.

Sutton/Weaver bridge SJ 534788. Electrically operated steel-girder swing bridge of 1923 carrying A56 over River Weaver Canal. Swings on roller bear-ings on south-western side, driven by steel ropes and pulleys. Timber control house with pyramidical roof, iron road gates at each end.

SWETTENHAM

Swettenham Corn Mill SJ 811673. Very interesting mill building, partly brick-built, partly timber-framed, with dates 1675, 1714, 1765. Drying kiln. Pitchback 14 ft (4·3 m) diameter water-wheel. Still much as described by Nor-ris in 1969. Now used only for wood-working. Long millpond to east and race to weir on Midge brook.

TETTON

Township south of Middlewich cros-sed by Trent & Mersey Canal.

Moston Corn Mill SJ 731622. On east bank of canal north of Crows Nest bridge. Three storeys, brick-built, early 19C, loading openings on canal front. Unusual because driven by water from overflow weir above canal lock (cf. Conder Mill, *Thurnham*, Lancashire).

Crows Nest lock. Typical Trent & Mersey, single upper, double lower gates, ground paddles at upper, gate paddles at lower gates. Brick side walls, masonry coping. There are two similar locks to north.

THREAPWOOD
Threapwood windmill SJ 443452. Brick tower with remains of wooden cap and tail wheel.

TILSTONE FEARNALL
Tilstone Corn Mill SJ 567594. Three-storey brick-built mill, with iron-framed small-paned windows, being restored as residence. Had two waterwheels, fed by river Gowy and tributary. Large pond east of road. Tail race alongside canal to west.

Nearby is **Tilstone lock** on Shropshire Union Canal. Brick side walls, stone coping, double gates each end, brick balance-arm treads. At upper end on south bank, circular brick hut with central chimney or ventilator.

TIVERTON
Bate's Corn Mill (Horton Mill) SJ 532602. On south side of Shropshire Union Canal west of Beeston. Three-storeys, brick and stone-built, central loading doors and hoist beam, being restored and extended as residence. Internal 14 ft (4·3 m) diameter breast-shot waterwheel at south end, iron buckets. Some machinery and millstones survive. Pond fed by river Gowy, by-pass with sluice, tail race.

UTKINTON
Utkinton Corn mill SJ 566649. Spectacular site in gorge below large millpond. Ruins of sandstone-and-brick mill: in 1969 Norris reported three storeys and scratch marks of large wheel on gable.

WALTON (near **Warrington**)
Acton Grange viaduct SJ 389857.

High-level, skewed, steel-girder viaduct built across Manchester Ship Canal 1893 on the LNWR line to Crewe and GWR/LNWR joint line to Chester.

WARDLE
Barbridge Junction SJ 613570. On Shropshire Union Canal: junction of main line (Chester Canal opened 1779) and Middlewich branch, opened 1833.

WARRINGTON
Warrington's position at an important crossing of the river Mersey, near the Lancashire coalfield and about half-way between Manchester and Liverpool led to the development of a wide variety of industries, including cotton, sail-making, velvet cutting, copper, iron and steel, file and tool-making, wire-drawing, pin-making, engineering, glass, tanning, flour milling and brewing. It is also of great interest from the point of view of transport. The river Mersey was improved up to Bank Quay, west of the town, by Thomas Patten at end of 17C, and above Warrington after 1720 as part of the Mersey & Irwell Navigation, who in 1799–1804 made the direct cut from Latchford to Runcorn. The Bridgewater Canal had a wharf at Stockton Heath, and the Manchester Ship Canal, opened 1894, passes through the sandstone along the southern boundary. There is a great deal of information in Shelagh Grealey, ed., *The Archaeology of Warrington's Past*, 1976.

CENTRE

Warrington bridge SJ 607878. The present bridge was opened by King George V in 1913: single span of ten concrete arches with balustrade. Had several predecessors: earliest reference to a bridge 1305, rebuilt 1364, stone bridge built by Earl of Derby 1495, damaged in Jacobite rising of 1745, stone Victoria bridge 1837. To south are two causeways first built across Mersey marshes on stone arches in 17C:

Wilderspool causeway and Latchford causeway (Knutsford Road).

Arpley Station SJ 606878. Former junction of St Helens & Runcorn Gap Railway's line from Widnes, opened 1854, and Warrington & Stockport Railway's line to Altrincham, opened 1853. Closed 1958. Surviving is five-storey brick-built warehouse, 14 by 4 bays, wide windows, three loading slots each side with gables at top.

Warrington Museum SJ 604879. Collections include clocks and watches made by Warrington manufacturers, hand-made files from Holdens' Reliance Works, 1900–05, coloured glassware made by Robinson's Mersey Glass Works at Bank Quay 1869–1925. A glasshouse in Warrington was mentioned in 1696 and there were 12 glass works in 1828.

Mersey Tannery SJ 609880. In Mersey Street. In use by 1825, two-storey 11-bay building remains with arch to yard and building occupied by firm of curriers. Tanning was an important industry in Warrington from 17C, partly because of brine supplies from Cheshire, partly because of cattle trade from Ireland.

File and tool works. Also in Mersey Street, latterly occupied as furniture store. Warrington was a main centre of a domestic/small workshop industry (often organised on putting-out basis) producing a wide variety of tools from 17C. The best known firm was that of Peter Stubs, working originally from the White Bear Inn in Bridge Street and after 1802 from workshops and warehouses in Scotland Road. Stubs's career is described in T. S. Ashton, *An Eighteenth Century Industrialist: Peter Stubs of Warington, 1756–1806*, 1939.

Cockedge Mill SJ 609884. Only surviving cotton mill in town, started 1831, latterly spinning yarn for the carpet trade. Four storeys, brick-built, mainly late 19C, engine house with date stone 1878. Now occupied by variety of firms.

Central Station SJ 608886. Built 1873–74 on the CLC Manchester–Liverpool line. On viaduct, single-storey yellow-brick station buildings, red and blue-brick decoration, pairs of semi-circular arched windows, wood and glass canopies over platforms on cast iron pillars with ornamental brackets. To north-east is goods station with handsome warehouse, three storeys, 13 by 5 bays, patterned brickwork with pilasters between windows, three loading slots on each front. Names of railway companies on stone plaques: CLC, GNR, GCR and Midland.

NORTH

Dallam Lane Station SJ 605886. Was the original terminus of the Warrington & Newton Railway, opened 1831. Little remains except the Three Pigeons Inn in Tanners Lane, said to have been the booking office. The station was moved to Bank Quay in 1837, following the opening of the Grand Junction Railway from Birmingham.

Tanners Lane SJ 605887. At Winnerton Street end are former tannery buildings now occupied by number of firms. There was a tannery on the site by 1772, marked as Guests' Tannery on OS map of 1851, Tanners Lane Tanning Co. 1903.

Dallam Forge SJ 602889. Started 1840 making bar-iron plates and railway axles. Established Warrington Wire Iron Co. to make rods for the wire-drawing trade. Later amalgamated with Pearson & Knowles, colliery owners, of Wigan. Now Lancashire works of British Steel Corporation, Scunthorpe Division, who took over from Lancashire Steel Corporation.

Dallam Brewery SJ 605889. Started in 1850 by Peter Walker, who had brewery in King Street in 1846: Warrington Ales. Now modern plant of Tetley-Walker. Older buildings include interesting engine house with yellow-brick decoration, circular windows on top floor, ornamental front with clock, date stone 1868.

Longford Street SJ 607894. Pair of long two-storey brick-built workshops, formerly used for velvet cutting.

EAST

Rylands Wire Works SJ 614887. Extensive buildings north of Church Street. Started by George Ainsworth and Nathaniel Greg at end of 18C. John Rylands replaced Ainsworth as partner before 1812. Wire drawing developed as a major industry in 19C Warrington and has given the nickname 'Wire' to the local Rugby League team. The old method was to pull rolled iron rods through holes of varying dimension and cross section in cast-steel wortle plates, now replaced by continuous drawing through tungsten carbide dies.

Howley Quay SJ 617882. Quay of early 19C origin on Mersey & Irwell Navigation. Three-storey early 19C agent's house: James Dawson was agent in 1825. Two warehouses: one of two storeys, three aisles, internal structure of cast iron pillars and beams, loading canopy over river and travelling gantry inside. See *Archaeology of Warrington's Past*, pp. 61–3. To east is former Union Tannery. To south, Howley suspension bridge, footbridge of 1912, giving access to Victoria Park.

Howley Cut SJ 615877. Made before 1761: walls of lock and upper gate survive.

Mersey Flour Mills SJ 614877. Originally early 19C water-powered mill with race from weir above Howley Cut. Later five-storey brick-built steam-powered mill has also been demolished. Recent elevator survives and two tail openings for mill race.

SOUTH

Manor lock SJ 624879. Start of Runcorn & Latchford Canal, masonry side walls, double wooden gates each end, gate paddle gear, swing bridge to south. Feeder from Woolston Cut enters here. North of **Black Bear bridge** SJ 621874 is

two-storey, brick-built warehouse, six bays long, two loading openings on canal front, small windows, row of stone corbels which formerly supported loading canopy over canal. Canal continues to **Twenty Steps lock** SJ 613865 and junction with Manchester Ship Canal.

Latchford locks SJ 637873. On Manchester Ship Canal. Large lock 600 ft by 65 ft (183 m by 20 m), smaller lock 300 ft by 45 ft (107 m by 14 m). Operated hydraulically from power station to west, which also worked swing bridges, brick-built engine house, boiler house and accumulator tower. To west is a high-level steel-girder bridge on the LNWR (Warrington & Stockport) line built at time of construction of Ship Canal. On north bank of Ship Canal opposite locks is **Richmond Gas Cooker Works**, started 1906 for manufacture of cooker castings.

Knutsford Road bridge SJ 629870. Hydraulically operated steel-girder bridge over Ship Canal, turning on roller bearings with rack-and-pinion drive, brick-built control tower. There are similar bridges on **Northwich Road** SJ 614864 and **Chester Road** (Stag Inn), SJ 604861.

Wilderspool Brewery SJ 612865. Started by Peter Greenall of St Helens soon after 1761. Now modern works of Greenall Whitley, with older buildings west of Wilderspool Causeway, including four-storey buildings with circular tower with ornamental roof and clock.

Greenalls' Maltings SJ 608574. Circa 1850, building of great interest on west side of Wilderspool Causeway. Main range three storeys, brick-built, nine by three bays, central pediment, small windows with stone sills, brick lintels, criss-cross panes. Malt kiln at right-angles at south end, maltster's house at north end. There is a full description in *The Archaeology of Warrington's Past*.

New river diversion SJ 606876/

Greenall Whitley maltings, Wilderspool Causeway, Warrington, west front, 1979

601865. Straight cut on river Mersey parallel to Chester Road made in 1884. The old course of the river parallel to Wilderspool Causeway was intended for use as a dock after the opening of the Manchester Ship Canal in 1894: it has now been filled in.

Walton Lock SJ 607865. Adjusts the water level between the Ship Canal and the surviving stretch of the old river Mersey.

WEST

Bank Quay Station SJ 600878. The first station was built in 1837 when the Grand Junction Railway was opened from Birmingham and linked with the Warrington & Newton Railway and so with Liverpool and Manchester. Re-built 1868. In use, with late 19C buildings modernised. The low-level station on the St Helens & Runcorn Gap Railway was closed in 1963 and has been demolished. To south are two viaducts over the Mersey: a twelve-arch viaduct on the original GJR line and a later high-level steel-girder bridge.

Bank Quay Foundry SJ 598875. Started 1834, made parts for Conway and Britannia (Menai) tubular bridges on Chester & Holyhead Railway in 1840s.

Crosfield's Soap Works SJ 599880. Works started in 1814 by Joseph Crosfield on site of iron foundry and wire works, using coal from Haydock and Parr, soda from St Helens and Widnes, salt from Cheshire. In 1880s, 23 soap pans in use, eight frame rooms. Modern Unilever factory on site. There is a railway transporter bridge of 1916 within the works. There is a full account of the history of the firm in A. E. Musson, *Enterprise in Soap and Chemicals*, 1965.

Whitecross Wire Works SJ 597883. West of railway near Bank Quay. Started in 1864 by Frederick Monks, who had been an apprentice with Rylands (see above). In late 19C employed 800–1,000 hands and works included a foundry, rolling shops for making iron rods, annealing, tempering and galvanising shops, drawing shop. Made wire ropes and netting as well as ordinary wire. Drawing by old wortle-plate method until recently.

WIDNES

A 'new' 19C town and port created by the soap and chemical industries, following the making of the link with the coalfield through the extension of the Sankey Canal from Fiddler's Ferry and the opening of the St Helens and Runcorn Gap Railway in 1833.

Seven chemical works were started between 1847 and 1855, mainly in the area north of West Bank Dock and along the line of the canal. John Hutchinson established a works between the dock and canal in 1847 and a second works east of Waterloo Road. One of his managers was Harry Deacon, who moved to his own works between the canal and the railway to Garston in 1853. William Gossage started an alkali works on opposite bank of canal from Hutchinson's first works in 1850. He also had a soap works and was the inventor of the Gossage tower for condensing waste hydrochloric acid gas in the Leblanc process. James Muspratt, who earlier had a works in Liverpool, started a works in 1852 on the north bank of the canal east of the docks. All these works were for the manufacture of soda (sodium carbonate) by the Leblanc process in which sodium sulphate,

made from the reaction of salt (sodium chloride) and sulphuric acid was burned in furnaces with lime and coal to produce soda ash, which was purified in iron pans and then evaporated. There are still a number of chemical works, including ICI Mond Division Widnes Works on the site of the former United Alkali plant at Moss bank, Laporte Chemical at Farnworth on the site of a works started by Peter Spence in 1919.

Transporter bridge SJ 509838. Built 1905 by Widnes & Runcorn Bridge Co. and taken over by Widnes Corporation in 1911. Former stone-built ticket office and approach road with commemorative tablets survive, as do Runcorn Transporter Bridge Offices at corner of Mersey Street and St Mary's Road, two storey, machine brick, curved front.

West Bank. Mid-19C housing area now being redeveloped. Houses north of Irwell Street have mostly been demolished: Mersey Road is most complete of older streets. Hartland Wesleyan chapel, 1882, and St Mary's Church, 1884, survive.

Old Dock SJ 515843. Opened as terminus for St Helens & Runcorn Gap Railway, 1833. For vessels up to 300 tons. 200 tons of coal per day shipped

Old dock, West Bank, Widnes, 1979

from dock in early years. Stone side walls and entrance lock survive and the area is now being conserved, with the beginnings of an industrial archaeology trail. To the west the double locks into the Sankey Canal survive. The canal and railway companies were amalgamated in 1844.

Widnes South Station SJ 512848. The first Runcorn Gap Station nearer the dock was closed in 1852 when the line was extended to Garston (and to Warrington in 1853–54). The South Station was closed in 1962, site of platforms still visible. The railway approaches from the east on a long brick-built viaduct.

Central Station SJ 510850. On the GCR/Midland joint line from Widnes East Junction on CLC, opened 1873, extended to Hough Green, also on CLC, 1879. Closed 1964. Cobbled road approach, embankment and Central Hotel survive.

Widnes North Station SJ 513871. On CLC line to Liverpool, opened 1873 and still in use. Typical CLC station buildings: another example at **Hough Green Station** SJ 485865.

WILLASTON (WIRRAL)

Willaston Windmill SJ 327784. Early 19C tower mill replacing former post mill. Five storeys, brick-built, 60 ft (18·3 m) high, wooden boat-shaped cap, iron cross for mounting sails, iron tail wheel for turning cap into wind. Converted to residence in late 1950s. Extended c. 1870 to drive nine pairs of stones (four in tower) with steam engine and new machinery: brick chimney survives. Ceased to work as flour mill c. 1911, animal feeds until c. 1930. One of two Wirral flour mills working when Milford Abraham wrote in 1903.

Hadlow Road Station SJ 330773. On Birkenhead Railway (GWR/LNWR joint) line from Hooton to Parkgate, opened 1866. Closed to passengers 1956, goods 1962. Preserved and fur-

nished in 1950s style as part of Wirral Country Park. Level-crossing gates on cast iron posts, portion of track, platform and platform furniture, single-storey booking hall and two-storey stationmaster's house, brick-built with ornamental stone window sills and lintels, stone-framed doorways. Date stone '1866' on road side. Before 1959 as many as 58 trains stopped in a day and there was a station staff of six.

WILMSLOW

There was considerable activity in textile production in 18C and early 19C: making of silk buttons, jersey spinning, silk and cotton hand-loom weaving. There was formerly a silk mill on the river Bollin in the Carrs, SJ 843817, burned down 1923, worked as laundry in later years. There is a photograph in Hodson, *Portrait of Wilmslow*, 1974. For a useful introduction see Wilmslow Historical Society, *Wilmslow of Yesterday*, 1970.

Wilmslow Station SJ 851811. On Manchester & Birmingham Railway, opened 1842, rebuilt on opening of Styal loop line, 1909. Single-storey brick building on west platform and at road level, modernised. Impressive **Railway Hotel** near by. To north are twin **Bollin viaducts**, twenty-three arches: M&BR viaduct of 1842, red brick, on east; Styal line viaduct, 1909, blue brick, on west.

Fustian-cutting workshop, Bollin Walk SJ 850813. Fustian cutting was an important domestic and small-workshop industry in late 19C Wilmslow, employing women and children, supplying Manchester merchants. The Bollin Walk workshop was used by a Mr Clare who later moved to Hawthorn Street. Two storeys, brick-built, loading openings in east end wall.

Bollin Corn Mill SJ 848817. Four-storey 19C mill building survives, used by firm of builders. Powered by over-shot waterwheel, removed c. 1955.

Ceased production 1949. Long mill race 900 yd (823 m) from weir on river Bollin at SJ 857811.

Manchester Road SJ 849814. Former fustian-cutting shop started by a Mr Dearden 1951–61. Four storeys, brick-built with three-storey building at right angles, large blocked windows on north end wall. Occupied by dairy furnishers.

Hawthorn Street SJ 842809. Former fustian-cutting workshop behind houses on north side. Started by Mr Clare (from Bollin Walk) *c.* 1900 and worked by Platt family 1910–20. Two storeys, brick-built, nine bays long, large rectangular windows. Occupied by furniture removers.

WINCHAM

Formerly busy salt township north of Northwich, with several rock-salt mines and evaporation works in later 19C.

New Cheshire Salt Works SJ 676754. The only one still in use, a vacuum works, with remains of older works to west and name 'SELVA' on one of two circular brick chimneys. Marked as 'Wincham Works (salt)' on OS map of 1882. The near-by Sunbeam Salt Works was in use as open-pan plant with brine pumped by horizontal steam engine until about ten years ago. West of New Cheshire Works are abutments of canal bridge on Salt Branches Railway from Northwich, opened 1867.

Ashton's Flashes on west side of township are on site of former Ashton's rock-salt mine.

Wincham Corn Mill SJ 685747. Buildings of 19C steam-powered mill occupied by North West Farmers. On west, three-storey building with loading openings, two-storey building and kiln. On east, three-storey building parallel to road, with stone tablet inscribed 'Wincham Corn & Bone Mills J. K. and W. Hesketh 1870'. Near by is **Wincham aqueduct** carrying Trent &

Mersey Canal over Wincham brook, twin arches, blue brick on stone piers.

WINCLE

Folly Mill SJ 971664. Remains of water-powered paper mill in deep valley on Clough brook just north of its junction with river Dane. Started *c.* 1790, though there are references to paper-makers in Wincle before that date (1764, 1770, 1786). Run in early 19C by Thomas Hope, who had another mill on the river Dane at **White Lee** SJ 955642. Advertised to let in 1849: water power, machinery for finishing paper, making coarse brown and blue papers.

WINSFORD

Developed as a major salt-producing centre following the improvement of the river Weaver to Winsford bridge in 18C. There was a line of salt works either side of the river of which there is now comparatively little trace. White's *Cheshire Directory* in 1860 talks of '. . . Salt Works more numerous than in any other place in England', 416 pans, over 1,000 workers. Brine was pumped from a depth of 150–210 ft (46–64 m) and rock salt was mined in large quantities. There was considerable ship repair and building activity in the area around Winsford bridge.

Over & Wharton Station SJ 657665. Terminus of LNWR branch from Wharton Greeen, opened 1882, closed to passengers 1947. Surviving wooden station building, painted LMS red and yellow, blue-brick chimneys, sidings to west. North Western Hotel on opposite side of High Street.

Winsford & Over Station SJ 653664, west of river, terminus of CLC branch from Cuddington, opened 1870, closed 1930, has been demolished and tracks removed.

Birkenhead and Liverpool Salt Works SJ 653668. Foundations only of buildings of two works on east side of river Weaver. To north, at Wharton

Lumpman filling salt tubs, Salt Union open-pan works, Winsford, 1923.
Courtesy Cheshire County Museums

Works, buildings are still occupied: there was a rock-salt mine and a twelve-acre works in 1915.

Meadowbank Salt Works SJ 654681. The only rock-salt mine still open in Cheshire, worked by ICI. Mining started with two shafts in 1844 and continued until 1892. Reopened by Salt Union 1928 when the last Northwich mine closed: further shafts bored 1940 and 1964. Workings at depth of approx. 500 ft (150 m) over area of 250 acres. Face undercut by machine, blasted, salt loaded into diesel dumper trucks and carried to primary crusher before being lifted up shaft by electric winding gear. Output mainly bought by local authorities for road clearing. In 1950s rail transport was still used underground.

In old workings roof supported by leaving salt pillars 12–36 yd (11–33 m) square, in later workings 18 yd by 6 yd (7·3 m by 5·5 m). There is a detailed account in *Mine and Quarry Engineering*, May–June 1956. There are still traces of the railway branch from the Cuddington–Over line and of a dock on the west side of the Weaver.

New Bridge SJ 652687. Site of former double locks on Weaver, removed 1897. Iron swing bridge between west bank and lock island, turning on roller bearings on circular track, operated by capstan driving shaft and cogwheel geared to rack moving in curved opening in masonry. Small brick control house.

WINWICK

Winwick Quay SJ 595918. Canal basin, wharf and repair yard on Sankey Canal. Dry dock with stepped sandstone walls south of yard on west bank, Quay Fold Cottages to north. Workshops and stores, mostly single-storey, along north side of yard; 1841, brick-built, stone decoration, semi-circular arched windows. Single-storey shed on east, former soaking pit for bending timbers on south. Remains of narrow-gauge railway system and of crane supports.

Holme lock SJ 597914. Sandstone and brick side walls, double wooden gates, footbridge on brackets on upper gate, side weir between lock and lock keeper's cottage. The canal in this area has largely been filled in.

WISTASTON (CREWE)

Wistaston Corn Mill SJ 696541. On Wistaston brook, south of Crewe–Nantwich road. Three storeys, brick-built, windows with semi-circular arched heads, wheel house at west, being restored as residence. Millpond at rear partly dried up, overflow with rack-and-pinion sluice gear. In 1969 Norris reported two wheels, one over-shot, 12 ft (3·6 m) diameter, one breast-shot 15 ft (4·6 m) diameter, at one time assisted by horizontal steam engine.

WOOLSTON

Woolston Old Cut. Made in early years of Mersey & Irwell Navigation from below New Woolston weir, SJ 653885, 700 yd (640 m) west, cutting out long bend running south to Thelwall.

Woolston New Cut. Replaced Old Cut in 1821, a mile and a half (2·4 km) from Martinscroft lock, SJ 654888, partly filled in, to Paddington lock (see *Poulton with Fernhead*). Lock keeper's house at Martinscroft occupied, line of cut and side walls clearly visible to west.

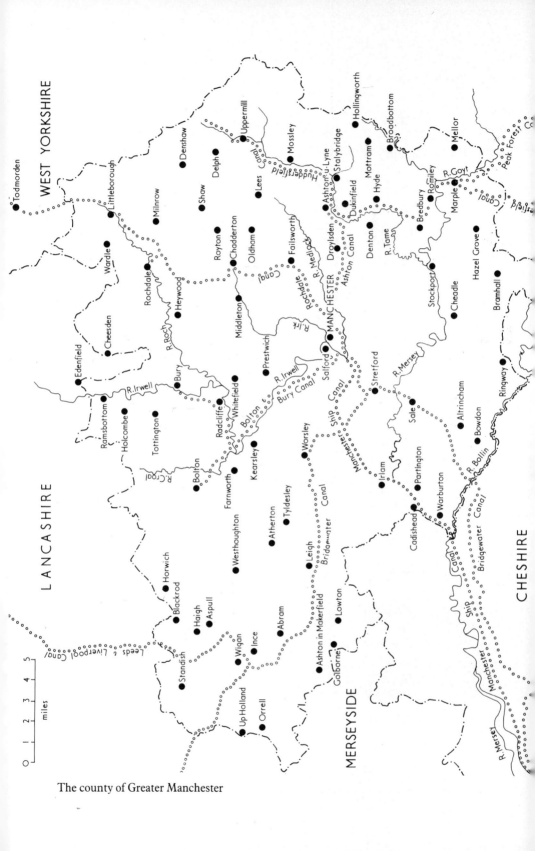

The county of Greater Manchester

Greater Manchester

The new metropolitan county of Greater Manchester consists essentially of the old cotton area of south-east Lancashire and north-east Cheshire, with an incursion into Yorkshire and the woollen industry through the inclusion of Saddleworth. With a population of nearly 2¾ million it is the most densely inhabited area in the region. The county is divided into ten metropolitan boroughs, but in this gazetteer the old townships have been used. To help readers who may want to work on the new basis a list of townships in each metropolitan borough is given at the end.

ABRAM
Former coal-mining township south-east of Wigan, collieries of Abram Coal Co. before nationalisation. None working.

Abram Colliery SD 628016. Spoil heaps and pit-head buildings; railway sidings and line to Bickershaw and to LNWR at Hindley Green in use. Community of rows of two-storey brick cottages to north in Bolton Fold Road. Five shafts sunk 1870 onwards. In 1892 four steam winding engines, two steam haulage engines, two steam air compressors, large Guibal ventilation fans, 21 Lancashire boilers, extensive workshops with fitting shop, smithy, carpenter's shop and wagon shop. Abandoned by 1918.

Maypole Colliery SD 614011. Site still occupied, with some new buildings. Traces of spoil heaps, concrete foundations of head gear, brick pit-head buildings, circular brick chimney, traces of railway lines to Platt Bridge Colliery and to GCR at Park Lane Junction. Nearly 1,600 workers in 1954, producing about 350,000 tons a year.

ALTRINCHAM
Altrincham Station SD 770879. The Manchester South Junction & Altrincham Railway from Manchester London Road was opened in 1849, with an Altrincham Station in Stockport Road north of the present site and Bowdon Station in Lloyd Street to the south. The line was a major factor in the suburban development of the area, as White wrote in 1860, '. . . causing numbers of merchants and manufacturers to fix their abode in this pleasant and salubrious locality . . .'. The line was linked with Warrington by the Warrington & Stockport Railway to Broadheath, opened 1853, and with the Cheshire Lines following the opening of the Stockport Timperley & Altrincham Railway and the Cheshire Midland line from Altrincham to Knutsford and Northwich, opened 1862–63. The present station was built in 1881 between the old Altrincham and Bowdon stations as traffic developed, with four platforms, two for the Manchester line, two for the CLC. The single-storey red-brick buildings with blue and yellow-brick decoration survive, though

hidden by unattractive modern bus station built on front. Also surviving is the clock tower, which stood behind the railings of the old station yard, between the two entrance gates. The line from Manchester was electrified in 1929–31 by the LMS and LNER on a 1,500 V d.c. overhead system, changed in 1969 to 25 kV a.c.

ASHTON IN MAKERFIELD

Former coal-mining township, earlier known for manufacture of nails (community at Downhall Green), locks and hinges. Collieries mainly operated by Garswood Coal & Iron Co. on lease from Lord Gerard of Garswood Hall; some 2,500 employed in late 19C.

Park Lane Colliery SD 571018. Pithead site east of lane is built on, to west is line of railway to Middle Place Colliery and High Brooks Colliery. Park Lane had branch from LNWR Wigan–St Helens line, opened 1869. Pits sunk from 1877. Five shafts in 1892, four steam winding engines, steam pumping engine, steam air compressor, seven haulage engines, bar sorting screens, workshops with fitting shop, smithy with ten hearths, steam hammer, carpenters' shop, wagon shop.

Garswood Hall Colliery SD 576008. No. 5 pit sunk 1880 with winding engine made by Haigh Foundry. Area now landscaped. Near-by community at Bryn: Garswood Mines Insitute on Wigan Road demolished. To southeast, traces of Long Lane pits, two shafts in use in 1890s.

ASHTON UNDER LYNE

A medium-sized cotton town which developed on the basis of earlier domestic manufacture of linens and woollens: noted for fustians and checks in 17C and 18C. Early water-powered mills were built on the river Tame and its tributaries: there were four mills on the Cock brook, which now runs though Stamford Park. The Ashton and Hud-

dersfield Canals provides a location for many of the mid-19C mills: there is a surviving line from Guide Bridge in the west to Whitelands in the east. There were formerly a number of collieries, some quite close to the present town centre. There is a detailed account in Owen Ashmore, 'The industrial archaeology of Ashton under Lyne', *Victorian Ashton*, ed. S. E. Harrop and E. A. Rose, 1974, pp. 86–107.

CENTRAL AREA AND SOUTH

Bankfield Mills SJ 936986. Five storeys and basement, brick-built, octagonal staircase tower built round chimney at south-eastern corner, 48,000 spindles and 1,550 looms in 1903.

Ashton New Wharf SJ 934985. At junction of Ashton Canal, opened 1796, and Peak Forest Canal, opened 1797. Towpath bridge of 1835 over Peak Forest Canal: fine example, single arch, stone-built, twenty arch stones each side of keystone, path surfaced with stone setts, parapet of stone flags. Three-arch sandstone aqueduct over river Tame, arched in plan, with buttresses. Foundations only of brick-built warehouse of 1834 in Portland Place, destroyed by fire 1973.

Ashton Old Wharf SJ 941988. Original wharf at junction of Ashton and Huddersfield Canals: the latter was opened partly in 1798, throughout in 1811. The wharf is clearly visible but the arm off the canal has been filled in. To the east are the remains of an arm from the Huddersfield Canal to a warehouse, and of Whitelands tunnel, 150 yd (137 m) long, opened out before 1911, and Whitelands locks. West of the wharf is the site of **Park Parade Station** on the Sheffield Ashton under Lyne & Manchester Railway (later MSLR) line from Guide Bridge to Stalybridge, opened 1845. Approached by a long curved thirty-three-arch stone viaduct across the Tame valley, scene of a collapse during construction in April 1845. The Station Hotel survives, the former goods yard is still an open space and below in Lower Wharf Street are the foundations of a former warehouse which was a rail, road and canal interchange.

Charlestown Station SJ 939994. Now the only station on the LYR Manchester–Stalybridge line, opened 1846. Late 19C yellow-brick buildings, former goods station to west.

NORTH

Alger Mill SJ 947999. Late spinning mill, four storeys and basement, machine brick, rectangular windows in threes with white-tile decoration, six-bay engine house also with white tile decoration at north-west, ornamental water tower. 81,000 mule spindles in 1928.

Cedar Mill SJ 947001. Similar period to Alger, five storeys, machine brick, large rectangular windows in groups of two or three, yellow-brick decoration, ornamental water tower, engine house, boiler house and chimney on east. 77,000 mule spindles in 1911. Occupied by Courtauld's Northern Textiles.

Hurst Mill SD 949002. A horse-driven carding mill was started by John Whittaker from Oldham in 1806: later spinning jennies and hand mules. New mill in 1847 powered by two beam engines. In 1908 86,000 mule spindles, 1,130 looms. Four-storey brick-built mill on east side of Queens Road, large windows. Ornamental brickwork below parapet, water tower with clock at north-east corner. Associated community: housing, school, Methodist chapel.

Oldham Road Station SJ 936995. Site of former station on Oldham Ashton & Guide Bridge Railway, opened 1861. Line of platform visible. Route can be followed north as earthwork to Oldham boundary. Signal box west of Oldham Road bridge with name 'OA&GB Junction' still on it.

Atlas Mill SD 935001. Late-period spinning mill at Waterloo, four storeys, machine brick, large rectangular windows in threes, yellow-brick decoration, Hotel-de-Ville style water tower, six-bay engine house, boiler house and chimney on north. In use by Courtauld's Northern Textiles. Near by Rock Mill has been demolished.

Bardsley Mill SD 931014. Former water-powered spinning mill on river Medlock, occupied since 1896 by Thomas Kerfoot & Co., manufacturing chemists. Kerfoot's were pioneers in the introduction of machinery for making pills and tablets.

Park Bridge Iron Works SD 940025. Outstanding example of an industrial community associated with wrought iron manufacture and textile machinery making. Started *c.* 1784 by Samuel and Hannah Lees on site of former corn mill on river Medlock, making rollers and spindles for the new cotton mills. Continued by Hannah's sons and considerably extended in later 19C: new roller-making shop, rolling sheds, drop forge. Four-storey cotton-doubling mill on site of first works, now becoming derelict. Later rolling shop on hill above. Five-aisle single-storey rolling mill for wrought iron bar production in valley to east, now used for storage. Brick-built gas works and site of drop forge, now cleared. Dean House on hillside is former home of Lees family: stables and out-buildings round yard. Two rows of late 19C brick-built workers' cottages in Dingle Terrace, earlier cottages in Dean Terrace with St James's Church of 1866 and school. Branch line on incline from OA&GBR into works: viaduct and Park Bridge Station demolished. The road to the works follows line of former tramroad, horse-drawn in early days, later locomotives used until *c.* 1880, to branch of Ashton Canal at Fennyfield bridge, SD 935017, now partly filled in. Near by at the former **Fairbottom Pit** is the site of an early Newcomen pumping engine removed to Dearborn, Michigan, by Henry Ford in 1929. North of Park Bridge is site of **Rocher Pit** SD

944024 with remains of stone-built engine house, formerly served by Park Bridge Tramroad.

WEST AND SOUTH-WEST

Wellington Works SJ 929991. Site by side of OA&GBR taken over in 1889 by Henry Nield Bickerton for manufacture of gas engines: National Gas Engine Co. Produced two-cycle engine, different from the four-cycle Otto engine made in Britain by Crossley Bros of Openshaw. Widely used in electric power plants, mainly overseas, cotton mills, corn mills and other works. Later made diesel engines and became part of Mirlees Bickerton & Day (Hazel Grove Works, 1908).

New Row, Little Moss SJ 917999. Row of late 18C cottages which were formerly hand-loom weaving community. Described by the local historian, Butterworth, in 1823 as occupied by muslin weavers.

Ryecroft Mills SJ 927983. Mills started by Buckleys with associated community described by Reach in 1849 as a '. . . snug little colony', with rents of 3s, 3s 9d and 4s 6d according to number of rooms, some houses with gardens. 55,000 mule spindles in early 20C. Six-storey brick-built mill with engine house and chimney at rear survives.

Oxford Mills SJ 930979. Two six-storey brick-built spinning mills, 1845 and 1851, built by Thomas and Hugh Mason, windows with stone sills and lintels, internal structure of cast iron pillars and beams, brick arches, formerly internal engine houses for beam engines, later engine and boiler houses on canal side. Adjoining the mills between Oxford Street and Stockport Road is the workers' community built by the Masons from 1845 onwards. Smallest four-roomed cottages in Ann

Oxford Mills community, Ashton under Lyne

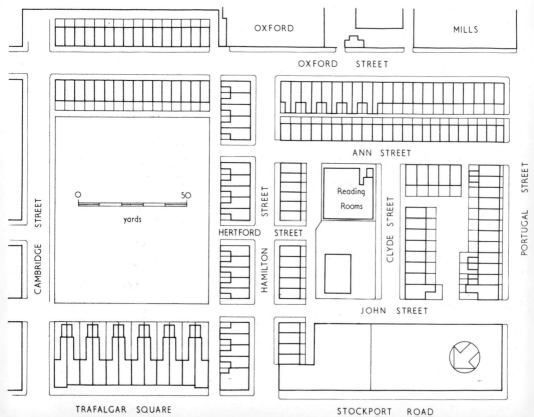

Street, five and six-roomed cottages in Oxford Street and Hamilton Street, more ornamental rows in Gibson Terrace, 1869, and John Bright Terrace, 1871 (Hugh Mason was a leading Liberal and for a time MP), very large houses with five to seven bedrooms in Trafalgar Square. In Ann Street is institute of 1868 with 'Venetian' tower: it included swimming bath as well as library and reading room. The community is described in Angus Bethune Reach's reports for the *Morning Chronicle* in 1849 (*Manchester and the Textile Districts in 1849*, ed. C. Aspin, 1972). See also Owen Ashmore and Trevor Bolton, 'Hugh Mason and the Oxford Mills and community, Ashton under Lyne', *Trans. Lancs. & Ches. Antiq. Soc.*, vol. 78, 1974.

Birch Mills SJ 928977. Four and five-storey mid-19C buildings. Windows with stone sills and lintels, corner pilasters, later four-storey building with blue-brick decoration to west.

Guide Mills SJ 926976. Late 19C three-storey brick mill with older building to north. Engine house, boiler house and chimney on canal side. Built by Kershaw's, who provided houses for the workers, described by Reach in 1849 as having parlour and kitchen, good range with oven and boiler, yard and privy at back. There is a wide variety of examples of Victorian worker's cottages in this part of Ashton, both north and south of Stockport Road.

Guide Bridge Spinning Co. SJ 923978. Late 19C mill, five storeys, large windows with stone sills and brick-arch lintels, projecting engine house, square water tower. 157,000 mule spindles in 1911.

Guide Bridge Station SJ 926697. Where the railway first reached Ashton when the Manchester–Sheffield line was opened in 1842. Became junction for lines to Stalybridge and Huddersfield, Stockport and Oldham. Substantial late 19C station buildings and two-storey range of offices, indicating the importance of the junction.

Ashton Moss Colliery SJ 920979. Two pits sunk 1875 and 1882, 2,850 ft (870 m) deep. 530 men employed in 1954. Spoil heaps and remains of buildings, including former pit-head baths, south of Manchester Road.

ASPULL

Like the neighbouring township of Haigh, Aspull had colliery workings from 16C. Some drained by famous Haigh Sough, which reached its eastern limit at **Aspull Pumping Pit** SD 626082 in 1866. North of Bolton Road in the village is square brick chimney for ventilating shaft of **Cullett Pit** SD 616079. Numerous traces of workings between Bolton Road and Leeds & Liverpool Canal.

Duke's Row SD 608079. Good early example of colliers' houses south-east of Wigan Road. Row of fifteen two-storey stone-built cottages with prominent chimneys, stone-framed doorways and windows. Adjoining is **Moss Pit Row**, six stone-built cottages, later. A little farther along Wigan Road is site of bridge on railway branch from LYR at Hindley Junction to Aspull Collieries.

Kirkless Iron & Steel Works SD 607065. On east bank of Leeds & Liverpool Canal, now used as store and workshops by NCB. Started by Earl of Crawford and Balcarres, owner of Haigh Collieries, in 1858, taken over by Wigan Coal & Iron Co., 1865. In 1890 ten blast furnaces with annual output of 125,000 tons and rolling mills for bar and rod iron. In 1908 also had five open-hearth steel-making furnaces, steel-rolling mills, and three batteries of Solvay coke ovens producing tar and ammoniacal liquor as by-products. There were also a brick works and lime kilns. Site of Kirkless Colliery to south.

Top Locks SD 608068. Top of the famous Wigan flight carrying Leeds & Liverpool Canal up 200 ft (61 m) from

Wigan to junction with southern arm of Lancaster Canal. Locks have masonry side walls, double gates at each end, gate paddles on both, ground paddles also at upper end, variety of paddle-operating mechanisms, wooden lock-end footbridges, iron bollards. A walk down the locks affords fine views of the area and is of great historical interest. At No. 1 lock is two-storey stone-built lock keeper's house and single-storey brick-built tollhouse; at No. 2 lock Kirkless Hall Inn and to south **Cale Lane bridge**, 1816, stone-built, single arch, humped, bowed in plan, projecting string course below parapet, wooden rubbing rollers each side; between locks 4 and 5, abutments of former railway bridge from LNWR at Whelley to Kirkless Hall Works; at bottom of No. 5 lock, **Kirkless Hall bridge**, also 1816.

ATHERTON

Well known for nail-making from 17C to 19C: one shop working in early 1900s. Coal-mining community in 19C: collieries of Fletcher Burrows & Co. before nationalisation. Three collieries working in 1950s, now none.

Atherton Central Station SD 684037. On LYR line from Pendleton to Hindley, opened 1887–88, still in use. Single-storey yellow and red-brick booking office with hipped slate roof and two chimney stacks. Three platforms, one on south disused, canopies on cast iron pillars. Brick-built goods shed to west.

Laburnum Mills SD 682038. Good example of twin early 20C cotton-spinning mills, in use by Carrington Vyella Yarns. East mill 1905 (date on tower), four storeys and basement, brick-built, rectangular windows in pairs, in threes on top storey, thirty-six bays long, water tower with stone decoration, balustrade and dome at north-east, large engine house on south with semi-circular arched windows and square windows above, tall circular brick chimney. Ornamental single-storey brick and stone office in Upton Road. Later mill in similar style to west.

Gloucester Street Mill SD 673033. Another large early 20C spinning mill in use by Carrington Vyella. Four storeys and basement, yellow-brick decoration over windows and on top storey, 36 by eight bays, single-storey carding extension on south, large engine house, tall circular brick chimney, ornamental flat-roofed water tower at north-east. On opposite side of Factory Street is slightly earlier mill, also occupied by Carrington Vyella, with recent buildings added at west.

Gibfield Colliery SD 666035. At side of Bolton & Leigh Railway, used as coal yard and most of buildings gone. 800 men employed in 1954, 250,000 tons a year. In 1892 two shafts with steam winding engines, two steam pumping engines, one steam haulage engine, fan ventilator, six-bar sorting screens, washery, extensive fitting repair shops. Near by was **Bag Lane Station**, closed 1954 and demolished.

Howe Bridge Colliery SD 662021. Pit-head site occupied by Lancashire United Transport as garage and repair works. 460 men in 1954. Three shafts in 1890s. The line of the **Bolton & Leigh Railway**, opened 1828–31, runs north to south along the west side of the township. Closed and track removed. Clearly visible at Wigan Lane, SD 663061.

BARTON See *Eccles*

BILLINGE WITH WINSTANLEY

Coal mining from 16C, particularly by Bankes family of Winstanley Hall. See J. H. M. Bankes, 'Records of mining in Winstanley and Orrell', *Trans. Lancs. & Ches. Antiq. Soc.*, vol. 54, 1939.

Winstanley No. 4 Pit SD 548018. Winding-engine house, steel lattice-girder head gear, brick pit-head buildings. Self-acting incline on Bankes Colliery Railway, built 1836–45, 4 ft (122 cm) gauge, mounted on stone blocks from local quarries. Ran north-east to **No. 3 Pit**, SD 552025, spoil heaps, foundations of head gear. Near by in Pemberton Road is **New Houses**, row of cottages built by Meyrick Bankes in late 18C and early 19C. Railway then ran east to **Clap Gate Colliery**, SD 562033, under Pemberton Loop Railway at Goose Green, via Stonehouse Colliery and across river Douglas to Wigan Pier. Locomotives used from 1878. Line now difficult to trace in built-up areas. Detailed account in J. H. M. Bankes, 'A nineteenth-century colliery railway', *Trans. Hist. Soc. Lancs. & Ches.*, vol. 114, 1963.

BLACKROD

Huyton Bleach Works SD 607128. Group of stone and brick buildings with brick enclosing wall and tall brick chimney. Mill race half mile (805 m) east of works on river Douglas: water colour of 1816 reproduced in *Concerning the Bleaching Industry* (Bleachers' Association, 1925) shows waterwheel. Started 1812. Gallimore Liddell & Co., calico printers in 1825. Later Davies & Eckersley, bleachers, taken over by Bleachers' Association 1900. Huyton House, owner's residence, on south. Formerly had siding from Bolton & Preston Railway. Blackrod was a considerable coal-mining township and there are old shafts and traces of spoil heaps of 19C colliery sites: **Dark Lane** SD 607112, **Ackers Colliery** SD 612109, **Blundell Lane** SD 603107, **Marklands Colliery** SD 613118, **Sibberings Colliery** SD 610104, with Copperas House near by, marking site of former copperas works, for making ferrous sulphate used in manufacture of sulphuric acid from iron pyrites, marked on OS map

of 1844. There are traces of the former branch from the Bolton & Preston Railway to collieries north of Blundell Lane.

BOLTON

One of the major Lancashire cotton towns, with interesting contrasts in industrial archaeology. There are many examples of mid- and late Victorian mills, and some larger ones of later date. The streams running down from the northern moors into the river Croal—Dean brook, Eagley brook, Astley brook, Bradshaw brook, river Tonge—provided power and processing water for the bleach works which were a major feature of the area. Samuel Crompton's invention of the spinning mule provided the basis for the start of an important textile machinery-making industry. Bolton also had the first public railway in the region, the Bolton & Leigh, opened 1828, also giving a stimulus to engineering development.

CENTRE

Trinity Street Station SD 720087. Originally terminus of Manchester & Bolton Railway, opened 1838, taken over by Manchester & Leeds Railway 1846. Rebuilt by LYR 1871 and 1899–1904: present buildings belong to latter period. Two long island platforms: on west two-storey 23-bay building, red brick on upper storey, yellow brick and glazed red brick below, semi-circular arch doorways and windows; on east four single-storey yellow and red-brick buildings, window inscriptions showing former use – ladies' second and third-class waiting rooms, general waiting room, telegraph office. Office building on viaduct across north end of station, blackened with smoke on northbound side, pillared entrances from Trinity Street, ornamental clock tower with cupola. Goods shed on east, 1904, three aisles, 24 by 12 bays, four loading openings on roadside, two on railway side.

Great Moor Street Station SD 715088. Site of former terminus of Bolton & Leigh Railway, opened 1855, rebuilt 1874, demolished and now used as car park. Lecturers Closes, south of Crook Street, where line originally terminated, is now built on. West of Fletcher Street is the beginning of the **Daubhill incline** on the earlier line and the LNWR deviation line of 1885, both with track removed. The incline is clearly visible both sides of Rothwell Street, SD 713083.

Atlas Works SD 714083. Iron works of Thomas Walmsley & Sons, who made wrought iron by the puddling process, patented by Henry Cort in 1784, from 1866 until recently: reverberatory furnaces, iron stirred by hand tools, reheating forges and rolling mills. Older plant being transferred to Blists Hill Open Air Museum (Ironbridge Gorge Museum) in Shropshire. Now steel stock holders.

91–109 Great Moor Street SD 715087. Row of ten three-storey shop buildings with clear traces of double windows of former domestic workshops in basement along entire length of rear wall.

Flash Mills SD 714088. Good example of cotton mills of early Victorian date, three, four and five storeys, brick-built, rectangular windows with stone sills and lintels, projecting latrine towers on mill to east.

Croal viaduct SD 722093. On Bolton Blackburn Clitheroe & West Yorkshire Railway (LYR from 1857) line to Blackburn, opened 1848. Four cast iron arches of 76 ft (23 m) span on stone piers, segmental stone approach arches each side. The terminus of the Bolton branch of the Manchester Bolton & Bury Canal to south has been lost in recent road development.

Shiffnal Street Bus Garage SD 720089. Built by Bolton Corporation as depot for electric trams from 1899 on site of former horse-tram stores and stables: generating station in Spa Road. Two-aisle main garage with traces of

Shiffnall Street tram/bus depot, Bolton, 1973

tram tracks and name 'Bolton Corporation Tramcar Depot' over entrance. Near by is Carlton Street Works, built 1911–13 for repairs and maintenance. Buses from 1923: thirty garaged in 1928. Also still in use is **Bridgeman Street Garage** SD 716082, built 1909, extended 1925 (for 64 trams), 300 ft (91 m) long.

SOUTH AND SOUTH-EAST

Beehive Mills SD 726073. Outstanding example of late brick-built cotton mills. No. 1 at north, 1902, four storeys, large rectangular windows, yellow-brick decoration, 26 bays long, ornamental tower. No. 2 at south, five storeys, 26 by eight bays, rectangular windows in pairs, in threes on top storey with pillars between, yellow-brick decoration, corner pilasters, water tower with balustrade and pyramidical roof. Group of earlier mills in **Lever Street** area. Oldest is **Grecian Mills** SD 717079, five storeys, windows with stone sills and lintels, corner pilasters, ten by four bays. Later, with large windows and brick-arch lintels, are **Lever Street Mills** with notable ornamental three-storey office, and **St Mark Street Mills** with internal structure of cast iron pillars, lengthwise and crosswise iron beams, brick arches.

Damside viaduct SD 726083. On LYR line to Bury opened 1848. Steel lattice-girder spans on stone piers. The near-by Damside aqueduct on the Manchester Bolton & Bury Canal was demolished in 1965: the canal is empty and landscaped to east towards Smithy Bridge.

SOUTH-WEST

Swan Lane Mills SD 708076. Arguably the outstanding example of spinning mill building in Bolton. At south, five storeys and basement, large windows with stone sills and brick-arch lintels, yellow-brick decoration, 56 bays long, twin water towers on south front, large engine house at rear. To north later and unusual seven-storey mill with

segmental-arched windows, rounded corners. Described by J. and J. Nasmith in *Recent Cotton Mill Construction*, 1909: nearly 200,000 mule spindles, combed Sea Island (100s to 130s counts) and combed Egyptian (60s and 80s counts) sections, 250 carding engines, 200 drawing and roving frames. Near by is Swan Lane bridge over LNWR Bolton & Leigh deviation of 1885: tracks removed.

Sunnyside Mills SD 703074. Extensive spinning and weaving mills of Tootal Broadhurst & Lee, started 1868. Ornamental engine house with frieze showing cotton processes. Sunnyside Institute in Adelaide Street with clock tower and blue-brick decoration.

Daubhill SD 705076. West of Adelaide Street is site of top of Daubhill incline on Bolton & Leigh Railway, where there was a 20 h.p. stationary winding engine. There is a water colour showing former Daubhill Station at Sunnyside Mills. West of St Helens Road is **Daubhill Junction**, where later line of 1885 deviated from original route: track removed from both.

Crown Brewery SD 708079. Former Magee Marshall brewery in St Helens Road. Late 19C and early 20C ornamental building of traditional brewery style with five-storey section for gravity processing at west; ornamental tower at east. There is material relating to the brewery in Little Bolton Town Hall Museum.

Lostock Junction SD 674084. Junction of Bolton & Preston Railway, opened 1841, and LYR line to Liverpool, opened 1848. Brick and timber signal box, brick-built engine shed, Junction Hotel. Station closed 1966 and demolished.

NORTH-WEST

Falcon Mill SD 707111. In Handel Street, 1903, five storeys and basement, large windows in threes, yellow-brick decoration, 33 by 16 bays, ornamental water tower with name of mill. In use for cotton spinning.

Atlas Mills SD 701101. On south side of Chorley Old Road. Group of six spinning mills built by Musgrave Spinning Co. from 1862, in square around reservoirs, three, four and five storeys, windows with stone sills and brick-arch lintels, internal structure of cast iron pillars and beams. In engine house of No. 3 mill in Mornington Road is **Museum of Northern Mill Engines Society**: vertical overhead-crank engine by Barraclough of Barnsley c. 1860; double-beam engine from Crosfield Mill, Wardle, Rochdale; horizontal tandem compound engine by Pollitt & Wignall of Sowerby Bridge, 1896; another by J. & W. McNaught of Rochdale, 1902, from Wasp Mill, Wardle; compound non-dead-centre engine by Musgrave's of Bolton, 1893, from Park Street Mill, Radcliffe.

Halliwell Bleach Works SD 696114. Group of mid-19C buildings still occupied. Started by Peter Ainsworth, who was a crofter in Little Bolton and acquired bleachcroft at the Moss, Halliwell, in 1739. Grandson, Richard Ainsworth, went over to chlorine bleaching, employing two French chemists. Taken over by Bleachers' Association, 1900. Reservoirs to west, including Victoria Lake.

Barrow Bridge SD 689116. Fine example of industrial community associated with Dean Mills of Gardner & Bazley, started c. 1830, with 42 ft (12.8m) diameter water wheel. Mill site only: reservoir, later used for boating, has been filled in. Six rows of six two-storey stone-built cottages along First, Second, Third, Fourth and Fifth Streets, row of six cottages with three storeys and basement at east. Occupied and being improved. Sir Thomas Bazley also provided a school and an institute with news room and library.

Smithills Moor. Old coal shafts and workings from Smithills Dean north along valley of Dean brook and towards Winter Hill television mast. Coal Pit Road runs from Smithills Moor to Smithills Dean. Two rows of miners' cottages: **Colliers Row** SD 681124, originally six two-storey stone-built cottages, late 18C; to east, **Colliers New Row**, four cotttages with school of 1885.

NORTH AND NORTH-EAST

Dobson & Barlow SD 718101. Site of Kay Street works of famous firm of textile machinery makers, where they moved in 1846. Started by Isaac Dobson and Peter Rothwell, 1790, in Blackhorse Street for manufacture of spinning mules. In later 19C made wide range of preparation, carding, drawing, roving and spinning machines with export to many parts of the world. 4,000 employees in 1890. Moved to Bradley Fold, Radcliffe, 1906. For history see *Samuel Crompton, 1753–1827*, published by the firm in 1927.

Tonge viaduct SD 724102. Long viaduct on railway line to Blackburn, stone piers and side walls, brick interior to arches, branch to former goods station north of Waterloo Street.

Textile Museum, Tonge Moor Library SD 728106. Collection of early machinery, including carding engines from Arkwright's mill in Cromford and Strutt's mill at Belper, jack frame by Isaac Dobson c. 1830, bobbin-winding machines, warp reel and sizing trough, 60-spindle spinning jenny, jersey and Saxony spinning wheels, Arkwright lantern and water frames, hand mule with twelve spindles used by Crompton in King Street, models of self-actor mule headstock and of mill steam engines.

Firwood Fold SD 732110. House where Samuel Crompton, inventor of the spinning mule was born 3 December 1753. To east is **Firwood Bleach Works** on Bradshaw brook, started by Thomas Hardcastle for chlorine bleaching 1803. Taken over by Bleachers' Association 1900: Frank

Hardcastle became vice--chairman of the Association. Group of single-storey buildings, tall brick chimney, extensive reservoirs used by local anglers.

Meeting of the Waters Bleachworks SD 721111. At junction of Eagley brook and Astley brook. Started 1870. Eden & Thwaites, taken over by Bleachers' Association 1900. Number of stone buildings, still partly occupied.

New Eagley Mills and community SD 724122. Water-powered cotton mill on Eagley brook built by John Ashworth 1802–03 with 17 ft (5.2m) diameter wheel, 4,500 mule spindles. Extended by Henry and Edmund Ashworth in 1820s: 40 ft (12.2m) diameter waterwheel of 45 h.p., 28,000 spindles, 280 employees. Weaving shed with 290 looms. Now little trace. To west is community of **Bank Top**. Seventy-one cottages by 1867, school, library, news room, two shops, cricket ground and recreation field. Cottages of different types and sizes, yards with privies at back, piped water from 1835, gas supply. Described enthusiastically by Cooke Taylor on his visit to Lancashire in 1844 and by Lord Shaftesbury, the factory reformer. Rows of six and 15 cottages survive in Hugh Lupus Street, six in Eleanor Street with middle pair gabled. In Ashworth Lane three rows of cottages, one at corner of Hugh Lupus Street with shop, United Reformed Church and school. There is a full history of the Ashworths and of life in the community in Rhodes Boyson, *The Ashworth Cotton Enterprise*, 1970.

Sharples Hall Mill SD 717123. On east side of Blackburn Road, good example of large, late spinning mill, 42 bays long, domed water tower, two-storey carding extension on east.

BREDBURY

Pear New Mill SJ 912908. Large cotton-spinning mill built by Pear New Mill Co., opened 1912. Plans show it was intended to build second mill,

Apple Mill, using same engine house: never constructed. Mule spinning until 1961, closed 1976. Five storeys and basement, machine brick with terracotta decoration, two-storey carding extension on west, ornamental water tower with pear-shaped roof, engine house at east, tall circular brick chimney. Internal structure of cast-iron pillars, double lengthwise beams, concrete floors. Powered by Saxon twin tandem compound horizontal steam engine, removed 1961. Some of mill records are preserved in Stockport Central Library and Stockport Museum.

BROADBOTTOM

In the Etherow valley, east of Hyde: mixture of former woollen domestic workshops and later cotton mills.

Summerbottom Row SJ 991937. Row of twelve three-storey stone-built cottages with stone flag roofs. Four cottages at west end have long four-light mullioned windows on third floor and bridges at back giving access to doors of weaving shops.

Broadbottom Mills SJ 993936. Ruins only, remains of square stone chimney, millpond to east. Stone-built workers' cottages to north in Temperance Street, Old Street and Well Street. 60,000 spindles, 850 looms in 1884.

Limefield Mill SJ 997935. On west bank of river Etherow with weir near by. Three storeys, stone-built, beam-engine house at south-east corner, square stone chimney, single-storey boiler house with two boilers. At west, Lymefield Terrace: row of six two-storey brick-built cottages.

Etherow viaduct SJ 996938. Originally built, like Dinting viaduct, of laminated wooden arches on Sheffield Ashton under Lyne & Manchester Railway, opened 1845. Replaced about twenty years later by wrought iron structure, and later still by present viaduct of steel riveted girders and plates on stone piers with additional brick piers inserted. **Broadbottom station**, to west, has good three-storey stone station buildings with projecting porch.

BURY

Until 1800 Bury's textile industry was mainly in woollens, based on domestic production of yarn and cloth, water-powered fulling mills. Cotton took over to a large extent in 19C, with the rivers Roch and Irwell and their tributaries providing power for early spinning mills and processing water for the finishing trades. This was also an important factor in making Bury a centre for paper making in 18C and 19C.

CENTRAL AREA

Bury Museum SD 803105. Has a number of items relating to local industries, including a Whitworth planing machine from a local brickworks, small steam engines, a cast iron hand loom made by Robert Hall, a local textile machinery firm, paper moulds, calico-printing pattern books, brick-making materials, cloggers' and shoemakers' equipment.

Bury Ground SD 800112. By river Irwell north of Bury bridge, site of calico-printing works started by Haworth & Yates c. 1770, joined by Robert Peel (later Sir Robert Peel, first baronet) a few years later. With their other cotton mills in the area the firm were major employers in the town in early 19C. In 1840, Hardman & Price: seven printing machines, 178 block-printing tables.

Canal terminus SD 797109. The Bury branch of the Manchester Bolton & Bury Canal was opened in 1808, linking Bury with the Irwell Navigation in Manchester. The two arms at the terminus have now been filled in and the fine three-storey warehouse demolished.

Bolton Street Station SD 802107. The East Lancashire Railway was opened from Clifton Junction on the Manchester–Bolton line to Rawtenstall in 1846, and Bolton Street Station became the company's headquarters, with an impressive office building, now demolished. All that remains is the approach, paved with stone setts, and the surrounding stone walls. The station is now the terminus of the line from Manchester, electrified in 1916 by the LYR on a 1,200 V d.c. third-rail system. The goods station north of Bolton Street was closed in 1965 and is now the home of **Bury Transport Museum**, opened 1972, run by East Lancs. Railway Preservation Society with collection of industrial locomotives, rolling stock and road vehicles, open week ends.

Knowsley Street Station SD 803103. On the LYR line from Rochdale to Liverpool, opened 1848. Station closed 1970 and track west of Knowsley Street taken up except for curve to Bolton Street Station. Remains include platforms built on curve, station approach, brick-built ticket office at street level in use as shop. Goods station demolished and area being landscaped. To east is Market Street bridge, with four segmental brick arches, steel-girder span and two iron-girder spans.

Rochdale Road Bus Depot SD 809107. Between Foundry Street and George Street, built for electric trams 1906–07 and later extended for buses. Main garage along Foundry Street with four-aisle extension to north-west. Workshop with two rows of cast-iron pillars, steel beams and iron roof truss. Single-storey offices on Rochdale Road, opposite former electricity works.

Bentley & Jackson's SD 810107. Former works of well known firm of paper machinery makers south-east of bus depot. 'B & J est. 1860' on chimney. Many of their machines survive in paper mills in the area.

Derby Street Mills SD 809109. Three-storey brick-built mill on east side of Derby Street, engine house near car park, traces of weaving shed are surviving remains of extensive woollen mills started by James Kenyon, son of Richard Kenyon of Crimble, in 1841. Near by is **Earl Street Mill**, a cotton mill purchased by Kenyons in 1904: the older part is the building they bought, on the east is their extension. For an account of the Kenyon mills see Augustus Muir, *The Kenyon Tradition*, 1964.

SOUTH-EAST

Bridge Hall Paper Mills SD 829108. Historically the most interesting papermaking site in Bury. Largely recent buildings of Transparent Paper Co. on banks of river Roch around core of earlier buildings dating back to at least 1861. Earliest reference is to George Warburton, paper maker, in 1716, probably on site of fulling mill. Eight pairs of moulds, vat and spout for hand making of paper in 1721. Worked by Thomas Crompton *c*. 1766–1810: up to two vats, water-powered beaters for making pulp. Large-scale development by James Wrigley & Sons from 1810: Fourdrinier paper-making machine installed 1814–17. World-wide trade: eleven paper-making machines in late 19C, warehouses in Manchester and London. Made newsprint (e.g. for *Times* and *Manchester Guardian*) and wide variety of fine-quality stationery, about 600 employees. Decline after first world war: bought by Transparent Paper Co. for manufacture of cellulose film for packaging. There is a detailed history: Martin Tillmanns, *Bridge Hall Mills: Three Centuries of Paper and Cellulose Film Manufacture*, 1978.

Roch viaduct SD 817101. At Pinhole, seven-arch brick viaduct on LYR line from Heywood, opened 1848.

Pilot Mill SD 813100. East side of Albert Street. Good example of late cotton-spinning mill, four storeys, large rectangular windows, ornamental pillars between windows on top floor, water tower with pyramidical roof at north-east corner, engine house, single-storey weaving shed to north.

NORTH-EAST

Mossfield Mill, Chesham Fold SD 819114. Woollen mill marked on OS map of 1851. Two four-storey stone-built blocks, 11 and ten bays, rectangular windows with stone sills and lintels. Square stone chimney. In use by woollen spinners. The fine three-storey row of domestic workshops south of the mill has been demolished.

Hudcar Mill SD 813117. Early cotton mill purchased by Gregs of Quarry Bank Mill, Styal, Cheshire, in 1827 and sold *c*. 1850: two steam engines in 1833. Surviving building is considerably later, five storeys, brick-built, large rectangular windows, corner pilasters, ornamental brickwork below parapet.

Freetown is an industrial community associated with Hudcar and other mills in the area. Streets of brick-built cottages. In Haslam Street two rows of 12 two-storey stone-built cottages, dated 1877 on southern row.

NORTH

Walmersley Dyeworks SD 809134. On Pigs Lee brook in Mather Road. Fulling mill and tenter field in 1851: there was another fulling mill on the brook south-west of Walmersley Road. Three-aisle single-storey stone-built shed, with early three-storey brick building to north.

Burrs Mill SD 799127. Water-powered cotton mill and community on banks of Irwell, started by Haworth Yates & Peel in 1780s. Surviving building is later: three storeys and basement, brick-built, ten by three bays, windows with stone sills and arched brick and stone lintels, projecting brick piers between windows, open cast iron water tank on top. To east are ruins of row of 20 two-storey stone-built back-to-back workers' cottages with stone-flag roofs. Mill ponds to north and weir on river 720 yd (658 m) upstream. Canal feeder for Manchester Bolton & Bury Canal

Mill race and former openings to waterwheel pits, Wood Road mill, Bury, 1966

was taken from weir, along side of mill and then over river on three-arch blue-brick bridge. Sluice for supply to mill ponds. There is information about living conditions at the mill in Frances Collier, *The Family Economy of the Working Classes in the Cotton Industry, 1784–1833*, 1964, chapter 4.

Fern Hill Mills SD 807116. East side of Hornby Street. Occupied by woollen manufacturers. Late single-storey weaving shed at north, three-storey brick-built mills with dates 1860 and 1871 over ornamental doorway. Good example of mid-Victorian period. To west is site of former Fernhill Colliery.

Peel Mills SD 803114. Gordon Street. Most impressive of Bury's large cotton-spinning mills. Late 19C four-storey mill at south, 23 by 12 bays, corner turrets, ornamental water tower, large engine house on north, circular brick chimney. To north, early 20C extension in Accrington brick, 24 bays long, very large window area.

WEST

Atlas Works SD 796110. Extensive works of Beloit Walmsley, paper-machinery makers, in area of Victoria Street and Wood Street. Started by Charles Walmsley *c*. 1860 for manufacture of pumping machinery, steam engines, mill gearing, artesian wells and

paper-making machinery.

Irwell viaduct SD 795104. On LYR line to Bolton, opened 1848. Five arches, skewed, stone-built, turrets at each end, plain stone parapet.

Elton Paper Mills SD 796106. Started 1856 by J. R. Crompton, who moved from Stoneclough Mill, Kearsley. Six paper-making machines in 1889, twelve steam engines, bleaching, washing, beating and dyeing plants; glazing, cutting, reeling and embossing machines. Made tissue paper, copying paper, cigarette papers, toilet paper, greaseproof paper.

Elton Reservoir SD 789095. About 1,000 yd by 400 yd at widest (914 m by 366 m), built to supply Manchester Bolton & Bury Canal. Feeder can be traced from north end of reservoir through Daisyfield, under Bolton Road, Ainsworth Road, Tottington Road and Brandlesholme Road to weir on river Irwell at Burrs. Textile-finishing sites along Elton brook, Walshaw brook and Kirkless brook, some still occupied: **Elton Bleachworks** SD 786110, on OS map of 1851; **Bolholt Mills** SD 785117, printworks by 1825, four printing machines and 78 block-printing tables in 1840, bleach and print works 1848; **Dunster's Bleach Works** SD 790122, on OS map of 1851, remains of reservoirs and feed from weir upstream; **Woolfold Bleach Works** SD 791118, also on 1851 map, two reservoirs, buildings occupied by Olives Paper Mill Co., whose **Woolfold Paper Mills** upstream were first mentioned in 1856.

The former LYR **Bury–Holcombe Brook railway**, opened 1882, electrified 1912–13, closed 1952, can be traced through Woolfold. Cuttings with track removed each side of Brandlesholme Road at Woodhill, SD 769117. Kirkless viaduct, SD 790121, has been demolished: embankments remain each end. Site of Woolfold Station at north-west end now inaccessible.

Wood Road Mill SD 795141. Surviving three-storey stone-built mill originally powered by two waterwheels in basement supplied by race from weir on river Irwell, with vertical-shaft drive to upper floors. Internal structure of cast iron pillars and timber beams. Steam engine installed later: date 1847 on plinth of chimney.

CADISHEAD See *Irlam*

CHADDERTON

West of Oldham and much of the same character, with many former cotton-spinning mills and traces of earlier coal mining. In the valley of the river Irk in the north are sites of former water-powered mills and finishing works.

Fernhurst Mill SD 911063. Early 20C spinning mill, five storeys, 32 by 18 bays, water tower at south-east corner, engine house on south. Occupied by luggage manufacturers. In Victor Street, SD 911059, group of three large spinning mills: **Kent** and **Manor Mills**, both early 20C, four storeys, engine houses and chimneys at rear, ornamental water towers, long frontages on street, both formerly driven by Saxon cross-compound steam engines; **Falcon Mill** to south was built for velvet manufacture, single-storey buildings, date 1895 on chimney; **Magnet Mill**, one of the last mule-spinning mills in the area, now demolished, used to stand opposite the other three. Northern Mill Engines Society have preserved a Saxon barring engine from this mill.

Middleton Road SD 909052. Group of earlier brick-built mills. **Sun Mill**, 1868, built by one of first joint-stock companies in the area, five storeys, 42-bay frontage, internal engine house with twin semi-circular arched windows, circular brick chimney, occupied by office equipment makers. **Stockfield Mill** to west, four storeys, square water tower with pyramidical roof, later engine house added. **Melbourne Mill** to north, four storeys, 15 by 14 bays, large arched windows, circular brick chimney, seven-bay building at north-west corner.

Field New Road SD 906044. **Chadderton Mill** at north, late Victorian, five storeys, corner pilasters, square tower. **Nile Mill** on west side of road, good example of early 20C spinning mill, four storeys, large rectangular windows, yellow-brick decoration. Of same period on east side of road are **Mona Mill**, five storeys with five-bay engine house, and **Ramsey Mill**, with late brick tower, partly demolished. **Bay Tree and Laurel Tree Mills** SD 889054. At Middleton Junction by side of Rochdale Canal. Pair of very fine large early 20C spinning mills, machine brick with elaborate terracotta decoration, especially on central engine house and boiler house, located between the two mills, which were designed to produce different types of yarn.

COMPSTALL

Site of one of the North West's most interesting industrial communities based on spinning and weaving mills and a calico printing works established by the Andrew family from 1820. The history is told in R. E. Thelwall, *The Andrews and Compstall their Village*

(Cheshire Libraries & Museums), 1972. The Etherow valley, including the mill reservoir, is now part of a Country Park.

Compstall Print Works SJ 964908. Slight remains only of site where Andrews began hand-block printing in 1820s. Two printing machines in 1840, fourteen in 1890. Taken over by Calico Printers' Association in 1899, closed down 1901.

Albert and Victoria Mills On east side of Andrew Street opposite print works, parallel to river. Four storeys, brick-built, Victoria Mill older, latrine turret at east end. Weaving sheds on south and along Andrew Street. Remains of former North and Scotland Mill buildings near Country Park car park. Site of early 19C North Wheel between two mills: sluice gear survives. Large iron waterwheel installed by Fairbarn & Lilley 1838–39, 50 ft (15 m) diameter, 17 ft (5·2 m) wide, replaced by water turbines 1881–82. Wheel removed 1906 and site occupied by engine house for new steam engine. Spinning ceased 1926, weaving 1961. Very large reservoir fed by canalised mill race from large weir three-quarters of a mile (1,200 m) above mill: race used for navigation by iron boats carrying coal from pits in the area. Much of the housing and community institutions established by the Andrews family survives, mostly built in 1820s and 1830s. Two long rows of four-roomed two-storey stone-built cottages in **Montague Street**, another row behind in **Thomas Street**. To east is **Edith Terrace**, row of later two-storey brick-built cottages. **St Paul's Church**, built by George Andrew I 1839–41, Sunday school to south-east. **Athenaeum** in Andrews Street built in 1860s by George Andrew II with library and reading room, used for concerts and education classes. Reading room in George Street: now county library branch.

DENTON

With Stockport one of the two great hat-making centres of the North West. Described by Aiken in 1795 as '. . . a long straggling village . . . increased much of late and . . . principally occupied by hatters, cotton spinners and colliers'. Twenty-five hat manufacturers listed in Baines's *Lancashire Directory*, 1825. Small-workshop industry in 18C and first half of 19C, gradually mechanised and concentrated in factories in later 19C. Local firms produced the machinery, e.g. blowing, planking and forming machines. One of the first was Turner Atherton (John Turner of Denton, Giles Atherton of Stockport) in 1860. Well known firm of Oldham's Batteries started in general engineering and developed into production of hat-making machinery. For a general introduction to the industry see J. H. Smith, 'Felt hatting', in *The Great Human Exploit*, ed. J. H. Smith, 1973.

Many hat factories were built around the town centre in later 19C and early 20C, mostly now used for other industries or demolished. **Wilson's Hat Factory** SJ 923957 on north side of Wilton Street, now Associated British Hat Manufacturers, making cloth hats, four storeys, brick-built, 22 by 8 bays, impressive street frontage, water tower with cast iron tank, older three-storey building to north, tall octagonal brick chimney. Name 'Wilsons' on east gable. There are photographs of processes in the works *c.* 1900 in H. C. Caffrey, *Hatting in Denton*(Tameside Museum Service), 1976. Also in Wilton Street are the works of the Denton Hat Co., started 1927, making wool hats, and of Burgess & Co., as well as two former works on the south side no longer used for hat-making.

Moores Hatworks SJ 918954. In Heaton Street south of Manchester Road with very long frontage. Started by Jonathan Moores and his brother in 1862.

Hat finishing, Denton, late nineteenth century

Dane Bank SJ 909949. Off Windmill Lane, interesting group of buildings, becoming derelict, illustrating change from domestic to factory production in the hat trade. Joseph Wolfenden made felt hats in a workshop adjoining Dane Bank Farm from *c*. 1830 and later built a three-storey factory, which was extended in 1873. In near-by Joseph Street and Danesford Street are rows of cottages built for the workers and three larger houses for members of the family. See D. M. Smith, 'The hatting industry in Denton, Lancashire', *Industrial Archaeology*, vol. 3, No. 1, February 1966.

Denton Colliery SJ 925944. Remains of workings both sides of Stockport Road and branch line from LNWR Stockport–Guide Bridge line, 2,400 yd (2195 m) to junction at SJ 905941.

Haughton Glass House SJ 941947. Glass works referred to in 1636 and 1644. On west bank of river Tame, excavated by Pilkington Glass Museum 1969–70. Furnace transitional between wood-fired and later coal-fired reverberatory type. Three chambers associated with firing of crucibles to hold molten glass. Produced green, blue and black domestic glass, including decorated vessels, bottles and window glass *c*. 1600–43.

DROYLSDEN
Lumb Mill SJ 911994. On east bank of Ashton Canal. Mid-Victorian cotton-spinning mill, six storeys, brick-built, 12 by 10 bays, later extension at south, single-storey weaving shed.

Saxon Mill SJ 905988. Also on canal side, typical large cotton-spinning mill of 1907, ornamental water tower, engine house (former engine was Adamson horizontal cross-compound).

Christy's Towel Works SJ 903982. In Ashton Road west of canal bridge (canal filled in). Building of 1913 fronting road, much older buildings to east, three and four storeys, windows with stone sills and lintels, projecting latrine tower. Started as hat works by Christy's of Stockport and changed to towel-making.

Double locks, Ashton Canal SJ 900979. Two sets of locks which were doubled after the opening of the canal, older locks have masonry sides, later locks brick. Double gates at lower, single gate at upper end, wooden lock-end bridges, stone steps at lower end, cast iron bollards, stone treads for balance arms. At the eastern pair single-storey brick-built tollhouse, two-storey lock keeper's house, and at west end fine humped single-arch stone footbridge with parapet of stone flags (cf. towpath bridge at Ashton New Wharf). On north bank long stone-built boat-house with date 1833 over shipping entrance. Immediately east of locks is junction of main line with Hollinwood and Fairbottom branch, opened 1796–97.

DUKINFIELD

Former cotton town between Ashton under Lyne and Hyde. Worrall's *Textile Directory*, 1884 and 1897, records some 14 spinning mills varying from 5,000 to 130,000 spindles. Interesting group of mills in Tame Valley area north of Park Road. **Tower Mill** SJ 951982, *c.* 1890, four storeys, brick-built, large rectangular windows, narrow brick piers between, yellow-brick decoration, ornamental tower on south front with mill name in yellow brick. **Tame Valley Mill** SJ 950983, earlier, three and four storeys, tall engine house at south end, circular brick chimney, added water tower. 25,500 spindles in 1897, still in use for spinning. **River Mill** SJ 947983, intermediate in date between Tower and Tame Valley, four storeys, large windows with stone sills and brick-arch lintels, corner pilasters, 20 by 12 bays, added water tower.

Two mills side by side in Park Road, SJ 945984: **Park Road Mill**, five storeys and basement, very large windows with arched lintels, corner turrets, two projecting towers on south front with date 1893 on one, thirty bays long, iron dog-leg fire escape on west front. Park Road Spinning Co. in 1897 with 92,000 spindles. Now used by computer firm. To west is **New Mill** on site of former

Dukinfield Old Mill, also late 19C, five storeys, tower at south-east corner, tall circular brick chimney. Occupied by plastic-foam manufacturers.

Peak Forest Canal railway bridge SJ 934982. Six cast iron arches in halves bolted at centre, tied by system of struts, skewed, 50 ft (18 m) span, dated 1845, when the Sheffield Ashton under Lyne & Manchester Railway's line from Guide Bridge to Stalybridge was opened. Dukinfield Central Station was closed 1959 and has been demolished. The LNWR line from Denton to Dukinfield opened 1882, extended to Stalybridge 1893, was closed 1950, track has been removed and area landscaped. No trace of buildings at Dukinfield & Ashton Station, abutments of bridge over Wharf Street, two-storey brick-built goods shed south of Wharf Street.

Chapel Field Rope Works SJ 937981. Firm started 1866 by William Kenyon, son of a weaver from Hurst, with his three sons, making cotton ropes. Purchased Chapel Field site in 1875. Patented rope-making machine in 1893. Export trade to India, USA and Canada. Opened factory in Armentières, France, in 1900.

Queen Mill SJ 947978. North side of Foundry Street, post-1900, good example of period, four storeys and basement, large rectangular windows in pairs, narrow brick piers, terracotta decoration, ornamental Hotel-de-Ville style water tower at south-west corner with name of mill, engine house at east.

Daniel Adamson's Engineering Works SJ 944966. By side of Manchester Sheffield & Lincolnshire Railway at Newton Wood. Famous in later 19C for production of steel Lancashire boilers and steam engines, many of which were installed in Lancashire cotton mills. Daniel Adamson was a leading promoter of the Manchester Ship Canal.

DUNHAM MASSEY
Dunham Hall Mill SJ 734873. Elizabethan mill with overshot waterwheel, now being restored and put into working order as sawmill by Dr Cyril Boucher on behalf of the National Trust.

ECCLES
Monks Hall Museum SJ 775988. Local museum in Wellington road, containing items relating to James Nasmyth and the Bridgewater Foundry. Steam hammer (patent by Nasmyth, 1842), two machine tools made 1851–56 for Earl Fitzwilliam's colliery workshops at Elsecar, near Barnsley: slotting machine with adjustable tool head and moveable circular table; shaping machine with cast iron frame, belt drive to two-speed cone pulley, sliding work table with adjustable tool head.

Bridgewater Foundry SJ 763989. Started 1836 by James Nasmyth in partnership with Holbrook Gaskell of Liverpool at a site near the junction of the Bridgewater Canal and the Liverpool & Manchester Railway. Nasmyth trained with Henry Maudsley in London and had a small works in Manchester before moving out to Patricroft. Established new type of engineering works making machine tools on a ready-made basis, with printed catalogues and a planned factory layout with buildings in line, railway lines through shops and overhead cranes. Also made locomotives, steam engines, pumping engines and hydraulic presses. From 1856 Nasmyth Wilson & Co. Sold to Ministry of Supply 1939 and became Royal Ordnance Factory. See A. E. Musson, 'James Nasmyth and the early growth of mechanical engineering', *Economic History Review*, 2nd series, vol. 10, No. 1, August 1957, pp. 121–8.

Gardner's Barton Hall Works SJ 755980. Diesel-engine works established 1898 by sons of Laurence Gardner, who himself started 1868 in works off Stretford Road, making machine tools, dentists' chairs and hot-air engines. First oil engine in 1894. Closely associated with Foden's of Sandbach, Cheshire.

Barton aqueduct SJ 767976. Famous swing aqueduct on the Bridgewater Canal, built 1893 when the Manchester Ship Canal was constructed, to replace the 600 ft (183 m)-long three-arch stone aqueduct of James Brindley, completed 1761, of which the abutments remain on the north side. Iron trough 18 ft (5·5 m) wide, 7 ft (2·1 m) deep, 235 ft (71 m)

Nasmyth shaping machine, Monks Hall Museum, Eccles. Photograph taken at Elsecar Colliery, Barnsley, 1961. *Courtesy Royal Commission on Ancient Monuments (Scotland)*

long, swinging full of water on roller bearings operated by drive from hydraulic engines. Rubber-faced tapering wedges each end to keep trough watertight. On island to west is operating machinery: two Mather & Platt electrically driven plurivane pumps to provide hydraulic pressure, two Mather & Platt monovane pumps to bring water from canal to storage tanks, two twin-cylinder tandem hydraulic oil engines by Hydraulic Co. of Chester. To west is **swing road bridge**, 195 ft (60 m) long, turning on 64 steel rollers, operated by two three-cylinder hydraulic engines, dating from opening of bridge.

Barton locks to west on the Ship Canal. Two locks: 600 ft by 65 ft (183 m by 20 m) and 350 ft by 45 ft (107 m by 14 m) with a rise of 16 ft (4·9 m). Before the building of the Ship Canal there were locks on the river Irwell and Barton Corn Mill. There are traces to the north of the old course of the Irwell before 18C improvements.

FAILSWORTH

Failsworth's cotton mills can profitably be studied by walking along the Rochdale Canal from the Manchester boundary to Wrigley Head. The canal itself, including Failsworth locks, has been effectively landscaped by Greater Manchester Council.

Marlborough Mills SD 889009. Pair of fine large early 20C spinning mills, No. 1, 1905, No. 2 (to east), 1908, now used as mail order and discount warehouses. Four storeys and basement, large window area, narrow brick piers, each mill over forty bays long. No. 2 mill has large engine house, boiler house and circular brick chimney on canal side. Ceased production 1955.

Regent Mill SD 895014. In similar style, with ornamental water tower, built 1906, ceased production 1966, occupied by electrical firm.

Failsworth Mill SD 895013. On opposite bank of canal to Regent Mill,

considerably earlier, four storeys, built of dark brick, large windows with stone sills and arched lintels, 20 by 12 bays, chimney and water tower on canal side, occupied by wine merchants.

Ivy Mill SD 897017. North of Oldham Road bridge, 1886, ceased production 1934, now mail-order warehouse. Five storeys and basement, of dark brick with blue-brick decoration, 20 by 12 bays, corner turrets, water tower, internal engine house, boiler house and chimney on canal front. To north is **Wrigley Head Mill**, pre-1890, ceased production 1959.

Hollinwood branch of Ashton Canal On east side of township is fine series of canal works along line opened 1796, now part of Daisy Nook Country Park in the Medlock valley. **Tunnel** SD 921007, opened out c. 1914, brick side walls survive. At its north end **Medlock aqueduct**, fine example, single arch, deep inward curve in plan, bowed outer walls, buttresses. North of aqueduct are two sets of two staircase locks, now filled in, stone and brick side walls, side weirs. Water was formerly pumped to top of locks by a beam engine, erected 1798 and demolished c. 1960. Immediately above locks is **double basin**, one on Hollinwood branch, one on Fairbottom branch, with line of former tramroad to Bardsley Collieries and site of coal tippler for loading boats. West of basins is **Crime Lane aqueduct**, 1859, single arch, stone-built, walls battered outwards, buttresses each side of arch, canal carried in iron trough. Beyond **Crime Bridge** SD 915012 the canal is visible only as an earthwork, identifiable by nature of the vegetation.

FARNWORTH

Small industrial town south of Bolton famous for its links with the development of the Lancashire paper industry and with the Crompton family. There is a reference to a Crompton holding a paper mill in 1674: presumably on site of **Darley Mill** SD 745068, by river Irwell, now demolished and area landscaped. Robert Crompton was paper maker in Lower Darley in early 18C. John Crompton, grandson of Adam Crompton of Greaves Paper Mill, Little Lever, came to Darley in 1780s. John died 1807 and mill passed to his sons, John and Thomas. T. B. Crompton developed the continuous drying process in the paper-making machine, using steam-heated copper cylinders, a major factor in the growth of paper-making in the Irwell valley in the 19C.

Long Causeway SD 740054. Good examples of cotton-mill building, including Gladstone Mill, two four-storey buildings with beam-engine house, internal structure of cast iron pillars and timber beams, and **Causeway Mill**, four storeys, brick-built, windows with stone sills and lintels, corner pilasters.

Bolton Textile Mill SD 732065. One of group of mills in Moses Gate area. Late 19C, five storeys, large rectangular windows, 30 by 17 bays, large engine house with semi-circular arched windows, circular brick chimney. Near by in Lorne Street is **Horrockses' Mill**, dated 1915 on east front, five storeys, large window area, ornamental water tower, later-style engine house, now used by mail-order firm.

Moses Gate Station SD 733067. On Manchester & Bolton Railway (later LYR), opened 1838. Late 19C brick-built single-storey booking office, booking hall with lantern roof, original wooden ticket office. Two-storey stone-built station master's house. Goods yard cleared but three-storey brick-built goods shed survives.

GOLBORNE
Golborne Colliery SJ 604983. Still working, in conjuction with Bickershaw and Parsonage Collieries (see *Leigh*). Two sets of steel lattice-girder head gears, brick-built winding-engine

houses. Later pit-head baths. 950 employed in 1954, output of 250,000 tons a year.

Kenyon Junction Station SJ 643964. Where Leigh & Kenyon Junction Railway joined Liverpool & Manchester tracks in 1831. Leigh line closed, station demolished. Two brick-built, humped and bowed road bridges in 'canal bridge' style to east.

HAIGH
North-west of Wigan: another early coal-mining area associated particularly with the pits of the Bradshaigh family of Haigh Hall, later Earls of Crawford and Balcarres. Haigh Hall itself is now a country park and will shortly have re-erected wooden pit-head gear of *c.* 1890 from Gauntley pit, near Bispham Hall, Billinge with Winstanley.

Haigh Sough. Outstanding example of early mine drainage, constructed by Sir Roger Bradshaigh 1653–70 with outlet on Yellow brook in Haigh Hall plantations, SD 591071. Runs 1,120 yd (1,024 m) east to Park Pit. Extended in 19C to pits in Aspull.

Haigh Windmill SD 605089. In field near Haigh village, small brick-built tower mill with four common sails at base of cap. Used for pumping water to near-by brewery.

Haigh Colliery workshops SD 602073. On north bank of Leeds & Liverpool Canal west of Wigan Road. Built 1839–41 as central workshops for Balcarres's Haigh and Aspull collieries. Long range of stone buildings with two wings, including forge, smithy, fitting shop and carpenter's shop, with machinery driven by steam engine. Only central office section survives, restored and cleaned, two storeys with cupola, later Georgian style. After formation of Wigan Coal & Iron Co. in 1865, used as sawmills for collieries and for Kirless Iron and Steel Works. Near Wigan Road entrance is **Packet House**, two storeys, stone-built, with stone-flag roof, and, to north, row of six two-storey workers' cottages. Crossing Wigan Road is line of **Springs Branch Railway**, opened 1838, which ran from Haigh and Aspull to North Union Railway at Ince Moss.

Basin Quay SD 594080. Off west side of Leeds & Liverpool Canal at east end of Hall Lane, marked on OS map of 1844. Basin survives, but boathouse has been demolished. Typical single-arch stone-built canal bridge to south.

Red Rock SD 585099. Single-arch stone bridge over canal, from where there was a tramroad east to William Pit in Haigh. **Red Rock Station** to west on Lancashire Union Railway's line from Boars Head (north of Wigan) to Adlington on the Bolton & Preston Railway. Opened 1849, closed 1949. Brick-built goods shed survives.

HAZEL GROVE

Active silk-weaving community in 19C, supplying Macclesfield merchants: still some 200 hand-loom weavers at beginning of 20C. Workshops in basements, attics or extra rooms with large windows at back and sides. Examples in older cottages on both sides of Buxton Road (A6): in streets off **Commercial Road**, including **Spring Gardens** SJ 919872, 1858, row of six two-storey brick-built cottages with basement workshops, double windows at front, some blocked; in **Mount Pleasant** area SJ 906874, and in Hatherlow Lane, SJ 920869, where there are single-storey workshops with large windows at the rear of some cottages. There were also a number of silk mills: one building survives by the car park off Commercial Road, brick built, three storeys, early 19C, later used as hat works.

Wellington Mill SJ 927875. Cotton mill in Bosden Fold started in 1830s and worked by Hollins Mill Co. of Marple in early 20C.

Norbury Colliery SJ 938856. Originally one of Lord Vernon's collieries (see *Poynton*, Cheshire). Engine house for beam-pumping engine survives, converted to private residence.

HEYWOOD

Mutual Mills SD 862111. Fine group of three late 19C/early 20C cotton-spinning mills, five storeys, large windows, patterned in ornamental brick-work, water towers, large engine houses, date 1900 on more southerly mill in Aspinall Street. Still used for spinning man-made fibres.

Hooley Bridge Mill SD 854117. Five-storey brick-built mill, twenty-six bays long, windows with stone sills and lintels, internal engine house, structure of cast iron pillars and beams, brick arches. From 1902 to 1954 driven by Buckley & Taylor compound beam engine. On site of earlier water-powered mill started by Joseph Fenton 1826. Centre of industrial community of which some cottages survive.

Crimble Mill SD 866116. Four-storey, brick-built mid-Victorian mill in remote situation on north bank of river Roch. On site of water-powered woollen-fulling mill taken over by Richard Kenyon of Castleton 1761. Sold 1776: mill, four houses, two fulling stocks, waterwheel, perching mill, tentering frames in Crimble Brow, coal mine. Bought back by Kenyon's 1781: cotton spinning from *c.* 1815, supplying hand-loom weavers in wide area around. Went back to woollen finishing in later 19C: James Kenyon & Son. See Augustus Muir, *The Kenyon Tradition*, 1964.

Sites of water-powered mills in the valley of the **Cheesden brook**, which runs down to river Roch on north side of township: **Birtle Dean Mill** SD 833137, cotton mill by 1845, foundations of stone buildings, chimney, shafts of old coal workings on hillside above, with chute down to site of boiler house; **Kershaw Bridge Dyeworks** SD 842134, known as Nab Wife Mill in 1845, foundations, remains of reservoir to west; **Simpson Clough Mill** SD 853121, paper mill of J. R. Crompton Bros on site of early 19C fulling mill, only site in Cheesden valley still in use.

Heywood Station SD 863103. On LYR Rochdale–Bury line, opened 1848. Closed 1970, single-storey decorated brick building, becoming derelict. Stone-built goods shed still used by transport firm. The near-by basin at the terminus of the Heywood branch of the Rochdale Canal, opened 1834, is filled in, as is most of the line of the branch.

HINDLEY
Between Wigan and Westhoughton, well known for nail-making in 17C, 18C and early 19C, and for coal mining, which has now ceased.

Hindley Green Station SD 641027. On LNWR Eccles–Wigan line, opened 1864. Closed 1961. Traces of platforms, track removed.

Hindley Green Collieries SD 625032. Traces of workings, spoil heaps and railway lines south of Atherton Road. Sovereign Pit sunk by Wigan Coal & Iron Co. in 1908 was one of earliest to have underground electric haulage.

Hindley Field Colliery SD 624024. South of LNWR tracks, shafts and spoil heaps visible north of Bickershaw Lane.

Platt Bridge Colliery SD 608028. Site of workshops visible north of Bickershaw Lane. Railway link south to Maypole Colliery and to GCR, north to Ambersswood Colliery and Springs Branch Railway.

Strangeways Hall Colliery SD 610036. Between Liverpool Road and Strangeways Junction. Late 19C group of miners' cottages in twelve rows east of Liverpool Road. Earlier housing at Low Green to south-west.

Hindley South Station SD 612035. On Wigan Junction Railway, later GCR, opened 1884. Closed 1964 and demolished, track removed. Also gone

is **Platt Bridge Station** SD 605031 on LNWR Eccles–Wigan line, closed 1961. Railway Hotel survives at junction of Moss Lane and Liverpool Road.

Hindley Station SD 620052. On LYR Bury–Liverpool line, opened 1848, two-storey brick station building on disused south platform.

HOLLINGWORTH
Moorland township in the Etherow valley, east of Mottram and below Manchester's Longdendale Water Works.

Albion Mill SK 001961. Four-storey cotton mill, stone-built, two aisles, 25 bays long, rectangular windows with stone sills and lintels, stone-flag roof. 'Albion Mill 1859' on cast iron beam over entrance. Occupied by shoe manufacturers.

Arrowscroft Mill SK 006962. On south side of A57, four storeys, stone-built, large rectangular windows, six-storey staircase and water tower at north-west corner, two-storey extension to north, engine house at each end, circular stone chimney. 'New Hollingworth Spinners & Manufacturers Ltd 1876' at west end. 44,000 spindles (cotton spinning) in 1884.

Hollingworth Print Works SK 001961. On river Etherow at Woolley Bridge, mainly single-storey stone-built sheds of early 19C origin. Thomas & John Dalton in 1840: five printing machines, 30 block-printing tables.

HORWICH
Historically two towns: older community, mainly in north, based on cotton mills, finishing works and coal mines, new community of late 19C along Chorley New Road associated with the LYR works. See B. J. Turton, 'Horwich: the historical geography of a Lancashire industrial town', *Trans. Lancs. & Ches. Antiq. Soc*, vol. 72, 1962, pp. 141–50.

Bottom o' th' Moor SD 661112. South of Chorley Old road, row of eight three-storey cottages with basements with double windows, partly blocked, indicating use as domestic workshops.

Montcliffe Colliery SD 653123. Shaft and spoil heaps of small colliery worked for coal and fireclay until late 1960s. Further colliery workings to north at Burnt Edge and Wildersmoor. Extensive sandstone quarries around Montcliffe.

Wallsuches Bleachwork SD 653118. Started *c.* 1775 by John and Thomas Ridgway, who moved out from Ridgway Gates, Bolton. Early pioneers of chemical bleaching, installed 10 h.p. Boulton & Watt steam engine in 1798 to drive calenders, mangles, etc. Taken over by Bleachers' Association 1900. Range of two, three and four-storey stone buildings, one with bell turret, tall stone-built engine house. Cleaned and restored, occupied by engineering firm.

Club Houses SD 644114. Community of early 19C stone-built workers' cottages arranged in grid pattern of streets south of Church Street. Built through terminating building society on land provided by Ridgways. Three rows on Church Street, 22 cottages, 15 with possible basement workshops for hand-loom weaving. Row of nine cottages in Nelson Street, two rows of ten in Duncan Street, row of eight in George Street, all with double-windowed basements, some converted to garages, and steps up to front door. Rows of two-storey cottages without basements in Chapel Street, Wood Street and Back Owen Street, twenty in all. 150 houses in 1851, with inhabitants including many crofters, stovers and bleachers. Holy Trinity Church 1830–31 with monument to Joseph Ridgway, National School 1832.

Horwich Vale Print Works SD 626112. On river Douglas, started *c.* 1799. Seven printing machines and 151 hand-block printing tables in 1840. Jolly & Jackson, bleachers, from 1864, taken over by Bleachers' Association 1900 and still in use. Premises partly occupied by paper manufacturers.

L&Y Railway Works SD 638108. Built 1884–87 nearly a mile from old town centre, 3,000 men employed by 1894. Three long lines of brick-built sheds with railway connections to LYR Horwich branch (closed 1966) and internal 18 inch (46 cm) gauge transport system. Original foundry, forge, smithy and boiler shop on north; pattern shop, joiners' shop, fitting shop and signal shop in middle range; erecting and repair shops on south. Built locomotives 1889–1962, diesels after 1957. In use by British Rail Engineering.

Near by on both sides of Chorley New Road is railway workers' community, with houses built on land provided by the company, along streets named after famous engineers. At least three types of houses along streets south of Chorley New Road, many now being demolished, larger houses on north. Some 420 houses survive. Railway Mechanics' Institute of 1888, later Horwich Technical College, has been demolished.

HYDE

Cotton town above all associated with Ashton Bros, a local yeoman family, who went into the textile trade in the 18C. Benjamin Ashton was a putter-out for the well known merchants Touchett's. His son, Samuel (1742–1812), started a cotton mill at Gee Cross in late 18C. Samuel's seven sons were the brothers who built up the business on a large scale. Prior to 1821 they were operating four mills: Apethorn, Carrfield, Greencroft and Newton, and a print works at Newton Bank. The partnership was dissolved 1821–23: Samuel took Apethorn and then built Woodley Mill, Thomas took Carrfield and then built Bayleyfield Mill, John and James took Newton Mill, Benjamin and Robert the print works. In the 1860s Ashton's had mills in Hayfield, New Mills and Stockport, as well as three large mills at Flowery Field. The firm became a limited company in 1885 and was taken over by Courtauld's in 1968. (I am indebted to Dr. J. H. Smith of Glossop for much of the above information.) Hyde was a major hat-making centre in 19C and there were a number of works in production around town centre and in Gee Cross in the 1880s and 1890s. The town was also known for its leather trade, especially the dressing of chamois leather and glove-making. Middleton, in his *History of Hyde*, refers to thirteen firms, of which three or four are still working.

CENTRAL AREA

Hyde Wharf SJ 943951. The Peak Forest Canal runs north–south along the west of the township, built on the east side of the Tame valley. It is crossed near the wharf by Manchester Road bridge, a roving bridge, widened three times, but with original stone arch surviving. At the wharf is a fine brick-built warehouse of 1828, two storeys and basement, five by three bays, semi-circular arched windows, central opening in road front blocked, loading opening on canal front with windows each side.

Greencroft Mill SJ 946951. Five-storey brick-built spinning mill and weaving shed, on site of mill occupied by Ashton Bros. in early 19C. Hibbert & Aspland in later 19C: 26,000 spindles, 500 power looms in 1884.

Hyde Central station SJ 944949. On MSLR Hyde branch from main line at Newton, opened 1858, extended to Marple 1863. Approach on stone-built viaduct from north, brick building including booking hall with lantern roof and long staircase window, tunnel under tracks lined with glazed white and yellow bricks.

Bury & Hopwood SJ 946948. In Boardman Street, chamois-leather dressing and glove-making works started by Ebenezer Bury and George Hopwood 1904.

Joseph Adamson & Co. SJ 944946. Engineering works started 1874 by Joseph Adamson, who was earlier apprenticed to his uncle, Daniel Adamson, in Dukinfield. Famous for manufacture of steam boilers for textile and other industries, later of electrically driven cranes and overhead travellers. Dates 1885, 1896, 1898 on long ranges of workshops by side of railway.

Newton Bank Printworks SJ 952952. Started by Benjamin Ashton 1812 and run with his brothers Robert and Joseph until 1856, then Robert's nephew, Francis William Tinker, who took name Ashton. Taken over by Calico Printers' Association 1899 and still working. five printing machines and sixteen block-printing tables in 1840.

James North & Sons SJ 952947. Douglas Street. James North began chamois-leather dressing in Colne, Lancashire, and his sons started in same business in Hyde in 1876. Developed into glove-making with export trade to Germany, North America, West Indies and Scandinavia. Provided gloves for polar expeditions of Nansen and Shackleton.

Slack Mills SJ 954945. Between Market Street and Back Lane. Three and four-storey late 19C buildings, water tower, engine house, remnant of octagonal brick chimney. Older four-storey building on east, large weaving shed to north. 54,000 spindles and 800 power looms in 1884. On site of mill started very early in 19C.

Spring Bank Mills SJ 953943. Four-storey mill taken over 1906 by Wilfred E. Redfern for manufacture of rubber heels for shoes, later cycle tyres and tubes. Made gas-mask mouthpieces in first world war. Still in use as rubber works.

NORTH

At **Flowery Field** is core of Ashton Bros enterprise, with three mill buildings in use by Courtauld's. **Carrfield Mills** SJ 947954, west of Newton Street, taken over by Thomas Ashton in early 19C, three and four-storey buildings, windows with stone sills and brick-arch lintels, old two-storey office building in Newton Street, with added 20C block to north. Adjoining on north, **Bayleyfield Mills**, started in 1820s by Thomas Ashton, mid-Victorian building of five storeys and attic with later building to north-west, larger windows, tower at west corner with date 1890 over door, free-standing engine house to north. **Throstle Bank Mills** SJ 942955, west of Dukinfield Road on side of Peak Forest Canal. Built by Thomas Ashton jr. and John Alcock c. 1870. Five storeys and basement, brick-built, large windows, two projecting towers on road front with cast iron water tank on north west, 24 bays long. On canal front six cast iron beams with date 1869 over former loading openings. Large single-storey weaving shed at north.

Around the mills are surviving parts of the **Flowery Field community** developed by Ashton Bros in mid- and late 19C. In **Throstle Bank Street** two rows of two-storey brick-built cottages with yards and privies at the back. **Flowery Field View**, 1871, in Furnace Street, brick-built, windows with stone sills and lintels, stone-framed doorways. In **Well Meadows** to south, two rows of cottages, one each side, two storeys at front, three at rear; at south end on west side, row of 13 earlier cottages. Opposite Bayleyfield Mills in **Newton Street**, row of ten larger houses with bay windows, presumably for managerial or supervisory staff. **Westfield Terrace** on east side of Old Road, 1888, ten cottages with deep stone sills to windows, ornamental stone lintels. Opening off Old Road on west is a series of streets with flagged surfaces, central drainage channel and rows of late 19C houses: Gair Street, Bryce Street, White Hart Street, Bramall Street.

Ashton's also provided religious, educational and community institutions. **Flowery Field Church**, east side of Newton Street, 1878, by Thomas Worthington. **Flowery Field Sunday School**, Spring Gardens, two two-storey and one single-storey stone buildings, becoming derelict, date 1872 on building at west end.

NORTH-EAST, EAST

Hyde Mill SJ 951965. East of Ashton road, 1905–06, good example of cotton-spinning mill of period, four storeys, machine brick, large rectangular windows, 48 by 16 bays, domed water tower with name of mill. Occupied by tobacco manufacturers.

ICI Rexine SJ 963964. At Newtonhurst, works started by British Leather Cloth Manufacturing Co. on site of earlier soap works. Impregnated cloth with mixture of nitrocellulose, solvents and pigments, inventing name 'Rexine'. Taken over by ICI 1926.

T. Wall & Sons SJ 966949. Ice-cream works at Godley in premises of former margarine works started 1879 by John Broomer, taken over by Lever Bros and business transferred to Bromborough, Wirral, 1921.

SOUTH

Gee Cross Mill SJ 942936. Late 19C and early 20C cotton-spinning mill on east bank of Peak Forest Canal. Four storeys and basement, large window area, ornamental water tower, separate engine house. Near site of former Apethorn Mill. There is earlier housing to east, including square of two-storey stone-built cottages and much older Mill Cottage opposite mill gates. To west by weir on river Tame are traces of former **Gibraltar Mill**, built before 1800.

INCE IN MAKERFIELD

Former coal-mining township south of Wigan, famous at one time for its landscape of spoil heaps and flashes, otherwise known as 'Wigan Alps and Lake District', crossed by bewildering maze of railway lines, many now disused. They include LNWR main Warrington–Wigan line, Eccles–Wigan line, Wigan–St Helens line and branch to Whelley, Springs Bank Railway to Haigh and Aspull, LYR Bury–Liverpool line and Pemberton loop, GCR Glazebrook–Wigan line, and various colliery branches.

Ince Colliery SD 615055. Spoil heaps and shafts. Line of railway from LYR to collieries at Aspull. There was formerly a tramroad running south-west to Leeds & Liverpool Canal at Higher Ince.

Wigan locks, Leeds & Liverpool Canal. Sixteen locks of flight (Nos. 6–20) are in Higher Ince. For fuller information about locks see *Aspull*. At **Lock 9** SD 601061 are abutments of bridge which carried LNWR line from Ince Moss to Whelley, opened 1869.

Rose Bridge Colliery SD 599059. Reclaimed site of colliery shown on OS map of 1844. Down to 2,445 ft (745 m) by 1869: one of deepest in England at time. Three shafts working 1894, wharf on canal, sidings from Springs Branch Railway.

Ince Hall Colliery SD 593050. Site of former colliery, coke ovens and chemical works south of Leeds & Liverpool Canal, now reclaimed as William Foster Playing Fields. Line of former branch canal can be followed on east side of playing fields to **Whelley's Basin** on south bank of canal between locks 17 and 18.

Moss Colliery SD 589035. Spoil heaps and pit-head buildings, railway sidings from LNWR. 650 workers in 1954, producing 160,000 tons per annum. From Taylor Lane bridges near by there is a good view of the elaborate railway system.

IRLAM

Cadishead Interesting example of a community where velvet or fustian cutting was carried on until after the first world war. The cloth, usually cotton and woven with a loop, was brought from Manchester, stiffened with flour paste and lime paste and stretched tightly on tables or cutting frames, 27 ft to 30 ft (8·2 m to 9·1 m) long. The cutting was done, usually by women, by a long, thin steel blade inserted into a guide and sheath, with a wooden handle, which was run along the line of loops by the cutter, walking along the table. After cutting, defects were put right by 'enders and menders'. See also *Lymm* and *Wilmslow* in Cheshire. There is a considerable variety of workshops. **Academy Row, Liverpool Road** SJ 708918, brick-built cottages, two storeys at front, three at rear, with common attic used as workshop. **Jacksons Row** SJ 710921, off Green Lane, 'traditional' three-storey row of four cottages with top-storey workshops from front to rear. In same area is a row in **Hayes Road** with a cutting shop at the end marked by twin windows below the gable, and an outbuilding for storage. **Albion Hall** near by is a two–storey purpose-built cutting workshop with no domestic accommodation, seven windows on each floor each side to provide light for cutting tables. **Fir Street** SJ 709722, at corner of Devon Road, row of cottages with two-storey workshop at end, three windows on each floor. Built 1888–90 by master fustian-cutter. **Moss Lane** SJ 710923, workshop specially built *c.* 1890 for cutting, two storeys, six windows each side on upper floor, ground floor used for storage. Later used as dance hall and Cadishead's first cinema.

Irlam Steelworks SJ 718925. 20C works of Lancashire Steel Corporation, closed in recent contraction of industry and being demolished. Had four blast furnaces, eight open-hearth furnaces for making steel, battery of coke ovens, private wharf on Ship Canal. To south is high-level steel-girder bridge on CLC line from Baguley to Glazebrook, opened 1873. To north, traces of former moss railway built in connection with drainage of Chat Moss, running via series of farms to Liverpool & Manchester Railway at SJ 698972.

Father along Ship Canal near Mersey View Farm is gap in embankment with traces of old course of Irwell and site of wharf on Mersey & Irwell Navigation. There were two locks on the Irlam stretch: Calamanco and Sandiways.

Irlam Ferry SJ 729944. Old ferry across the river Irwell, now used only for pedestrians. Boathouse Inn nearby. To south is another high-level steel-girder viaduct on the CLC line.

KEARSLEY

Kearlsey Mill SD 752057. Late-period cotton-spinning mill, five storeys and basement, red brick with yellow-brick decoration, large windows in pairs, 24 by 17 bays, ornamental water tower at south-east.

Stoneclough Paper Mill SD 759057. Started as bleachworks by Ralph Crompton at Prestolee, 1823. Taken over by nephews James and Roger, who changed to papermaking 1829 and developed Stoneclough village. After their death in 1844 and 1859 respectively the manager, Robert Fletcher, bought the business: firm of Robert Fletcher & Son. Made tissue, copying and cigarette papers in later 19C: seven machines. Limited company 1897; taken over by Imperial Tobacco Co., one of main customers, in 1936. Extensive range of buildings between Ringley Road and river Irwell. Kearsley Vale House opposite works, now social club, was residence of Crompton and Fletcher families. Full account by member of firm in C. G. Hampson, *150th*

Prestolee aqueduct, Manchester Bolton & Bury Canal, Little Lever, 1979. Kearsley cotton mill is in the background

Anniversary of Robert Fletcher & Son Ltd, 1973.

Ringley Old Bridge SD 763053. Fine two-arch stone bridge over river Irwell between Stoneclough and Ringley, with triangular opening in parapet wall each side. Scheduled as ancient monument.

Kearsley Station SD 753053. On Manchester & Bolton Railway (later LYR), opened 1838. Late 19C blue and yellow-brick booking office. Deep single-arch stone bridge in 'canal aqueduct' style over Stoneclough Road. To northwest is Clammerclough tunnel, 295 yd (270 m) long, part of original engineering.

LEES

Cotton-spinning (earlier woollen) township between Oldham and Saddleworth, losing much of its character as mills are demolished. Contrast of vernacular stone-built housing with mainly brick-built mills. There were early water-powered sites along the river Medlock and Thornley brook of which little trace remains.

Acorn Mill SD 954047. In St John's Road, good example of stone building tradition, L plan, four storeys, early single-storey, seven-aisled weaving shed to west.

Leesbrook Mill SD 950045. 1884, illustrates later Victorian mill style, four storeys and basement, brick-built, large windows with stone sills and brick-arch lintels, tall circular brick chimney.

Two fine examples of later spinning mills: **Athens Mill** SD 951047, 1905, one of most impressive in area, five storeys, machine brick, narrow piers between large rectangular windows, separate engine house on east, 260 ft (79 m) high brick chimney demolished 1968. Now empty. **Owl Mill** to east, 1898, five storeys, engine house at north, still occupied.

LNWR Oldham–Greenfield line, opened 1856, partly remains as embankment west of St John Street.

Sites of Lees Station and goods warehouse cleared.

LEIGH

Cotton and coal-mining town with quite a significant silk industry in 19C: two collieries still working. Outstanding feature is line of spinning mills along Bridgewater and Leeds & Liverpool canals.

Bus depot SD 666003. Between Holden Road and Pownall Street. Built as munitions factory *c.* 1916 and taken over by Leigh Corporation Transport for bus garage and workshop, 1930. Office range on north with date stone 1930, three-bay main garage 300 ft (91 m) long.

Leigh Station SD 662002. On LNWR Tyldesley–Pennington line, opened 1864, closed 1969. On viaduct: buildings demolished. Leigh now has no railway station open, an astonishing result of Beeching and after.

Charles Street SD 661004. Two early spinning and weaving mills. The one on the west, three storeys, windows with stone sills and lintels, is marked as a silk mill on OS map of 1844.

Bedford New Mills SD 666001. Large, late five-storey spinning mill, long rectangular five-light windows, engine house at north, tall circular brick chimney, water tower with tiled, domed roof. Reservoir to east. In use by Courtauld's.

Leigh Spinners SJ 674997. Fine twin spinning mills of 1907 north of Bridgewater Canal. Five storeys, red brick with yellow-brick decoration, large window area, ornamental water/staircase towers (with dome on east mill), with circular windows, engine house for each mill, tall circular brick chimney and two-aisled boiler house between mills. Still used by Leigh Spinners, tufted-carpet manufacturers.

Alder Mill SJ 671997. Early 20C spinning mill, five storeys and basement, decoration of terracotta bands,

Cross-compound horizontal steam engine of 1893 by J. & E. Woods of Bolton, Brooklands Mill, Leigh. *Photograph A. E. Dennis*

ornamental-arched windows, decorative brick and terracotta water tower at north-east, 36 by 15 bays, large engine house on south, single-storey carding extension, ornamental office building. Similar in style to Butts Mill. In use by Carrington Vyella Yarns.

Butts Mill SJ 667995. 1907, on south side of Bridgewater Canal, five storeys and basement, yellow-brick decoration, ornamental corner turrets, main water tower similar to that at Alder Mill, large engine house with terracotta decoration at west, shortened brick chimney. Occupied by electrical manufacturers.

Brooklands Mill SJ 664996. Plain five-storey brick-built mill of 1893 on south side of Bridgewater Canal, water tower with pointed roof, engine house on canal side, circular brick chimney with decorated cap. Until quite recently driven by 1,200 h.p. cross-compound

steam engine by J. & E. Woods of Bolton. Occupied by camping equipment makers. **Hall Lane Mill** to west is of similar date.

Mather Lane bridge SJ 663997. Good example of single-arch Bridgewater Canal bridge, bowed in plan, humped, brick with stone course over arch and stone coping, fixed wooden rubbing posts. Navigation Inn near by.

Leigh bridge SJ 656997. Carries St Helens Road over Leeds & Liverpool Canal, stone arch with iron extension, date 1903 on parapet wall. Bridgewater Hotel, 1868, to north, wharf to west. To east is junction of Leeds & Liverpool Canal Leigh branch, opened 1820, and Bridgewater Canal Leigh branch, opened 1799.

Bolton & Leigh Railway SD 650000. On north bank of Leeds & Liverpool Canal is site of wharf at original terminus of line, opened 1828. Line is visible to north, as is that of later Leigh & Kenyon Junction Railway to south, on which bridge span over canal has been removed.

Parsonage Colliery SD 620005. Still working, now in conjunction with Golborne and Bickershaw collieries, to which it is linked underground. Spoil heaps, concrete pit-head buildings, two sets of concrete head gear with twin pulleys. Two pits sunk during first world war on site where there has been mining since *c*. 1840. No. 1 shaft still has twin-cylinder horizontal steam winding engine by Galloway's of Manchester, 1920, 40 in. (102 cm) cylinders, 6 ft (183 cm) stroke. Similar engine at No. 2 shaft by Markham & Co. of Chesterfield, also 1920, replaced by electrically driven winder 1978. Had railway links south to Leeds & Liverpool Canal, north to LNWR Tyldesley–Hindley line.

Victoria Mills SD 653009. Three spinning mills of mid- to late 19C date. Oldest on west, four storeys, brick-built, rectangular windows with stone lintels and sills, corner pilasters, 24 bays long, internal engine house at south end. In use by Courtauld's Carpet Yarns.

Firs Cotton Mill SD 642005. Surviving mill of group of three north of Firs Lane. Four-storey brick building of 1902, triple semi-circular arched widnows on top storey, water tower at north-west with four clock faces. To north-west is site of **Fir Tree Colliery**, formerly linked by tramroad to **Higher Hall Colliery**, which with site of Albert Colliery is now being developed as major open-cast working by NCB.

Bickershaw Colliery SJ 633997. Now used for winding all coal from Bickershaw, Parsonage and Golborne group. Two pits sunk in late 19C. Still has a number of steam engines: No. 1 shaft, twin-horizontal winding engine of unknown make, 36 in. (91 cm) cylinders, 6 ft stroke, Worsley Mesnes brake engine; No. 3 shaft, twin-horizontal winding engine by Walker Bros of Wigan, 1891, 32 in. (81 cm) cylinders, 7 ft stroke, 18 ft (5·5 m) diameter rope drum; steam compound air-compressor engine by Walker Bros, supplying 3,000 cu ft. per minute at 80 p.s.i. At No. 4 shaft is oldest British-made electrically driven winding engine, with two 1,800 h.p. d.c. motors by Walker Bros, 1936. Large flash to south, now being used for recreational purposes.

LITTLEBOROUGH

North-east of Rochdale, on road to Todmorden. Like Milnrow and Wardle, former centre of woollen manufacture. Examples of domestic workshops survive and sites of former water-powered mills along river Roch and its tributaries: Shore brook, Featherstall brook, Clough brook, Longden End brook. Littleborough is also of great interest from point of view of transport, with early packhorse roads over the moors, and the later turnpike, canal and railway following the Summit Gap at the watershed of the Roch and Calder into Yorkshire.

SOUTH AND WEST

55–63 Smithy Bridge Road SD 928152. Row of five three-storey, stone-built cottages, with workshops on top floor, mullioned windows.

Dearnley Lower Mill SD 925156. Derelict three-storey stone-built mill with stone-flag roof, weir on river Roch. Marked as woollen mill on OS map of 1848.

Stubley Mill SD 930158. Also formerly water-powered mill, traces of tail race, tenter ground to north-east on 1848 map.

18–20 New Road SD 925159. Pair of three-storey, stone-built domestic workshops with long mullioned windows. Another pair at **Smith Field**, Whitelees Road, SD 933165.

Higher Shore Mill SD 923173. Site

of early water-powered woollen mill, with remains of pond and foundations, tenter field to north on 1848 map. **Lower Shore Mills** SD 927171, four-storey brick-built mill and two weaving sheds on site of earlier water-powered woollen mill.

Littleborough Station SD 938163. Single-storey late 19C stone station buildings. Commemorative plaque of opening of Manchester & Leeds Railway on outside wall of booking office. To north-east handsome six-arch stone viaduct, with opening for footpaths, over Halifax Road.

NORTH

Fothergill & Harvey SD 947179. Line of mill buildings along Rochdale Canal, one notable of four storeys, stone-built, 16 bays long, decorative stonework, corner towers, internal engine house, weaving shed to south.

Summit tunnel SD 945182. On Manchester & Leeds Railway (later LYR), built 1836–41. George Stephenson and T. L. Gooch, engineers; resident engineer, Barnard Dickenson. 2,885 yd (2,638 m) long, lined with five to ten rings of brickwork, series of 14 shafts for excavations, deepest 320 ft (98 m). Cost £251,000. Longest railway tunnel in Britain when opened. Southern entrance approached in cutting, rusticated stone arch projecting in front of side walls. Spoil heaps and numerous ventilation shafts along line.

Salley Street SD 944186. In Calderbrook Road, row of six two-storey stone-built cottages, 1808, formerly used for domestic woollen manufacture, privies on opposite side of road.

Reddyshore Scout Road. Fine example of packhorse road to Burnley and Todmorden, with views over the valley. Can be walked from Calderbrook Road near Dean Head, SD 945190. Evidence of road engineering, including embankments, bridges and partial paving. At top, early milestone marked 'Rochdale 5 Burnley 9 Halifax 10 Todmorden 2'.

Calderbrook Road. Itself is part of early turnpike to Halifax: the later road of the 1820s follows the valley bottom. At junction of two roads is **Steanor Bottom Bar**, SD 945198. Two-storey, hexagonal, stone-built tollhouse, being restored. Toll board removed for preservation.

Long Lees lock SD 946200. On Rochdale Canal, opened fully 1804, with ninety-two locks in thirty-three miles. Masonry side walls, lock keeper's house on east, remains of coal and stone wharf to south.

EAST

Hollingworth Lake SD 9314/9315. One of a number of reservoirs built to feed Rochdale Canal. Long feeder can be followed to summit level of canal via Syke and Owlet Hall. Water was pumped by a steam engine to raise it from lake level. The lake became a popular recreational centre in the Victorian period, with hotels (Beach Hotel survives), refreshment rooms, boating, rowing club, regattas. Now a country park. For detailed account see A. W. Colligan, *The Weighvers' Seaport*, 1977. At south-eastern end of lake, series of mill sites along **Longden End brook**: **Longden End Mill** SD 955140, **Booth Hollings Mill** SD 952139, both marked as fulling mills on 1848 map; **Tunshill Hey Mill** SD 948137, woollen mill in 1848; **Rakewood Mill** SD 945142, still used for woollen finishing, waterwheel pit at south-east, pond, 500 yd (152 m)-long mill race.

LITTLE LEVER

Lever Bank Works SD 762064. On north bank of river Irwell west of Mount Sion Works (see *Radcliffe*). Operated in late 18C and early 19C as paper works by John Grundy, son of James Grundy, mentioned as paper-maker in Little Lever, 1767. Closed 1835. Bleach works on OS map of 1848. Buildings demolished and site being cleared.

Ladyshore Colliery North of Lever Bank Works, pits sunk in 1830s, closed 1951. Also produced clay for terracotta used in buildings in area. Remains of engine bed of winding engine, workshops, offices and stables. Boatbuilding yard and wharf on canal.

Creams Paper Mill SD 757064. Range of late 19C and early 20C buildings, worked by Trinity Paper since 1968. Crompton family in 18C and early 19C: references to Adam Crompton, paper-maker, 1739, 1773, Joseph Crompton 1777, Adam Crompton 1781, 1793, Adam and Joseph Crompton 1797, 1812.

Prestolee aqueduct and locks SD 753063. On Manchester Bolton & Bury Canal. Four-arched stone-built aqueduct over river Irwell, three river piers. At north-western end, sharp right-angled turn to locks, overgrown masonry remains of two staircases of three locks each taking canal to upper level from where Bolton branch ran west, then north, Bury branch east. Just east of top of locks are retaining walls in canal embankment built to repair breaches in 1914 and 1936. Traffic on the upper level ceased by 1951 and the canal was abandoned in 1961.

MANCHESTER

CENTRAL AREA

North West Museum of Science and Industry SJ 845071. Grosvenor Street. The major industrial museum of the region. Collections include early textile machinery, textile finishing machinery, steam, gas and oil engines, photographic equipment, hand paper-making equipment, exhibits relating to Manchester scientists. Education service for teachers and classes. Open weekdays.

The city centre is ringed with major transport sites. On the south-west at **Castlefield**, SJ 831975, is the terminus of the Bridgewater Canal, built from 1764 on land of Hulme Hall estate, near junction of rivers Medlock and Irwell. Site of basin and early wharves crossed by Bridgewater viaduct, opened 1841. There were eventually seven warehouses, of which only two remain: **Merchants' Warehouse** in Castle Street, five storeys, brick-built, small semi-circular arched windows, twin shipping holes with mezzanine floor above, loading openings on canal and street front, hoists in roof truss, damaged by fire a few years ago; **Middle Warehouse**, built before 1845, two large shipping holes, approach channels filled in. Just west of Bridgewater viaduct is site of former **Grocers' Warehouse**, built before 1789, demolished 1960, traces against sandstone bluff of arches which gave access to interior and housed waterwheel to drive hoists. Near by is former passenger quay from which regular services ran to Worsley and Runcorn until mid-19C. The **Potato Wharf**, opening off basin on north side, has largely been filled in but there are traces of covered transit sheds.

The Rochdale Canal, extension opened 1805, joins Castlefield basin north of Merchants' Warehouse, with entrance lock crossed by humped single-arch stone bridge. To east is **Deansgate tunnel** SJ 833976, later opened up except for short stretch under Deansgate itself. At west end of basin are **Hulme locks**, to link canal with Mersey & Irwell Navigation. In Chester Road are **Canal offices**, two-storeys, brick-built, Georgian, with two pediments on front.

In **Water Street** SJ 830980 warehouses on river Irwell – Victoria, Albert, New Botany, Marshall's Side – brick-built, small windows, loading openings on river front with direct loading on and off boats alongside. The improvement of the Mersey & Irwell was completed in 1740, and Quay Street to north commemorates site of main Manchester wharf. Near Water Street warehouses are traces of lock entrance from river Irwell to **Manchester & Salford Junction Canal**, promoted by Mersey & Irwell Co, and Rochdale Canal Co., opened 1839, avoiding Bridgewater terminus at Castlefield. The canal ran under what is now the Granada TV building and Central Station, under a surviving bridge in Lower Mosley Street, to join the Rochdale Canal near Great Bridgewater Street.

Liverpool Road Station SJ 831979. In the same area, original terminus of Liverpool & Manchester Railway, opened 1830. Became goods station 1844 (closed 1975) following extension to Hunts Bank and building of Victoria Station. Two-storey passenger station building, three classical-style doorways, three-storey agent's house at west end. Platform at first-floor level, wooden canopy on cast iron pillars, early booking office. Restored in connection with 150th anniversary of railway and likely to become museum site. Opposite is goods warehouse, built at same time,

three storeys, divided into bays by internal transverse walls, pitched slate roofs, wooden beams, joists and roof trusses supported by wooden pillars, impressive series of three-storey loading openings on road side, wide openings for wagons on railway side, capstans, cranes, hoists and remains of hydraulic power system. To east, tracks continue to later transit sheds in area of Lower Byrom Street. To north in Grape Street is **Bonded Warehouse** of 1860s, six storeys, brick-built, access for wagons by three tracks and turntables, internal structure of three rows of cast iron pillars, lengthwise and crosswise iron beams, brick arches. There is a detailed account in R. S. Fitzgerald, *Liverpool Road Station, Manchester*, 1980.

Manchester Central Station SJ 837977. Opened 1880, terminus for CLC and Midland lines. Single-span roof 210 ft (64 m) wide, made of segmental wrought iron arches cantilevered out from side walls, constructed by Handyside's of Derby. Six platforms

Manchester and Salford: railways and canals

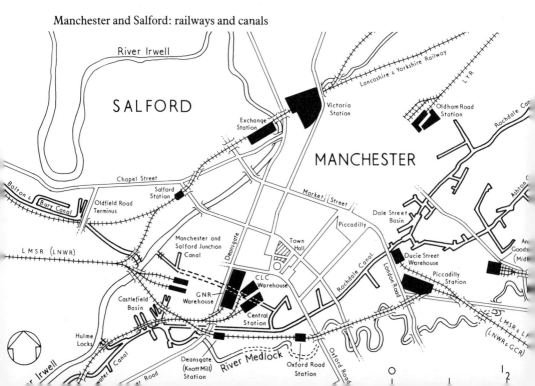

Old goods warehouse, Liverpool Road station, Manchester, from Water Street, 1965

and 'temporary' wooden buildings, never in fact replaced. Closed 1969 and since used for car parking. Brick-arched undercroft below for goods traffic: hydraulic lifts to sidings. Opposite station approach is **Midland Hotel** by Charles Trubshaw, 1898.

Great Northern Railway Warehouse SJ 836978. Built 1895–98, providing road, rail and canal interchange. Goods station at two levels inside warehouse, four platforms and turntables at each level, connected by inclines with hydraulic haulage, marshalling yards to south, approach viaduct from CLC tracks. Hoists to canal below. Internal structure of steel pillars, lengthwise and crosswise riveted steel beams, brick jack arches. 267 ft by 217 ft (81 m by 66 m). Interesting line of shops and offices along Deansgate with names of destinations served by the company.

Another important area south-east of centre is **Bank Top** (London Road). Two canal termini: **Ashton Canal**, opened 1796, in **Ducie Street** SJ 848981

with aqueduct over Store Street, stone side walls, brick tunnel, triangular openings off parapet each side; **Rochdale Canal** in Dale Street SJ 847982, linked with Ashton terminus, basin filled in and used as car park. **Salt Warehouse**, four storeys with basement and attic, stone-built, loading openings in south wall, two large shipping holes at basement level on east, internal structure of two rows of cast iron pillars on each floor, side brackets supporting timber beams. Hoists formerly worked by waterwheel. To north is **Tariff Street Warehouse**, 1836, five storeys, brick-built, small semi-circular arched windows. There are two locks and five single-arch stone bridges with later widenings on extension to Castlefield, opened 1805.

Piccadilly Station SJ 848978. Former London Road Station, opened by Manchester & Birmingham Railway 1842, afterwards used jointly with Manchester Sheffield & Lincolnshire Railway. Rebuilt as joint station 1865–66: companies had separate platforms, offices and passenger accommodation. Enlarged 1880–82. MSLR side used also by Midland Railway 1867–84. Late 19C train shed partly survives but concourse and offices were rebuilt 1959–66. At south end of station approach is **London Warehouse**, built by MSLR 1867. Seven storeys, brick-built with stone quoins, internal structure of large cast iron pillars in eight rows of nine, riveted wrought iron crosswise beams, cast iron lengthwise beams, brick arches. Wrought iron roof truss: four-aisled roof. Only survivor of group of four warehouses and two goods sheds built MSLR and LNWR.

Victoria Station SJ 841990. North of city centre at Hunts Bank, built 1845 as terminus for Manchester & Leeds Railway, later LYR. The original terminus was at Oldham Road where the station buildings were demolished in 1968. Part of original single-storey building at Victoria survives north of Hunts Bank, alongside platform 11, which was linked by long platform to Exchange Station in 1929. There was a three-aisle train shed and five sets of tracks. Extended to south in 1854–55 for trains to Oldham and Ashton under Lyne, to north 1861–65 for trains to Bolton and Salford: new single-span roof, surviving pillar in concourse by Ardwick Iron Works, 1864. New extension 1876–81, five platforms connected by subway, new roof. The 1854–55 section was re-roofed 1882–84, approach road from Long Millgate, total of thirteen platform faces. Rebuilt 1898–1904, new station buildings 1903–09 with LYR monogram and names of destinations. Tiled map of LYR system in entrance hall. Fine cast iron arched bridge across Ducie Street to **Exchange Station**, built as separate terminus by LNWR 1884, triple train shed, Italianate buildings, severely bomb-damaged in second world war; closed 1969.

EAST

Immediately east of the centre is **Ancoats**, one of the earliest concentrated industrial areas in the region, now being redeveloped. **Royal Mill** SJ 850986, on site of McConnell & Kennedy's cotton-spinning mill, started 1797, one of great pioneering firms in Manchester (see C. H. Lee, *A Cotton Enterprise, 1795–1840*, 1972). Taken over by Fine Cotton Spinners' & Doublers' Association, 1898. Present building in 1912, five storeys, brick-built, brick and stone decoration, corner pilasters, domed tower at north-west corner. Adjoining on north-east along line of Rochdale Canal are earlier **Union Mill**, eight storeys and basement, internal structure of cast iron pillars and beams, brick arches, and **Murrays Mill**, partly early 19C, six storeys and basement, internal structure of cast iron pillars and timber beams. **William Fairbairn's Ancoats Works**. Still some remains of works started by Fairbairn, who came to Manchester in 1814, and manufactured iron waterwheels, mill gearing, steam boilers, constructional iron work for bridges and buildings, iron ships. Four-storey building south-east of Cannell Street, Shooters Brook Iron Works between Ducie Street and Store Street.

Line of early and mid-Victorian cotton mills along Ashton Canal from Great Ancoats Street to Holt Town and between Pollard Street and Mill Street. Mostly six or seven storeys, brick-built, older ones have windows with stone sills and lintels.

Pin Mill Works SJ 855978. At junction of Great Ancoats Street and Fairfield Street. Pin manufacturing in late 18C. Later cotton mill run by firm of J. & J. Thompson, and dyeing and calico-printing works. In 1903 engraving works of Edmundson Bros, part of Calico Printers' Association, engraving copper rollers for printing machines.

Hyde Road Bus Depot SJ 859970. Oldest part built for trams 1904, with structure of cast-iron pillars, steel box-girder beams, iron roof trusses, rebuilt in 1920s. Tramcars built in works beyond depot until 1932: engineering shop, body shops, saw mill, cabinetmaker's shop, paint shop (32 coats of paint on a new car), signwriter's shop, coach-trimming shop.

Beyer Peacock's works SJ 883967. In Gorton, site of works started by C. F. Beyer and Richard Peacock, first locomotive superintendent of the MSLR. Works produced thousands of locomotives which were exported all over the world, including the famous Garratt articulated locomotives. Closed 1966: papers, drawings and photographs preserved at North West Museum of Science & Industry. Workshops north of Gorton Lane: Steelworks Tavern at corner of Preston Road. To north was the Gorton Works of the MSLR (later GCR) itself.

Joseph Whitworth's Engineering Works SJ 878972. Whitworth started his machine-tool works in Chorlton Street in 1833 and moved out to Openshaw 1880. Famous for pioneering work in accurate-measurement equipment and standardised screw threads. Site partly occupied by Openshaw Technical College, partly by Corporation Direct Works Department.

Crossley Brothers SJ 873973. Pottery Lane, Openshaw. Started 1882 by Frank and William John Crossley, who earlier made pumps and hydraulic presses, for manufacture of Otto-

Locomotive erecting shop, Beyer Peacock works, Gorton, Manchester, 1903.
Courtesy North Western Museum of Science and Industry

Langen gas engine, later oil engines. Two early gas engines, an Otto-Langen vertical of 1869 and a four-cycle engine of 1889, are preserved in North Western Museum of Science & Industry.

Park Works, Newton Heath SJ 873998. Mather & Platt: started in Chapel Street, Salford (Salford Iron Works) by William and Colin Mather, making rollers for textile machinery. Later specialised in machinery for textile-finishing trades, many examples of which would be found in bleaching, dyeing and printing works all over the region. Moved to Newton Heath from 1900: development of production of Edison–Hopkinson dynamo for growing electricity supply industry.

Queens Road Garage SD 846006. Built as tram depot 1901. Now site of bus museum run by Manchester Transport Museum Society, open Sundays. **Rochdale Road Garage** SJ 849992 was built 1938 for trolley buses.

NORTH

ICI Organics Division, Blackley SD 850029. Mainly modern works developed from Ivan Levinstein's dyestuff works at Hulton House (now site of New Hexagon House), started 1864. Levinstein also took over works started by Delauney's in late 18C. Manchester was an important centre of the early artificial dyestuffs industry. Charles Dreyfus from Alsace started the Clayton Aniline Co. (now Ciba-Geigy UK) in 1976. ICI have considerable collection of historical material about the early days of the dyestuffs industry. There were a number of bleaching, dyeing and printing works along the river Irk in Crumpsall and Blackley.

SOUTH

A group of early cotton-mill buildings survives off Oxford Road, in the area of Chester Street and Hulme Street, SJ 840973 : **Chatham Mill** in Chester Street, seven storeys, brick-built, 1820s; **Chorlton Mills**, started by Birley's 1808, six-storey mill in Hulme Street, internal structure of cast iron pillars and beams, brick arches. Later became part of works of Charles Macintosh & Sons, now Dunlop. Macintosh came from Glasgow in 1824 to make waterproof clothing, using rubberising technique, in partnership with Birley's.

MARPLE AND MELLOR

Former industrial communities of great interest, with evidence of domestic production in woollens and later cottons, hat-making, water-powered and later steam-powered textile mills, major canal works. There is a detailed survey in, *Historic Industries of Marple and Mellor*, ed. Owen Ashmore (Metropolitan Borough of Stockport Recreation and Culture Division), 1977.

Mellor Mill SJ 967884. The story of the cotton-spinning mill established by Samuel Oldknow 1790-92 is told in a classic of industrial history: George Unwin *et al.*, *Samuel Oldknow and the Arkwrights*, 1924, reprinted 1968. Oldknow developed not only the mill but the whole Bottoms Hall estate in the Goyt valley. Six-storey mill destroyed by fire 1892: foundations and traces of two waterwheel pits, one for Wellington Wheel 22 ft (6·7 m) diameter, the other for Waterloo Wheel, 20 ft (6·1 m) diameter, tunnels for tail races. Extensive millponds, one in Linnet Clough valley, the other on the Goyt involving diversion of river and known locally as 'Roman' Lakes. Bottoms Hall, southeast of mill, had farm machinery driven by water power.

SITES ALONG LINE OF MELLOR BROOK

Dove Bank Mill SJ 988886. At Moor End, started in 1820s, by Thomas, Ralph and Samuel Waller, six-storey spinning mill until 1929, now only foundations, gateposts and former bobbin shop.

Damsteads Mills SJ 979883. In use, built for manufacture of cotton wool and wadding c.1890 by William Jowett.

Made 'Kinetogene' as competition to 'Thermogene'.

SITES ALONG MILL BROOK VALLEY

Hollyhead Bleachworks SJ 989899. Started by Ralph and John Wood in 1840s on site of earlier water-powered cotton mill. Taken over by Bleachers' Association 1928 and closed 1930. Remains of stone buildings, chimneys, engine beds, three mill ponds.

Holly Vale Mills SJ 981897. Remains of industrial community started by Samuel Ratcliffe in early 19C. Eventually three mill buildings, one used as bleach works, others for cotton spinning, four rows of cottages, two larger houses and a farm. Worked until c.1900. Had two beam engines as well as waterwheels in later 19C. Foundations of mills only: stone plaque with inscription 'Holly Vale Mills 1846' marking date of extension. Two rows of three-storey cottages south of mill with signs of use as domestic workshops, including blocked loading openings at top-floor level. Six brick-built cottages of 1876, two storeys at front, three at back, on main road through Mill Brow.

Primrose Mill SJ 977893. Started as 18C woollen-fulling mill, then cotton spinning. Worked 1897-1924 by a Mr Warburton making Ramie gas mantles, which were bleached and knitted and then taken to Victoria Mill, Bredbury, to be impregnated. Later dyeing, then rubber and plastics. Two early 19C stone buildings, millponds, sluices, tail race.

Clough Mill SJ 975893. Ruins of stone-built cotton-spinning mill started in early 19C by William Stanney, later candlewick and cotton waste. Closed in 1890s. Evidence of five storeys, site of waterwheel pit and head race, engine house for steam engine installed after 1840, foundations of chimney.

Spade Forge, Marple Bridge SJ 966892. Forge of early 19C origin which made spades, pickaxes and other implements, using tilt hammer. Worked by Yarwood family until 1920. Two waterwheels, of which larger one survives, 15 ft (4·6 m) diameter, 4 ft (1·2 m) wide, iron axle, hubs and rims, wooden spokes, buckets gone, tail race in tunnel. Millpond above.

SITES ALONG LINE OF CANALS

The Peak Forest Canal was built 1794-1800 from Ashton under Lyne to Buxworth in Derbyshire, where it was linked with tramroad from limestone quarries north of Buxton. It is joined at top of Marple locks by the Macclesfield Canal, opened 1831, providing a link with the Trent & Mersey Canal to the Potteries and the Midlands.

Goyt Mill SJ 958876. Fine cotton-spinning mill on bank of Macclesfield Canal at Hawk Green. Built 1905 by Goyt Spinning Co. for mule and ring spinning, 120,000 spindles. Closed 1960 and now used for plastic-foam manufacture. Six storeys, machine brick with yellow-brick decoration, large window area, ornamental water tower, office with name of company on windows. Engine house on south with green and white-tiled interior decoration,, formerly housed 2,400 h.p. engine by Carel Frères of Ghent, Belgium. Boiler house with five Lancashire boilers, one by Yates & Thom of Blackburn, 1905. Internal structure of rows of cast iron pillars supporting twin H section steel beams. Rooms 250 ft by 150 ft (76 m by 46 m). Filled-in arches on canal side, presumably used for coal for boilers.

Macclesfield Canal wharf SJ 961884. Near junction of two canals, two-storey stone-built warehouse, stone-flag roof, internal waterway, stone steps to first floor at north-eastern end. Bridges each side of wharf – Church Lane and Junction – are roving bridges, carrying towpath across canal. **Tollhouse** opposite top lock with scale of charges on board.

Lime kilns SJ 963884. On east side of Peak Forest Canal near top of locks.

Tunnel for access to bottom of kiln, Marple limekilns, 1972

Built by Samuel Oldknow 1797-1800, now 'preserved' but almost out of recognition. Loaded from basin at top, coal from near-by pit. Kilns 36 ft (11 m) deep, unloaded from bottom grates by series of stone-lined tunnels 20-100 ft (6-40 m) long, then run out by wagon to transit buildings for loading on to road carts or boats. Traces of former dwellings above tunnel entrances with Gothic tracery in windows. Worked until early 20C, latterly by Buxton Lime Firms. Near-by was a mineral mill, producing plaster of paris, etc., which was worked in late 19C by J. & M. Tymm, who then had the kilns.

Marple locks SJ 961884/958900. Flight of 16 locks with fall of 210 ft (64 m), 13 ft (4 m) per lock. Stone side walls, large pounds between, some surviving lock houses. Until locks were completed in 1804 a tramroad connected upper and lower levels of canal: surviving embankment across recreation ground between Strines Road and Arkwright Road, then along line of St Martin's Road. Near top of locks is site of Jink's Boatyard, dry dock converted to garden, traces of slipway and boat-building shed.

Possett bridge SJ 961887, where Marple–New Mills turnpike crosses canal. Three openings: one for main line of canal, one for branch to lime kilns, one for horses to walk along towpath.

Hollins Mill SJ 960887. Weaving sheds partly survive from large cotton-spinning and weaving mill near new shopping centre. Built 1830 for William Thomas Walmsley, later Thomas Carver and from 1865 Hollins Mill Co. 82,000 spindles and 1,500 looms at maximum. Closed 1956, largely demolished 1957. Line of canal branch traceable, with surviving bridge parapet east of car park. Hollins Terrace to north: row of ten two-storey brick-built workers' cottages with gardens at front.

Samuel Oldknow's warehouse SJ 962890. By lock 10. Fine example, now occupied by firm of architects. Three storeys, stone-built, putched stone-flag roof, shipping holes for access to lowest level, semi-circular arched windows, loading openings on canal and road side, remains of chain hoist in roof truss, with cast iron roller, operated by large handwheel.

Goyt aqueduct SJ 955901. At bottom of locks, built by Benjamin Outram 1794-1900, stone, three arches, 309 ft (94 m) long, 100 ft (30 m) above river. One of major aqueducts of the region. Side by side with it is twelve-arch stone-built railway viaduct on the MSLR line from Hyde Junction to New Mills, opened 1865. At the south-eastern end is junction to Marple & Macclesfield line, closed 1970 beyond Rosehill Station, and then junction to former transfer wharves on canal.

MIDDLETON

Formerly had many domestic work-shops used for cotton and silk hand-loom weaving, especially in Boarshaw Road and streets to west. Nearly all demolished during last ten years, though one small group survives in Morton Street. For details of houses with basement and ground-floor work-shops surveyed by W. J. Smith see Owen Ashmore, **The Industrial Archaeology of Lancashire**, 1976, pp. 31-4.

Warwick Mill SD 871057. In Oldham Road, large early 20C cotton-spinning mill, five storeys and basement, big window area, ornamental brickwork on top storey, Hotel-de-Ville style water tower, superb engine house at rear, which formerly had Saxon cross-compound horizontal steam engine, stopped 1964. Other spinning mills of same period are **Times Mill** SD 877056, two mills in **Soudan Street** SD 854063 and **Cromer Mill** SD 877064, built for ring spinning.

Line of textile finishing works along river Irk and its tributaries from **Stake Hill Bleachworks** SD 891081, on Whit brook in north-east, to **Boothroyden Bleachworks** SD 848049, near Manches-

ter boundary. Ten marked on OS map of 1848, including four bleachworks, four printworks, a dyeworks and a logwood mill. Much the most important was **Rhodes Printworks** SD 853053, started by Daniel Burton in 1784, taken over by Sales Schwabe & Co. 1833, ten printing machines, 80 hand-block printing tables, five steam engines in 1846. Taken over by Calico Printers' Association 1899, now industrial estate. One of tallest chimneys in north west, due to be demolished. Six reservoirs to east.

Hopwood Hall Colliery SD 870082. Embankment of tramroad built 1828 from pits near the Hall to canal wharf in Heywood, best seen in area of Oaken Bank Road, clearly shown as tramroad on OS 6-inch map of 1848, about a mile and a half (2,930 m).

Hopwood Hall Corn Mill SD 878082. On Whit Brook, in grounds of De La Salle College of Higher Education, remains of stone buildings, wheel pit, wooden axle, part of iron pit wheel, millpond.

Higher Boarshaw bridge and locks SD 885070. On Rochdale Canal, good example of single-arch, bowed and humped canal bridge, lock with masonry sides. Basin on west side of canal, formerly connected by tramroad with collieries, filled in and built on.

Slattocks SD 885086. Two more locks on Rochdale Canal, and Ship Inn, near to former boat-building yard.

MILNROW

Township east of Rochdale, formerly centre of woollen manufacture, later cotton spinning.

Milnrow Mill SD 928127. Dale Street, early two, three and four-storey stone buildings with red and yellow brick additions of 1907. Still used for cotton spinning. Near by in Dale Street (Nos. 55-65, 101-129) are rows of three-storey stone-built cottages with signs of use as domestic workshops, including long mullioned windows. In Major Street above mill, two rows of 14 and 15 two-storey stone-built cottages, separated by octagonal brick mill chimney.

Ellenroad Ring Mill SD 931116. 1892, fine example of large cotton-spinning mill still working. Five storeys and basement, brick-built, 40 by 18 bays, corner turrets, three projecting towers on south front, large windows, tall circular brick chimney. On north, engine house with triple-expansion horizontal steam engine by J. & W. McNaught of Rochdale, rebuilt as twin tandem compound 1916, cylinders 23½ in. and 43¾ in. (59·7 cm, 111·1 cm) diameter, Corless valves on high pressure, piston valves on low pressure, driving 28 ft (8·5 m) diameter rope drum. At **Mount Green** north of mill is example of three-storey domestic workshop.

Butterworth Hall Colliery SD 932124. Site of pit-head buildings with line of former tramroad east across golf course to Higher Tunshill.

Mather & Platt calico-printing machine, Buckton Vale printworks, Mossley, 1967

MOSSLEY

In Tame valley between Stalybridge and Saddleworth. Like Stalybridge, had earlier woollen industry based on domestic production and small carding and spinning mills, later cotton industry with line of mills along river valley and Huddersfield Canal.

Buckton Vale Print Works SD 991009. Large works in valley below Buckton Moor, started *c.* 1825, two printing machines in 1840. Gartside's in later 19C, taken over by Calico Printers' Association 1899, now Tootall's Calprina Works. Large reservoirs to east, late 19C and early 20C stone-built single-storey sheds including former grey cloth warehouse, singeing room, bleachcroft, printing shop and engraving shop.

Carrbrook Industrial community adjoining Buckton Vale Works. Mainly late 19C stone-built cottages: row of nine in Carr Rise; along Castle Lane two rows of eight, Oak Bank and Thorn Bank, plain with gabled houses each end; to south, Beaconsfield Terrace, seven larger cottages with two semi-detached houses at south-eastern end, recreation ground opposite; in Carrbrook Road, running up to works, Long Row, 27 earlier cottages, some with three storeys at back, yards and privies; to south, South View, rows of six and five cottages with large house, West View, at end; Castle Terrace, seven also quite substantial cottages. Village institute of 1893 with ornamental roof. West of Buckton Vale works are sites of early water-powered woollen mills along **Carr Brook**: Carr Mill, Castle Mill and, just west of Huddersfield Road, Castle Clough Mill, SD 982016.

Domestic workshop SD 981017. At junction of Stayley Road and Cemetery Road, three storeys, stone-built, long mullioned windows in former top-storey workshop.

Micklehurst brook. Another line of former water-powered woollen mill sites. Clough Mill, SD 987021, east of Huddersfield Road and, to west, Vale Mills, SD 984020, three storeys, stone-built with brick shed to north, Doctors Mill (demolished), Squire Mill, also three storeys, stone-built. All working as woollen mills in 1880s. Near junction with Carr brook is Hollins Mill, SD 980019, five storeys, stone-built, projecting central six-storey tower, circular brick chimney.

Brunswick Mill SD 978018. Cheshire Street, late woollen mill, four storeys, brick-built, yellow-brick decoration, large rectangular windows, ten-aisle roof; at north, stone-built engine house and octagonal brick chimney on stone plinth, ornamental water tower. Still used for wool carding and spinning.

Croft Mill SD 976020. Long four-storey stone-built cotton mill on east bank of Huddersfield Canal with internal engine house. Worked by Robert Hyde Buckley with Woodend Mill in late 19C: 166,000 spindles and 450 looms in 1884.

Bottoms Mill SD 975021. Early water-powered site on river Tame, marked on Burdett's map of Cheshire, 1777. Present building four storeys, stone-built, windows with stone sills and lintels. In later 19C John Mayall, who also had Britannia, Southend and Scout mills.

Mossley Station SD 974020. On LNWR Manchester–Huddersfield line, opened 1849, runs on west side of Tame valley. Ornamental stone station building with semi-circular arched windows, steep pitched slate roof. Bridge at south end by St Helens Foundry 1882. The Diggle loop line on the east side of the valley, opened 1885, now closed, surviving building in Station Road of **Middlehurst Station** SD 977021, closed to passengers 1907, goods 1962.

Carr Hill Mill SD 976025. Cotton mill between river Tame and canal north of Mossley Bottom. Mill marked on OS map of 1850. N. Buckley & Sons in late 19C: 63,700 spindles and 790 power looms in 1884. Present building is four storeys, brick-built, late date.

Milton Mill SD 977025. Late four-storey brick-built woollen mill, ornamental brickwork below parapet, large windows with arched lintels, ornamental tower at north-east corner, engine house and boiler house on west, circular brick chimney with name of mill. Worked with Brunswick Mill.

Tollhouse SD 978027. On east side of Manchester Road, single-storey, stone-built, slate roof, projecting front for visibility along road, Gothic windows and doorway.

Woodend Mill SD 978027. Near weir on river Tame, four-storey cotton-spinning mill, stone-built, 18 by ten bays, five-aisled roof, yellow-brick water tower added, older building to east, ornamental Gothic office. Worked with Croft Mill by Robert Hyde Buckley in late 19C.

OLDHAM

The cotton-spinning town *par excellence* of the North West where the mills remain a dominant feature of the landscape, though mostly used for other purposes, including mail order, plastics, office furniture, school equipment, catering machinery, luggage manufacture, meter-making, motor engineering, packing materials, wallpaper manufacture. Few early 19C mills survive, but many mid- and late-Victorian and early 20C examples: evidence of major building activity in 1870s, 1890s and early 1900s. Little water power: horse power used in early spinning and carding mills. Local coal mines enabled rapid development of steam power: 65 steam-driven mills by 1825. There were over forty collieries in 1841, the Chamber Colliery Co. was operating seven in 1890s. Oldham & District Historical & Antiquarian Society published a very good survey of the mills in Oldham and the adjoining townships: *The Cotton Mills of Oldham* (Oldham Libraries, Art Galleries & Museums), 1979.

CENTRAL AREA

Oldham Local Interest Centre Greaves Street, opened 1972. Ground-floor museum, including section of Platt Bros mule from Elk Mill, models and manuals of cotton machinery, photographs of processes, hat samples, hat-making tools (Oldham was an important hat-making centre in 19C), clogs and clogmakers' tools, locally made Bradley sewing machines.

Wallshaw Street Bus and Tram Depot SD 933053. Older part between Wallshaw Street and Car Street built 1902 for electric trams (previously there were steam trams), domed tower at south-western corner, two-aisled garage. To north, bus garage of 1928, seven aisles, 420 ft by 320 ft (128 m by 97·5 m), 'modernistic' decoration on front.

Greenbank Mills SD 936048. Early 20C building surviving from group of three marked on OS map of 1848. Run by Lees family 1816–86, then Wrigley's, closed 1958. Over 400 employees in 1840s.

Commercial Mill nearby, started early 19C, said to have had first power looms in Oldham, closed 1932, used for aircraft assembly during second world war. Five storeys and attic, water tower, 1870s.

Soho Iron Works SD 939053 Part of Oldham's important textile machinery-making industry, supplying preparation, carding and spinning machinery to many parts of the world. Started by Samuel Lees, 1816, for manufacture of rollers and spindles for new textile machines: firm of Asa Lees & Co. Near by was **Hartford Works** of Platt Bros (see **Hartford New Works**, under Western area).

EAST

Waterhead SD 952057. On Old-ham–Lees boundary, group of three late 19C/early 20C spinning mills: **Cairo** 1906, **Orme** 1907, **Majestic** 1890s. Four and five storeys, brick-built, ornamental water towers, yellow-brick decoration on Majestic, separate engine houses, circular brick chimneys. Cairo and Orme, both now used by Ferranti, formerly driven by vertical triple-expansion steam engines; Majestic still used for spinning. In same area is **Orb Mill** north of Huddersfield Road, 1907, five storeys, Hotel-de-Ville style tower, occupied by school equipment manufacturers.

Springhey Mill SD 949059. 1840, formerly Equitable Spinning Mill, five storeys, brick-built, eleven by three bays, pitched slate roof, rectangular windows with stone sills and lintels, square brick chimney at corner, later extension on west.

Bank Top SD 948047. Bank Top and Egyptian Mills, mid- and late Victorian buildings, but both mills on OS map of 1844. Bank Top Mill still used for spinning and doubling.

Sett Mill SD 947045. Earlier mill on south side of Lees Road, 1840s, five storeys and basement, brick-built, windows with stone sills and lintels, pitched slate roof.

NORTH
Granville and Prince of Wales Mills SD 941060. In Vulcan Street, north of Greenacres Hill. Both four storeys and basement, large windows with stone sills and brick-arch lintels, engine houses, boiler houses and circular brick chimneys at rear, ornamental water towers. Granville 1885, Prince of Wales 1875, extended 1886.

Oldham Edge North of town centre, area of early coal pits, now landscaped.

WEST
Burnley Brow SD 918060. Just west of Rochdale Road, two impressive late 19C mills, **Werneth** and **Pine**. Werneth Mill notable for elaborate stone decoration on main fronts of four-storey build-

ings, on three-storey office block and on towers, including triple Norman-style windows on top two storeys. Pine Mill is more typical of period, four storeys, large windows with arched lintels, seven-bay engine house and chimney at rear. Occupied by catering equipment manufacturers.

Main Road SD 915055. Cotton mills each side of road: Gresham Mill, 1862, extended 1905, five storeys, corner towers. Osborne Mill, 1873, with later building of 1913 to west.

Hartford New Works SD 914048. Henry Platt moved from Uppermill in 1822 to Hartford Works, making carding engines, roving billies and looms. As a result of rapid growth in export trade in late 19C, Platt Bros moved out to new site near Werneth Station. Had their own foundry, forges, smithies, pressing shop, machine shops, erecting shops, railway sidings. Some of the older stone buildings still survive, including six-storey former Oxford Mill with name 'Hartford Works' above top-floor windows, canteen of 1894, two-storey office building on Featherstall Road, now empty. Now Platt Saco-Lowell, assembling spinning-mill machinery with automatically controlled machine tools.

Werneth Station SD 916047. On LYR line from Middleton Junction, opened 1842. West of station is Werneth Incline with gradient of 1 in 27, worked by rope and balance wheel until 1851. East of station are Werneth and Central tunnels, 471 yd and 449 yd (430 m and 410 m) to former Central Station, closed 1966, and to Mumps Station, which still has two-aisle four-storey goods warehouse. The LNWR Oldham–Greenfield line, opened 1856, closed 1955, operated after 1862 from Clegg Street Station, which was also the starting point of the Oldham Ashton & Guide Bridge Railway, opened 1861. Both can be followed for much of their length and have been partly landscaped.

SOUTH-WEST

Chamber Mill SD 913035. Heron Street, mainly 1880s and 1890s, on site of earlier mill, four storeys, large windows with arched lintels, twelve by ten bays, water tower, circular brick chimney. To south is group of three mills north of Hollins Road, SD 916031, **Dunbar** and **Heron**, both 1905, and **Brook**, earlier, similar in style to Chamber Mill and marked on OS map of 1894.

Fox Mill SD 912025. 1908, at Lime Gate, four storeys, corner water and staircase tower with circular windows at top, separate engine house for former Saxon combined horizontal and vertical compound steam engine. In use for rayon spinning.

Bradley Bent Basin SD 905025. Near junction of Manchester Road and Hollins Road. On Hollinwood branch of Ashton Canal, opened 1796, traffic until 1920s. Basin filled in but line of canal visible to south. There was formerly a tramroad running east to **Oak Colliery**, still in production in 1950s. The canal continued north to a basin near Butler Green.

Ferranti Works SD 902024. Former cotton mill taken over 1896 by Sebastian de Ferranti for manufacture of power-generation equipment. Ferranti's have a substantial collection of archives, relating to the early electrical engineering industry.

SOUTH

Some of best surviving examples of cotton-spinning mills are in Hathershaw area either side of Ashton Road. **Belgrave Mills**, SD 932035, four buildings; No. 1, 1881; Nos. 2, 3 and 4, 1908–14, domed water tower. **Maple Mills** SD 931033. No. 1, 1904, four storeys, rectangular windows in threes, corner tower. No. 2, 1915, five storeys and basement, impressive front with long windows and narrow brick piers, Hotel-de-Ville style tower. Illustrates dramatically steel and concrete structures, where outer wall becomes almost a curtain. **Earl Mill** SD 929032, originally 1860, rebuilt 1890, four storeys and basement, large windows with arched lintels, tower at north-western corner.

Iris Mill SD 925031, in Hatherlow Lane west of Ashton Road. 1907, four storeys, brick-built with terracotta decoration, ornamental water tower and office, built for ring spinning on site of earlier mill of Hathershaw Spinning Co., destroyed by fire 1896. In use by firm of meter manufacturers.

Bell Mill SD 927027. 1904, one of more decorative examples, five storeys, flat roof, large twin rectangular windows with narrow brick piers between, terracotta decoration over windows, below parapet and in form of pillars between windows on top storey. *B*s in shields above top-storey windows on north. Ornamental water tower with dome at north-east corner. Now used as mail-order warehouse.

Wood Park Colliery SD 928021. Site of colliery which had over 400 employees in 1954, producing 89,000 tons per annum. Traces of former tramroad running south-west to basin on Fairbottom branch of Ashton Canal. (see *Failsworth.*)

ORRELL

Well known for nail-making in 18C and 19C, especially **Far Moor**, where there was at least one nailer working in early 20C. Orrell Collieries from Gathurst in north to Longshaw Common in south were extensively worked in 18C and first half of 19C: there is a full account in Donald Anderson, *The Orrell Coalfield, Lancashire, 1740–1850,* 1975.

Clarke's Tramroad. Built by John Clarke and opened 1812, edge rails, 4ft (122 cm) gauge, on stone blocks. Robert Daglish carried out experiments with a Blenkinsop-type steam locomotive on this line 1812–16. Ran from collieries to Leeds & Liverpool Canal at

Crooke SD 554072. Visible south of Crooke towards Kit Green, and in Hall Lane east of Winstanley Road.

Hustler's Railway. Opened 1830 from pits in Far Moor area to Leeds & Liverpool Canal at Gathurst, SD 541073. Line visible in Gathurst Wood to south. Ran under small arch of Gathurst Bridge on LYR Wigan–Southport line 1855.

Gathurst Station SD 541072. Two-storey stone station building with steep pitched slate roof, gable and bays, similar in style to Appleby Bridge Station in Shevington.

RADCLIFFE

Small textile and former coal-mining town between Bury and Bolton, noted for coloured-cloth weaving in late 19C, crossed east–west by river Irwell and Bury branch of Manchester Bolton & Bury Canal. The Irwell and its tributaries provided power and processing water for the important local textile-finishing and paper works. For a general introduction see K. Howarth, 'The industrial archaeology of Radcliffe and the Irwell gorge', *Industrial Archaeology*, vol. 11, No. 2, May 1974, pp. 14–34.

SOUTH

Chapel Field Former bleach works, all marked on OS map of 1851, on streams draining into Irwell: **Crow Oak Bleachworks** SD 795064, in use for finishing; **Nursery Bleachworks** SD 791061, north of Stand golf course, approached by stone-sett road from Chapel Field, one, two and three-storey brick buildings, octagonal brick chimney on hill above, reservoir to west, now dry and used for tipping; **Cawdaw Clough Bleach Works** SD 788064, largely demolished, surviving two-storey brick-built office with clock tower.

Clough Side Colliery SD 777058. Spoil heaps, remains of pit-head buildings and former railway sidings of one

of a number of collieries working in Radcliffe at end of 19C. Marked as colliery on OS map of 1851. To north is site of Outwood Colliery. To west is line of East Lancashire Railway from Clifton Junction to Rawtenstall, opened 1848, track removed, deep cutting becoming overgrown each side of Ringley Road. Four-span iron-arch bridge over river Irwell, SD 782067, immediately north of which was Radcliffe Bridge Station, closed 1958.

EAST AND NORTH-EAST

Wilton Mill SD 791072. Large cotton-spinning mill of 1907, originally driven by Galloway triple-expansion steam engine, taken over by Lancashire Cotton Corporation 1929, four storeys, brick-built, rectangular windows in threes, yellow-brick decoration, corner pilasters, 36 by 10 bays, six-bay engine house on south, circular brick chimney on square ornamental plinth, domed water tower. Now used by East Lancashire Paper Co.

East Lancashire Paper Mill SD 792074. First reference 1860, on site of former calico-printing works marked on OS map of 1851. Part of late 19C expansion of paper industry in Bury area. Six paper-making machines by Bentley & Jackson and Walmsley's of Bury in 1908. Formerly had 2,500 h.p. horizontal compound steam engine by Musgrove's of Bolton, driving 800 kV generator, used as standby. Mill still working, reservoirs to east. This book is printed on paper made by East Lancashire Paper Co.

Radcliffe Station SD 788073. On LYR Manchester–Bury line opened 1879, electrified 1916 on 1,200 V d.c. third-rail system, with power station at Clifton Junction and substation on south bank of canal in Radcliffe, turbine alternators by Dick Kerr & Co. of Preston. Approached by fine 12-arch stone-built viaduct over river Irwell. Station buildings modernised. Branch to Bradley Fold on Bury–Liverpool line closed 1970, track removed. Goods station north of Spring Lane closed 1966, school built on site.

Bealey's Bleachworks SD 798078. East of Dumers Lane. Started by William Bealey & Sons, who were whisters in Radcliffe by 1750, using bleachfields near parish church. Eight water wheels in 1794. Bealey's also had their own chemical works where they made sulphuric acid by the lead-chamber process from 1791 (6 chambers in 1799), chlorine and bleaching powder. Taken over by Bleachers' Association 1900. In use by A. C. Bealey & Sons, dyers and bleachers. Engine house dated 1879. Bealey's Goit, to provide water power and processing water, can be traced from weir on river Irwell, near Bury boundary, about 2,500 yd (2286 m). The Close, adjoining the works, now child welfare centre, was Bealey's family house: grounds have become a public park. Opposite Bealey's is **Broad Dumers Paper Mill**, started *c*. 1860.

Withins Lane Colliery SD 790084. Traces of spoil heaps of colliery operated by Andrew Knowles & Sons in late 19C, three shafts in 1892. **Withins bridge** and **Hams bridge** are good examples of Manchester Bolton & Bury Canal bridges, brick with stone coping, single arch, humped, bowed in plan.

WEST AND NORTH-WEST

Sun Mill SD 783075. Seddon Street, good Victorian example, three storeys, brick-built, windows with stone sills and arched lintels on ground floor, stone lintels on upper floors, corner pilasters. Occupied by plastic-foam manufacturers.

Bolton Street Mills SD 779073. Between Water Street and canal. Late four-storey cotton-spinning mill, 26 bays long, single-storey north-light weaving shed. Occupied by paper merchants. To west on canal bank is former mill of J. C. Hamer, which once had over 900 looms: earlier two and three-storey brick buildings, weaving shed.

Water Street/Unsworth Street SD 777074. Small mid-19C three-storey brick-built mill, windows with stone sills and lintels, former internal engine house at east, ten-aisle single-storey weaving shed to north. Marked as fustian and shearing mills on OS map of 1848. Occupied by lampshade manufacturers.

Allens Green Colliery SD 778068. Spoil heaps and remains of pit bank of colliery worked from *c*. 1820. Knowles's in late 19C: two shafts sunk 500 yd (457 m) deep to Cannel seams, produced steam, gas-making and household coal, furnace ventilation, workshops with carpenters' shop, smithy and fitting shop, triple sorting screens, coal washery, dock on canal, railway branch from LYR.

Mount Sion Paper Works SD 767067. On north bank of river Irwell, with reservoirs to east. Former bleach works of Whittaker's started 1859 on site of calico-printing works marked on 1848 OS map. Taken over by East Lancashire Paper Mill for manufacture of straw pulp, later esparto pulp, then manilla pulp. Occupied by manufacturer of paper-makers' materials. Two good examples of canal bridges between Allens Green and Mount Sion: Camm Lane (with iron-bar rubbing post) and White.

Red Bank Mills SD 776081. Pilkington Road. Two-storey building *c*. 1880 along road, later three-storey building and single-storey weaving shed to west. Row of 17 two-storey brick-built workers' cottages to north: look to be of same date as older part of mill.

Hardman Street Mill SD 777088. Good example of more ornamental late 19C style, five storeys, 17 by 10 bays, rectangular windows in pairs on main floors, smaller twin windows on top storey with semi-circular arched lintels, blue-brick decoration and cast iron pillars between lights, square water tower with pyramidical roof at south east.

Bradley Fold SD 762085. Textile machinery works established by Dobson & Barlow, who moved out from Bolton 1906 to new 40-acre site with branch from LYR Bury–Liverpool line. Gradually extended 1906–26. In 1926 foundry, dressing department, casting store, grinding department, machining shop, erecting shop, joiners' department, roller department, sheet-steel department. See *Bolton*. Near works is two-storey former turnpike tollhouse at corner of Bradley Fold Road and Radcliffe Road.

RAMSBOTTOM

'New' 19C industrial town in Irwell valley created by growth of textile-finishing works, cotton mills and paper mills. Earlier it was part of the old manor and forest of Tottington. See also in *Lancashire* section.

Old Ground Printworks SD 793168. Near present town centre was site of works started by Haworth Yates & Peel 1783–4, sold 1806 to Grant Bros, who came from Scotland and played a leading role in the industrial history of the town, used as prototypes of Cheeryble brothers, benevolent capitalists, in Dickens's *Nicholas Nickleby*. Moved works to *The Square* SD 792165, 1821–22, with buildings arranged round central yard, six printing machines, 88 hand-block printing tables, two steam engines in 1846, site cleared and occupied by haulage contractors.

Ramsbottom Station SD 793168. On East Lancashire Railway's line from Bury to Rawtenstall and Accrington, opened 1846–48. Closed 1972. Level crossing, timber and brick signal box, stone abutments and steps of footbridge, platform on west, no buildings.

Holcombe Paper Mills SD 794167. First reference 1865, date 1875 on surviving engine house. Older stone buildings with recent extensions. Pap-

er-making machines by Smith & Law and Bentley & Jackson of Bury, beaters by Bury firms, including Walmsley's. Weir to north on river Irwell, mill race and sluice. In use as paper mill.

Cobden Mill SD 792166. South of town centre, three storeys, stone-built, rectangular windows with stone sills and lintels, eleven bays long, two storey building at south-east.

Hazelhurst Engraving Works SD783157. West side of Bolton Road, three-storeys, stone-built, continuous mullioned windows along top floor front and rear, square stone chimney. Part of building at south appears older. Reminiscent of style of Pennine domestic workshops. Still used by engravers to calico printers, for engraving patterns on copper rollers for printing machines.

Holcombe Brook Station SD 781152. Site now occupied by shopping centre: only parapet of bridge remains. Single-track line from Bury was opened by Bury & Tottington District Railway Co. in 1882, transferred to LYR 1888. Electrified 1912–13 by Dick Kerr & Co. of Preston with d.c. overhead 3,500–3,600 V supply, converted to third rail 1,200 V d.c. 1917–18. Closed to passengers 1952.

Brooksbottom's Mill, Summerseat SD 796152. Industrial community started by John Robinson Kay from Burnley 1829, taken over by Isaac Hoyle, who married Kay's daughter. Mill of 1874–76 replacing original mill. Four storeys, stone-built, L plan, elaborately ornamented façade on river front, internal structure of cast iron pillars and beams and brick arches. Single-storey weaving shed at rear, tall chimney. Traces to east of mill race which formerly supplied waterwheel from weir higher up river: classic water-power site where river Irwell cuts through rocks in deep gorge. Stone-built cottages, some older than mill. To west, north of Roby Street, ten rows of

Brooksbottoms mill, Summerseat, Ramsbottom: line of former mill race alongside river Irwell, 1966

two-storey, forbidding-looking blue-brick workers' cottages, narrow streets between, no yards, now becoming empty.

Lee Hill Bleachworks SD 805175. On Cross Bank brook at Shuttleworth. Foundations of mill, line of rectangular tanks with stone-flag sides, site of waterwheel pit.

ROCHDALE

From the late Middle Ages until 19C major centre of woollen manufacture, based on domestic production in surrounding area with wool staplers, clothiers and dyers in the town, trading with Yorkshire, especially Wakefield and Halifax. Water-powered fulling mills built along river Roch, Naden brook, river Spodden, Sudden brook and tributaries, some later became spinning mills. Mechanisation of textile processes during industrial revolution led to development of wool scribbling and spinning mills, but also to change-over to cotton, which was employing nearly four times as many as wool by 1835. Many of domestic workshops built in 18C and early 19C, including fine examples in Smallbridge area, have been demolished. Mills present a contrast: small number of early and mid-Victorian brick-built steam-powered mills, a number of late 19C/early 20C large spinning and weaving mills.

CENTRAL AREA

Drake Street Basin SD 898130. Former basin at end of branch from main line of Rochdale Canal near Oldham Road. Filled in, but still traceable. Two-storey stone-built warehouse survives, but fine six-storey flour warehouse has gone. In Drake Street area are examples of what appear to be former domestic workshops: the 'Hotel' in Drake Street, buildings in Henry Street and at corner of Richard Street and Machine Road.

Rochdale Station SD 899127. Opened 1839, on Manchester & Leeds Railway, later LYR, near present goods yard. New station on present site built 1887–91, with subway under all platforms, booking office on town side, two long island platforms with two bays. Southern platform now disused. Being modernised: new booking office at platform level. Surviving yellow-brick single-storey platform buildings, with red-brick decoration.

Holfus Foundry SD 896138. Whitehall Street, with preserved single beam engine by John Petrie & Co., 1840–41, moved from Whitelees Mill, Littleborough, where it worked until 1942. Cylinder 25½ in. (65 cm) diameter, 5 ft (1·5 m) stroke, 16ft (4·9 m) diameter flywheel. Near by in Toad Lane is **Co-operative store** opened by Rochdale Pioneers in 1844, one of the earliest co-op retail stores, preserved as museum.

Crawford Street SD 905124. Mills along line of Rochdale Canal varying in date from early Victorian to early 20C: **Grove Mill**, four storeys *c.* 1870; **Norwich Street Mill**, later three-storey mill, single-storey weaving shed, in use by bed-linen manufacturers; **Crosfield Mill**, typical mill of 1870s.

South of canal two large spinning mills: **State Mill** SD 909124, four storeys and basement, brick-built, yellow-brick decoration, rectangular windows in threes, ornamental tower, 28 by 16 bays, large engine house, two-storey carding extension. To west, **Moss Mill** slightly earlier, 44 bays long, in use by John Bright & Bros.

Petrie & McNaught SD 907125. Crawford Street. Firm started by Alexander Petrie, who moved from Bury to Rochdale 1816 and established Phoenix Foundry in Whitehall Street. William McNaught, who developed a technique of converting simple beam engines to compounds by addition of high-pressure cylinder, was superintendent of Phoenix Foundry before establishing his own firm. Both Petrie's and McNaught's produced many steam engines for mills in area.

SOUTH

Eagle Mill SD 902116. Queen Victoria Street. Large 18-aisle single-storey weaving shed, in use by Courtauld's.

Buersil SD 908114. Two surviving examples of domestic workshops: **Buer-**

Toll board, Steanor Bottom Bar, Rochdale–Todmorden road, Rochdale, 1965 sil Grove, row of nine three-storey stone-built cottages, mostly with long mullioned windows on all floors, some lights blocked, two cottages at east end later, chimneys suggest they may have been back-to-back. **Fairplay Court**: row of four three-storey stone-built cottages, stone-flag roofs, mullioned windows, partly modernised.

SOUTH-WEST: CASTLETON

Castleton has many surviving mills, including a line along Rochdale Canal north from Castleton Station. **Arrow Mill** SD 886109, good example of late spinning mill, 1907, four storeys, large window area, ornamental staircase and water tower in Hotel-de-Ville style, large engine house. Formerly driven by McNaught marine-type triple-expansion vertical steam engine. **Ensor Mill** SD 888111, two storeys, late brick buildings, formerly Cyril Lord's, now industrial estate, large double-engine house which contained Sharples horizontal tandem compound engine of 1908 and Yates & Thom horizontal cross-compound engine of 1915. **Crest Mill** to north, similar in style, very prominent engine house.

March Barn bridge SD 886110. On Rochdale Canal near Arrow Mill, single-arch stone bridge, skewed, crossing waterway at 60°, winding courses of masonry, 1797. Two late-period cotton-spinning mills west of Manchester Road in area of **Nixon Street** SD 878111. **Marland Mill**, five storeys, machine brick, large rectangular windows in threes, 36 by 14 bays, ornamental water tower, engine house on south, in use by Marland Spinning Co. **Mars Mill** immediately north, five storeys and basement, 24 by 12 bays, ornamental tower, late engine house at south, date 1906 on office, in use by Courtauld's Northern Spinning Division.

WEST AND NORTH-WEST

Oakenrod Mill SD 888131. On river Roch, south of Bury Road. Fulling mill in 1825, woollen mill in 1848, three storeys, stone-built, traces of weir and mill race.

Standard Mill SD 887129. Corporation Street, late 19C cotton-spinning mill, still in use, five storeys and basement, brick-built, large windows, ornamental water tower.

Mellor Street Bus and Tram Terminus SD 887136. Offices of 1904, with tram garage, extended 1964, behind. Workshops on opposite side of street. Rochdale had horse buses from 1856, steam trams on 3 ft 6 in. (1·1 m) gauge from 1883, taken over by corporation and electrified from 1902. Electric trams ran until 1932, when buses took over.

Carter's Rest SD 888138. Pub in Spotland Road at corner of Silk Street which shows signs of having been domestic workshop, three storeys, brick and stone-built, long mullioned windows, partly blocked.

Shawclough Mill SD 889147. Cotton-waste spinning mill on river Spodden. Formerly had two horizontal tandem compound steam engines, one by McNaught's, 1907, one by M. E. Robinson of Openshaw, 1912. In earlier 19C there were a number of water-powered mills on Shawclough brook and Spodden brook, including three fulling mills, a cotton mill and a dyeworks.

TBA, Spotland Mill SD 883146. Cotton-weaving mill started 1855 by Samuel Turner, son of John Turner of Passmonds, farmer and hand-loom weaver. Samuel and his three sons, John, Samuel II and Robert, as firm of Turner Bros went into the manufacture of cotton packings (e.g. for valves, glands). In 1879 started spinning and weaving asbestos which by then was being imported from Canada and proved a better material for packings. By 1900 making asbestos yarns and cloth, hair belting as well as packings. Rapid expansion in early 20C and in 1920 formed firm as Turner & Newall with Washington Chemical Co. in County Durham, Newall's Insulation Co. and J. W. Roberts of Leeds. In 1925 acquired Ferodo of Chapel en le Frith, Derbyshire, manufacturers of brake linings. Part of original mill survives by river Spot, with late 19C and early 20C four-storey stone buildings and single-storey weaving sheds. Equipped with modern asbestos carding, spinning and doubling machines and looms, plaiting machines.

Norden. On Rochdale's western boundary, where Naden brook and Mill Croft brook provided power for a number of water-powered fulling and spinning mills in early 19C. Shepherd Mill, near Edenfield Road, was a fulling mill. Lower down were Black Pits Mill, Coal Bank Mill and **Ashworth Mill** SD 854134, foundations and part of walls of four-storey stone-built woollen mill, remains of waterwheel pit, large stone-built weir, mill ponds. There were formerly tenter fields east of shepherd mill, and the names of 'tenter house' and 'lower tenter house' occur south of Edenfield Road.

NORTH AND NORTH-EAST

Fieldhourse Mills SD 898148. East of Whitworth Road, works of John Bright & Bros. Earlier buildings on east: four storeys, brick-built, rectangular windows with stone sills and lintels, ten-aisled single-storey weaving shed in Whitworth Road. Later three-storey mill with stone-decorated water tower with pyramidical roof. Works formerly had branch from LYR Rochdale–Bacup line. Bridges and viaducts on Rochdale–Bacup line, opened to Facit 1870, Bacup 1881, closed and track removed: **Yorkshire Street bridge** SD 903140, steel-girder bridge with original cast iron abutments of 1869, LYR coat of arms; **Roch viaduct** SD 907137, 18 arches, stone-built; **Spodden viaduct** SD 881159, high, eight arches, stone with iron or steel-girdered span at south end.

Late-period cotton-spinning mills in Halifax Road area: **Eclipse Mill** SD 905148, five storeys, forty-one by fourteen bays, large window area, ornamental water tower, engine house on east; **Dale Mill** SD 909144, Albert Royds Street, similar date to Eclipse, carding extension on south-east; **Croft Mill** SD 908139, Hamer Lane, with older four-storey mill opposite.

ROYTON

Cotton-mill town north of Oldham with traces of earlier water-powered sites, including fulling mill along Royley Clough in west. Traces of former domestic workshops e.g. two houses with basement workshops in High Street.

Group of three late Victorian cotton-spinning mills in Shaw Road, north of railway: **King Mill**, 1897, north of road, four storeys and basement, brick-built, large windows with stone sills and brick-arch lintels, water tower, five-storey building to west; **Bee Mill**, south of road, 1899, four storeys, 24 by 12 bays, six-bay engine house and circular brick chimney on south, occupied by flexible-foam manufacturers; next to it **Lion Mill**, 1889, five storeys and basement, ornamental tower, separate engine house, in use by cotton-wool manufacturers. The site of **Royton Station** SD 921076 is built on: LYR branch from Royton Junction opened 1863, closed 1966.

Diamond Rope Works SD 929082. Hardman & Ingham, closed. Inverted-vertical compound steam engine by Scott & Hodgson of Guide Bridge 1912, 14 in. and 30 in. (35·5 cm and 76 cm) cylinders, 250 h.p., 12 ft (3·7 m) diameter flywheel/rope drum, 14 rope grooves. In care of Northern Mill Engines Society.

Fir Mill SD 922077. North of Barn Street, 1905, four storeys, engine house and circular brick chimney at rear, in use by catering equipmment manufacturers and renamed Vernon Works.

Group of three mills east of Rochdale Road, SD 919082: **Park Mill**, 1912, built by Shiloh Spinners, five storeys, large rectangular windows, 25 by 13 bays, ornamental water tower; to east, **Larch Mill**, earlier named Highfield Mill, built 1872, older building than Park, windows with stone sills and brick-arch lintels, corner pilasters, water tower; north of Larch Mill is **Sandy Mill**, 1912, four storeys, large rectangular windows with narrow brick piers between, water tower with circular windows. Farther out along Rochdale Road is **Roy Mill** SD 916087, also Shiloh Spinners, started 1906.

Three mills south of Middleton Road, SD 916073: **Delta Mill**, 1902, five storeys and basement, 44 bays long, engine house and chimney at rear, ornamental tower and office with 'Delta Mill Co. Ltd' in windows; **Vine Mill**, 1897, four storeys, large rectangular windows, older building at rear, in use by blanket manufacturers; next to it, **Grape Mill**, built as No. 2 to Vine, 1905, formerly Royton Textile Corporation (closed 1964), four storeys, water tower with triple windows, separate engine house.

Monarch Mill SD 919068. South of Broadway, 1901, four storeys and basement, red brick with yellow-brick decoration over large rectangular windows, Hotel-de-Ville style tower, separate engine house, circular brick chimney. Near by was site of Royton's windmill, attacked in food riots 1795, on OS map of 1894, described as 'in ruins' 1923–25.

Elk Mill SD 912069. At Holden Fold, 1926, one of last cotton-spinning mills built in Lancashire, designed to be driven by Parsons steam turbine. Mule spinning until 1974. Four storeys, machine brick, large rectangular windows, water tower, engine house and circular brick chimney at rear. In use by Shiloh Spinners, who started at near-by **Shiloh Mill**, 1874, second mill built 1900–01, demolished 1967–76.

SADDLEWORTH
Moorland township east of Oldham brought into Greater Manchester from the West Riding of Yorkshire. Crossed north–south by the river Tame, which, with its numerous tributaries, provided water power for the mills. Traditional woollen industry based on domestic

Delta cotton mill, Royton, from south-west, 1979

production, with notable surviving examples of workshops, water-powered fulling mills, later scribbling, carding and spinning mills in the valleys. Until later 19C predominance of hand-loom weaving and jenny spinning. Cotton introduced during industrial revolution.

Important for transport between Manchester and Oldham and West Riding woollen area around Huddersfield and Halifax; packhorse and cart roads over tops, later turnpikes, canal and railways following Tame and Diggle valley.

I am indebted for information to Bernard Barnes of Grasscroft, whose *Local History Trails*, Nos. 1–6, published by Saddleworth Historical Society, are a very useful guide.

GRASSCROFT

Royal George Mills SD 983040. Woollen mill on river Tame built by Whitehead Bros from 1835 on site of earlier water-powered fulling and scribbling mill. Described by Angus Bethune Reach in *Morning Chronicle* 1849 (see *Manchester and the Textile Districts in 1849*, ed. Aspin, 1972, pp. 114–16) as '. . . country factory in deep cleft of a wooden glen', with comfortable, clean cottages for workers. Known for manufacture of bunting and flags: putting-out system for sewing them together. In use. Three and four-storey stone buildings, ornamental turret with clock, later brick-built extensions. Ponds to east fed from weir on river, tail race survives south-west of mill joining river near canal aqueduct. At **Mann's Wharf** near by on Huddersfield Canal is Mann's Cottages, row of ten houses, two storeys and basement, stone-built, projecting gables on central pair, yards and privies at back. Whitehead's also took over in 1850s near-by **High Grove Mill**, which was used for cotton spinning.

Grasscroft Clough SD 981045. Number of stone-built domestic work-

shops: **Beech Hill**, four storeys, three bays, five-light mullioned windows on top floor, cleaned and modernised; **Nettle Hole** , three storeys, three bays with oldest part at west, taking-in door at back.

Lydgate tunnel SD 979044. On LNWR Oldham–Greenfield line, opened 1856, closed 1963, track removed. 1,334 yd (1,220 m) long, east portal approached by overgrown cutting, four air shafts along line to west portal at **Grotton** SD 968044, where there are also remains of Grotton & Springhead Station in area being landscaped as part of Medlock Valley improvement.

GREENFIELD

Greenfield Mill SE 009037. In valley of Chew brook, started in late 18C as textile mill, later became bleach works, and in 1920 was bought by Robert Fletcher & Son of Stoneclough Paper Mill, Kearsley, for paper-making with two Fourdrinier machines. Major extensions since 1950s. Three to four-storey stone-built mill and single-storey sheds survive among later buildings. On hillside to south, **Hey Top**, row of 23 two-storey stone-built workers' cottages.

Waterside Mill SE 002039. Long millpond and race to east. Built by Bradley's in 1830s for cotton spinning, four-storey stone-built mill, row of workers' cottages to west. In use by cotton and canvas manufacturers.

Tunstead Clough Mill SE 004042. Former water-powered woollen mill built in 1790s. Two-aisled stone building with house on south-east side, millpond to west.

Domestic workshops on higher ground on north slope of Chew Brook valley: **Shepherds Green** SE 006043, four-storey stone building added to older three-storey building, 16 lights in one top-storey mullioned window, taking-in door and outside staircase at rear, former tenter field behind; **Bunkers** SE

004047, long row of three-storey work-shops, now cottages, blocked-up win-dows in gable ends; **Fir Lane** SE 002047, two three-storey buildings at right angles, 13 and 14-light mullioned windows in top storeys, date stones of 1715 and 1750, long occupied by Shaw family; **High Kinders** SE 000046, com-munity once occupied by some seven families, three and four-storey build-ings, taking-in doors and outside stair-cases, bridge access from rear, gradual-ly extended from mid-17C to late 19C, former dyehouse opposite.

Oakview Mill SD 995040. Four storeys, stone-built, projecting tower on north front, engine house at east. Used in early 19C by Whitehead's, in use by textile manufacturers, dried-up pond on south. Higher up Warlow brook is site of **Bolt Meadow Mill**, demolished before 1900.

Wellington Mills SD 994047. Wool-len mill with older stone buildings facing Wellington Road and Chew Val-ley Road, later three-storey mill to north-west with five-bay brick-built en-gine house for horizontal steam engine. In use by firm of wool spinners. At Frenches to north is site of former dye works built on site of early 18C fulling mill.

Tollhouse SD 992047. On branch of Oldham–Standedge road, single-storey, stone-built, Gothic windows, central chimney, early 19C.

Greenfield Station SD 992046. At junction of LNWR main line to Hud-dersfield with line from Oldham. Mod-ernised, no buildings, wooden signal box at west, single-arch skewed stone bridge at east.

UPPERMILL

Saddleworth Museum SD 997055. High Street, in part of former Victoria Mill, collections relating to local textile industries and transport.

Alexandra Mill SD 997055. Built in 1860s. J. Bradbury & Co., flannel manufacturers, four storeys, stone-built, 13 bays long, small-paned win-dows, stone-built engine house, square stone chimney.

Uppermill Station SD 999054. Site of former station on LNWR Staly-bridge–Diggle loop line, opened 1885, closed 1965, which runs along east side of valley, partly built on, partly land-scaped.

Albion Mill SD 999057. Like Alex-andra Mill in use by Bradbury's, 1850s, five storeys, stone-built, 12 by 3 bays, internal engine house, octagonal stone chimney, mill dam to north. Used for cotton spinning in 19C. On site of former Damhead Mill, woollen scrib-bling mill started in 1780s.

New Street SD 998058. Row of five three-storey stone-built domestic work-shops, with seven-light mullioned win-dows on top floor and blocked taking-in doors at rear.

Buckley New Mills SD 997059. East side of High Street, occupied by J. F. & C. Kenworthy, flannel shawl makers, from *c.* 1876. Three storeys, stone-built, water tower with open cast iron tank, engine house, octagonal chimney, single-storey weaving shed. The old Buckley Mill was east of High Street

Lime Kiln lock SD 996063. Remains of lock on Huddersfield Canal with handsome stone-built single-arch lock-end bridge. The locks generally have been landscaped or filled in.

Saddleworth viaduct SD 996063. Carries LNWR Manchester–Hud-dersfield line, opened 1849, across Tame valley, built on curve, 18 semi-circular arches, stone-built, later rail-ings on top of parapet walls.

Saddleworth Station SD 996064. At north end of viaduct, closed 1968; on west are two-storey station buildings with gable and bay window, ornamental roof, verandah with cast iron pillars, in use as residence.

Saddleworth Fold SE 005061. Group of domestic workshops forming community, described by Reach in

Morning Chronicle, 1849, hand-loom weaving and jenny spinning, population of 70–80.

Heathfields Mill SE 002057. Remains of woollen mill started c. 1790, demolished in 1960s. Wheel pit with remains of waterwheel 36ft (11m) diameter 3ft 6in (1.1m) wide.

Church Bank Mills SE 007065. Site of two former water-powered mills in Church Bank Clough below Saddleworth Church. Mill ponds, wheel pits, ruins of buildings.

DIGGLE

Dobcross Loom Works SE 003076. Famous textile machinery works started by Hutchinson & Hollingworth in 1861, making Dobcross woollen and worsted power looms with chain-operated mechanism for changing shuttles in weaving patterned cloths. Closed 1967. Long range of stone-built machine shops, two-storey Gothic office with clock tower.

Huddersfield Canal approaches summit level by a series of eight locks from Woolroad, mostly landscaped, with basins between. The canal was diverted 1846–49 in connection with construction of railway tunnel: on the old line a small section and remains of an aqueduct are visible opposite the school at Kiln Green, SE 007079.

Standedge tunnel is the longest canal tunnel in Britain, 3 miles 176 yd (4·99 km) originally, later 3 miles 418 yd (5·21 km), no towpath. Took boats an hour and twenty minutes to leg through. Built 1796–1811 by John Evans and Benjamin Outram with nine waterwheels and four steam engines to pump water or move spoil. Four passing places. Up to 600 ft (183 m) below surface. Cost £160,000.

Standedge railway tunnel SE 007081. Entrances immediately north of Diggle Station, closed 1963, on LNWR Manchester–Huddersfield line. Longest railway tunnel in Britain, 3 miles 66 yd (4·89 km) until opening of Severn tunnel in 1886. On east are two earlier single-track tunnels, first opened 1849, second 1871. West of platform is double-track tunnel opened 1894. On moors above are numerous ventilation shafts and remains of beam-engine houses used for drainage or removal of spoil during construction.

Harrop Green SE 006082. West of Diggle Station: former community of weavers' cottages.

Diggle village SE 008051. Cluster of stone-built cottages with mullioned windows and evidence of former domestic workshops.

Diggle Mill SE 017081. On Diggle brook, still partly occupied, stone buildings, separate stone chimney on hillside, millpond to east. Famous for former 64 ft 8in. (19·7 m) diameter waterwheel installed in 1847. There are traces of three or four millponds lower down the brook.

Dean Head Mill SE 008093. On Thurston Clough brook, remains of stone building and pond, industrial hamlet in 19C worked by Rhodes family: fulling and carding mill by 1818. There are two other identifiable mill sites lower down Thurston Clough and three or four sites in Brun Clough. The three-storey stone-built farm at **Dean Head** SE 009096 was formerly a domestic workshop and dyehouse. Photograph in Ammon Wrigley's *Songs of a Moorland Parish*, taken c. 1912, showing spinning jenny and hand looms.

DOBCROSS

Brownhill Bridge Mill SD 996064. At junction of Diggle brook and river Tame. Built as woollen fulling and scribbling mill in 1770s, later spinning. Three storeys, stone-built, long mullioned windows, openings with wooden slats on west showing use as tannery in late 19C. Arched opening for tail race from former waterwheel pit.

Dobcross village SD 992066. Streets lined with three and four-storey stone buildings with mullioned windows in traditional Pennine vernacular. Many have blocked doorways, suggesting former use as domestic workshops.

LNWR branch line from Uppermill to Delph, opened 1851, closed 1955, can be followed as earthwork on west side of Tame valley. Single-arch skewed stone bridge near site of **Dobcross Halt** SD 989062. There was also a halt at **Measurements Mill** SD 986067, opened for employees 1932, mill still used for making meters, five storeys, concrete, large windows.

DELPH

Bailey Mills SD 985074. Near Delph Station, unusual building of *c.* 1865, stone-built, three aisles, two nine-bay sections, appears to have seven or eight storeys from outside but probably two windows to each floor. Square stone chimney, water tower. In use by woollen manufacturers.

Delph Station SD 986074. Terminus of branch from LNWR at Uppermill, closed 1955. Once a busy line: 19 trains each way Oldham–Delph in 1927. Remains of single-storey stone station building and platform on north, stone-built goods shed on south.

Delph village SD 986079. Like Dobcross has numerous traditional stone buildings, including domestic workshops, of which there are good examples in **St Ann's Square**, three three-storey cottages, six and seven-light mullioned windows, openings in gable ends; east of Bull's Head Hotel and at corner of Grains Road. South of St Ann's Square is a three-storey stone-built workshop with pairs of rectangular windows with small panes, stone-flag roof, outside staircase to first floor, appears not to have had domestic accommodation.

Scribbling Mill SD 986079. East of Delph bridge on river Tame, early water-powered mill used for scribbling

Wool scribbling mill, near Delph bridge, Saddleworth, 1979

Front Elevation

Side Elevation

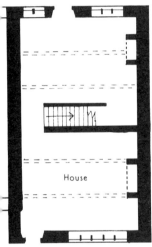

House

Ground Floor

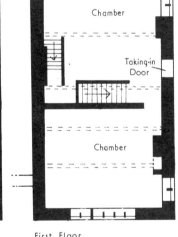

Chamber

Taking-in
Door

Chamber

First Floor

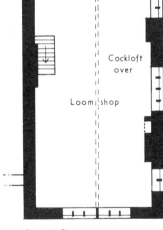

Cockloft
over

Loom shop

Second Floor

No.5 New Tame.
Saddleworth.
c.1810.

0   5   10   15
⌊ιιιι⌋_____⌊_____⌋ feet

WJS.

Domestic workshop, Delph, Saddleworth

(equivalent to carding) wool. Three storeys, stone-built, four six-light mullioned windows, stone-flag roof, sluice at bridge for race, arched opening to wheel pit, tail race to mill below.

Eagle Mill SD 985081. Near junction of Hall brook and river Tame, site of early 18C fulling mill, later spinning, bleaching and dyeing, three storeys, stone-built, tail race carried in iron trough to brook. There were other water-powered sites higher up Hall brook, some now lost in Castleshaw reservoirs.

Pingle Mill SD 979081. In upper Tame valley, started as scribbling mill in 18C, later spinning. In use as mule-spinning woollen mill, pond filled in, but traces of weir and sluices.

Linfitts Mill SD 974083. Foundations and remains of pond with weir a quarter of a mile up river Tame. Started mid-18C as fulling mill, worked by Buckleys from 1850s, later Byrons, making flannels and shawls, closed in 1930s. Notice of sale 1901 in Manchester Central Library: two mills, three storeys and attic, engine and boiler houses, mill race, dyehouse, tenter stove, warehouse, office, stable, single-cylinder horizontal steam engine, beam engine, waterwheel, three cottages and Linfitts House.

New Tame SD 974082. Community of former domestic workshops, developed from older farmhouse from late 18C, many long multi-light windows, taking-in doors. Other good examples of domestic workshops at **Grange** SD 987090, worked by Schofields in 19C, population of nearly fifty in 1870s; **Heights** SD 981090 **Old Tame** SD 968096, worked by Wrigleys in 18C.

DENSHAW

Denshaw Vale Printworks SD 974102. On site of early 19C Calf Hey Mill. Calico printing from 1830. Stone buildings, now partly derelict. To west on A672 Printer's Arms and former hand-block printing workshop at Friarmere Lodge.

Junction Inn SD 974106. Coaching and posting inn at important junction of turnpike roads connecting Milnrow, Saddleworth and Oldham with Huddersfield and Halifax, built from 1795 onwards. Short distance to east along A640 is single-storey stone-built **tollhouse**. West of New Years Bridge Reservoir are traces of the old route before the reservoirs were built (1875–83) and between two reservoirs cast iron milestone of Huddersfield Newhey Trust. South-east of reservoirs at SD

989102 is junction of six earlier roads leading from Denshaw and Delph towards Huddersfield.

Denshaw Mill SD 977103. Traces of foundations and millpond of woollen mill, started as fulling mill. Similar site in same valley at **Longroyd** SD 982104 and in **Lumb Hall Clough** at least two mill sites and spoil heaps of former coal workings with traces of tramroad.

SALFORD

Old Quay SJ 833985. Quay Street, running south from Chapel Street, marks site of Old Quay on Salford side of Mersey & Irwell Navigation, built 1755. Open quay enclosed on three landward sides with warehouses and dwelling house.

Salford Iron Works. North-east of Quay Street in area of Brown Street is site of engineering works started by Colin Mather in 1830s. Moved out to Park Works, Newton Heath, in later 19C: Salford site sold to Threlfall's Brewery. Plans and elevations of buildings in Salford Local History Library.

Salford Station SD 831984. Originally terminus and offices of Manchester & Bolton Railway, opened 1837, built at end of long brick viaduct and fronting on to New Bailey Street. When LYR built line to Manchester Victoria 1863–65 Salford became a through station. Extended in 1880s when line to Windsor Bridge was widened, with new blue-brick arch over river Irwell. Columns supporting Bailey Street bridge show work of different periods of construction.

Salford Goods Station SJ 827982. East Ordsall Lane. Established 1837–38 on land near Irwell extension of Manchester Bolton & Bury Canal. Crossed by Liverpool & Manchester Railway's line to Manchester Victoria in 1844, connecting line built in 1860s. Extended 1868–73 on to site of former New Bailey Prison, which was demolished. Closed 1967. Surviving five-storey brick-built goods warehouse in East Ordsall Lane, five loading slots on road side with hoists at top, small rectangular windows with stone sills and lintels. The LYR had a locomotive works between Ordsall Lane and Oldfield Road, started 1839 and shown on 1851 OS map.

Adelphi Ironworks SJ 827989. Engineering works of James Farmer & Co., now Sir James Farmer Norton & Co. Well known in late 19C for manufacture of steam engines, bleaching, finishing, dyeing and calico-printing machinery.

Oldfield Road Basin SJ 823984. Terminus of Manchester Bolton & Bury Canal, opened 1808, now largely filled in and built upon. Linked to river Irwell by line going under Oldfield Road and Ordsall Lane, with series of locks, still traceable in part.

Manchester Docks Built as terminus for Manchester Ship Canal, opened 1894. Manchester soon became the third port of the country in terms of traffic.

Pomona Docks SJ 820968. Four docks (Nos. 1, 2, 3 and 4) opening off east side of Ship Canal east of Trafford Road bridge, 600–700 ft (183–213 m) long by 120–150 ft (37–46 m) wide.

Main Docks SD 810973. Four docks, Nos. 6–9, first three opened 1894, No. 9 in 1905, on site of old Manchester Racecourse, with large grain elevator of 1915. No. 6 dock 850 ft by 225 ft (260 m by 68 m), No. 7 1,160 ft by 225 ft (354 m by 69 m), No. 8 1,340 ft by 250 ft (408 m by 76 m), No. 9 2,700 ft by 250 ft (822 m by 76 m). Some of the original 37 steel and concrete transit sheds survive. There were also 13 seven-storey warehouses and some 200 hydraulic steam and electric cranes. For a full account of the construction see Sir Bosdin Leech, *History of the Manchester Ship Canal*, 2 vols, 1907.

The LYR built a dock branch from Windsor bridge to site near No. 8 dock, opened 1898, with three tunnels en route. The Docks Station at the end of the line was used for racecourse traffic until 1901.

Museum of Mining SJ 798994. **Buile Hill No. 1 Drift**, drift mine and pit yard of 1930s, blacksmith's shop, lamp room, fan room, part of endless-chain haulage system from Old Meadows Colliery, Bacup, Lancashire, tippler and conveyor, cast iron plateway with four-wheel bogies for man riding, pit-head baths, hand-worked coal face on pillar-and-stall system, hand tools. **Buile Hill No. 1 Pit:** lamp room, pit cage, roadway with conveyor to coal face, mid-19C hand-worked face with hand tools and simple prop-and-bar roof support, coal tubs as hauled by pit ponies, long-wall working of 1940s, coal-cutting machine, face conveyor and gate conveyor, hydraulic roof props.

Frederick Road Tram & Bus Depot SJ 821998. Built 1902–07 by Salford Corporation for electric trams, later extended for bus garage. Main garage of six bays with double entrance, workshops to rear. Formerly had tram-car axle shop and driven by line shafting.

Broughton Depot SD 827012. Former northern terminal depot for horse-tram services of Manchester Carriage Co., taken over by Corporation 1901. Garage and stables. There is a similar surviving building of Manchester Carriage Co. at southern end in Rusholme, Manchester.

Kersal Bar SD 823021. Turnpike tollhouse at junction of Bury New Road and Moor Lane, single-storey, stone-built, three-sided bay window projecting on road side, stone-flag roof, in use as shop.

SHAW

Fine example of small cotton town

with landscape dominated by spinning mills of late 19C and early 20C. Four mills (Ash, Briar, Dee and Lilac) still spinning, remainder in use for variety of other purposes including manufacture of carbon, electric transformers, electric light bulbs, stretch covers, warehousing and mail order.

Four mills are good examples of 1880s, four storeys, dark brick, large windows with stone sills and brick-arch lintels, corner pilasters on turrets, water towers, usually external engine houses: **Ash Mill** SD 944090, 1883, added water tower with dome; **Duke Mill** SD 939088, 1883, closed 1916, now GEC heavy transformer works; **Elm Mill** SD 944094, Linney Lane, 1889, renamed Newley Mill 1932, closed 1972; **Fern Mill** SD 939093, west of Milnrow Road, 1884, internal engine house, ceased production 1938.

There are eight mills built in period 1900–15, machine brick, very large window areas, ornamental staircase and water towers, large external engine houses, tall circular brick chimneys, usually one or two-storey carding extensions. **Cape Mill** SD 939085 at Moss Hey, 1900, ceased production 1939, used for light bulb assembly; **Dawn Mill** SD 940088, 1901, closed 1965, used as discount warehouse, yellow-brick decoration; **Lilac Mill** SD 943087, 1915, forty bays long, in use by Courtauld's Northern Textiles; **Briar Mill** SD 942088, south of Beal Lane, 1906, thirty-nine bays long, also in use by Courtauld's; **Dee Mill** SD 944091, north of Ash Mill, 1907, very important because it still has double tandem-compound horizontal steam engine by Scott & Hodgson of Guide Bridge, 1907, 1,500 h.p., two 18 in. (45.7 cm) diameter high-pressure cylinders, two 42 in. (106·7 cm) diameter low-pressure cylinders, 5ft (1·5 m) stroke, 60 r.p.m. Corliss valves on high pressure, piston valves on low pressure, stopped in 1967, preserved and in care of Northern

Mill Engines Society; **Lily Mills** SD 943093, No. 1 1904, No. 2 1914, closed 1977, No. 1 has terracotta decoration; **Rutland Mill** SD 943094, 1907, ceased production 1965, 'modernistic' dome of water tower looks like later addition, name 'Rutland Mill Ltd' in windows of office.

SHEVINGTON
Gathurst bridge SD 541074. Leeds & Liverpool Canal, single segmental arch, stone-built, humped, bowed in plan, iron eyes each side to hold wooden rubbing posts, Navigation Inn on south, former wharf and terminus of Hustler's Tramway (see *Orrell*).

Dean locks SD 535074. Double locks, staggered, masonry sides, stone sett pavements, double gates top and bottom, gate paddles on both, side-lever paddles at top, iron bollards, wooden lock-end bridges. Two-storey stone-built lock house. Former lock connecting canal with Douglas Navigation has been filled in.

STANDISH WITH LANGTREE
Crooke SD 551074. Community and wharf on Leeds & Liverpool Canal with line of former railway from **John Pit** SD 552081. Still working in 1950s. To east is side cut from canal, visible south of Crooke Road, leading to **tunnel** built in late 18C running 1,100 yd (1,006 m) north via Taylor Pit towards Standish Hall, 9 ft (2·7 m) wide, masonry sides, boats legged through, disused by 1845.

Victoria Pit SD 576094. Sunk by Wigan Coal & Iron Co. 1908, with electrically driven underground haulage, fan ventilation, mechanically driven shaking screens, employing 1,200 in 1954. Now industrial estate: large brick-built former engine house and other pit-head buildings.

STALYBRIDGE
Former woollen manufacturing area which became cotton town from early

19C: 22 cotton-spinning mills by 1825. Contrast of older stone buildings to north with later brick-built mills around and west of town centre.

NORTH

Millbrook Mills and community SJ 978996. **Millbrook Old Mill** on Swineshaw brook east of Huddersfield Road, largely demolished, surviving three-storey building and two-storey offices, later yellow-brick engine house, Millbrook Spinning Co. in 1884, 61,000 spindles. **Millbrook New Mill** to north, in use by firm of bleachers, four storeys, stone-built, 23 bays long, castellated water tower with date 1851, octagonal stone chimney at rear. Interesting **community** of houses between mills and Huddersfield Road: at north **Oak Wood**, five two-storey stone-built cottages 1892; two sets of four-roomed cottages with stone-flag roofs arranged round squares with openings from streets to central yard where privies were located: **Oak Square** on north, 13 houses in Huddersfield Road and Stanford Street, six in Oxford Street and Goss Street; **Victoria Square**, 15 houses in Huddersfield Road, 12 in Stanford Street, six in Grenville Street, now open south side; **Cambridge Terrace**, between squares, long row of 27 large two-storey cottages with grass and trees in front looking on to Huddersfield Road; at south end of Stanford Street and in Grenville Street, L-shaped block of 21 houses, formerly with yards behind and stone-built privies. East of Huddersfield Road is St James's Church, 1861–63, former Church of England school (now youth and community centre). Methodist chapel in Fitzroy Street.

Copley Mills SJ 973988. Long stone-built range running east–west along valley, four and five storeys, engine and boiler houses projecting from south front, date 1871, octagonal brick chimney. James Wilkinson cotton spinner, in 1848. 51,000 spindles in 1884. Housing on opposite side of Huddersfield Road and in Copley Street north of mill row of 16 two-storey stone-built workers' cottages.

Staly New Mill SJ 971986. Demesne Street, main building six storeys, stone-built, stone-flag roof, octagonal stone chimney on tall stone plinth. 'Staly New Mill 1824' over entrance on south front. James Adshead & Bros, 1825, 1848. 56,000 spindles in 1884. In use by cotton-waste merchants. Housing in Demesne Street: row of ten two-storey stone-built cottages with stone flag roofs.

CENTRE

Castle Street Mills SJ 962985. By side of river Tame, range of three and

Workers' cottages, Oak Square, Millbrook, Stalybridge, 1978

four-storey brick buildings, rectangular windows with stone sills and lintels, stone-flag roof on older parts, 24 bay front on west, internal engine house, date 1820 over arched entrance. George Cheetham & Son, cotton spinners and manufacturers, 1848. 85,000 spindles and 1,240 looms 1884.

Stalybridge Station SJ 958986. Original terminus of MSLR line from Guide Bridge, opened 1845, LYR line from Ashton under Lyne, opened 1846. LNWR to Huddersfield opened 1849, loop line to Diggle 1885. Both lines leave central area by stone-built viaduct and tunnels of 800 yd (731 m) and 350 yd (320 m), ventilating shaft north of Stamford Street.

WEST

Bridge Street Mill SJ 958982. Late 19C, brick-built, five storeys and basement, corner pilasters, windows with stone sills and brick-arch lintels, tower at north-west corner on site of earlier mill.

Aqueduct Mills SJ 955982. In Tame Street, on south side of canal. Higher Mill, three storeys, brick-built, rectangular windows with stone sills and lintels, eleven bays long. Lower Mill, similar style, two five-storey buildings at right angles, late 19C engine house, remains of octagonal brick chimney, water tower with open cast iron tank. In 1848 Stalybridge Doubling Co., 55,000 spindles, John Wagstaff & Co., 52,000 spindles.

Ray Mill and Victor Mill SJ 952983. Tame Street. Two good examples of early 20C cotton-spinning mills still in use, five storeys, machine brick, large rectangular windows, narrow brick piers, ornamental water towers, external engine and boiler houses, tall circular brick chimneys.

Tram and bus depot SJ 952981. Built 1903 as tram depot and electricity works (separated 1948). Three-storey brick-built offices with 'SHMD 1903' (Stalybridge Hyde Mossley & Dukinfield Joint Transport), above them later large arch with 'modernistic' decoration each side, fronting works building. Garage on east.

STOCKPORT

Old Cheshire market town at junction of rivers Tame and Goyt with Mersey, industrialised in 18C and 19C, first through water-powered silk-throwing mills, then cotton-spinning and later weaving mills. Famous also for felt hat-making industry, which was a major employer in 19C and early 20C. For a detailed account see Owen Ashmore, *The Industrial Archaeology of Stockport*, 1975.

CENTRAL AREA

The Carrs SJ 899902. Valley of Carr brook or Tin brook, where silk-throwing mill was built in 1750s. Later three cotton mills, of which two partly survive. Lower Carr Mill: older five-storey mill built across stream demolished, five-storey mill of 1826 survives, internal structure of cast iron pillars, timber beams, joists and floors. Remains of pond to south.

Christy's Hat Works SJ 899898. In Middle Hillgate, now Associated British Hat Manufacturers, only hat works still working in town. Taken over by Christy's, who had works in Bermondsey, London, 1826 from local firm of T. & J. Worsley. Oldest buildings at Canal Street end, four and five storeys, 1840–64. On Hillgate side, Victoria Mill of 1882 on site of former Hillgate Cotton Mill, with long late 19C range to east. Offices are in Georgian house, once occupied by Samuel Oldknow, who moved to Stockport 1784 and conducted a putting-out business in cotton based on a warehouse in Hillgate and eventually employing over 300 weavers. Later moved to Mellor to start water-powered cotton-spinning mill (see *Marple* and *Mellor*).

Two survivors of Stockport's many breweries (at least 12 in 19C or early 20C). **Unicorn Brewery** SJ 898904, started by Robinson's 1854, still in production, earliest surviving buildings late 19C, traditional brewery lay-out; **Royal Oak Brewery** SJ 898895, built before 1872, traditional five-storey structure, later mineral water works to west.

Wellington Mill SJ 893902. Good example of earlier 19C cotton mill, built 1830–31 by Marsland Hale Lingard & Cruttenden. In later years used for hat-making by William George Ward. Now let out to several firms. Seven storeys plus attic, brick-built, pitched slate roof, circular staircase tower with tank at top, internal structure of two rows of cast iron pillars, cast iron beams and brick arches. Tall circular brick chimney on south.

Mersey viaduct SJ 891902. West of town centre the Mersey valley is crossed by one of the most impressive railway viaducts in the region, built by G. W. Buck for Manchester & Birmingham Railway, opened 1842. 1,680 ft (512 m) long, 26 arches, parapet 111 ft (34 m) above river. Widened on west 1882–89, division between two periods of brickwork clearly visible.

WEST: BRINKSWAY, EDGELEY,
CHEADLE HEATH

Weir Mill SJ 891902. Partly under railway viaduct. Started before 1800 by Thomas Fernley, originally water-powered. Taken over by Fine Cotton Spinners & Doublers: 60,000 spindles and 900 power looms in 1892. Earliest building on east, six storeys, brick-built, rectangular windows with stone sills and lintels.

Brinksway Mill SJ 884899. Another early water-powered cotton mill site, established by Joseph Heaward before 1790. Traces of weir, entrance to head race with grille and sluice controls. Waterwheel was still working in 1843: 20 ft (6·1 m) diameter undershot. J. & G. Walthew c. 1870 to 1930s, became part of Fine Cotton Spinners & Doublers. 32,000 spindles 1908. Collapse of part of cast iron structure reported in

Stockport Advertiser, 2 August 1850.

Edgeley Bleach Works SJ 884890. Started 1793 by William Sykes of Wakefield: open-air bleaching, servicing hand-loom weavers in Adswood, Cheadle and Cheadle Hulme. Water for power and processing from wells and from Hempshaw brook. Became part of Bleachers' Association 1900. Typical range of late 19C and early 20C single-storey buildings, very tall chimney at west, large reservoir to east.

Cheadle Heath Station SJ 876894. Three platforms and remains of goods warehouse of station on Midland Railway's direct line from New Mills to Manchester Central, opened 1902, station closed 1968.

NORTH-WEST: HEATON NORRIS,
HEATON MERSEY

Stockport Ring Mills SJ 882901. Three mills built for ring spinning 1892–1911, some 200,000 spindles when complete. Became part of Lancashire Cotton Corporation. Typical buildings of period, large windows, ornamental brickwork, external engine houses.

Heaton Mersey Bleachworks SJ 867901. Works established by Samuel and Thomas Oldknow 1785–86, outdoor bleaching, hand-block printing. Taken over by Samuel Stocks and later by Melland & Coward, who became part of Bleachers' Association in 1900. Stockport Library has a large-scale plan of the works in 1848, when it included spinning mill and weaving shed. Water power used until 1920s: weir and traces of mill race. Related housing in Vale Road area.

Heaton Norris Goods Warehouse SJ 888908. Wellington Road North, LNWR, rebuilding after fire in 1877. Fine example: four storeys and basement, brick-built, irregular plan, loading openings in north and south walls, internal structure of five rows of steel box-girder pillars, lengthwise and crosswise riveted steel beams, timber floors. Hand-operated gravity hoists in roof trusses. Remains of hydraulic power system including capstans, turntables, hoists, piping, engine house with pumps made by Hydraulic Engineering Co. of Chester, accumulator tower. To south are site of former Heaton Norris Station and CLC goods warehouse, two aisles, three storeys, stone-framed windows in pairs (demolished 1981).

NORTH: LANCASHIRE HILL, REDDISH

Albion Flour Mill SJ 894913. On top of Lancashire Hill. Modern roller-milling works of William Nelstrop & Co., built 1893, to replace mill of 1820 destroyed by fire. Originally steam-powered: 14 pairs of stones in 1834, two steam engines. Grain was brought to the mill by the Stockport branch of the Ashton Canal, now largely filled in, with terminal basin and wharves to south. There is an impressive line of cotton-mill buildings along the line of the canal in Reddish.

Albert Mill SJ 894922. Started 1848 by Robert Hyde Greg, second son of Samuel Greg of Quarry Bank Mill, Styal, Cheshire. In 20C specialised in production of fancy yarns. Still R. Greg & Co., though no longer owned by family. 50,000 spindles in 1911. Mill of 1848 survives, four storeys, brick-built, rectangular windows with stone sills and lintels, hipped slate roof, internal

structure of two rows of fluted cast iron pillars, cast iron beams and brick arches. Doubling extension with north-light roof on west. Two-storey mill of 1907 on north-east with further two storeys added 1925, three-storey mill of 1920 on north-west.

Broadstone Mill SJ 892930. Survivor of two mills built 1903–07 by Broadstone Spinning Co.: 260,000 mule spindles. Two engines in one engine house. Closed 1959: now used by mail-order firm. Typical of period, large window area, yellow-brick decoration, ornamental domed water tower.

Reddish Mills SJ 891933. One of most striking mill buildings in Stockport. Built 1863–65 by Henry Houldsworth, who bought land in Reddish Green and moved business out from Manchester. Taken over by Fine Cotton Spinners & Doublers, 1898. 140,000 spindles in 1920. Two large four-storey mills linked by office block, flanked by staircase towers. Internal structure of large-diameter cast iron pillars, cast iron beams, brick arches. Boiler house, chimney and reservoir on canal side. Adjoining mill is industrial community whose streets of workers' houses have recently been demolished. Row of more substantial houses with bay windows and gardens, presumably

Interior of mule-spinning room, Orrell's Mill, Stockport, showing structure of cast iron pillars and beams and brick arches, 1977

for managerial staff, survives opposite mill, as do community buildings by Alfred Waterhouse: St Elisabeth's Church, 1882–83, rectory, school, and Working Men's Club in Leamington Road, with prominent bow windows, ornamental roof with dormers and gables.

Reddish Spinning Co. SJ 891937. Built 1870 for mule spinning by company in which Houldsworths were involved, and which also became part of Fine Cotton Spinners' & Doublers' Association 1898. More developed cast iron structure in middle mill: six rows of 17 cast iron pillars with winged castings on top bearing on to lengthwise brick arches. Water and staircase tower between north and middle mills.

Reddish Vale Printworks SJ 905933. On river Tame with large reservoirs and weir to north-east. Typical group of single or two-storey buildings associated with bleaching and printing. Started before 1800. Becker Bros had four printing machines and 118 block-printing tables in 1840. Taken over by Bradshaw Hammond & Co. of Levenshulme, Manchester, 1862, and by Calico Printers' Association in 1899. Now industrial estate.

Tame viaduct. North-east of Reddish Vale Printworks. Fine tall brick-built 14-arch viaduct on Sheffield & Midland Committee's line from Romiley to Ashbury's opened 1875. On same line is **Reddish North Station** SJ 897948, with original single-storey station building with three-bay iron and glass verandah.

EAST: PORTWOOD, OFFERTON
Portwood developed as concentrated industrial area in early 19C, following bringing of water power into area by **Portwood Cut**, which partly survives, from weir on river Tame at SJ 907918.

Portwood Mills SJ 899911. Started by Howard family in early 19C, originally water-powered, remains of wheel house at north, which later housed water turbine. Waterwheel still in use 1842, together with two beam engines. Marsland Street Mill, six storeys plus basement, rectangular windows with stone sills and lintels, corner pilasters, internal structure of cast iron pillars and beams, brick arches, c. 1850. Three mills along Water Street, four and five storeys plus basement, mainly later 19C, but middle building looks earlier. 110,000 spindles in 1908, mule spinning until 1960s. Taken over by English Sewing Cotton Co. (Richard Arkwright & Co.) (being demolished July 1981).

Hope Mills SJ 898910. Irregular range of buildings in use by rubber manufacturers, between river Tame and Portwood Cut. Notable for systems of tunnels, brick arches, natural sandstone side walls, taking water power to site. Stockport Museum has photographs.

Meadow Mill SJ 899913. Fine example of late 19C mill, c. 1880, built for T. & J. Leigh, cotton and wool spinning. 120,000 spindles in 1914. Twin six-storey brick-built mills with ornamental engine house between, cast iron pillars between windows on top storey. Internal structure of single row of cast iron pillars, lengthwise and crosswise iron beams, brick arches between lengthwise beams.

Henry Street Mill SJ 899909. Good example of early small mill building, started before 1820. Cotton spinning on throstles until 1903, then purchased by Thomas Coppock, paint maker. Three storeys and attic, projecting curved staircase tower on north.

Palmer Mill SJ 903907. Built by Palmer Spinning Co. Late 19C five-storey building, 200 ft by 150 ft (76 m by 39 m), large windows, ornamental top storey, water tower at north-west corner, corner turrets at other corners, large external engine house. 180,000 spindles in 1920.

Vernon Mill SJ 904908. 1902 rebuilding of mill built in 1880s, 190,000 spindles in 1914. Four storeys, machine brick, flat roof, large rectangular windows in pairs, terracotta decoration, ornamental water tower, external earlier engine house, boiler house and circular brick chimney.

Stockport Museum SJ 907906. Vernon Park. Collections include local industrial material, in particular reconstructed hat block-making workshop of Walter Plant, which operated in Ancoats Lane, Manchester.

Offerton Hat Works SJ 911895. Hempshaw Lane, built by Battersby's for manufacture of felt hats 1886, rebuilt 1906 after fire. Prominent water tower.

STRETFORD
Trafford Park. The first British trading estate developed on land belonging to the former Trafford Hall and run by the Trafford Park Estate Co.,

with Marshall Stevens, first managing director of the Manchester Ship Canal Co., as managing director 1896. Took active part in promoting building of grain elevators, warehouses and cold storage plants. By 1912 there were on the estate ten timber firms, two flour millers (Greenwood's and Hovis), six foodstuffs firms (including three lard refiners), eight oil importers or refiners, seven engineering firms, including the Ford Motor Co., seven electrical engineering firms, seven metal processing firms, two marine engineering firms, eight building firms, five chemical manufacturers, three textile importers, two coal merchants and five warehouses (three operated by private companies, two by railways).

GEC Power Engineering SJ 794960. Site of electrical engineering works started by American, George Westinghouse, in 1901 for production of power-

Coil winding, British Westinghouse works, Trafford Park, Stretford, *c.* 1903. *Courtesy GEC Ltd*

supply equipment. Carried out electrification of Mersey Railway 1903. Near by was site of first Ford motor works in Britain built 1911–12 and closed when the company transferred to Dagenham, Essex, in 1929.

SWINTON AND PENDLEBURY

Agecroft Colliery SD 802013. One of group of four sizable collieries (others were Clifton Hall, Pendlebury and Pendleton) operated in late 19C by Andrew Knowles & Sons. Two shafts with furnace ventilation sunk 1844. Abandoned 1913–15, but reopened after second world war by NCB in connection with Agecroft power station.

Clifton Junction Station SD 793028. Junction of Manchester & Bolton Railway, opened 1838, with East Lancashire Railway's line to Bury and Rawtenstalll, opened 1848. Scene of a famous 'battle' between the two companies on 12 March 1949. To north is Irwell viaduct, 13 arches, 80 ft (24 m) above river.

Pilkington's Tiles SD 790033. Works started 1891 by four Pilkington brothers, who in 1889 had sunk two trial coal-mining shafts which revealed possibility of clay working. Also made moulded vases, including the well known Royal Lancastrian pottery, developed at the time of the Arts and Crafts movement, particularly by the Burton brothers as pottery managers. William Burton became the focus of a 'cultural centre' at Clifton. The pottery was made until 1957 and examples survive in the Monks Hall Museum at Eccles.

Chloride Batteries SD 795030. Works started in 1893 for manufacture of batteries and accumulators by Chloride Electrical Storage Co., in the formation of which Mather & Platt took a leading part.

Clifton aqueduct SD 791034. Three-arch stone-built aqueduct over river Irwell on main line of Manchester

Bolton & Bury Canal. On south side is start of **Fletcher's Canal**, built 1791 by local colliery owner, Matthew Fletcher, from Wet Earth Colliery and running parallel to river.

Wet Earth Colliery SD 774042. Started *c*. 1750 by Fletcher family. Scene of ingenious water-power system installed by James Brindley 1752–56, with weir on river Irwell at Ringley, SD 764048, 800 yd (731 m) tunnel to siphon under the river, then race on south side of Irwell to drive waterwheel which operated a series of pumps. Line of race which also supplied water to Fletcher's Canal is still visible. At colliery site are old shafts and a brick chimney. See A. G. Banks and R. B. Schofield, *Brindley at Wet Earth Colliery*, 1968.

TOTTINGTON

Textile finishing sites along Kirklees brook: **Kirklees Bleach Works** SD 784128, marked on OS map of 1851, mostly recent buildings, reservoirs north and west; **Kirklees Print Works** SD 783133, five printing machines and 60 block-printing tables in 1840, foundations and remains of three reservoirs; **Tottington Bleach Works** SD 777136, in use by finishing firm, formerly had railway branch from Bury–Holcombe Brook line; **Tottington Mill Print Works** SD 780137, started by Joshua Knowles 1820, five printing machines and 95 hand-block printing tables in 1841, seven machines, including two six-colour machines, in 1846. Overgrown foundations and machine beds. Large reservoir crossed by nine-arch stone viaduct of LYR Bury–Holcombe Brook line. Also on the line are sites of **Tottington Station** SD 778132 and **Greenmount Station** SD 778142.

TURTON See also in *Lancashire*.
Bradshaw Hall Bleachworks SD 734129. Started by Thomas Hardcastle, who also had Firwood Bleach Works, and moved to Bradshaw Hall

1784. Farm originally provided land for open-air bleaching. Taken over by Bleacher's Association, 1900. Reservoirs to north.

Eagley Mills SD 717132. Four cotton mills of period 1860–1900 built along Eagley brook on Turton–Bolton boundary. Formerly Chadwick's, later Coats' of Paisley. Industrial community to south in area of Park row, Andrew Lane, Park View and Playfair Street.

Dunscar Bleachworks SD 712135. Started 1750 by Thomas Slater on farm near Dunscar bridge, opposite present works. Chlorine bleaching from 1790s, but still some open-air bleaching until late 1830s. Firm of G. & J. Slater taken over by Bleachers' Association, 1900. Still working.

Egerton Mill SD 708145. Cotton mill started by George Bowden & Co. 1826 and bought in 1829 by Henry Ashworth of New Eagley Mill, Bolton, in partnership with Fairbairn & Lillie, engineers, of Manchester, who installed 62 ft (19 m) diameter waterwheel of over 110 h.p. Machinery included thirty-two pairs of mules by Dobson's of Bolton: 56,000 spindles in 1854. Became part of English Sewing Cotton Co., 1898. Fine stone buildings: four storeys on south side with four-aisled roof, three storeys on north with six-aisled roof, ball finials on gables. Opposite is two-storey building, site of wheel pit and water-feed system, also site used by Deakin's Bleachworks. As at New Eagley, Ashworth provided houses for workers in Egerton village, many of which survive: about a 100 in 1844, with library, news room and school. See Rhodes Boyson, *The Ashworth Cotton Enterprise*, 1970.

TYLDESLEY

Former coal-mining town with five collieries working in 1950s, including two of largest in North West: Mosley Common and Astley Green, each then employing over 2,000 workers and pro-ducing over 700,000 tons per annum. None now working.

Mosley Common colliery SD 725017. Pits sunk early 20C and modernised on a major scale after second world war: closed after failing to meet NCB ouput target in 1960s. Spoil heaps and abutments of bridges for railway branches.

Astley Green Colliery SJ 705999. Two pits sunk 1909–12 to depth of 2,500–2,650 ft (762 m–870 m). No. 2 pit had cross-compound steam winding engine by Foster Yates & Thom of Blackburn 1918, scrapped 1971. At No. 1 pit winding engine survives in large brick-built engine house with tall semi-circular arched iron-framed windows, steel lattice-girder head gear with twin pulleys. Engine is horizontal double-tandem compound also by Foster Yates & Thom, 1912, Corliss valve gear, cylinders 35 in. and 68 in. (89 cm 172 cm), 6 ft (1·8 m) stroke, 300 h.p., large bi-cylinder conical winding drum running at maximum of 58 r.p.m. One of largest winding engines installed: there are still hopes of preservation.

Hough Lane bridge SD 705019. Provides good view of abandoned track of LNWR Eccles–Wigan line, opened 1864, closed 1969. Little trace now of Tyldesley Station to west.

Cleworth Hall Colliery SD 701023. North-east of Manchester Road, spoil heaps, landscaped. Three pits working in 1958, with 670 workers producing some 160,000 tons per annum. To north-west is site of former Shakerley Colliery.

Barnfield Mill SD 689023. Handsome cotton-spinning mill of 1894 started by Caleb Wright & Co. and taken over 1898 by Fine Cotton Spinners' & Doublers' Association. In use by Courtauld's. Five storeys and basement, brick-built, long rectangular four-light windows, corner pilasters, ornamental water tower at south-east with dome and circular windows, turret at north-east. Two

Engine house for Foster Yates & Thom winding engine, and headgear, Astley Green Colliery, Tyldesley, 1979

engine houses at rear. Seven-bay ornamental single-storey office.

Nook Colliery SD 688007. Pit-head baths, in 'modernistic' style with tower for water tank, site of pit bank and concrete foundations of head gear. Two pits working 1954, 1,800 workers, production of about 440,000 tons per annum. Had two horizontal steam winding engines, one by Worsley Mesnes Ironworks of Wigan, 1898, one by Musgrave's of Bolton 1911.

Gin Colliery SD 680011. North of Nook, also working 1950s, 500 workers. Near by is community of Gin Pit Village with eight surviving rows of two-storey brick-built cottages and school.

URMSTON

Two typical CLC-style stations with cottage buildings with gables, ornamental woodwork and slate, twin pointed windows, verandah between gables: **Urmston Station** SJ 766946; **Flixton Station** SJ 747942.

WARBURTON

Warburton Mill SJ 704888. On river Bollin east of Warburton bridge, modern buildings around older four-storey brick-built mill, mill race under buildings at north end. Gothic-style mill house. Two pairs of millstones in yard. In use, of medieval origin. Had Francis water turbine by Escher Wyss & Co. of Zurich, 1905, 49 h.p., replacing two waterwheels (Information from J. H. Norris.)

WARDLE

Recent building development, somewhat out of character with the vernacular tradition of the area, has removed much of the former evidence of domestic industry and early water-powered woollen mills.

Knowle Syke SD 911172. Two three-storey stone-built cottages, mullioned windows, top-floor workshop, blocked taking-in openings and windows in gables, formerly belonged to Wardle Mill. To west in Knowle Syke

Street is so-called 'flannel mill' of 1815, three storeys, stone-built, central loading openings on south front, mullioned windows at rear, eastern part modernised and converted to residences.

Wardle Mill SD 911170. Only substantial survival of the early woollen mills, oldest stone building on south with date stone 1815, occupied by firm of tanners and leather dressers. There were a number of other water-powered sites on Wardle, Clough House and Knowle Syke brooks: three were covered when Water Grove Reservoir was built.

WESTHOUGHTON

Noted as nail-making centre in 18C and early 19C. There were at least twelve collieries operating in the late 19C and early 20C: the last one closed in 1937.

Chequerbent SD 674061. A site of major importance on the former Bolton & Leigh Railway. The embankment of George Stephenson's original track of 1828 can still be seen north of Manchester Road. On the road is the station/crossing house dated 'Hope House 1828'. To the south is the Chequerbent Incline, which was operated by a 50 H.P. stationary steam engine at the top. Many of the stone blocks on which the track was laid throughout can be seen, approximately 23 in. (58 cm) square and 9 in. (23 cm) deep, with two holes to fix chairs. Contemporary documents in Lancashire Record Office show that the blocks were laid every two yards along each rail. To west is LNWR deviation line of 1884 which goes under Manchester Road, closed 1965; site of station and line in cutting to south visible, track removed.

Daisy Hill Corn Mill SD 652039. Three-storey brick-built mill, 11 bays, loading openings on front, stone-flag roof, pond filled in. After ceasing to work as corn mill became bleach works, cotton-waste factory, then pickle factory.

Dams Head, Bolton Road SD 652039. Surviving example of nailmaker's shop entered from 18C cottage, which may have had water power. There is another example in **Haworth Street** SD 657058. Timber-framed house with workshop at right angles.

Hart Common Colliery SD 637055. Concrete supports for head gear, brick pit-head buildings, rows of miners' cottages along Wigan Road, colliery community until 1920s. There are traces of workings and spoil heaps of other collieries: Brinsop Hall, SD 630084; Four Gates, SD 641078; Wingates, SD 661070; Snydle Hall, SD 668067.

WIGAN

One of the medieval royal boroughs of Lancashire, which became a considerable industrial centre in the early modern period, with brass, bell and pewter-making workshops and the beginnings of coal production. In 19C mixture of coal mining on large scale, engineering and textiles, with Douglas Navigation, Leeds & Liverpool Canal and later the railways providing an important transport network.

CENTRAL AREA

Powell Museum SD 585055. Station Road. Displays illustrating Wigan's history from earliest times, including much of industrial interest. 17C pewter ware by local manufacturers, watches by Wigan makers, coal-mining equipment, information and photographs relating to collieries, engineering workshops and forges.

Central Station SD 585057. Terminus of Wigan Junction Railway (later GCR) from Glazebrook on CLC from 1892, when line was extended from earlier station south of Darlington Street. A plan to continue the line to Blackpool was never implemented. Closed 1964–65, buildings demolished, site is now car park on top of former embankment.

Wallgate Station SD 580056. On LYR line from Bury to Liverpool, opened 1848, and line to Southport, opened 1855. Two-storey brick building with semi-circular arched stone-framed doorways and windows, verandah on cast iron pillars in front. Built 1896 when station was moved from site to west. Long island platform with bay at west. Goods station closed 1968, track removed.

North Western Station SD 582053. Entirely modernised. Site where railway first reached Wigan when Wigan Branch Railway from Parkside on Liverpool & Manchester Railway was opened, 1832. Joined with Preston & Wigan Railway to form North Union Railway, opened north to Preston 1838.

Wallgate Basin, Leeds & Liverpool Canal SD 577053. Perhaps the most important historical site in Wigan, widely known as 'Wigan Pier'. The canal line from Liverpool was completed by 1780, but it was another 36 years before the northern section to Blackburn was finished. The basin is an arm off the main line near Pottery bridge and was the terminal of a number of colliery tramroads, including the well known Bankes's Colliery Railway from Winstanley, first section opened 1822 with short wooden pier. At the end of the arm is a stone-built terminal warehouse, two storeys and basement, with twin shipping holes for boats to enter, loading openings above and on Pottery Road and Wallgate fronts, being restored and re-roofed. To west are three other warehouses: three storeys, stone-built with stone-flag roof, early 19C with later corrugated iron hoist covers on cast iron supports; three storeys and attic, brick-built, arched windows, hoist covers similar to one on east, mid-19C; two storeys, brick-built, late 19C, two projecting hoist covers, canopy over canal above ground floor.

Trencherfield Mills SD 578051. Large cotton-spinning mill of 1907 on site of earlier mill on side of canal. Four storeys and basement, brick-built, stone decoration including pillars between windows on top storey, large window area, 31 by 6 bays, ornamental water tower, tall circular brick chimney. Branch dock from canal alongside two-aisle boiler house. Large brick-built engine house on north-east side with four-cylinder triple-expansion horizontal steam engine by J. & E. Woods of Bolton, 1907, one high-pressure, one intermediate pressure and two low-pressure cylinders, 2,500 h.p., large rope drum and rope race. Stopped 1968 but still preserved. Mill used by Courtauld's Northern Weaving Division and Household Textiles.

Swan Meadow Mills SD 577051. On opposite side of canal to Trencherfield. Three late 19C four-storey brick-built cotton mills. Started by James and William Eckersley in early 19C, spinners and manufacturers in 1850. Formerly driven by horizontal tandem compound steam engine by Musgrave of Bolton, 1884. Occupied by fashion-wear firm.

Wigan bottom lock SD 579051. Lock 23 on Leeds & Liverpool Canal, bottom of Wigan flight (see *Aspull*), masonry side walls, double gates each end. To east is dry dock and boat repair yard, to west British Waterways offices.

SOUTH AND SOUTH-WEST:
POOLSTOCK, WORSLEY MESNES,
PEMBERTON

Lock 22, Leeds & Liverpool Canal SD 582049. Immediately east of Henhurst bridge, early 19C two-storey lock-keeper's house on north, small brick toll office to east, milepost. To east is aqueduct over river Douglas and junction with Leigh branch, opened 1820.

Western Mills SD 577049. Two large late 19C cotton-spinning mills of Eckerley's in Fourteen Meadows Road, large engine houses at rear of each mill, partly derelict.

Poolstock Mill SD 577046. Earlier four-storey brick-built cotton mill, windows with stone sills and lintels, corner pilasters, 14 by 9 bays, octagonal brick chimney. Two buildings on OS map of 1894. Adjoining community of Poolstock with St James's Church, 1866.

Pemberton Colliery SD 560035. Remains of extensive collieries of Jonathan Blundell & Son, worked from 1815 until 1946. Spoil heaps from Highfield to Clap Gate, pit banks, remains of workshops, frame for sorting screens, washery. Three pits working in late 19C, (King, Queen and Bye pits) when there were two compressor houses, two sets of screens, three banks of coke ovens and extensive repair and maintenance workshops. The history and operation of the collieries along with others operated by Blundell's is described in detail in D. Anderson, 'Blundells' collieries', *Trans. Hist. Soc. of Lancs. & Ches.*, vol 116–18, 1965–68. There was an early tramroad to Seven Stars bridge on the Leeds & Liverpool Canal.

Pemberton Station SD 557040. On LYR Bury–Liverpool line, opened 1848. Small late 19C yellow-brick booking office blackened by smoke, single-storey red-brick buildings on platform. The Pemberton loop line on the east, built to avoid Wigan in 1889, is closed and the track removed.

May Mill SD 556036. Large late 19C cotton-spinning mill, some fifty bays long with projecting centre section. In use by Courtauld's.

NORTH AND NORTH-WEST:
WHELLEY, GIDLOW, MARTLAND

Alexandra Colliery SD 595071. Spoil heaps and remains of workings north of Whelley, Alexandra Hotel on south side of road. Worked by Wigan Coal & Iron Co. in early 20C, one of deepest in Wigan area. Had land-sale depot in Whelley Lane and railway sidings from LNWR Standish–Whelley line. Producing about 40,000 tons a year in 1954.

Gidlow Mill SD 578067. Late 19C mill of Joseph Rylands & Sons, now occupied by mail-order firm. Rylands started as linen yarn merchants in early 19C and developed into linen and cotton spinning and manufacturing. First mill was north-west of present site, north of Buckley Street. Rylands also had a colliery near the site of the later mill: two pits marked on OS map of 1844 and tramroad to canal along line of Gidlow Lane.

Frog Lane bridge SD 577058. On North Union Railway's line to Preston, opened 1838. Tall stone-built single-arch bridge with substantial side walls in 'canal aqueduct' style.

Pagefield Iron Works SD 570061. Between Leeds & Liverpool Canal and LYR line to Southport. Well known engineering works of Walker Bros, now Beloit Walmsley. In 1890 three main shops 120 ft long and 40 ft wide (37 m by 12 m), five travelling cranes, total area of four and a half acres, siding from LYR. Made wide variety of mining and tunnelling machinery for firms in Britain and overseas, including air compressors, ventilating fans, haulage machinery, locomotives, steam winding and pumping engines, bailers, coal-sorting machinery, pit cages, constructional iron and steel work. Made ventilating machinery for Severn railway tunnel and Mersey road tunnel.

Ell Meadow Lock SD 563068. On Leeds & Liverpool Canal. Doubled in 1863, rebuilt following subsidence in 1903. In early 19C there was a tunnel running north-east to Douglas Bank Colliery in the Beech Hill area.

WORSLEY

Of major importance as the starting point of the Bridgewater Canal to Manchester built under an Act of Parliament of 1759 by the 'partnership' of Francis Egerton, third Duke of Bridgewater, James Gilbert, the Duke's agent, and James Brindley, the canal engineer. See F. Mullineux, *The Duke of Bridgewa-*

ter's Canal (Eccles & District Historical Society), 1961, and Hugh Malet, *Bridgewater: the Canal Duke*, 1978.

Worsley Delph SD 748005. Canal basin with twin entrances to system of underground canals developed from 1760 onwards, with main level, two lower levels, side arms to coal workings. Different levels connected by shaft and in one instance by an underground inclined plane built 1795–97 with iron cradle to raise and lower boats. Eventually a total of 46 miles (73 km) reaching up to Dixon Green, Farnworth. Iron rings in roof for use of sling harness to propel boats up the tunnels, sluices to sail boats down. Last transport of coal in 1887. See F. Mullineux, 'The Duke of Bridgewater's underground canals at Worsley', *Trans. Lancs. & Ches. Antiq. Soc.*, vol. 71, 1971, pp. 152–9.

Packet House SD 748004. Starting point of passenger services established soon after opening of canal. Flight of steps down to landing point, 18C brick building with later 'black and white' additions *c*. 1850. To north-west is **Court House** built by the first Earl of Ellesmere 1849 for meetings of Court Leet. In same area Barber Road crosses the Leigh branch of the canal opened 1799, widened but with original single brick-arch surviving and a 19C hand crane on the towpath nearby.

The Granary SD 749003. Built in 1850s but used in fact for storage of oil rather than corn for which it was intended. To south on same side of canal is Boat House.

Dry docks SD 751004. Two of three 18C dry docks survive with stepped sides. These were part of the boat repair yard. To north on Worsley Green is a memorial to the third Duke of Bridgewater made out of the base of a chimney for the forge in the repair yard. Some of the houses in this area were built in the early 20C very much on the Port Sunlight model. On the opposite side of the canal are the remains of an 18C lime kiln and a warehouse which was rebuilt from a former forge.

Worsley Old Hall SD 742010. Sixteenth-century timber-framed building which was the headquarters of the Duke, Gilbert and Brindley during the construction of the canal.

Boothstown Canal Basin SD 728004. Rectangular basin on north side of Leigh branch of Bridgewater Canal. Remains of mechanical tipper, including brick end wall, wooden supports and sleepers. Railway line (formerly tramroad) to Mosley Common Colliery and to Worsley–Bolton line. To west is site of entrance to former tunnel linking collieries to north with canal.

Greater Manchester townships mentioned in gazetteer, arranged by metropolitan boroughs

Bolton MB Blackrod, Bolton, Farnworth, Horwich, Kearsley, Little Lever, Turton (part), Westhoughton

Bury MB Bury, Radcliffe, Ramsbottom (part), Tottington (part)

Oldham MB Chadderton, Failsworth, Lees, Oldham, Royton, Saddleworth, Shaw

Rochdale MB Heywood, Littleborough, Middleton, Milnrow, Rochdale, Wardle

Salford MB Eccles, Irlam, Salford, Swinton and Pendlebury, Worsley

Tameside MB Ashton under Lyne, Broadbottom, Denton, Droylsden, Dukinfield, Hollingworth, Hyde, Mossley, Stalybridge

Trafford MB Altrincham, Dunham Massey, Stretford, Urmston, Warburton

Wigan MB Abram, Ashton in Makerfield (part), Aspull, Atherton, Billinge with Winstanley (part), Golborne, Haigh, Hindley, Ince in Makerfield, Leigh, Orrell, Shevington, Standish with Langtree, Tyldesley, Wigan

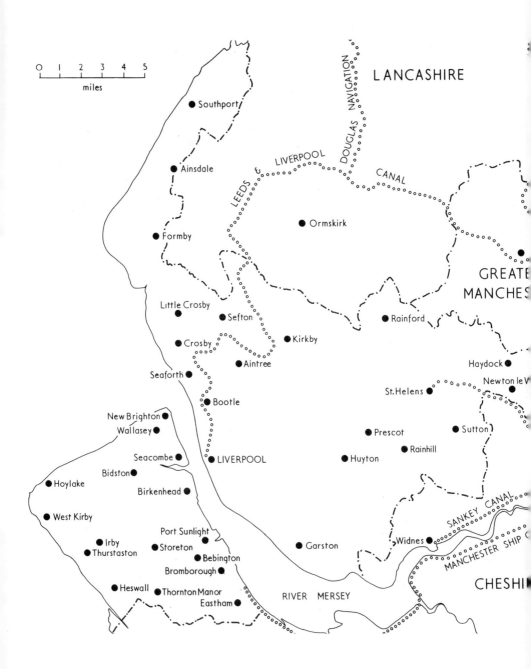

The county of Merseyside

Merseyside

The metropolitan county of Merseyside was created from the northern part of the Wirral peninsula, the city of Liverpool, the coastal area from Bootle to Southport and the south-west part of the Lancashire coalfield centred on St Helens. The emphasis of the industrial archaeology is on ports, transport installations, coal mining and related industries, including glass, soap and chemicals. There is an excellent introduction and list of sites published by the North-Western Society for Industrial Archaeology and History, *A Guide to the Industrial Heritage of Merseyside*, second edition 1978, to which I am indebted for much information.

AINTREE
Aintree Sefton Arms Station SJ 366978. On LYR Liverpool–Preston line, opened 1850, adjoining racecourse, single-storey brick buildings, canopy on cast iron pillars over platform, yellow-brick booking office in Park Road, brick-and-timber signal box to north. To west, CLC Aintree Central Station on Hunts Cross–Aintree line, opened 1879, was closed 1960 and demolished.

BEBINGTON
Merseyside township between Birkenhead and Eastham very much affected by late 19C and 20C development and with two important industrial communities.
Lever Bros and Port Sunlight SJ 337839. W. H. Lever, who began by selling soap, started a factory in Warrington and moved to a new site by Bromborough Pool in 1888. His great success was in developing the sales of branded toilet soaps and, later, powders: Sunlight soap, Lifebuoy soap, Lux and Vim. The office buildings of 1888–89 and 1913–14 remain with frontage on Wood Street. Adjoining the works is the internationally famous model village built by Lever's from before 1890 to 1930s with brick-built houses in a wide variety of styles, open-plan gardens, landscaping, church, school, library, art gallery, inn and social centre: a major landmark in town-planning history. It is fully described in Pevsner, *Buildings of Cheshire*, 1971. Port Sunlight railway station, SJ 336841, has wooden cottage-style buildings in keeping with the atmosphere of the village.
Price's Candle Works and village SJ 345845. New works started 1853 by William Wilson and his sons, James and George, on land at edge of Bromborough Pool. William Wilson had moved from Scotland, where his family had an iron works in Lanarkshire (Wilsontown), to London and in 1830 established a candle and nightlight making works in Battersea in partnership with a Mr Lancaster, from whose aunt the name Price in Price's Patent Candle Co. came. From 1936 the Bromborough

Houses in Manor Place, Bromborough Pool village, 1979

works concentrated on fatty acids and is now occupied by Unichem. Some of the candle-making machinery is in the care of the Cheshire Museums Service. The outstanding feature is the model village developed by the Wilsons, who had earlier undertaken a similar experiment in Battersea. By 1901 there were 142 houses, of which over 100 survive and are inhabited. The oldest, built 1853–58, are in York Street and Manor Place: rows of four two-storey brick-built cottages with rear extensions and gardens, some houses with bay windows, water-borne sanitation from the start. There are also a number of later houses in Manor Place, built 1872–78, when 12 houses were also built in South View. The final period of building was in 1896–1901, to which most of the houses at the east end of Manor Place and those in South View belong: semi-detached plan, gables to road, bay windows. The population of the village was 460 in 1858, 728 in 1901. Commun-

ity institutions include the first school of 1858 in York Street, yellow-brick with barrel roof over large schoolroom; later school of 1898 built of local sandstone, still in use; St Matthew's Church, 1889–90. There were also allotments, a cricket field and bowling green.

Storeton Quarry Tramroad ran from wharf at side of Bromborough Pool, SJ 341843, along line of Wood Street, by tunnel under railway, then along line of Quarry Road East and Quarry Avenue, over Cross Lane (line visible), across playing fields of Wirral Grammar School, SJ 323839, along boundaries of back gardens of houses in Ferns Road, under Mount Road to quarries. The tunnel under Mount Road is no longer visible but the line can be followed south and north of Rest Hill Road, which it crosses at SJ 313846. The quarries, which closed in 1907, had supplied stone for many buildings in Liverpool and Birkenhead, including the houses in Hamilton Square, Birkenhead.

Bromborough Corn Mills SJ 345832. Traces of pond only of former tide mill by side of Bromborough Pool. Mitford-Abraham recorded an undershot waterwheel in 1903, four pairs of stones and steam power. There was formerly a windmill on the bank above.

Raby Corn Mill SJ 331812. Site only of water-powered mill at north-eastern end of Raby Mere, which became popular boating lake. Already derelict in early 20C. Mill House cottage survives.

Good examples of Birkenhead Railway (GWR/LNWR joint) early 20C brick station buildings at **Bromborough** SJ 343810, **Spital** SJ 339830 and **Bebington & New Ferry** SJ 333850.

BILLINGE

Billinge Hill Coke Ovens SD 521017. Site of early 19C coke ovens on the west slope of the hill. OS 6-inch map of 1848 shows inclined planes running west to Crank Road.

Billinge Hill Quarry SD 526015. Very extensive stone quarry developed from 18C and still in use.

BIRKENHEAD

A new 19C town, growing rapidly in the 1840s and, after a set back, in the later part of the century, in relation to the development of the docks and the shipbuilding industry, and other related industries, including iron-founding, engineering, tanning, flour milling and brewing.

CENTRAL AREA

Woodside SJ 329892. **The Woodside ferry** is the only one still working in Birkenhead. Of early 19C origin, it was taken over by the Woodside Birkenhead & Liverpool Steam Co., 1835, and by Birkenhead Corporation, 1858. The floating landing stage survives, with two walkways from the booking hall, which has seven wooden ticket kiosks and, on the road front, a

five-bay canopy on cast iron pillars. Near by is the Woodside Hotel, Georgian, three storeys, brick-built, with recent extension. **Woodside Station** was opened in 1878, linked by tunnel to the Chester & Birkenhead Railway (later GWR/LNWR joint), replacing Monks Ferry Station to south. Trains used to run through to London from Woodside. It was closed in 1967, and there is now a car park on the site, the outer walls survive and the tunnel entrance is visible.

Hamilton Square Station SJ 326891. The Mersey Railway was originally promoted as a pneumatic railway in 1866, but built as a steam line from James Street, Liverpool, to Green Lane, Birkenhead, opened 1886, extended to Rock Ferry 1891. The tunnel under the river was constructed at the same time as the GWR's Severn tunnel. The line was electrified by George Westinghouse, whose works were in Trafford Park, with a power station in Spa Road and reopened 1903; it is now part of the Merseyrail system. The building at Hamilton Square is of three storeys in brick and terracotta, with Norman-style windows and arcading, timber booking hall with glass roof. The platforms are 100 ft (30·5 m) below. At the north is the accumulator tower for the hydraulic power system for lifts, hoists, etc.: three storeys with balcony. Also surviving is the pumping station in Shore Road, Woodside, for removing water from the tunnel, three storeys, brick-built, hipped slate roof, Norman-style windows and arcading, terracotta detail. The pumps were originally steam-driven by a Hawthorne-Davy horizontal engine and two compound grasshopper engines, replaced by electric motors 1926, though one grasshopper engine remains as stand-by.

Monks Ferry SJ 331887. The Birkenhead ferry dates back to the Middle Ages, the rights being purchased by the near-by Birkenhead Priory in 1282. Monks Ferry was connected by rail with the Chester & Birkenhead Railway (opened 1840) by a tunnel from Grange Road, and a new station built 1844. Monks Ferry Station was closed in 1878 when the new extension was built to Woodside. The tunnel entrance survives at the Grange Road end.

Cammell Laird's SJ 330887. William Laird established his first shipbuilding yard on the banks of Wallasey Pool in 1827 and moved to the site near Birkenhead Priory in the late 1850s, with graving docks south of Monks Ferry. The yards were later extended farther south, and in the 1920s Cammell Laird's were employing 10,000–14,000 men. They have built many famous ships, including the *Alabama*, which figured prominently in the American Civil War, the *Ark Royal* and the *Mauretania*.

Mersey Tunnel SJ 326887. Queensway, the road tunnel under the Mersey between Liverpool and Birkenhead, was built between 1925 and 1934. At the Birkenhead entrance is a 60 ft (18·2 m) high black granite memorial column with illuminated head, recording the names of the architects, engineers and contractors. There are three ventilating stations, with tall, brick 'modernistic' towers: Woodside, SJ 329824; Taylor Street, SJ 322893; Sidney Street, with twin towers, SJ 325892. The electrically driven fans were provided by Walker Bros of Wigan at Woodside, by the Sturtevant Engineering Co. of Leeds at Sidney Street and Taylor Street. Impure air was drawn from slotted arching in the roof of the tunnel, up the towers, and into the atmosphere.

Birkenhead Central Station SJ 323884. On Mersey Railway. Stationmaster's house and station buildings of 1886: two storeys, brick-built, Dutch-style dormer windows, pediment, single-storey building to south, wooden canopy on cast iron pillars at entrance, original wooden ticket offices. Platforms in cutting below. Mersey Railway offices of later date in Argyle Street to south. South again is site of GWR/LNWR **Hinderton Road Goods Station**, closed 1970, tracks removed.

NORTH

Birkenhead Docks. The first plans were promoted by William Laird in the 1820s, but were then held up until 1844 by Liverpool Corporation, who took them over in 1855. The docks were built in the Wallasey Pool, which runs inland for two miles (3·2 km) and provided the necessary deep water. The engineer in the early years was J. R. Rendel, after 1857 J. B. Hartley, son of

Birkenhead and Wallasey docks

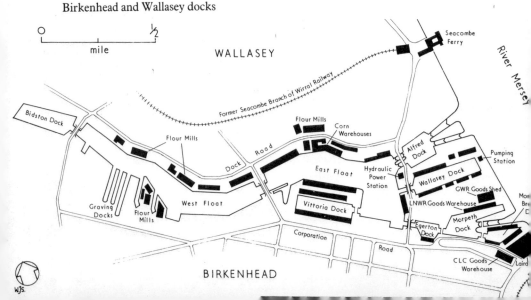

GWR goods shed, north compound, dock estate, Birkenhead, 1979

Jesse Hartley, the famous Liverpool dock engineer.

Morpeth Docks SJ 325896. The original dock near the river entrance was opened in 1847, then extended and the Branch Dock built 1866–68. Single-storey brick-built transit sheds along the wharves. North of Morpeth Dock is the roofless shell of the former LNWR warehouse and stables, and the GWR three-aisle goods shed, with four platforms and corrugated roof supported on five rows of cast iron pillars. North-east of the railway warehouses was the **Wallasey landing stage**, used for bringing ashore cattle from Ireland and North America, which were then moved along an elevated walk to the Woodside lairage, whose buildings survive north of the present bus station.

Morpeth Branch Dock and Mersey Tunnel ventilating station, Birkenhead, 1979

Some 350,000 cattle, 450,000 sheep and lambs and 100,000 pigs were landed in 1913.

CLC warehouse SJ 327892. Between Shore Road and Canning Street. On north, three-aisle, single-storey shed of 1871 with names of CLC's owning companies: GNR, GCR and Midland. On south three-storey, brick-built extension with date 'CLC 1889' on west front. The warehouse was connected with the GCR line from Hawarden at Bidston. Near the east end is the original dock entrance gateway of 1866.

Egerton Dock. Small dock west of Morpeth Dock and also opened in 1847. At each end are examples of the fine series of hydraulically operated counterweight lift bridges, operated by rack-and-pinion drive, with wooden central tower over the roadway. The former rail link from Grange Road on the Chester & Birkenhead line is visible from Bridge Street, south of the dock.

The Great Float SJ 320898, running for nearly a mile and a half (2·4 km) inland from Wallasey and Egerton Docks, was opened between 1851 and 1860 and divided into East and West Floats by Duke Street bridge, SJ 312902, another example of a counterweight lift bridge. Graving docks were built on the south side of the West Float in 1864 and 1877, SJ 302904. To east are remains of **Canada Works**, engineering works established 1853 by Thomas Brassey for shipbuilding and constructional ironwork, including work for the Grand Trunk Railway of Canada. Near by are the roller flour mills (Rank's, Vernon's and Spiller's) which were built in relation to the dock development.

Vittoria Dock, SJ 316898, with entrance from south side of East Float, opened 1909. Two and three-storey brick-built warehouses on south side.

Tramway carriage works SJ 318896. Some of the buildings survive in Cathcart Street, occupied by a firm of steel-plate manufacturers. Birkenhead

had one of the earliest systems of horse trams in Britain, starting 1860. There is a model of one in the Williamson Museum.

Birkenhead Park Station SJ 310895. On the joint Mersey Railway/Wirral Railway line from Hamilton Square to Birkenhead North. Two island platforms, rebuilt red-brick buildings. To east in Aspinall Street is the entrance to the long tunnel which runs under Beckwith Street and Hamilton Street to Hamilton Square.

NORTH-WEST
Birkenhead North Station SJ 298903. Opened in 1866 by the Hoylake Railway, which became the Wirral Railway, with links to Wallasey and New Brighton, 1888, and a branch to Seacombe in 1895. The station was rebuilt in the 1880s: single-storey, red-brick buildings, stone-framed windows and doorways, on north island platform wooden canopy on cast iron pillars with ornamental capitals and brackets.

Bidston Dock SJ 298910. The last addition to the docks, opened 1933, at inland end of Wallasey Pool. Between the dock and West Float is Poulton Road swing bridge, built by Francis Morton & Co. of Liverpool, 1926.

Bidston Station SJ 284908. Originally opened on Hoylake line, 1866. Island platform, wooden station buildings, brick and timber signal box. Bidston was also the junction for the GCR line from Hawarden, Flintshire, opened 1896: this part of the station was closed in 1968.

Bidston Hill lighthouse SJ 286899. At north end of Bidston Hill. Three-storey stone-built tower and keeper's house, built 1873 to replace earlier lighthouse.

Bidston windmill SJ 287894. Best surviving example in Wirral. Late 18C tower mill, replacing earlier post mill, brick-built, three storeys, wooden boat-shaped cap, wooden tail wheel operated by rope to turn cap, four common sails, cast iron cross on windshaft, wooden vertical main shaft, clasp-arm wallower wheel, great spur wheel driving two pairs of stones, drive to sack hoist and auxiliary machinery. Ceased working *c.* 1875. Restored 1894. In care of Wirral Borough Council.

WEST

Craven Street Electric Power Station SJ 314888. Between Craven Street and Bentinck Street, brick-built, two storeys, nine bays on Bentinck Street, pediment and date stone 'Electric Lighting Station 1902'. Nine-bay building in Craven Street with name 'Electricity Generating Station' on front. In use by MANWEB.

Oxton Road Brewery SJ 314883. Three and four-storey brick buildings of mid-19C on south-eastern side of the road, stone quoins, rusticated stone arches at entrances, malting towers with ventilators.

Williamson Art Gallery and Museum SJ 309881. In Slatey Road. Wirral Maritime Collection, including some 60 models of ships and dock installations made by Cammell Laird's, models of Mersey ferry boats, from late 19C paddle steamers, *Cheshire* and *Birkenhead* to motor vessels of 1960s, prints and water colours of ferry buildings and landing stages. There is also a collection of porcelain, including some from Liverpool potteries and of textiles from the local firm of Lee Fabrics, including furnishings for the *Queen Mary*. Behind the museum is the site of the former Spring Hill Water Works, now demolished.

Tranmere Pumping Station SJ 314875. In Borough Road, two-storeys, sandstone, classical style with ornamental cornice, date stone 'Tranmere Water Works 1861' on south front. The water works in Birkenhead were established by a private company in 1841 and taken over by the town's Improvement Commissioners in 1858. Water was pumped up from wells to tanks and reservoirs on the hills in Prenton, Tranmere and Flaybrick.

Prenton water tower SJ 309861. Waterworks tower at junction of Tower Road and Reservoir Road on 250 ft (76 m) hill, rectangular, stone-built with turret, covered iron tank on top.

SOUTH

Tranmere Tannery SJ 327878. Four-storey, brick-built works in Chester New Road with typical wooden shuttering on upper storeys, in use by British Leather Co. Marked on OS 6-inch map of 1882.

Tower Hill Waterworks, Tranmere SJ 318871. Square stone-built water tower, three storeys, pairs of semi-circular arched windows and arcading, iron water tank on top. Tank with pitched cover to west: inscription 'Erected 1882, W. A. Richardson, civil engineer, Wm Hamer & Sons, engineers'. Reservoir with sandstone walls.

Rock Ferry SJ 335868. Purchased in 1857 by private company, who built the half-mile (800 m) -long esplanade. Steam ferries ran to and from Liverpool about every half hour in 1860. The Royal Rock Hotel has been demolished, though some of the 'elegant' villas which were built in the area survive. There are the remains of a sandstone slipway, and an extended pier on iron pillars, now used for oil-dock repairs. The Tranmere Oil Dock is to the north on the site of the mouth of Tranmere Pool.

New Ferry SJ 339861. The buildings of the New Ferry Hotel are still occupied, but not as an hotel. The site of the pier can also be identified.

BOOTLE

A bathing place in early 19C, described by Baines in 1825 as 'a pleasant maritime village'. Developed as industrial town in later 19C mainly as a result of the northern extension of the line of Liverpool docks.

Three docks were opened in 1881: **Brocklebank Dock** SJ 333942, north of Canada Dock, with pump house of 1906, steam-powered until *c.* 1950. Inland in Millers Bridge are Brocklebank bonded warehouses, five storeys, brick-built, small windows, recessed loading openings; **Langton Dock** SJ 330946, with ornamental pump house with stone tower, originally steam-powered; **Alexandra Dock** SJ 330950. with three branches.

Hornby Dock SJ 328953. Opened 1884. Electrically driven hydraulic power station of 1920s.

Gladstone Dock SJ 3395. Last to be built before the recent Seaforth Container Dock, opened 1975. Graving dock with pump house 1913, main dock 1927, Nos. 1 and 2 branch docks 1930. Good examples of three-storey concrete transit sheds.

Harland & Wolff's SJ 336944. Former shipbuilding and engineering works, nine-aisle single-storey brick-built workshops, long semi-circular arched windows with iron frames, two-storey office block. Occupied by Mersey Docks & Harbour Co.

CLC goods station SJ 333953. North of Lister Road, linked by rail to Halewood–Aintree line. Closed but three-aisle, single-storey warehouse survives, red brick with yellow brick decoration.

In general the former railway links to the Bootle docks and the goods warehouses have gone.

Bootle Museum and Art Gallery. In Stanley Road, with collections including pottery and porcelain, models of ships and ships' engines.

CALDY
Birkenhead Joint Line. The track of the GWR/LNWR joint line from West Kirby to Parkgate, opened 1886, closed 1962, runs along the west side of the township. There are the side walls and abutments of a bridge at SJ 223849, with an embankment overlooking the golf course to the south.

There was some shipping from Caldy in 19C and a boat repair yard between Caldy and West Kirby.

CROSBY
Windmill SD 329005. Early 19C tower mill in Moor Lane, Great Crosby, brick-built, worked until 1960s. In later dates had steam engine and then oil engine. Converted to residence. Yates's map of Lancashire, 1787, shows post mill in Little Crosby, south-west of the Hall.

EASTHAM
Eastham locks SJ 370810. Entrance Locks from the river Mersey to the

Former ticket office, Eastham Ferry, 1979

Manchester Ship Canal, built 1887–92, using steam navvies. Three locks side by side: large 600 ft by 80 ft (183 m by 24 m), intermediate 350 ft by 50 ft (106 m by 15 m), small 150 ft by 30 ft (46 m by 9 m). Sluice machinery by Ransome & Rapier of Ipswich. Engine house, boiler house and accumulator tower for hydraulic power system. Eastham Dock to west with a separate lock entrance from the river is a modern structure, built for oil traffic, approx. 300 yd (274 m) square.

Eastham ferry SJ 365818. One of the old Mersey ferries, certainly operating in the 16C, always in private hands. Steam boats from 1816, meeting coaches to Chester, Holyhead and Shrewsbury. Service continued until 1929. Single-storey sandstone ticket office, now converted to toilets, with blocked bow windows overlooking site of landing stage, date stone 'Eastham Ferries 1856.' Eastham Ferry Hotel, three storeys, Georgian. Stables to north near present car park. Popular recreation area in 19C, now Country Park with information centre.

FORMBY

Two stations on LYR Liverpool–Southport line, opened 1850: **Formby Station** SD 291069, early 20C brick-built booking office, timber roof to booking hall and office structure, timber and glass covered staircase to platform with earlier single-storey brick buildings. **Freshfield Station** SD 291083, level crossing, brick-and-timber signal box, two-storey brick-built crossing keeper's house, brick-and-timber station buildings.

GAYTON

Gayton windmill SJ 277812. At junction of Mill Lane with A540. Circular sandstone tower, derelict and partly covered with creepers. Built before 1760, worked until late 1870s. Mitford Abraham in early 20C called it the '. . .

oldest tower mill in Wirral'.

Tollhouse SJ 282809. At junction of Chester Road and Gayton Lane. Single-storey, brick-built, rendered, hipped slate roof, ruinous. There is a Cheshire County Council cast iron milestone of 1896 100 yd (91 m) south.

Gayton Lane bridge SJ 268803. On disused Birkenhead Railway line from Hooton to Parkgate. Single arch, dark-blue brick.

There was formerly a ferry across the Dee from Gayton.

HAYDOCK

Formerly an important coal-mining community, with collieries operated in late 19C by Richard Evan & Co.: eight at the peak in 1890. None now working.

Haydock Colliery SJ 557967. After closure became site of NCB workshops. Had a single-cylinder beam engine, originally used for pumping, then until 1954 for driving workshop machinery, preserved in care of Merseyside County Museums.

Lyme Colliery SJ 563961. Spoil heaps only. Had two steam winding engines which worked until early 1960s.

New Boston Colliery SJ 568972. Three shafts, two beam engines in late 19C. Wooden head gear. Pit-head buildings now occupied by NCB Area Training Centre.

Wood Colliery SJ 572967. Had three steam winding engines, including a twin-cylinder horizontal by Robert Dalglish & Co. of St Helens Foundry, 1891, working in 1968. Site now cleared.

Sankey Canal runs along the southern boundary, with traces of former tramroads from collieries. Clipsley Tramroad ran along line of Wigan Lane from SJ 547969 to the canal near Haydock lock. There was a tramroad along the line of Cooper Lane from the canal near Boardmans Brow to pits at Haydock Green, SJ 560967.

There are remains of LNWR branch line from Earlestown to Haydock Colliery and Broad Oak, with branches to Old Boston, New Boston and Wood Collieries. The St Helens & Wigan Junction Railway line from Lowton to St Helens, opened 1895, now closed, crosses the township north-east to south-west, with line visible at **Pule Road** SJ 561972 leading to a tunnel.

HESWALL

Heswall Hill quarries SJ 260820. An important source of sandstone for buildings in the area in 19C.

Birkenhead Railway (GWR/LNWR joint), now part of Wirral Country Park, runs along west side of township. Typical single-arch, blue-brick bridge on Delavon Road/Park Lane, SJ 258816. The site of Heswall Station, SJ 265809, is built on: cutting to south. There is a row of railway cottages at the junction

of Davenport Road and Station Road.

Heswall Hills Station SJ 286819. On GCR line from Hawarden to Bidston, opened 1896. Raised timber platforms on embankment, timber signal box at west. Four-bay yellow-brick booking office at bottom of approach from B5137.

HOYLAKE

Boat-building and fishing village at the north end of the Wirral peninsula, which became a popular seaside resort in late 19C and a populous residential area in 20C.

Hoylake Station SJ 217888. Modernistic 'London Transport'-style station buildings of 1938 on Wirral Railway, built when line was electrified. Concrete and brick, circular tiled booking hall with glass domed roof. Hoylake was the terminus until 1879, when the line was extended to West Kirby. Man-

Upper lighthouse, Hoylake, from south, 1979

or Road Station, SJ 223893, and Meols Station, SJ 234898, have buildings in similar style.

Upper Lighthouse SJ 215892. Valentia Road. Octagonal brick tower with recessed patterning on walls, balcony with iron railings, octagonal iron lantern, ball and weather vane on top. Occupied as residence.

HUYTON WITH ROBY

Roby Embankment. Two-mile (3·2 km)-long embankment on Liverpool & Manchester Railway, built with stone excavated from Olive Mount cutting, between Broad Green, SJ 408903, and Roby, SJ 432907. Some of the original narrow bridges over crossing roads survive. There are stone blocks from the original L&MR track built into the wall near the entrance to **Huyton Station**, SJ 440907.

LIVERPOOL

The great port of the North West, which played a major role in the economic development of the whole region. The outstanding feature is the long line of docks and associated structures stretching from Herculaneum Dock in the south to the new Seaforth Container Dock of 1975 in the north. The first or Old Dock was built by Thomas Steers at the mouth of the Pool (on the line of Paradise Street) and opened in 1715. By the end of the 18C there were seven docks south of the present pierhead. The big expansion took place in the 19C, with growing trade leading to demand for more dock space, wharfage and warehousing. Larger ships and, later, steamships, increased the demand and much greater emphasis was placed on security. John Rennie recommended a doubling of the dock area in 1811, but the central figure in the mid-19C expansion was Jesse Hartley, dock engineer 1824–60, who left a line from Brunswick Dock in the south to Canada Dock on the Liverpool–Bootle boundary in the north. To him more than anyone else is due the separation of the dock area from the city, the building of the great dock wall, the gates with their castle-style features, the dock railway along the city side of the wall, of which there are still some traces. Liverpool also has a major place in railway history, following the opening of the Liverpool & Manchester Railway in 1830.

CENTRAL AREA

Lime Street Station SJ 352905. The only surviving main-line terminus in Liverpool. Opened 1836 by the Liverpool & Manchester Railway, to replace the former terminus at Crown Street. Rebuilt 1846–51, 1867–79. Train sheds of 200 ft (61 m) span built on curve. Remains of office block of second station on Nelson Street side, five storeys, classical stone front on two lower storeys, yellow brick above. On Lime Street front, former North Western Hotel by Alfred Waterhouse, 1868–71, now used as offices and station buffet.

Mersey tunnel entrance SJ 347907. Much-altered entrance to 2⅛-mile (3·4 km)-long road tunnel, opened 1934. There are three ventilation stations with towers in modernistic style on the Liverpool side: George's Dock, SJ 338902, south of the Dock Offices; North John Street, SJ 342903; New Quay, SJ 339905, with twin towers. See also *Birkenhead*.

Central Station SJ 350902. The CLC terminus, opened 1874, has been demolished. It also served, at a lower level, the Mersey Railway, opened 1886, and is still a station on the Merseyrail system.

Merseyside County Museum SJ 350908. William Brown Street. Important industrial collections, including material from Liverpool potteries and porcelain works; tools from file and watch-part and tool-making trades in Prescot and Liverpool, including material from Lancashire Watch Co. (see

Prescot), reconstruction of Prescot watchmaker's workshop; transport items, including Liverpool & Manchester Railway locomotive *Lion*, motor coach of 1892 from Liverpool Overhead Railway, traction engines, steam waggons, steam road roller, first Ford Anglia made at Halewood Works, 1963.

Exchange Station SJ 342907. The Lancashire & Yorkshire Railway's terminus, built for Liverpool Crosby & Southport Railway, opened 1850, and the East Lancashire Railway/LYR line via Ormskirk to Preston. Closed 1977, demolished 1978–79. Replaced by underground station on Merseyrail system. The Exchange Hotel survives unoccupied, with frontage on Tithebarn Street.

Princes landing stage SJ 338902. The floating stage of 1874 has been replaced by a concrete structure within the last four years. In the area are three striking examples of Liverpool's commercial buildings, the Royal Liver Building, 1908–10, the Cunard Building, 1913, and the offices of the Mersey Docks & Harbour Co., 1907, on site of former George's Dock, opened 1771, filled in by 1875.

South Docks Now largely disused and the subject of much planning discussion.

Canning Place SJ 344900, marks the site of the Old Dock of 1715. Filled in early 19C and Customs House, itself destroyed in 1941, built on site.

Canning Dock SJ 341899. There are still the half-tide dock which gave access to the Albert Dock and two graving docks built by Henry Berry in 18C and rebuilt *c*. 1815, stepped sides, rounded ends, granite huts for gatesmen.

Salthouse Dock SJ 343898. Built by Thomas Steers 1734–53 mainly for the growing Cheshire salt trade, with Blackburn's salt works nearby. Survives in reconstructed form of 1845.

Albert Dock. West of Salthouse Dock and perhaps the outstanding monument to Jesse Hartley's work. Built 1844–45, entrance from Canning half-tide dock, first enclosed dock, with high-security warehouses all round, five storeys, brick-built, supported at front on colonnade of cast iron columns, with wider spaces bridged by elliptical arches, loading openings over arches, small windows with iron grilles, internal structure of cast iron pillars and beams and brick arches, wrought iron roof trusses, roof coverings of iron slates. Hydraulic power system by Hydraulic Engineeering Co. of Chester. At north-east corner is Philip Hardwick's Dock Office with internal cast iron structure, portico entirely of iron, including columns, architrave, cornice and frieze. The conservation of this important site is now a major problem.

Duke's Dock. Entrance channel south of Albert Dock is the only trace of a dock built by the Duke of Bridgewater for traffic coming down his canal, opened 1773, with fine six-storey terminal warehouse, now demolished.

King's and Queen's Docks SJ 343892. South of Duke's Dock, opened in 1788 and 1796 respectively but with long side parallel to river: their present form with two branches at right-angles to the river is the result of alteration in early 20C. Queen's Dock has good examples of a stone gatehouse and a castellated, stone-built hydraulic accumulator tower.

Wapping Dock, which later became part of King's Dock, opened 1858, still has warehouses of 1857 built by Jesse Hartley, five storeys, brick-built, internal structure of cast iron pillars and beams; conical granite gatekeeper's lodge, castellated hydraulic tower. To east is site of former Wapping Goods Station, now demolished, connected by 2,280 yd (2,085 m)-long tunnel to Liverpool & Manchester Railway at Edge Hill.

Brunswick Dock SJ 347885. First

dock built by Jesse Hartley, opened 1832, on site of former tide-mill reservoirs. There is an hydraulic power engine house with an ornamental accumulator tower between Brunswick Dock and Toxteth Dock to south. Near by was the CLC Brunswick Goods Station, demolished.

Herculaneum Dock SJ 357873. Opened 1864. Near by are the remains of the Dingle tunnel which carried the Liverpool Overhead Railway to Dingle Station. The Overhead Railway, built as an electric line 1889–93 on a steel viaduct supported by steel columns, ran all along the line of docks from Herculaneum to Seaforth. It was demolished 1957–61, still well patronised, owing to cost of renewing the structure.

Jamaica Street SJ 348892. Inland from the South Docks in Jamaica Street and the adjoining streets is one of the best areas in Liverpool for studying warehouse development, from the early type with a narrow three-bay frontage and single loading slot on the street front to the fortress-like buildings of the mid- and late 19C with internal cast iron structures, small barred windows, often blue or yellow-brick decoration to relieve the forbidding impression of the façades. There are good examples of the earlier type in Bridgewater Street and Blundell Street, of the later type in Jamaica Street, Bridgewater Street (Metcalfe's Warehouse, 1874), Blundell Street. Also in Jamaica Street and Stanhope Street is the fine **Higson's Brewery**, completed 1902, red brick and terracotta, five storeys, ornamental tower, worked on old system of pumping the wort to the top of the tower and going through the processes downward floor by floor.

SOUTH

Garston Docks SJ 396840. A completely separate enterprise. The Old Dock was built by the St Helens & Runcorn Gap Railway at the end of an extension of its line from Widnes, opened 1853, mainly for coal trade. It is still in use, 1,100 ft by 350 ft (355 m by 107 m), masonry side walls, two-storey late 19C office, brick-built hydraulic power engine house and accumulator tower. There is a lock through to the North Dock, opened 1876. To south is Stallbridge Dock of 1909, with coal staithes and chute on north, line of former quayside railways. Adjoining is Garston Tannery with early 20C buildings. To south-east is the dock community with late 19C/early 20C housing and some streets named after Cunard liners. The docks are now operated by British Transport Docks Board

Bryant & May's match factory SJ 411841. Built 1919 by Maguire Patterson & Palmer, early example of functional, concrete structure.

There are a number of good examples of CLC cottage-style station buildings along the line into Liverpool Central: **Hunts Cross** SJ 431851, **Cressington Park** SJ 394850, **Mersey Road & Aigburth** SJ 384856, **St Michaels** SJ 367869, all built in cuttings.

North Docks. These continue to be used actively for shipping, with some new development taking place. The dock wall survives for much of the length along Waterloo Road and Regent Road, with granite gatehouses, often castellated, with gates running into slots.

Prince's Dock SJ 337908. North of Pierhead, opened 1821, following Rennie's dock report of 1811, 500 yd (457 m) long, converted to half-tide dock 1867. Octagonal brick-built hydraulic accumulator tower, with battlements and clock, on north entrance pier. West of the dock are remains of **Riverside Station**, opened by LNWR 1895, closed 1974, connected by Waterloo tunnel to Edge Hill.

Waterloo Dock SJ 336912. Opened 1834, designed by Jesse Hartley, originally single dock at right-angles to river, later east and west docks parallel to river. Corn warehouse of 1867 by G. F. Lister, five storeys, brick-built, front colonnade of square stone pillars supporting stone arches, pairs of small semi-circular arched windows, internal cross-walls dividing warehouse into six sections. The LNWR Waterloo Dock goods station has been demolished but the entrance to the 3,600 yd (3,290 m)-long Victoria tunnel to Edge Hill survives east of Great Howard Street.

Victoria Bell Tower SJ 333921. At entrance to Salisbury and Collingwood Docks, opened 1848. Granite, hexagonal, castellated, six-faced clock. This was also the entrance to Nelson and Bramley-Moore Docks to north, also opened in 1848, and to Stanley Dock.

Stanley Dock SJ 337921. The only dock east of Regent Road, linked by a branch and four locks with the Leeds & Liverpool Canal near Vauxhall Road. Fine warehouses by Jesse Hartley *c.* 1857, brick-built, five storeys on colonnade of cast iron pillars (18 pillars on north warehouse), small barred windows. In front of Hartley's warehouse on the south side is the imposing 13-storey brick-built tobacco warehouse of 1900. Good examples of granite gateposts and castellated hydraulic accumulator tower.

Huskisson Dock SJ 334933. Opened 1852 and used by larger steamers of period: eventually had three branches.

Canada Dock SJ 334939. Opened 1859 as timber dock, with yard on east where later branch docks were built. Gates and bridges moved by hydraulic machinery installed by Sir William Armstrong: accumulator towers along dock. The LNWR railway link from Edge Hill survives with a tunnel east of Bankhall Lane, station buildings and platforms on Derby Road. The other railway connections to the North Docks are closed and the viaducts and good stations largely demolished.

Inland from the North Docks between Waterloo Road and Great Howard Street is an area of warehouses and factories associated with the docks which would justify a major industrial archaeology project on their own. Particularly notable are: a warehouse at the corner of Waterloo Road and Gorton Street, SJ 337912; **Bibby's Flour Mills** SJ 337913, with mid-19C six-storey

Warehouse, Stanley Dock, Liverpool, from south, 1979

Olive Mount cutting, Liverpool & Manchester Railway, Liverpool, looking west, 1979

warehouses in Dundee Street and Barton Street, nine-storey modernistic-style building of 1933, two-storey brick-built Power House and eight-storey office block in Great Howard Street; **Bonded Tea Warehouse** SJ 338918, six-storeys, 12 bays on Great Howard Street, five storeys, 26 bays with ten loading slots between Dublin Street and Dickson Street, iron plates on corners to prevent damage by carts. East of Great Howard Street are the sugar refineries of **Fairrie's** SJ 343918, started 1847, now part of Tate & Lyle, and **Tate & Lyle** SJ 340915, started 1872, much extended.

Bankhall Quay SJ 343938. Four-storey brick-built warehouse of 1874 with shipping entrance from the canal. The Liverpool end of Leeds & Liverpool Canal was opened to Wigan in 1777 and is now filled in south of Chisenhall Street, SJ 341915. The terminus was in Leeds Street, just north of Exchange Station.

NORTH

Hartley's jam factory SJ 368964. In Long Lane south of Aintree race course, now mostly demolished. Surviving is the late 19C associated industrial village with rows of brick-built cottages in terraces of four, six, seven and eight, some with bays, extensions and yards at rear, arranged round a square.

EAST

Crown Street Station SJ 364898. Site only of original terminus of Liverpool & Manchester Railway (opened 1830) before building of Lime Street Station, tunnel towards Edge Hill, brick ventilation chimney for Wapping tunnel.

Chatsworth Street cutting. East of Crown Street, surveyed in detail and partly excavated by Merseyside County Museums and North Western Society for Industrial Archaeology and History. Remains of three tunnels, one to Crown Street (second one built in 1840s), one to Wapping goods station (see Wapping Dock), both worked by ropes and stationary engines until 1896, one to storage area. In the cutting itself are the remains of the much illustrated Moorish arch, which was a connection between two of the stationary-engine houses, including the inside wall of one engine house. Boiler houses, locomotive sheds and stores were cut into the sides of the cutting. There is now a plan for a permanent conservation area, with visitors' centre and rail trail. For a full account of the work on the site see Paul Rees, 'Chatsworth Street cutting', *Industrial Archaeology Review*, vol. 2, No. 1, autumn 1977, pp. 38–51.

Edge Hill Station SJ 372899. East of Chatsworth Street cutting, first opened 1830, rebuilt 1836 when the line was extended to Lime Street. Surviving structures include 1836 offices, two storeys, stone-built, in classical style, being restored, and stationary-engine house for hauling trains up the Victoria (Waterloo) tunnel from Waterloo Dock. **Edge Hill tunnel** to Lime Street, 2,025 yd (1,851 m) long, was operated by rope and stationary engines until 1870. When locomotives were used a ventilation shaft with a mechanical fan was added to remove the smoke. From 1881 sections of the tunnel were opened up into cuttings, which were later widened.

Olive Mount cutting SJ 394902. Famous as an impressive scene in early engravings of the line, 70 ft (21 m) deep into rock, formerly only 20 ft (6 m) wide at top, widened 1871.

NEWTON LE WILLOWS

The development of Newton is largely connected with the building of the Liverpool & Manchester Railway and the related engineering works.

Sankey viaduct SJ 569948. 1830, carrying Liverpool & Manchester Railway over Sankey brook and Sankey Canal, nine arches each 50 ft (15·2 m) span, brick with stone facings, frequent subject of early illustrations.

Viaduct Foundry. (Earlestown railway works) SJ 571949. At east end of Sankey viaduct, founded 1833 by Jones Turner & Evans for manufacture of railway wagons. Leased 1853 and bought 1860 by LNWR, rebuilt mainly by J. W. Emmett from 1863. Now industrial estate.

Earlestown. North of Earl Street is the railway community developed in connection with the works and named after Hardman Earle, Chief Mechanical Engineer of the LNWR. Houses now being demolished but long rows survive in Earle Street (opposite the works), 26 houses with central pediment, Lawrence Street, Chandos Street, Rathbone Street, Booth Street, Regent Street (rows of 46 and 49 cottages).

Earlestown Station SJ 578951. At junction of Liverpool & Manchester Railway with Warrington & Newton Railway, later Grand Junction Railway. Until 1842 trains from Birmingham divided here for Manchester and Liverpool. Triangular plan with Tudor-style stone-built waiting room with Gothic fireplace, iron bridge with beams made by Dallam Forge, Warrington. Remains of Haydock Colliery railway whose line crossed the Liverpool & Manchester tracks and passed between the two loops to join the Warrington–Newton tracks: used until 1960s, line visible at Heather Brae to north.

Vulcan Foundry SJ 585940. Railway engineering works founded 1832 by Robert Stephenson and Charles Tayleur by the side of the Warrington & Newton Railway, opened 1831. Made locomotive *Tayleur* for North Union Railway and three locomotives for Warrington & Newton Railway 1833. Later developed large export trade in locomotives to Europe, Africa, South America, India and the Far East. Taken over by English Electric Co.: manufacture of diesel-electric locomotives. Mainly modern buildings.

Vulcan Village. To south of foundry, with four rows of two-storey cottages parallel to works (London Row,

Chester Row, Sheffield Row, Liverpool Row), two rows running north–south to form sides of triangle (Manchester Row, Derby Row). School with Gothic features, Vulcan Inn converted to house, institute of 1907 adjoining works. Total of 114 cottages with two or three different styles. Vulcan Halt on the railway north of the works was closed in 1965.

Newton le Willows Station SJ 593953. Approached by long embankment and four-arch brick-and-stone viaduct over Newton brook and A49. Brick station building with stone details, waiting rooms on first floor, booking office below.

Newton Corn Mill. On Newton brook just south of railway viaduct. Remains of brick walls, bedstone, line of mill race with blocked openings in walls at each end of mill. Marked on OS 6-inch map of 1844.

Parkside Colliery SJ 602947. Still working, modernised, concrete pithead buildings, covered head gear, conical washery, railway sidings.

Parkside Station SJ 608956. On Liverpool & Manchester Railway, closed 1878, but with memorial commemorating place where Huskisson was killed by the *Rocket* at the opening of the line in 1830. At Parkside is junction with Wigan Branch Railway, opened 1832.

PRESCOT
Famous from 17C for tool and file-making and especially for manufacture of watch parts and tools. Small workshop trade, often organised on putting-out basis, supplying watch parts to London as well as locally and in 19C overseas, including United States. Highly specialised, with individual workshops concentrated on making springs, wheels, pinions, verges, hands, cases, watch files or broaches for reaming out holes in watch parts. Declined with development of American and Swiss Industries in later 19C. A number of former workshops survive in the central area, and Knowsley Metropolitan Borough have a proposal for a museum in one in High Street. There are collections of tools and reconstructed workshops in Merseyside County Museum, Liverpool.

Former watch-part making workshop, 20 Grosvenor Road, Prescot, 1979

Huckle's factory SJ 468928. Small watch-part factory at junction of Eccleston Street and Ackers Street, last operated by Mr Huckle, with range of treadle-operated machine tools for turning, wheel cutting, drilling, shaping and boring. Now used as clothing shop. Nearby in Eccleston Street is two-storey brick-built watch workshop, two large windows with small panes in upper storey. Built *c.* 1890. There are a number of surviving **workshops** in St Helens Road area, north of town centre: two-storey workshops behind houses on east side of St Helens Road between Rowson Street and Cross Street; 1–5 Cross Street, three-storey workshop attached to and at rear of houses; 20 Grosvenor Road, separate workshop at rear of house, two windows and two doors at first-floor level.

Lancashire Watch Co. SJ 472928. Watch factory built in 1888 in an effort to bring a number of small firms together to meet foreign competition, worked until 1910. Three-storeys, brick-built, with impressive long windows on each floor on Albany Street front, rather like an elongated version of the old watch workshops. Some machinery in Merseyside County Museum. Occupied by engineers and trade centre. There is a very good illustrated booklet, *The Lancashire Watch Company, 1889–1910*, published by Ken Roberts Publishing Co., Fitzwilliam, N.H., USA with an introductory article by Alan Smith.

Prescot Station SJ 470922. On LNWR Huyton–St Helens line opened 1871. Single-storey brick-built station buildings with hipped slate roof, two-storey stationmaster's house to west.

RAINFORD

Rainford Pottery SJ 493997. In Mill Lane, closed *c.* 1964. Tramway southwestward across Rainford brook to clay pit at SJ 486986, approx. 1,200 yd (1,097 m). Near clay pit is clay-pipe works excavated by Liverpool University Institute of Extension Studies and Merseyside Archaeological Society 1978–79, producing kiln material and some 10,000 pipe fragments. See *CBA Group 5 Archaeological News Letter*, No. 3, January 1979.

RAINHILL

For ever associated with the Rainhill trials on the Liverpool & Manchester Railway, held in October 1829 on track between Rainhill and Lea Green, won by Stephenson's *Rocket*. A cylinder from one of the other competing locomotives, Braithwaite & Ericsson's *Novelty*, is preserved in Merseyside County Museum, Liverpool, after driving machinery in iron foundry near Rainhill Station.

Rainhill Station SJ 492914. LNWR station buildings of 1860s west of earlier station site: single-storey, brick-built, hipped slate roof, platform canopy on cast iron pillars with ornamental brackets. At west end is single-arch, skew sandstone bridge by George Findlay, 1829, widened 1963, carrying Prescot–Warrington road over railway. Milestone with distances in Roman numerals to Warrington, Prescot and Liverpool.

Stoney Lane bridge SJ 485913. Possible site of stationary steam engine built for Whiston incline, but never used.

ST HELENS

The 'glass town' of the North West: a new 19C industrial town created out of the old townships of Windle, Sutton, Eccleston and Parr by the growth of coal mining, copper smelting, chemical and glass industries. The industrial growth is related to the development of transport facilities between the coalfield, the river Mersey, Liverpool and the Cheshire saltfield through turnpike roads, the Sankey Canal and the Weaver Navigation, and the St Helens & Runcorn Gap Railway. The history of

Spinning crown glass, Pilkington's works, St Helens, early twentieth century.
Courtesy Pilkington Bros Ltd

the town is fully described in T. C. Barker and J. R. Harris, *St Helens: a Merseyside Town in the Industrial Revolution, 1750–1900*, 1954.

CENTRAL AREA

St Helens Crown Glass Works SJ 511948. Started 1826 by partnership including James Brownlow, colliery owner, Peter Greenall, brewer, and William Pilkington for manufacture of window glass by the crown process. There were a number of such works in St Helens before the introduction of the drawn sheet process in the early 20C. Part of one of the cones which contained the glass furnaces survives together with part of the early buildings, and four-storey, brick-built warehouse of 1905. In use by Pilkington's for sheet glass production.

Sherdley Glass Bottle Works SJ 515947. Started by Carrington Shaw & Co., 1866, using hand blowing, mechanised 1897, using moulds and compressed air for blowing. Several works were started in the same period.

Beecham's Works SJ 508954. Building of 1886 with clock tower. Thomas Beecham, born 1820, started selling herbal pills in Wigan 1847, moved to St Helens 1858–59 and sold pills, using the slogan 'Worth a guinea a box'. Wholesale trade in many parts of the country by 1860s. Big expansion in 1880s, when the factory was built: producing a million pills a day in 1890. Thomas's grandson was the famous conductor, Sir Thomas Beecham.

St Helens Station SJ 516953. Built in 1871 to replace the earlier stations in Raven Street and Warrington Old Road: now recent buildings. The St Helens & Runcorn Gap Railway was promoted to provide an outlet for coal traffic with a new dock at Widnes, opened 1833, amalgamated with Sankey Canal Co. 1845, absorbed by LNWR 1864. The extension to Rainford, opened 1858, is closed and the line is being converted to a linear park. Branches were built to Eccleston 1859 with a tunnel at Greenbank, with a branch to

Ravenhead, and from Worsley Brow, Sutton, to Broad Oak and Blackbrook 1880.

Central Station SJ 512957. Former terminus of St Helens & Wigan Junction Railway (taken over by Great Central 1906), opened from Newton to St Helens 1895 with Sir Joseph Beecham as one of the promoters. Closed to passengers 1952, goods 1965. Magistrates courts and car park on site. Track traceable at north-east of town towards Haydock.

St Helens Museum and Art Gallery. In Gamble Institute, contains exhibits relating to coal, glass and clay-pipe industries, including locally made glass bottles, local earthenware, collection of pottery sherds from Gerards Bridge Pottery.

NORTH

Pocket Nook locks SJ 520962. Double lock at junction of Gerards Bridge and Ravenhead branches of Sankey Canal. The canal was promoted by a number of colliery owners and Liverpool merchants and built between 1755 and 1759, with Henry Berry, of Liverpool Docks fame, as engineer. There were eventually three branches: the third was to Blackbrook. Near the locks is the site of the former Double Locks Alkkali Works, one of a number established in St Helens in 19C for making soda from salt by the Leblanc process. Started by Muspratt & Gamble 1828, taken over by United Alkali 1890. There was formerly a plate-glass works in the area started by United Plate Glass Co., 1837.

Cowley Glass Works SJ 510966. Specially built by Pilkington's for manufacture of plate glass 1874–76.

EAST

Broad Oak locks SJ 536961. Double locks at the junction of the main line of the Sankey Canal with the Black Brook branch. The canal was abandoned in 1955 and is partially empty or filled in beyond this point.

Black Brook Quays The basin at the Lower Quay, SJ 535967, has been cleared and the area is being conserved. Nearby in Blackbrook Road is the Ship Inn. There are traces of the former tramroad running north-east from the basin to Pewfall Colliery in Haydock. At Blackbrook Upper Quay, SJ 533970, is the deserted basin with two small turning areas and wharves. East of the basin was the site of the former **Stanley Copper Works**, built by the Pattens of Warrington in 18C and taken over by Thomas Williams, the owner of the mines on Parys Mountain, Anglesey, from where the copper ore was transported via the port of Amlwch. Williams built another copper works at Ravenhead. There were tramroads to Laffack Colliery and to Blackley Hurst Colliery in Billinge and Winstanley, from which stone blocks survive at Carr Hill Reservoir.

Broad Oak Colliery SJ 537957. Spoil heaps and traces of workings north of Broad Oak Road of colliery which was in operation by 1832. Traces of branch railway with tunnel under Broad Oak Road to former wharf on Sankey Canal.

Ashton Green Colliery SJ 537948. Opened by 1828. Site landscaped. Line of tramroad to Sankey Canal at Haydock Wood visible near Derbyshire Hill Road.

Sutton Copper Rolling Mills SJ 536940. At Moss Nook, founded 1860. Corrugated and brick sheds with yellow-brick decoration, wall incorporating copper slag. Coppersmith's Arms and Roller Mill Lane near by.

SOUTH

Bold Colliery SJ 548935. One of two collieries in area still working. Opened in 1870s. Modernised: three concrete sets of head gear, brick and concrete pit-head buildings, power station adjoining.

St Helens Junction Station SJ 536933. On Liverpool & Manchester Railway: to west is loop to St Helens &

Runcorn Gap line. LNWR buildings of 1860s: brick-built single-storey platform buildings, stationmaster's house. Junction Inn and railway cottages near by. St Helens & Runcorn Gap Railway crosses L&MR line at Sutton, where there was at one time an incline worked by a stationary engine.

Sutton Oak Glass Works SJ 530937. Plate-glass works started by Manchester & Liverpool Plate Glass Co. 1837 with casting hall, three furnaces and 14 anealing kilns. Failed 1846: restarted by London & Manchester Plate Glass Co. 1,500 workers in 1860s. Last casting 1903. Now occupied by British Sidac.

Sutton Manor Colliery SJ 518908. Still working. The two shafts were sunk 1906-10 to a depth of over 2,300 ft (700 m). Two sets of lattice-steel girder head gear. The colliery still has a number of steam engines: two cross-compound winding engines, one by Fraser & Chalmers of Erith, 1907, one by Yates & Thom of Blackburn, 1914; two compound air compressors by Walker Bros of Wigan, 1912 (on stand-by) and 1943; one compound engine for driving 25 ft (7·6 m) diameter ventilation fan by Walker Bros, 1910.

Lea Green Colliery SJ 505921. Started 1877, closed 1964, now industrial estate on site. Had Manning Wardle 0-6-0 tank locomotive *Bellerophon*, 1974, which is now on the Keighley & Worth Valley Railway in Yorkshire.

WEST

Ravenhead Glass Works (Pilkington's) SJ 502945. Glass manufacture in St Helens started at Thatto Heath, west of Ravenhead, with one works established by John Leaf of Warrington, 1696, the other by John Heuzey, partner in a Prescot glass works, in 1721.

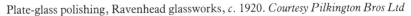

Plate-glass polishing, Ravenhead glassworks, c. 1920. *Courtesy Pilkington Bros Ltd*

The big step forward came with the introduction of plate-glass casting from France by the British Plate Glass Co. at Ravenhead 1773-76, achieving success from the time Robert Sherburne became manager in 1792. The works was taken over by Pilkington's in the late 19C. Unfortunately the remains of the old casting hall were destroyed by fire, but there are still the old Georgian manager's house and the stables. **Pilkington's Glass Museum**, open to the public, is easily the best place to study the history of the industry, showing the development of glass technology from the simple furnaces of the Kent and Sussex Weald to the modern float process. Outside the works is **Factory Row**, 26 two-storey brick-built cottages with date stone 1854. There was also a factory school.

Ravenhead Glass-bottle Works (United Glass) SJ 504944. Started by Nuttall & Co., 1840, joined with Carrington Shaw & Co. of Sherdley to form United Glass in 1913. Remains of furnace cone of 1890s.

Ravenhead road bridge SJ 509947. Railway bridge on Ravenhead branch of St Helens & Runcorn Gap Railway, with cast iron beams by Robert Daglish of St Helens Foundry. 1851. There is another one in Worsley Brow, Sutton.

Phoenix Colliery SJ 501941. Near Ravenhead Glass Works. Steel head gear on concrete foundations, brick winding house. Started by John MacKay in 1770s: merged with Pilkington's St Helens Colliery in 1876.

Royal Colliery SJ 495946. Octagonal brick shaft survives in French Street. Started by Brownlow's *c.* 1830, closed in late 19C.

SOUTHPORT

A 'new' seaside town developed as a resort with carefully planned layout in late 18C and 19C.

Chapel Street Station SD 338172. Opened as terminus of the Liverpool Crosby & Southport Railway, 1851: joined by LYR line from Wigan 1855. In use: multi-aisled train shed on cast iron pillars, recent buildings. Near by in LYR engine shed of 1891 in Derby Road is **Steamport Transport Museum**, with locomotive and road transport exhibits.

Central Station SD 343171. Opened 1882 as terminus of West Lancashire Railway's line from Preston. Two-storey frontage in brick and stone on Derby Road. Closed to passengers 1901, used for goods until 1960s.

Lord Street Station SD 331170. Opened 1884 as terminus of CLC line from Aintree. Closed 1952 and became bus station. Brick and sandstone offices, central porch, clock tower, train shed with ironwork by Handyside's of Derby (cf. Central Station, Manchester). The track has now been converted to a road between Central Station and Woodvale, north of Formby: line is visible to east where it crosses A565 at SD 312107

Ainsdale Station SD 311122. On LYR line from Liverpool: unusual black and white timber single-storey buildings, level crossing and signal box.

Botanic Gardens Museum, Churchtown SD 367187. Exhibits relating to weaving, car manufacture and shrimping industy.

STORETON

For Storeton quarries see *Bebington*.

Lever Causeway. Private road built by Lord Leverhulme, 1912-14. Runs over 3 miles (4·8 Km) from Storeton boundary, SJ 315856, to point between Clatterbridge and Thornton Hough, SJ 312819.

Facing Storeton quarry tramroad, north of Rest Hill Road, Storeton, 1979

THORNTON HOUGH

Thornton Hough estate village SJ 305810. Model village built by Joseph Hirst, textile manufacturer, and, after 1891, by first Viscount Leverhulme, using the architects who worked on Port Sunlight. Mixture of styles and materials: brick, stone and timber framing. Willshaw Terrace, 1870: row of six cottages and shop, Gothic details, castle-type tower. All Saints Church, 1867. St George's Congregational Church, 1906-07, in Norman style.

THURSTASTON

Thurstaston Station SJ 238835. On Birkenhead Railway's (GWR/LNWR joint) Parkgate–West Kirby line, opened 1886. Closed to passengers 1954, goods 1962. Two platforms, blue-brick side walls, single-arch blue-brick bridge. Now site of Visitors' Centre for Wirral Country Park, opened 1973: display includes model of 1690 Parkgate-Dublin packet boat. Car park and camping ground in former goods yard, which carried heavy traffic in its later years. The line has become a public footpath for most of its length.

Dawpool. Some shipping activity: Swift sailed from here to Ireland in 1707. Remains of jetty between Thurstaston and Caldy: Shore Cottages, SJ 236835, built for customs officers. In the early 1820s a scheme was promoted, and surveyed, for a ship canal from Dawpool across Wirral and along south side of Mersey via Frodsham, Lymm and Altrincham to Manchester. In 1827 there was a proposal for a canal link to Wallasey Pool which was stopped by Liverpool Corporation.

WALLASEY

An interesting mixture of dockland in the south (Poulton and Seacombe), Victorian and 20C residential areas in the north, with a touch of the seaside resort at New Brighton.

SOUTH

The Docks. Wallasey Dock SJ 325899, at the Mersey end, north of

Morpeth Docks. Opened 1877, entrance from East Float, single-storey brick-built transit sheds each side. Counterweight, hydraulic lift bridge in Tower Road at west end. Immediately north of the bridge is the central hydraulic power station for Birkenhead Docks, 1863, by J. B. Hartley, castellated engine house and accumulator tower. At east end is late 19C pumping station, with engine house, boiler house and chimney. **Alfred Dock** SJ 323902, north of Wallasey Dock. Opened 1866, lock entrances from East Float and river Mersey. Four-aisle single-storey brick-built transit sheds on south. Two road bridges at west end: swing bridge by Frances Morton & Co. of Liverpool, 1928, counterweight lift bridge of same type as that at Wallasey Dock. **West and East Float** Along north side are lines of single-storey brick-built transit sheds in rows of two or three, some single-aisled, some with two or three aisles.

Flour mills. Also along north side of the Great Float are late 19C and early 20C roller mills on both sides of Dock Road. **Spiller's** SJ 306904, with concrete grain elevator north of road, connecting bridge to five-storey early 20C brick building south of road, elevator to east; **Buchanan's** SJ 315904, older five-storey mill and 'modernistic' brick-built elevator north of road, recent building south, with bridges across; **Homepride** (Spiller's), SJ 317903, south of Dock Road, 20-bay, five-storey brick building of 1898, later buildings to west.

Corn warehouses SJ 316904. South side of Dock Road, two surviving blocks of three warehouses each built by Lyster, 1868, six storeys, 29 bays along Dock Road front, small window openings now mostly blocked, recessed loading openings, hoists, towers, partly used as silos by Spiller's Homepride Mills. The warehouses were formerly served by a canal arm from the East Float running between the blocks. One of the most impressive industrial monuments in the dock area.

Seacombe Ferry SJ 326908. Still in operation. Referred to as early as 16C, steam ferries from 1823. Attractive terminal buildings of 1930-33, single-storey, brick and stone, two three-bay colonnades on road front, hipped tiled roof, central brick tower, stone-arched entrance. Ticket hall with sandstone walls, timber roof structure, four ticket kiosks (disused kiosks to south), 1930s-style dark wood ticket offices inside, one disused. Iron walkways with wood-and-glass sides to floating stage. To north is recent ventilator station for Mersey Tunnel extension, two long air openings to river, tall concrete tower, looking like a massive piece of hi-fi equipment. The Seacombe branch of the Wirral Railway was opened in 1895, closed 1960-63, track removed and used for new road from Mersey Tunnel (Kingsway) to M53. There are flats and playground on the site of Seacombe Station, SJ 324908, bridges survive to west in Church Street and Wheatland Road. Between Seacombe Ferry and Alfred Dock there were formerly a number of shipbuilding yards, making and repairing vessels for Liverpool shipping lines.

Egremont Ferry SJ 320918. Started 1821 by Capt. J Askew, later Egremont Steam Ferry Co. and Ferry Hotel, taken over by Wallasey Local Board 1860. Stage rammed by a ship in 1941 and never rebuilt. Two-storey brick-built terminal building with hipped roof, converted to public toilets. Ferry Inn opposite.

NORTH
Wallasey Central Library and Museum SJ 307930. Earlston Road. Small maritime collection with models of Wallasey ferry boats, including paddle steamer of 1826, records and photographs, items relating to Perch Rock Battery.

Water tower, Goreshill waterworks, Wallasey, 1979

Gorsehill Waterworks SJ 303935. On hill above New Brighton octagonal stone-built water tower, Norman style, pairs of long semi-circular arched windows, pillars between, ornamental cornice, triple arcades above windows, battlements, side turret, Norman doorway. Three-storey brick-built engine house. Stone-sided reservoir at northwest. Plaque recording 'Wallasey Waterworks 1905. J. H. Crowther, engineer, John Cowley Liscard, contractor'.

Perch Rock lighthouse SJ 309947. Off New Brighton, brick tower, iron lantern, built 1827-30 to replace timber port marker. Perch Rock Fort also survives, built 1826-29 as defence for Mersey estuary, stone-built, four angle towers, imposing gateway, causeway connection to land.

New Brighton Station SJ 304939. Terminus of the Wallasey and New Brighton branch of the Wirral Railway, opened 1888. Main building of brick, two storeys, stone-framed windows and doorways, two gables, tall brick chimney stacks, five-bay single-storey building to south, double windows, ball finials on gables. Booking hall with high wooden roof and panelling. **Grove Road Station** SJ 290930 has buildings in similar style.

WEST

Leasowe Station SJ 271907 and **Moreton Station** SJ 260906 on Wirral Railway line to Hoylake have post-war brick and concrete buildings.

Leasowe lighthouse SJ 253914. 1763 (date stone over door), tall, tapering, circular brick tower, whitewashed, seven storeys, over 100 ft (30 m) high, cavity-wall construction, semi-circular arched windows, light openings blocked, iron-railed balcony below light on north-west side, last lit 1908, then used as café. In care of local authority.

WEST KIRBY

West Kirby Station SJ 213869. Two railway lines terminated in West Kirby. The Wirral Railway (then the Hoylake & Birkenhead Rail & Tramway Co.) was extended from Hoylake in 1878. The present terminus dates from 1896, red-brick buildings, stone-framed windows and doorways, single-storey building at west, clock tower, two-storey building with half-timbered gable and semi-circular arched windows, two-storey building with dormer windows. Island platform with recent canopy: circulation area with seven-aisle timber-and-glass pitched roofs supported on cast iron pillars. To east is site of former terminus of Birkenhead Railway's (GWR/LNWR joint) line from Parkgate, opened 1886, closed 1956. Recreation centre and car park on site. Line to south is start of Wirral Country Park. Bridges on Church Road and Sandy Lane: single arch, dark blue brick, stone string course and coping, buttresses each side of arch.

Grange Beacon SJ 223866. On top of Grange Hill by side of Coburn Road. Circular sandstone column with platform and ball finial at top. Erected by Liverpool Docks Trustees 1841 as landmark for mariners in Mersey and Dee. On or near site of former Grange windmill, post mill destroyed in gale, 1839, which previously served as landmark.

WHISTON

Formerly busy coal-mining area south of Prescot. References to workings in 17C and to installation of a Newcomen pumping engine in 1719.

Cronton Colliery SJ 475893. Only one still working, sunk 1914-18. Two twin-pulley steel lattice-girder head gears. Oldest electrically driven winding engines in use in Lancashire coalfield: both powered by twin 1,550 h.p. d.c. motors coupled direct to drumshaft, Siemens design, installed by English Electric Co., 1920–21, Worsley Mesnes brake engines. Railway branch from Liverpool & Manchester Railway at Huyton Quarry, built to Halsnead 1831, extended to Cronton 1918. Near this line to north-west are traces of shafts and workings of Halsnead Colliery, High Hey Colliery, Houghtons Hey Colliery, Ridings Colliery and Whiston Colliery.

Whiston incline. On Liverpool & Manchester Railway, mile and a half (2·4 km) from Platt's Bridge, SJ 467910, to Rainhill, rise of 1 in 96.

Merseyside townships and places mentioned in gazetteer, arranged by metropolitan boroughs.

Knowsley MB. Huyton with Robey, Prescot, Whiston.

St Helens MB. Billinge, Haydock, Newton le Willows, Rainford, Rainhill, St Helens.

Sefton MB. Aintree, Bootle, Crosby, Formby, Southport.

Wirral MB. Bebington, Birkenhead, Caldy, Eastham, Gayton, Heswall, Hoylake, Storeton, Thornton Hough, Thurstaston, Wallasey, West Kirby.

Lancashire

The new county stretches north from Ormskirk, Chorley, Darwen and Rossendale to the Cumbrian border north of Carnforth. It includes the industrial area of the old north-east Lancashire, the northern part of the West Lancashire plain, the Fylde, and the Bleasdale and Bowland fells, where a considerable area has been included from the old West Riding of Yorkshire.

(Map over page)

ACCRINGTON

A 'new cotton town' of the 19C created out of the townships of Old and New Accrington, areas of scattered farms and cottages, with a substantial domestic manufacture of woollens in 18C, water-powered fulling mills and early woollen-carding mills on local streams. Eventually had some 50 cotton-spinning and weaving mills and in many areas a grid pattern of streets with rows of stone-built workers' cottages. Like neighbouring Church, Clayton le Moors and Oswaldtwistle became major centre of calico-printing industry, which in turn affected change-over from woollens to cotton. There is a good detailed guide in M. Rothwell, *Industrial Heritage: a Guide to the Industrial Archaeology of Accrington*, 1979, to which I am indebted for much information.

CENTRAL AREA

Accrington viaduct SD 758289. Dominant feature of town centre is high curving stone-built viaduct of the East Lancashire Railway, built 1847, restored 1866-67, with 21 arches of 40 ft (12 m) span, height up to 60 ft (18 m). At south end is **Accrington Station**, triangular plan at junction of line from Ramsbottom with lines to Blackburn and Burnley, all opened 1848. Line from Ramsbottom closed 1966 and platform disused.

Globe Works SD 757283. Famous textile engineering works of Howard & Bullough, started 1853 by John Howard and James Bleakey, joined by James Bullough 1857. Started making cotton-spinning machinery in 1860s. Big extensions in later 19C with growth of export trade: 500 employed in 1866, 3,800 in 1902, 5,000 in 1915. Manufacture of openers, scutchers, drawing and roving frames, carding engines, ring-spinning frames and throstles, doubling frames, warping and sizing machines. Biggest employer in Accrington in 1920s. Did own moulding until 1960s. Became part of Textile Machinery Makers with other Lancashire firms in 1931. Now Platt-Saco-Lowell, with about 800 employees. Extensive brick and stone buildings in area bounded by Scaitcliffe Street, Richmond Street, Richmond Hill Street and Ormerod Street. Particularly notable is five-storey building of 1892-93 in Scaitcliffe Street. Howard & Bullough also took over **Charter Street**

Lancashire: the new county

Works SD 749282 in 1907 for moulding and machining: used 1906-07 by Alfred Hitchen for manufacture of Globe cars.

Broad Oak Mill SD 759283. Best surviving example of cotton mill in town. Built 1834-37 by Hargreaves Dugdale & Co. of Broad Oak Print-works for spinning and weaving. James & Robert Cunliffe from 1895. 3,800 mule spindles, 6,300 ring spindles and over 900 power looms in 1920. Cotton production ceased 1929: since used for manufacture of domestic machinery. Two 18-bay three-storey (originally four-storey) stone-built mills with engine house between, single-storey weaving shed.

SOUTHERN AREA: SPRINGHILL, WOODNOOK, BROAD OAK, BAXENDEN

Spring Hill Mill SD 746279. Stone-built weaving shed and two-storey preparation and warehouse block. Built by Pickup's in 1860s, closed 1930. Early housing in area.

Union Mill SD 746281. Brick-built weaving shed and preparation building of 1890. Over 1,000 looms in early 20C driven by horizontal steam engine by Wood's of Bolton. Introduced automatic looms in 1950s, closed 1964. In use by cable and wire manufacturers.

Spring Hill Works SD 748280. Built 1902-04 by Lang Bridge for manufacture of equipment for textile trade, including finishing machinery, fire doors and extinguishers, dust-removing apparatus. Closed 1967. Brick-built machine shops along Fairfield Street.

Woodnook Mill SD 759277. Large four to five-storey brick-built spinning mill, corner pilasters, octagonal brick banded chimney, engine house, remains of weaving shed to south. Was No. 2 mill of Accrington Cotton Spinning & Manufacturing Co., a co-operative venture, built 1889-90. No. 1 mill of 1862-65 is reduced to single storey. To south is site of earlier water-powered mill on Woodnook Water, started as carding and jenny mill *c.*

1780, mule and throstle spinning in early 19C, 24 ft (7·3 m) diameter water wheel. Eli Higham from 1870. Weaving only from 1909 to 1971. North of Woodnook Mill along Victoria Street are three stone-built mills and weaving sheds: **Victoria Mill**, started for mule spinning 1856, weaving shed, 1860, eventually 1,400 looms, ceased production 1962; **Ellesmere Mill**, closed 1960; and **Lodge Mill** to north with date 1879 on cast iron beam over boiler-house entrance, built by Eli Higham of Woodnook.

Broad Oak Printworks SD 767279. One of the major early calico-printing works of the area. Started in early 1790s by Taylor Fort & Bury of Oakenshaw Works, Clayton le Moors. Taken over in 1811 by Thomas Hargreaves, who had earlier worked at Sabden Print Works and Oakenshaw: firm of Hargreaves Dugdale & Co. Line of workshops with water-powered machines along valley of Warmden brook, steam power from 1816. In 1846 12 printing machines, 300 hand-block printing tables, 850 employees. F. W. Grafton & Co. from 1856. In 1880s two machine shops, bleachcroft, two dyehouses, finishing rooms, 30 printing machines of one to eight colours, about 1,000 employees. Taken over by Calico Printers' Association, 1899. Machine printing stopped 1958, engraving 1960, screen printing 1966, finishing 1970. Now industrial estate. A number of 19C stone buildings survive, including pre-1850 bleachcroft. Oak Hill Park, west of Manchester Road, is grounds of house built 1815 by Thomas Hargreaves. His eldest son, John, built Broad Oak, north of works in Sandy Lane, in 1839. In valley above works are remains of Broad Oak and Cat Hall collieries.

Baxenden Printworks SD 776259. In valley of Wodnook Water. Started *c.* 1790 as water-powered wool-carding and jenny-spinning mill by Benjamin

Wilson, who went over to printing and bleaching in 1799. Present works built in 1820s. Seven printing machines and 140 hand-block printing tables in 1846. Dyeing only from 1864: taken over by H. W. Kearns 1878 and still in use as dyeworks. Some of 19C stone buildings survive, including watch house and former printing shops. To north are remains of two former cotton mills built by Wilson's: **Alliance Mill**, 1854, mule spinning and weaving, **Victoria Mill**, weaving only, 1856. Workers' cottages in Alliance Street and Edward Street.

NORTHERN AREA

Queen Mill SD 764293. Large brick-built weaving shed of 1912 built by Accrington Mill Building Co. and leased to Queens Road Mill Co.: some 700 power looms. Closed 1964. To west in Queens Road is pair of two-storey stone-built cottages with stone-flag roof and traces of ground-floor weaver's workshop.

Hambledon Mill SD 761296. Also built by property company, Great Harwood Mill Properties Co., 1912-13, and leased to weaving firm with 760 power looms. Closed 1977: last weaving mill in Accrington. Long 20-bay two-aisle two-storey preparation and warehouse building on west, large weaving shed to east, tall circular brick chimney with cap.

Borough Corn Mill SD 758288. Built 1882-83 in Hyndburn Road for roller milling with 200 h.p. steam engine. Replaced adjoining old water-powered mill of medieval origin, which had six pairs of stones, steam engine and water-wheel in 1870s. Run by J. Greenwood & Sons 1895-1925, now occupied by plumbers' merchants. Five storeys and attic, brick-built with stone facade on south, central loading openings, earlier two-storey stone building at rear.

Bus and tram depot SD 756288. South of Hyndburn Road, built 1885-86 for Accrington Corporation's steam trams, with routes to Church, Clayton le Moors and Blackburn. Electrified 1906-07 and depot enlarged. Changeover to buses 1931-32. Three stone-built sheds with later brick-built shed on east.

Fountain Mill SD 756289. Brick-built weaving shed of 1899-1900 with two-storey preparation buildings and circular banded chimney. Over 1,000 power looms in early 20C. Closed 1959 and now used by engineering firm.

Ewbank Works SD 756289. New works taken over 1890-92 and greatly expanded in 20C. Old works in Paradise Street south of town centre was started c. 1862 for manufacture of water meters. Developed into general engineering by James Kenyon and James Entwistle, who started making washing machines and mangles in 1873, and the famous carpet sweepers in 1889.

Huncoat Colliery SD 772310. Huncoat is separate community north-east of Accrington. Spoil heaps north of Huncoat Station of colliery sunk 1889-92 by George Hargreaves & Co., company started in 1850s which ran all the collieries in the area. Two shafts over 850 ft (260 m) deep, fan ventilation, bank of 150 coke ovens. Nearly 500 workers in 1954 producing over 210,000 tons a year. Until it closed in 1968 had twin horizontal steam winding engine by Robert Daglish of St Helens, 1892. To south is site of **Huncoat Brickworks**, started 1894 for production of facing, ornamental and engineering bricks. Had tramway and later aerial ropeway to clay quarry south of Burnley Road.

ADLINGTON

Domestic workshops, 20-28 Market Street SD 601129. Row of five cottages with traces of multi-light windows front and rear at basement level.

Adlington Station SD 602131. On Bolton & Preston Railway, opened 1841. Late 19C station building, probably post-absorption by LYR and LNWR jointly. Two storeys, brick-built, steeply pitched slate roof, four chimney stacks each with two pots, windows with stone sills and lintels, eight bays. Four-bay single-storey building to south. North-west of station is single-arch skewed stone-built bridge, buttresses each side of arch, projecting course below parapet, slightly bowed in plan.

ALTHAM
Altham Corn Mill SD 775330. Former water-powered mill on river Calder east of Altham bridge. Early 19C, three storeys, stone-built, stone-flag roof, circular stone chimney (for late 19C steam engine), traces of waterwheel house on north. Miller's house and two cottages. Milling until 1880. Intended to become craft centre.

Calder Colliery SD 774332. Remains of last colliery opened by George Hargreaves & Co., 1903-08. 1,000 ft (310 m) deep, connected to workings of Huncoat Colliery, with aerial ropeway to Huncoat coke ovens. Closed 1958. Spoil heaps, pit banks, brick-built engine house for 600 h.p. winding engine, pit-head bath house of 1933, stables.

Moorfield Colliery SD 758313. Remains south of Leeds & Liverpool Canal. Sunk by Altham Colliery Co., 1881, scene of worst colliery explosion in area in 1883, when 64 were killed. Closed 1948-49. Beehive coke ovens by 1885. In 1928 gas and coke plant of Lancashire Foundry Coke Co. with 54 ovens, supplying Burnley and Great Harwood gas works, closed 1962.

Accrington Brick & Tile Works SD 756302. Built by Accrington Brick & Tile Co., 1887, following earlier small-scale operations. Famous for production of Accrington machine brick used for cotton mills and other industrial buildings and for houses throughout Lancashire. Also produced tiles and terracotta for decorative purposes. Run

1901-58 by Macalpine's, who owned the Altham Colliery Co.'s pits. Still working. Staffordshire continuous kilns, early tunnel kiln for terracotta, machine shops with brick-making machines. Large clay pits north of Whinney Hill Road. Whinney Hill Brickworks to west was started 1896-97 and also taken over by Macalpine's. Traces of mineral railway to Huncoat Station sidings and to Moorfield Colliery.

ANDERTON
Anderton Logwood Mill SD 630117. Weir on river Douglas and remains of stone-sided wheel pit mark site of mill for grinding logwood for dyeing, marked on OS map of 1848. To west is millpond at Anderton Old Hall Farm, supplied by race from below logwood mill and providing water power for farm machinery.

ANGLEZARKE
Lead mines Shafts, spoil heaps and drainage soughs of former lead workings on slopes of Anglezarke Moor east of Chorley above Rivington and Anglezarke reservoirs, e.g. at White Coppice, SD 623193, Lead Mines Clough, SD 632167. First developed at end of 17C by partnership including Sir Richard Standish, the landowner. Greatest activity in 18C, especially 1780s: numerous shafts, drainage works, smelting mill, smithy, waterwheels. Work continued until c. 1840. Shafts up to 240 ft (73 m) deep. Well known because of discovery of witherite, a barium carbonate used for glazing in porcelain industry, e.g. by Wedgwood.

BACUP
Township with typical Rossendale landscape: moorlands with old farms up to 1,200 ft contour, later industrial development of 18C and 19C along valleys of river Irwell and its tributaries from Weir in the north down to Bacup centre and west to Rawtenstall bound-

ary. Domestic woollen industry and fulling mills from later Middle Ages with change-over to cotton from early 19C. Many mid-19C stone-built mills with communities around them. In late 19C and early 20C introduction of felt, slipper and shoe-making, using former cotton mills.

CENTRAL AREA

Ross Mills SD 870220. Bacup's one example of a large, late, brick-built cotton-spinning mill, by side of railway from Rochdale. Six storeys, large arched windows with terracotta decoration above, ornamental water tower, decorated engine house on south, tall circular brick chimney on square plinth. In use by Joshua Hoyle & Sons.

Bacup Station SD 868224. Former terminus of East Lancashire Railway's line from Newchurch, opened 1852, and LYR line from Facit, opened 1881, both closed 1966. Goods and passenger stations demolished, buildings on sites. North and south of station site are good examples of stone-built 19C mills, including **Irwell Mills**, marked as cotton mill on OS map of 1848, which later became shoe factory.

SOUTH-EAST: BRITTANIA

Britannia Mill SD 880215. Typical local cotton mill with two, three and four-storey buildings and internal engine house for beam engine. Became shoe factory in 20C.

Hogshead Colliery SD 885222. Clear trace of workings, which are marked on OS map of 1848. Earthwork of tram-road can be followed from colliery site south-west to Rochdale Road, with bridge over Tong Lane.

Britannia Station SD 885215. Site only of what was highest point reached by LYR, 967 ft (295 m) above sea level. Line visible in overgrown cutting to west. West again is Bacup tunnel, 150 yd (137 m) long, single entrance blocked.

NORTH-EAST

Traces of 19C collieries, mostly drift mines, along valley of Greave Clough, including Greave Colliery, Change Colliery, Blue Ball Colliery, Copter Hill Colliery and Hilltop Drift, which worked until 1960s.

NORTH: UPPER IRWELL VALLEY

Waterside Mills SD 867234. Early-Victorian cotton mill, four storeys, stone-built, pitched slate roof, base of square stone chimney, date stone 1859 over archway. Became shoe factory and is still in use by shoe manufacturers.

To north on east side of valley is good example of industrial housing, with rows of two-storey stone-built cottages running up hillside in Hammerton Street, Gordon Street, Stanley Street, Abbey Street, Russell Street, Brown Street and Cooper Street.

Old Meadows Colliery SD 868238. One of last drift mines in area to close: pillar-and-stall workings with tubs pushed from coal face along rails to chain-operated incline. Only survival is part of incline, but one tub and part of chain system are preserved in Buile Hill Park Museum, Salford. On opposite side of valley was another drift working, Broad Clough Colliery.

Broad Clough Mill SD 868242. Originally water-powered mill started by John Lord: steam engine by 1838. 'JL 1835' on date stone over doorway. Three storeys, stone-built, internal structure of cast iron pillars, timber beams and floors. Square stone chimney. In early 19C there was another water-powered mill farther up the river at Higher Broad Clough.

Irwell Springs Printworks SD 874257. Calico-printing works developed from 1813 onwards on site of former woollen mill high up near source of Irwell. Two printing machines, three and four-colour, in 1844. Now partly demolished, but some of brick-built sheds survive.

Deerplay Colliery SD 871265. Another drift mine on Cliviger–Bacup boundary which worked until 1960s.

Coal tub and haulage chain, Old Meadows Colliery, Bacup, 1967. The colliery is closed and parts of the chain haulage system are preserved at the Salford Museum of Coal Mining.

Now marked by traces of spoil heaps. Formerly connected to coal depot on Burnley Road.

WEST: STACKSTEADS

Line of stone-built mills along the Irwell west from Lee Road: **Olive Mill** SD 862217, three storeys with single-storey weaving shed on north, taken over by Maden & Ireland for shoe and slipper manufacture, as were **Kilnholme Mill** and **Victoria Mill; Stacksteads Mill** SD 855218, typical stone-built cotton mill with internal beam-engine house, in use by Bacup Shoe Co., who also have **Rossendale Mill** SD 849216, a substantial four-storey mill with, to west, two rows of two-storey stone-built back-to-back cottages: Taylor Holme and Taylor Terrace.

BARNACRE WITH BONDS

Calder Vale Mill SD 533458. Cotton mill and community in middle valley of river Calder which was quite intensively used for water power. Mill 1835, four storeys, stone-built, latrine tower on west front, internal structure of two rows of cast iron pillars and timber beams, joists and floors, main rooms 95 ft by 45 ft (29 m by 14 m). Site of former waterwheel at south, tail race in tunnel, head race from weir and pond 300 yd (274 m) north. Replaced by water turbine. Mill also had a beam engine and later a National gas engine. Long row of two-storey stone-built cottages and Methodist chapel north of mill, other housing on hillside to west. Good example of textile development outside the main east Lancashire cotton area.

Barnacre Weaving Co. SD 531452. Built 1845, a mile (1·6 km) downstream from Calder Vale Mill. Weir and pond a quarter of a mile (400 m) upstream, water conveyed in pipe over entrance road to former waterwheel. Single-storey stone-built weaving shed, north-light timber roof structure on cast iron pillars, chimney for later steam engine on hillside above. Row of workers' cottages and owners' houses.

Iron forge SD 505459. At right-angled bend in road to Oakenclough, just west of railway and on small tributary of river Wyre. Single and two-storey building with high-breast waterwheel 20 ft (6·1 m) diameter, 2 ft (60 cm) wide, iron axle hubs, buckets and rims, wooden spokes, rim gearing. Marked as Forge on OS map of 1844.

BARNOLDSWICK

Like Earby a Yorkshire cotton town, now included in Lancashire. Grid pattern of streets with rows of stone-built workers' cottages, surrounded by some ten weaving mills, with large single-storey north-light sheds, two or three-storey preparation and storage buildings, separate engine houses and stone or brick chimneys.

Bancroft Mill SD 874461. Weaving mill of J. H. Nutter & Co., opened 1913-22, closed 1978. Two-storey stone-built preparation building with large rectangular windows, internal structure of cast iron pillars, timber beams, joists and floors. Two tape-sizing machines by Howard & Bullough of Accrington, 1903 and 1917. Engine house at north end, six bays, horizontal cross-compound steam engine by Wm Roberts & Co. of Phoenix Foundry,

Nelson, cylinders named 'James' and 'Mary Jane' after James Nutter and his wife, Corliss valves. Single-storey stone-built boiler house with Lancashire boilers. Tall circular dark brick chimney with iron banding. Single-storey weaving shed 225 ft by 200 ft (68 m by 61 m), eight rows of 22 cast iron pillars supporting timber north-light roof truss, drive from steam engine at north-eastern corner, shaft along north wall, cross shafts along line of pillars, pulley-and-belt drive to Lancashire looms, stone-flag floor. Capacity of 1,000 looms, about 500 when closed, including looms by Cooper's of Burnley and W. B. White & Sons of Colne.

Long Ings SD 884469. Three weaving sheds by Leeds & Liverpool Canal: Long Ings, Lower Barnsay and Clough Mills. To east is **Rainhill Rock**, former limestone quarry developed by canal company, with branch canal authorised 1796 and gradually extended in 19C with two short tunnels and a viaduct to carry an occupation road. Ceased working 1891. Overgrown line of cutting visible south of Long Ings Lane. Farther north along Leeds & Liverpool Canal is **Bankfield Shed** SD 882475, taken

Weaving shed, Bancroft mill, Barnoldswick, 1978

over in second world war by Rolls Royce for manufacture of aircraft engines.

Greenber Field locks SD 888482. Three locks on Leeds & Liverpool Canal north of Greenber Field bridge, replacing former three-rise staircase in 1820. At bottom lock brick-built tollhouse with pyramidical roof and stone-built lock keeper's cottage with stone-flag roof. At top of locks is discharge point of nine mile (14·5 km) long pipeline from Winterburn Reservoir, opened 1893.

Barnoldswick Station SD 878468. Car park on site of former terminus of branch from Leeds & Bradford Railway's (later Midland) line from Colne to Skipton at Kellbrook, opened 1848, closed 1965-66. Embankment clearly visible south-east of town.

BARROWFORD

Tollhouse SD 862398. At junction of Marsden-Gisburn road, turnpiked under Act of 1803, and branch road to Colne. Good example, two storeys, stone-built, stone-flag roof, twin stone-framed windows, built into angle of roads for visibility. Near by is weir on river Calder which provided power for Abraham Hargreaves's cotton-spinning mill in early 19C.

Barrowford Locks. Flight of seven locks raising Leeds & Liverpool Canal 50 ft (15·2 m) from south of Colne road, SD 868396, to Barrowford lock house, SD 869404, masonry sides, double gates top and bottom, wooden lock-end bridges. Wharf and single-storey stone-built warehouse above second lock south of Colne Road. Barrowford Reservoir east of locks was built 1885 to take surplus water from Foulridge Reservoirs.

BARTON

Barton Mill SD 525376. Former water-powered corn mill on Barton brook, shown on Yate's map of 1787 and OS map of 1848. Three storeys, brick-built on lower courses of sandstone, being rebuilt as residence, wheel pit at south end. Weir half a mile (800 m) upstream, tailrace under road.

Newsham bridges SD 504362. Single-arch stone-built bridge on Lancaster Canal, humped, bowed in plan. To east, wooden swing bridge with iron tension rods to hold platform supported on wooden posts near south side, iron side railings.

BICKERSTAFFE

Windmill SD 442048. Wide brick-built tapering tower in prominent, open position, re-roofed and being converted to residence. To east are traces of former Bickerstaffe Collieries both sides of A570 Rainford–Ormskirk road.

BILLINGTON

Abbey Mills SD 722357. Stone-built north-light single-storey weaving shed, three-storey preparation block with engine and boiler house in middle. Driven until March 1979 by cross-compound horizontal steam engine by Yates of Blackburn with flywheel and geared drive to shed: 80 Lancashire looms.

Judge Walmsley Mill SD 727361. Just west of Whalley railway viaduct and south of river Calder. Brick-built, north-light weaving shed, stone-built engine house, now industrial estate. Long rows of two-storey brick-built workers' cottages adjoining in Longworth Road.

BLACKBURN

A town with a long tradition of cotton manufacture, noted for its fustians in 17C and its grey cloth in 18C. Much evidence of domestic industry of 18C and early 19C: Timmins lists over 20 sites. Early water-powered mills and finishing works along river Darwen and Blakewater. Later steam-powered mills along Leeds & Liverpool Canal, e.g. in Nova Scotia and Audley. Specialisation in weaving in later 19C created north-east Lancashire landscape of single-storey sheds, two or three-storey preparation and storage buildings, engine and boiler houses, chimneys. Contrast of stone buildings of early and mid-19C with later brick-built sheds and one or two large spinning mills. Redevelopment has led to demolition of a number of mills and much of the older working-class housing.

CENTRAL AREA

Blackburn Station SD 685279. Originally built 1844-45 for Blackburn & Preston Railway, opened 1846. East Lancashire Railway's line from Accrington and line from Bolton were opened 1848, line to Chatburn 1850. Present station is rebuilding of 1885-88: two-storey brick-built office with triple stone-framed windows, stone parapet and clock; three-aisle booking hall, subway and ramps to two long island platforms with two bays at north, one at south. Twin train sheds with dividing wall and outside wall of yellow brick with twin semi-circular arched windows on town side, iron roof trusses. Single and two-storey yellow-brick platform buildings. Goods station to south with long three-aisle stone-built shed. Entrance to Blackburn tunnel, 434 yd (397 m) long, to north.

Bolton Road Station SD 681273. Original station of Bolton Blackburn Clitheroe & West Yorkshire Railway, opened to Bolton 1848, to Chatburn 1850. Closed 1859 on amalgamation of Lancashire & Yorkshire Railway and East Lancashire Railway. Stone-built goods shed survives. To north, Bolton Street is crossed by four-lane riveted steel girder bridge on large cast iron pillars with 'L&YR 1884' on stone abutments.

Salford Brewery SD 685281. Started *c.* 1808 by Thomas Dutton and his son, William, who had earlier worked at the New Brewery in Park Place. Now Whitbread's, but name of Dutton &

Son survives at top of loading openings. One of older buildings in High Street, behind which is ornamental tower of traditional brewery design. Duttons were pioneers of the tied-house system.

Star Brewery SD 687282. North of Eanam, almost entirely modernised. Started *c.* 1797 by David Thwaites and Edward Duckworth. Thwaites's keep up the tradition of delivering beer, now in metal casks, by horse-drawn dray to their houses in Blackburn.

Eanam Canal Basin SD 689282. Important wharf on Leeds & Liverpool Canal, now marina. Stone buildings, including two-storey stables at east, two or three-storey warehouses with wooden hoist covers and projecting loading canopies over canal, two-storey wharfmaster's house at west, iron base of former crane, single-storey office, boat-shaped in plan, with stone-flagged roof on Eanam. Higher up Eanam is Packet House Hotel, a reminder of the regular passenger services before the railway came.

Canal Foundry SD 689284. North of Eanam, started by William Yates 1826, making steam engines, boilers, pumping machinery, constructional iron work, mill gearing. William Thom became partner in 1880: Yates & Thom made many large mill engines for Lancashire cotton mills and winding engines for collieries. Foundry Arms survives at corner of Cleaver Street and Birley Street.

Lewis Textile Museum SD 682283. In Library Street near Town Hall. Given to town in 1934 by Thomas Boys Lewis, a local cotton manufacturer. Collection includes spinning wheel, hand looms, a spinning jenny, Arkwright water frame and a mule.

NORTH

Brookhouse Mills SD 687288. Cotton mills and community on Blakewater, west of Larkhill, started by John Hornby of Kirkham, who came to Blackburn 1779 to learn business of cotton merchant with Richard Birley: putting-out warehouse in Clayton Street. Size-house at Brookhouse 1809, first spinning mill 1828, second in 1832. W. H. Hornby & Co. employed over 1,400 in mid-19C. Three-storey building survives at south in Brookhouse Lane, four-storey brick-built mill and parts of stone-built mills to north. Housing has been cleared in redevelopment.

Roe Lee Mills SD 686303. West of Whalley Road. Duckworth & Eddleston, who also had Carr Cottage Mill, east of Whalley Road, took over old mill on north in 1902 and built new mill in 1906. Both have large weaving sheds. To west are four rows of two-storey brick-built late 19C workers' cottages. Still used for fancy weaving, which was started by Duckworth & Eddleston. **Vale Mill** SD 687306 and **India Mills** SD 691297 east of Whalley Road are examples of late brick-built weaving sheds.

Seven Acre Brook SD 672303. At Lammack. Long row of stone-built cottages with evidence of ground-floor loom shops, including blocked triple windows. There are other examples in Pleckgate Road and Revidge Road.

Northrop Loom Works SD 695288. Two and three-storey early 20C buildings in Moss Street, extensive later buildings to east now disused. Very important site in textile history, where in 1905 the sons of Henry Livesey of Greenbank Foundry started a works for the manufacture of the automatic loom patented by James H. Northrop of Keighley, Yorkshire, in 1894: based on mechanical replacement of weft in shuttle using cylindrical magazine for storage of cops or pirns. By 1960, 3,000 employees, producing 9,000 looms a year.

Greenbank Iron Works SD 697289. In Gladstone Street. Started 1864 by Henry Livesey of Withnell, who was a weaver at Hornby's Brookhouse Mill and demonstrated improved power looms at the Great Exhibition of 1851. Production of looms from 1874. Taken over after he died in 1896 by his sons, who also started Northrop Works.

Imperial Mill SD 700287. Blackburn's best example of a large cotton-spinning mill, c. 1900, four storeys, brick-built with yellow-brick decoration, large rectangular windows in threes, towers at north-west and north-east corners, six-bay engine house on canal side with long semi-circular arched windows, tall circular brick chimney. In use for spinning by Courtauld's. By contrast along canal are two stone-built mills of earlier date, **Burmah Mill** and **Greenbank Mill**.

Britannia Mill SD 701282. Brick-built weaving shed, dated 1913 by cast iron beams with names over entrances to engine house, boiler house, twist warehouse, size warehouse. Power plant installed by Ashton Frost & Co. of Blackburn.

Old Toll Bar Inn SD 703280. Former tollhouse in angle of Fecitt Brow, old road to Accrington, and Accrington Road, new turnpike of 1826-27.

Audley was a classic area of urban textile development with stone-built mills along the line of the canal and a gridiron pattern of streets with rows of workers' cottages. Now much of the housing has been cleared and some of the mills have been demolished. South of Audley Range are three good examples of weaving mills: **Prospect Mill** SD 698278, **Parkside Mill** SD 697277 and **Audley Hall Mill** SD 692275, with good row of brick-built cottages with gardens on north.

Cicely Bridge Mill SD 687278. Best surviving example in Higher Audley: four-storey, stone-built spinning mill, corner pilasters, ornament below parapet, four-aisled slated roof, stone-built engine house with date stone 'Cicely

Bridge Mill 1861'. Erected by John Baynes of Park Place Mills, still used for textile spinning and manufacturing. Traces of early buildings on sites of mills along canal to north: Alma, Bridgewater and Canton Mills. Stone-built mills and weaving sheds also in area north of Copy Nook, including **Jubilee Mill** of 1887, SD 693282.

SOUTH: NOVA SCOTIA, GRIMSHAW PARK, MILL HILL, EWOOD

Line of mills, mainly with stone buildings, along canal between Grimshaw Park Road and Infirmary Road. Nova Scotia still has its stone sett streets and long rows of workers' cottages, many now ready for demolition.

Nova Scotia Mill SD 682272. On north side of canal, started by Robert Hopwood. Four storeys, stone-built, 13 by 9 bays, windows with stone sills and unusual cast iron lintels.

Nova Scotia Locks Six locks on Leeds & Liverpool Canal between aqueduct south of Infirmary and Grimshaw Park. Masonry sides, double wooden gates top and bottom, iron bollards.

Ewood aqueduct SD 676265. Carries Leeds & Liverpool Canal over valley of river Darwen. Good example, now cleaned: stone-built, single arch, strongly bowed in plan, outward batter each side, buttresses both sides of arch, projecting string course below parapet, substantial side walls.

Albion Mill SD 674262. On south bank of canal east of aqueduct. Late four-storey brick-built spinning mill with tower at north-west corner, engine house and boiler house alongside canal. In use by Courtauld's Northern Spinning Division.

Waterloo SD 665258. Former hand-loom weaving community north of Livesey Branch Road. Six rows of two-storey stone-built cottages, with evidence of ground-floor and basement workshops.

WEST: BANK TOP, WENSLEY FOLD, GRIFFIN, WATERFALL

An area of early mill development with the Blakewater providing water power, e.g. at Wensley Fold Mill, the first in Blackburn, c. 1779, sold to William Eccles 1795. The area is being redeveloped but there are mid-Victorian buildings at **Phoenix Mill** SD 677277, five storeys, stone-built, at **Fir Mill** on opposite side of Blakewater and at **Bank Top Mill** near the old gas works.

Nova Scotia cotton mill and locks, Blackburn, 1979

South of Whalley Banks and Bank Top are sites of **Phoenix Foundry** SD 674274, former loom works of William Dickinson, started 1832-33; large LNWR **Galligreaves Street goods yard** SD 678723, closed 1970, perimeter wall and entrance gates survive, and to north LYR's **King Street sidings**, closed 1969, now coal depot.

Waterfall Mills SD 672268. Good example of large cotton-spinning mill with buildings from *c.* 1860 to early 20C. Four-storey brick buildings with corner pilasters, windows with stone sills and lintels, later engine house with name of mill.

BLACKPOOL

Little Marton Windmill SD 349342. Built 1838 on site of earlier mill, last worked *c.* 1928. Restored: four-storey, brick-built, whitewashed tower on low mound west of A583 from Preston, boat-shaped wooden cap, four common sails.

Blackpool North Station SD 306359. Original terminus of Poulton-Blackpool branch of Preston & Wyre Railway, opened 1846 as single line, doubled 1865. Station rebuilt 1896-98 when Blackpool was developing rapidly as a major seaside resort, with nearly 10,000 ft (3,050 m) of platform face, much of it for excursion trains from the cotton area of east Lancashire. Blackpool Central Station, near the Tower, closed 1964 and its site redeveloped, was built 1863 as terminus of Blackpool & Lytham Railway, rebuilt and line widened to four tracks 1899-1903. Terminus for trains from Lytham since 1964 is Blackpool South, opened 1863 as intermediate station, rebuilt as Waterloo Road Station 1903, when direct line from Kirkham avoiding Lytham St Annes was opened. Between the wars and in the immediate post-second world war period there was a large volume of traffic not only of holiday-makers but of commuters travelling to Manchester: club trains were introduced in 1896.

BOLTON LE SANDS

Bolton Mill SD 482687. Stone-built water-powered corn mill, working by 1825. Waterwheel replaced by turbine.

Packet bridge SD 484680. Where the old road through the village crosses the Lancaster Canal. Packet Boat Inn near by is reminder of regular passenger services on canal between Preston and Kendal, including express services in 1830s taking eight hours for full journey, three hours Preston to Lancaster. There were eleven sets of stables along the route.

Railway bridge SD 483688. On Lancaster & Carlisle Railway (later LNWR) opened 1846. Small bridge over lane to the Grange with original cast iron side beams by John Stephenson & Co., Lound Foundry, Kendal, 1845.

BORWICK

Wegber Quarry SD 530724. Large limestone quarry on east side of Lancaster Canal started 1805. Quay and dock on canal. Workers' cottages in New England village to south. Later served by Furness & Midland Railways line from Carnforth to Wennington, opened 1867. Became caravan site.

BRETHERTON

Tollhouse SD 463215. At junction of Liverpool–Preston road (A59) and Carr House Lane leading to Bretherton and Leyland. Single-storey, rendered, central chimney, projecting bay window on to A59.

BRIERCLIFFE

Harle Syke Cotton-weaving community on high ground east of Burnley with six stone-built weaving sheds with preparation blocks, separate engine and boiler houses, brick chimneys, interspersed with rows of stone-built workers' cottages each side of Burnley Road.

Queen Street Mill SD 868349. Large single-storey north-light weaving shed on west, two-storey preparation and storage block on east, tall circular brick chimney with name of mill, reservoir at south. Lancashire looms driven by belt-and-pulley drive from overhead shafting with direct drive from tandem compound horizontal steam engine by William Roberts of Nelson 1895, cylinders 16 in. and 32 in. (40 cm and 81·3 cm) diameter, Corless valves, 14 ft (4·3 m) diameter flywheel. One of very few working steam-driven mills in the North West.

BRIERFIELD

Small industrial town between Burnley and Nelson with line of cotton mills and weaving sheds along Leeds & Liverpool Canal.

Brierfield Mills SD 844365. One of most impressive groups of mill buildings in area, all of stone, mainly late 19C, but on site of earlier mill referred to in 1840. Fine five-storey cotton-spinning mill on side of canal, 44 by 8 bays, corner turrets, two-storey extension on west, four-bay separate ornamental engine house. Extensive single-storey north-light weaving sheds. Four-face clock tower with pryamidical roof and dormer louvres. Two-storey office in Coalpit Road, eleven bays, with later six-bay extension at north. Mill in use by Smith & Nephew (Textiles).

Brierfield Station SD 845364. On East Lancashire Railway's line from Burnley to Colne, opened 1849, in use. Stone-built gabled station house, white-tiled subway below tracks, brick-and-timber signal box, level crossing with wheel-operated gates, stone-built goods shed to south, Railway Hotel in Clitheroe Road. Near by are traces of **Marsden Colliery**, closed in 1870s.

BRYNING WITH WARTON

Warton windmill SD 417286. Timber post and side supports of post mill marked on Yates's map of Lancashire, 1787, and OS 6-inch map of 1844. Photograph in Bennett & Elton, **History of Corn Milling**, vol. 2, 1897, p. 284, shows brick-built round house, wooden mill with boat-shaped cap, four common sails, tail pole with wheel and paved circle for turning mill into the wind.

BURNLEY

Like Marsden and Colne, traditional centre of woollen manufacture which changed over to cotton in first half of 19C. Specialisation in weaving after 1850, hence preponderance of single-storey sheds in landscape. The Leeds & Liverpool Canal running east–west through the town has been a major factor in industrial location. Burnley was also an important coal-mining area: twelve collieries working in 1900, six in 1950, now only one – Hapton Valley. Roger Frost, **Along t'Cut**, (Lancashire County Council), 1977, is a useful guide to the industrial archaeology. For more detailed historical background see W. Bennett, *The History of Burnley*, part 3, 1948, part 4, 1951.

CENTRAL AREA

Burnley railway viaduct SD 837329. Fine 15-arch viaduct across Calder valley, stone piers, side walls and parapets, brick arches, 1,350 ft (411 m) long. On East Lancashire Railway's line from Accrington to Colne, opened 1848-49. Burnley Central Station at east end is entirely modernised.

Ashfield Shed SD 837328. Fourteen-aisle, single-storey, stone-built, north-light shed, three-storey preparation building, tall single-bay wide engine house with cast iron water tank on top. To north is **Calder Vale Shed** with larger engine house and circular stone chimney.

Weavers' Triangle. Area north and

south of Leeds & Liverpool Canal between Manchester Road and Westgate, where Burnley Industrial Museum Action Committee are undertaking recording and conservation: trail available. The sites are listed east to west.

Manchester Road Station SD 836321. On LYR line from Todmorden to Burnley and Gannow Junction on East Lancashire Railway. Closed 1961. Single-storey brick-built station building west of road, goods yard disused.

Manchester Road Wharf SD 838323. Major wharf on Leeds & Liverpool Canal, two-storey stone-built tollhouse on east, wharfmaster's house, two-storey stable block with stone-flag roof and arched openings, four-storey warehouse at west with wooden covered loading projection and wooden canopies on cast iron pillars. Earlier structures *c.* 1800.

Waterloo Shed SD 836324. North side of Trafalgar Street, typical stone-built shed, narrow engine house with water tank on top, circular stone chimney.

Trafalgar Mill West of Waterloo Shed. Four-storey stone-built spinning mill, tower at south-west corner with open cast iron water tank, weaving shed and stump of circular stone chimney.

Burnley Iron Works SD 836326. Started early 19C and became one of the town's major engineering firms, making a variety of products including steam engines for mills in the area and farther afield. Three-storey stone building in King Street now used by steel-construction engineers.

Clock Tower Mill SD 836325. On north side of canal east of Sandygate. Built *c.* 1840 as Sandygate Mill by George Slater. John Watts (Burnley) from 1890 to present. Impressive four and five-storey spinning mills along canal, monumental six-storey building, nine by five bays, with clock tower and name 'Watts' in white letters. Weaving shed on east.

Wiseman Street Mill SD 835326. Stone-built weaving shed, three-storey preparation block with internal structure of cast iron pillars and beams, brick arches, four-bay engine house, circular stone chimney on square plinth. Operated by Sutcliffe & Clarkson until March 1979 with Lancashire looms driven by overhead shafting from horizontal cross-compound steam engine by Yates of Blackburn *c.* 1890, 750 h.p., 10 ft (3 m) diameter flywheel, geared drive to main shaft, rope drum with eight grooves for drive to second shed. There are hopes that the engine may be preserved.

Slaters Terrace SD 834326. Exceptionally interesting row of mid-19C workers' cottages on south side of canal west of Sandygate bridge, associated with Slater's Sandygate Mill. Three storeys, stone-built, 10 or 11 two-storey dwellings above ground-floor warehousing, balcony at first-floor level for access to houses. Sandygate bridge is one of the original canal bridges.

Sandygate Shed North of Sandygate. *Circa* 1860, stone-built weaving shed, three-storey preparation buildings, tall stone-built engine house with semi-circular arched windows and open cast iron water tank on top.

Victoria Mill SD 833326. North side of Trafalgar Street, four-storey stone-built mill, built for throstle spinning in 1850s, seven-storey tower with pairs of semi-circular arched windows, small weaving shed. Three-stage dog-leg iron fire escape by J. Hall of Oldham. On opposite side of Trafalgar Street is **Woodfield Mill**, large weaving shed and three-storey brick-built mill, with date 1886 on engine house. On north bank of canal, **Bellevue Mill**, 1863, has a notable tall, narrow stone-built engine house.

EAST

Burnley embankment. Major engineering feature on Leeds & Liverpool Canal running 1,256 yd (1,148 m) from

Burnley embankment, Leeds & Liverpool Canal, looking north from Finsley Gate, Burnley, 1979

Finsley Gate, SD 843320, to Ormerod Road, SD 847331. Up to 60 ft (18·3 m) high. Partly built with spoil from Gannow tunnel and Whittlefield cutting. At south end is **Finsley Gate maintenance yard**, still used by British Waterways Board, two-storey five-bay stone-built warehouse with stone-flag roof, two arched loading openings, dock at side of canal. Cast iron bridge of 1885 carries Finsley Gate over canal. Half way along the embankment is **Yorkshire Street aqueduct** with metal trough replacing earlier stone structure in 1926. The Foulridge-Burnley section of the canal was opened in 1796, the section west to Enfield in 1801.

Finsley Mill SD 842321. West of Finsley Gate bridge, started as spinning mill in 1820s. Older three-storey building at west, later four-storey eighteen-bay building at east occupied by footwear manufacturers.

There is a line of cotton mills along the east side of the Burnley embankment: **Plumbe Street Shed**, still in use for weaving; **Dean Mills**, two and three-storey, stone-built, date 1906 on later part; **Central Mill**, late brick-built weaving shed used by furniture manfacturers; **Park Mill**, 1907, brick-built weaving shed, two-storey preparation and office building with stone detailing and ornamental tower each end.

Old Mill SD 847322. One of oldest surviving mill buildings in Burnley, on north bank of river Calder. Four-storeys, stone-built, 12 bays long with two projecting turrets, engine house and circular stone chimney, becoming derelict.

NORTH-EAST

Bank Hall Colliery SD 847336. Sinking started 1876, eventually four pits, down to 1,550 ft (470 m). 800 employed in 1954, producing over 220,000 tons a year. Closed 1967, shafts sealed, buildings demolished, site now a park. Line of former tramroad from Bank Top (Burnley Central Station) still visible, with stone abutment of canal bridge at SD 842334. Later standard-gauge branch is now a footpath. To south is **Sandyholme aqueduct**, extended on south to carry tramroad over river Brun. To north, line of cotton mills and weaving sheds along canal towards Reedley: **Daneshouse Mill** SD 841337, spinning mill and weaving shed built 1878 and taken over by Benjamin Thornber, whose firm also had Old Hall and Throstle Mills to north and south; **Livingstone Mill** SD 840342, 1888, and **Cameron Mill** SD 841342, also 1880s, both built by John Grey.

WEST

Gannow tunnel SD 827330. Major work on Leeds & Liverpool Canal built by Robert Whitworth 1796-1801, 560 yd (510 m) long, no towpath, at north entrance segmental stone arch with side buttresses and curved retaining walls. To east, three weaving mills along canal, including Cairo Mill of 1886.

Woodbine Mill SD 821327. Gannow Lane, north of canal. Brick-built north-light weaving shed, 1906, two-storey preparation and warehouse building, separate brick-built engine house, circular brick chimney, occupied by engineering firm. **Peel Mill** on south side of Gannow Lane was one of largest weaving sheds in Burnley, now used by makers of bakery equipment. Near by are three rows of early stone-built cottages, two with stone-flag roofs.

Globe Iron Works SD 812325. Late 19C brick-built sheds of former textile machinery making firm of Butterworth & Dickinson, who moved from Saunder Bank to Liverpool Road, Rose Grove. Closed 1972, now occupied by motor exhaust firm.

Hapton Valley Colliery SD 810313. Only colliery still working in Burnley coalfield, originally sunk 1853. Some 360 workers in 1958 producing 113,000 tons a year. There was formerly a tramroad running north-east along south side of present Burnley Cemetery to Barclay Hills Colliery, SD 821319, and thence to canal at Gannow Lane bridge: line visible at Rossendale Road crossing.

Lowerhouse Mill and Printworks SD 804329. Burnley's most interesting in-

dustrial community, started 1795 by Peel & Yates, who built two water-powered cotton mills. Run in early 19C by William and Jonathan Peel, sons of Robert Peel of Oswaldtwistle. Sold 1813 to Nathaniel Dugdale of Oakenshaw, Clayton le Moors, whose sons, John, James and William became partners. Began printing calicoes 1819, built new five-storey spinning mill 1836. In 1846 eight printing machines, 119 hand-block printing tables, waterwheel and five steam engines in print works. Gave up printing in 1860s and leased works to Crofton & Lightfoot of Broad Oak Printworks, Accrington, and from 1872 to Alexander Drew from near Loch Lomond. Cotton mill in late 19C had 60,000 mule spindles and 1,000 power looms. Taken over by Lancashire Cotton Corporation and closed 1933. Dugdales developed neighbouring community: over 180 houses and about 1,100 inhabitants in 1851, gas works, shop, Co-op store (in 1872), Sunday school, new day school (1876), Wesleyan chapel.

Foundations and parts of walls of cotton mill survive east of Lowerhouse Lane. At print works some of stone buildings, two reservoirs, stone-built weir. Rows of two-storey stone-built cottages with stone-flag roofs at Lowerhouse Fold, to south later row of 18 cottages and school of 1876. To west in Fox Street and Wellington Street two rows of stone-built cottages, 1866, running downhill from Bear Street, formerly known as Peel Terrace and Wellington Terrace. Early row of cottages at north-western end of Bear Street and long row running down to print works. Victora Terrace to north, row of five larger houses, presumably for managerial staff. There is a full account in Brian Hall, *Lowerhouse and the Dugdales* (Burnley & District Historical Society), 1976, to which I am indebted for information.

BURSCOUGH

Burscough Wharf SD 443122. On Leeds & Liverpool Canal east of bridge on A59, now British Waterways Board maintenance yard. Two-storey brick-built warehouse with small arched windows and two sets of loading openings on canal front. Two-storey office/toll-house, wharfmaster's house, single-storey workshop. Old swivel crane restored in yard. Packet House Hotel west of A59, renamed 'Lord Nelson', late 19C or early 20C with 'Billiard Room' 'Smoke Room' and 'Cyclists Room' on windows.

Burscough Station SD 444124. On LYR Wigan–Southport line opened 1855, with curves on east to Liverpool–Preston line opened 1849, making Burscough into an important junction. Only route from Preston to Southport until opening of West Lancashire Railway in 1882. Four-bay brick-and-timber signal box at west, two-storey stone station building on north platform with gable and bay, stone-framed windows, steep pitched slate roof. Stone and timber waiting room on south. Liverpool–Preston line served by **Burscough Junction Station** SD 444115.

New Lane canal bridge SD 426126. Good example of Leeds & Liverpool Canal wooden swing bridge, turned by long wooden arm on south side. To north is **New Lane Station** on Southport line, level crossing, two-storey stone-built station house, late 19C, with gables, bay window, dormers and projecting porch. Railway Hotel to south.

CARNFORTH

Carnforth Iron Works SD 497708. Built by Carnforth Haematite Co., 1864, at peak had five blast furnaces and two Bessemer converters for making steel. Site opposite Carnforth Station at junction of Lancaster & Carlisle Railway opened 1846, Furness Railway opened throughout to Barrow 1857 and Furness/Midland joint line from Carn-forth to Wennington opened 1867, providing link with the Midland's Skipton–Carlisle line and thus with West Riding industrial area. The ironworks affected the whole development of the town, shifting the centre of gravity west from old community along the road to Over Kellett. The works closed 1929 and were demolished, but perimeter wall survives along Warton Road.

Steamtown railway museum In Warton Road near the station. Ten to twelve steam locomotives, including **Flying Scotsman**, diesel locomotives, industrial locomotives, rolling stock, coaling plant and turntable.

CATON

Township south of river Lune and east of Lancaster where there has been considerable industrial activity and use of water power: at least six sites on Artle beck and another three or four on smaller streams, used at various periods for iron forging, cotton spinning, silk throwing, flax spinning, corn milling, bobbin making.

Low Mill. SD 527649. Good example of early water-powered cotton-spinning mill built 1784 by Hodgson's, using Arkwright water frames. Taken over 1817 by Samuel Greg of Quarry Bank Mill, Styal, Cheshire, uncle of Isaac Hodgson, son of the founder. Rebuilt after fire in 1837. Bought 1864 by Storey's of Lancaster, manufacturers of table baize and oilcloth. Four storeys, stone-built, rectangular windows with stone sills and lintels, semi-circular arched doorway with dates 1784 and 1838 above. Internal structure of cast iron pillars, timber beams, joists and floors. Waterwheel replaced by turbines.

CHATBURN

North-east of Clitheroe, chiefly noted for its limestone quarries from 17c.

Peach Quarry SD 763433. Grassed-over bank of at least three lime kilns south of road to Clitheroe, with quarry workings behind.

Bold Venture Lime Works SD 764436. Extensive quarry north of road to Clitheroe with railway sidings from Blackburn–Hellifield line. Old bank of lime kilns along the railway has been largely demolished. Stone-built warehouse, row of workers' cottages.

Chatburn Station SD 767437. Original terminus of Bolton Blackburn Clitheroe & West Yorkshire Railway, opened 1850. Rebuilt 1876 on extension of line to join Midland Railway's Skipton–Carlisle line at Hellifield, completed 1879. Closed 1962-64. Single-storey stone station building.

CHIPPING

Excellent example of use of water power: there were at least eight sites on Chipping brook from north of Wolfen Hall to junction with river Loud, used at different periods for cotton spinning, spindle-making, chair-making, corn milling, brass founding, nail-making.

Wolfen Hall Mill SD 612442. Highest site still in use. Corn mill, but may have been used for spindle manufacture in early 19C. In recent years dairy and cheese factory. Millpond to north.

Saunderrake Factory SD 614438. Cotton-spinning mill in 1824, marked on OS 6-inch map of 1844. Later became brass foundry. Recently demolished: foundations only.

Kirk Chair Manufactory SD 619437. Marked on OS map of 1844 as 'Chipping Factory'. Recent buildings east of road, older three-storey stone-built mill on west. Still used for furniture making.

Wharf Mill SD 623433. Corn mill just east of Chipping Church, marked on OS map of 1844. In use until 1960s. Now restored and converted to restaurant. Two and three-storey sandstone buildings, external breast-shot waterwheel, iron axle, hubs, buckets and rims, timber spokes.

CHORLEY

Bagganley Mills SD 596182. Late cotton-spinning mill on east bank of Leeds & Liverpool Canal north-east of town centre. Four storeys, machine brick, terracotta decoration and balustrade above top storey, large windows in pairs, threes on top storey, ornamental water tower at southwestern corner, engine house on east, ornamental single-storey office.

Chorley Station SD 587176. On Bolton & Preston Railway, opened 1841. Old station was south of Chapel Street and later became goods station. Level crossing, brick-and-timber signal box with pitched slate roof and ornamental woodwork, single-storey brick platform buildings.

Black Brook aqueduct SD 596174. Fine single-arch, stone-built aqueduct carrying Leeds & Liverpool Canal over Black Brook valley, strongly bowed in plan, curved retaining walls.

Cowling bridge SD 595169. North of Cowling Brow on Black brook is former **Cowling Bridge Print Works**, early four-storey and two-storey stone buildings, with later brick additions. Print works by 1825, marked on OS 6-inch map of 1844. South of the Brow is **Cowling Mill**, late cotton-spinning mill, four storeys, brick-built with terracotta decoration, including pillars between top-storey windows, ornamental engine house. The former stone-built spinning mill on the east bank of the Leeds & Liverpool Canal has been demolished.

Yarrow Road Mill SD 592168. Brick-built weaving shed of 1910, five-bay engine house with tall circular brick chimney. To south single-arch stone aqueduct-style railway bridge carrying Bolton & Preston line over Yarrow Road; south again, **Cowling Brook viaduct**, sandstone, eight arches.

Burgh Colliery SD 579148. Traces of workings of early 19C colliery south of Burgh Hall Farm. Tramroad running

Warehouse, Blackburn Road Wharf, Leeds & Liverpool Canal, Church, 1979

north to colliery yard in Pall Mall, SD 581167, is marked on OS 6-inch map of 1844. Line of embankment visible in area of Pleck Wood. Line of stone blocks south of Wellbank Lane appear to be for road rather than railway transport, as there are no holes for fixing rails or chairs.

Birkacre Printworks SD 571151. Large reservoirs south of main works site are chief survivals of print works started before 1800. Five printing machines and 40 hand-block tables in 1846. Taken over by Calico Printers' Association 1899, closed early 1950s. In this area Richard Arkwright had one of his early water-powered cotton mills.

CHURCH

See Michael Rothwell, *Industrial Heritage: a Guide to the Industrial Archaeology of Church*, (Hyndburn Local History Society), 1980.

Church Bank Printworks SD 745292. Started by William Peel, eldest son of Robert Peel of Oswaldtwistle, *c.* 1772. Sold in 1830s to Frederick Steiner, Frenchman who came to England in 1817 and was manager of chemical department at Broad Oak Printworks, Accrington. Five printing machines and 103 hand-block tables in 1846. In late 19C export trade to India, South East Asia, China, Japan and North Africa. 18 printing machines, 1,400 employees in 1890. Perimeter wall and many 19C buildings survive, but site is being redeveloped.

Peel Bank SD 744293. On Leeds–Liverpool canal, wooden swing bridge amd Peel Bank arm with opening off canal crossed by humped stone towpath bridge.

Church Wharf SD 742286. On north side of Blackburn Road at right-angled bend in Leeds & Liverpool Canal. Two stone buildings, four storeys and attic, with arched opening to wharf between them, loading openings on canal end of last building. Single-arch, stone humped bridge on Bridge Street.

CLAYTON LE DALE

Oaks Bar. SD 671335. Single-storey stone-built tollhouse at junction of Whalley–Preston road (A59) and Blackburn–Ribchester road (B6245).

CLAYTON LE MOORS

See Michael Rothwell, *Industrial Heritage: a Guide to the Industrial Archaeology of Clayton-le-Moors* (Hyndburn Local History Society), 1979.

Oakenshaw Print Works SD 742317. Reservoirs and one or two stone buildings are all that remain of major calico-printing works in valley of Hyndburn brook started by Jonathan Peel, fourth son of Robert Peel of Peel Fold, Oswaldtwistle. Sold to Taylor Fort & Bury 1787 and on dissolution of partnership in 1811 taken over by Fort's. In 1846 eight printing machines, 229 hand-block tables, two steam engines and large waterwheel. Works chemist and later partner was John Mercer (1791-1886) of Great Harwood, inventor of process of 'mercerisation' using hot caustic soda solution to give shiny finish to cloth.

CLAYTON LE WOODS

Tollhouse SD 579233. Clayton Green, at junction of Preston–Chorley road (A6) and road to Brindle. Two storeys, stone-built with projecting bay on A6 front. In the area are a number of former **weavers' cottages** with traces of ground-floor or basement workshops: on east side of Preston Road, SD 579236, in Radburn Brow on road to Brindle, SD 579233, in Sheephill Lane, SD 576233.

CLITHEROE

Old market town with Norman castle on hill above, headquarters of the great Honour of Clitheroe. Industrial development in 18C and 19C: cotton spinning and weaving, textile finishing, lime quarrying.

Primrose Mill SD 738407. Built as water-powered cotton-spinning mill by J. & J. Parker, 1787. Calico printing by James Thomson & Co. from early 19C; Thomson was chemist at Church Bank Works. In 1840 seven printing machines, 204 hand-block tables. Stone-built five-storey mill of early

date, with circular brick chimney, occupied by handling equipment manufacturers. Long reservoir on Mearley brook to east.

Greenacre Mill (Holmes Mill) SD 742414. Three-storey, stone-built mill along Greenacre Street, latrine tower at north-west corner, engine house, boiler house, circular brick chimney, weaving shed at north. On OS 6-inch map of 1844 as Holmes Mill. In use by firm of cotton doublers.

Claremont Mill. SD 749415. On Shaw brook, converted from brewery 1809 and marked as Brewery Mill on OS map of 1844. Three-aisle, two-storey stone building with weaving shed to north. Still in use for textile manufacture. Shaw Bridge Mill lower down the brook, started 1788, largely modernised.

Low Moor Mill SD 729418. Industrial community of great historical interest on river Ribble, west of Clitheroe. Water-powered cotton-spinning mill taken over by Jeremiah Garnett of Otley and Timothy Horsfall, 1799. In early 19C Garnett & Horsfall extended spinning mill on large scale and added weaving sheds in 1850s and 1860s. Three waterwheels by 1824, three beam engines by 1858. Waterwheels replaced by turbines in late 19C and beam engines by large 1,250 h.p. vertical engine in 1893-94. Garnett's ran the mill until it closed in 1930. The buildings were demolished a few years ago and the site has been developed as a new housing estate. The weir on the river Ribble survives but the three-quarter-mile (1,207 m) long mill race has been largely filled in.

Adjoining is the community of workers' houses developed by Parker's and Garnett's: 262 cottages, 1,057 inhabitants in 1861. Two-storey stone-built cottages survive in High Street, Queen Street, Nelson Street, Union Street: some were originally back-to-back, converted to through houses with yards and privies. Methodist chapel of 1866, United Methodist Free Church of 1892. There was also a National School adjoining the mill, now demolished. There is a detailed account in Owen Ashmore, 'Low Moor, Clitheroe: a nineteenth-century factory community', *Trans. Lancs. & Ches. Antiq. Soc.*, vol. 73–74, 1966, pp. 124-52. Two very interesting diaries survive from Low Moor: one by John O'Neill, a weaver, the other by James Garnett, one of the brothers who ran the mill in the later 19C and who lived at Waddow Hall on the opposite side of the river.

Coplow Lime Works SD 749432, **Horrocksford Lime Works** SD 749435. Extensive limestone quarries and works at Pimlico, north of Clitheroe. Ten kilns working in 1825: Baines's *Directory of Lancashire* lists six lime masters, including Thomas Coates & Co. at Cross Hill Quarry, south-west of Horrocksford. Railway branch from Horrocksford Junction, north of Clitheroe Station. Now large modern cement works.

Bellmanpark Limeworks SD 758434. Surviving bank of kilns and embankment of tramroad to Bellmanpark Quarry on other side of Chatburn Road.

COLNE
Old market town, with church of Norman origin, which became sizable centre of woollen manufacture in 17C and 18C, with its own Cloth Hall and commercial links with Yorkshire. Early sites of water-powered carding and spinning mills along Colne Water and its tributaries. Change-over to cotton in 19C with specialisation on weaving in later period.

SOUTH
Woolpack SD 890393. Off Larch Road on hill above the town. Row of five stone-built cottages, two storeys at front, three at back, blocked openings in gable-end wall, formerly used for hand-loom weaving.

Waterside Leather Works SD 892398. On Colne Water with weir at east end. Marked as tannery on OS 6-inch map of 1848 and still used for same industry. Two-storey, two-aisle stone building with large windows on upper floor. Colne had a well known leather and glove-making trade in 17C and 18C. Mill Green, north of the works, was site of Colne Corn Mill.

Spring Gardens Mill SD 888396. Five-storey buildings with weaving shed at north and separate engine house, occupied by felt-makers. North of Colne Water is three-storey **Stanley Mill** with three-aisled roof, and shell of **Walk Mill** with remains of weaving shed, on site of former fulling mill, marked on Yates's map of Lancashire, 1787.

WEST
Railway viaduct SD 881397. Six-arch stone viaduct carrying East Lancashire Railway from Burnley across Colne Water valley, opened 1849, in use. Colne Station to north now has no buildings. It was also the starting point of the Leeds & Bradford (later Midland) line to Skipton, opened 1848.

Line of stone-built mills and weaving sheds each side of Colne Water: **Primet Mill**, still in use for textile manufacture, with very large shed with drainage openings and pipes for north-light roof structure in end wall; **Holker Street Mill** to west used by Bass Charrington's as distribution centre; north of river, **Garden Vale Mill** with 24-aisle shed, and **Bankfield Mill**, both in use for textile manufacture. **Electricity works** SD 876394. Colne's first electricity works, near Greenfield bridge, stone buildings with blocked semi-circular windows and date stone 1901.

NORTH
Mills and weaving sheds on both sides of northern by-pass road. **Vivary Bridge Mill** SD 885402. Looks like oldest surviving textile site in the town, started *c.* 1800, marked on

OS map of 1848 as cotton mill. Two early buildings, three storeys, stone-built with stone-flag roofs, one on east with small windows, one on west larger windows with small panes. Engine house for beam engine with water tank on top. Possible traces of water power: sluice and stone-lined channel.

Derby Street Shed SD 887402. Three-storey stone-built mill with large weaving shed of Thomas Hyde & Co. Closed 1960; driven by 250 h.p. tandem compound horizontal steam engine by Ashton Frost & Co. of Blackburn, 1892.

EAST

Carry Bridge SD 897399. Site of early water-powered woollen mill on Colne Water, started in 1780s.

Ball Grove Mill SD 908402. Another water-powered site on Colne Water, but for cotton. In 1838 had blowing machines, willow and lap machine, 17 carding engines, 10 drawing and roving frames, 15 throstles, one pair of mules, 36 power looms. Near by Standroyd Mill, date stone 1876, is in use by Courtauld's Northern Weaving.

Laneshaw Bridge SD 923407. Two mills near junction of Shawhead brook and river Laneshaw. Two-storey, 24-bay mill and weir north of road, former weaving shed south. Row of early two-storey stone-built cottages with stone-flag roofs and small windows on Wycollar Road.

COPPULL

Coppull Mill SD 563147. Fine early 20C cotton-spinning mill west of Wigan–Preston railway line with former branch: two mills on OS map of 1955. Four storeys, machine brick with elaborate terracotta decoration, corner turrets, very ornamental water tower with dome and pinnacles, carding extension on west, separate engine and boiler houses, circular brick chimney. Name 'Coppull Spinning Co. (1906) Ltd' on east front, in use for cotton spinning.

Chisnall Hall Colliery SD 550124. Spoil heaps and remains of pit-head buildings of medium-sized colliery still working in 1950s: 1,300 workers in 1958, producing around 360,000 tons a year. Line of railway branch from Wigan–Preston line north of Coppull Mill visible east of Preston Road (A49).

CROSTON

Croston Mill SD 498179. Formerly water-powered corn mill on river Yarrow east of Croston Hall. Three storeys, brick-built on stone foundations, small windows, stone quoins, pitched slate roof. Weir and sluice at entrance to wheel pit. Mill house to south.

DARWEN

Nineteenth-century cotton-weaving town with earlier stone-built, later brick-built weaving sheds interspersed with rows of workers' cottages on either side of a long north–south valley. Notable as place where wallpaper printing was started by Charles and Harold Potter, 1839-40, using an adaptation of the calico-printing machine. Good deal of activity in coal mining and brick and tile manufacture.

SOUTH

Bowling Green Mill SD 696210. Three-storey stone-built mid-19C spinning and weaving mill with dressed stone front and pediment on Bolton Road, two-aisled roof. There are good examples of stone-built weaving sheds with two or three-storey preparation buildings, engine houses and chimneys at Waterfield Mill, SD 699207, Grimshaw Street Mill, SD 698211, Hope Mill, SD 695214.

Hilton's Paper Mill SD 695217. Paper works started by Richard Hilton, 1818, rebuilt 1836 by his sons, Christopher, Henry and Edward. Over 400 hands in 1842 producing 30 tons of paper weekly. Rebuilt by Wallpaper Manufacturers: recent brick buildings. Older three-storey stone building with water tower. In use by Reed Paper Group.

Belgrave Works SD 692220. Former weaving mill taken over by Charles and Harold Potter 1840 for paper printing. Still used by Crown Decorative Products, Potter Branch. For an account of the growth of the wallpaper printing industry see E. A. Entwistle, *Potter's of Darwen*, 1939.

India Mill SD 694218. The outstanding textile building in Darwen, erected *c.* 1870 by Eccles Shorrock & Co. Six-storey, stone-built spinning mill, 330 ft by 100 ft (100 m by 30 m), intended for 68,000 spindles, projecting central tower on west front, corner towers, semi-circular arched windows on top floor. Internal structure of three rows of cast iron pillars, transverse iron beams and brick arches. Ornamental stone-built engine and boiler houses. Unusual tall square brick chimney on stone plinth at south-west in Venetian style with slit windows in side walls and ornamental top. Preserved at gates is horizontal cross-compound steam engine by J. & E. Woods of Bolton, 1905, which worked in a local mill until 1970.

Greenfield Mill SD 704209. South of railway to Bolton, two-storey stone-built preparation building and north-light weaving shed, square brick chimney. Immediately west is **Spring Vale garden village** with groups of stone-built semi-detached cottages with gables, arranged in landscaped setting, e.g. five rows fronting on to an open green. Very much in same tradition as Port Sunlight (See *Bebington, Merseyside*).

Sough tunnel SD 707218. Just south-east of Greenfield Mill is entrance to tunnel on Bolton Blackburn Clitheroe and West Yorkshire Railway, opened 1848, 2,015 yd (1,842 m) long, on gradient of 1 in 74, rising to south, excavated from fifteen shafts up to 260 ft (79 m) deep. Castellated portal with turrets, spoil heaps clearly visible. Rails lowered 1880-81 when Manchester to Scotland services via Hellifield began.

NORTH

Darwen Station SD 694225. Opened 1847-48, rebuilt 1883: single-storey yellow-brick booking office with tiled hall and tiled approaches to platforms, where there are remains of formerly more extensive yellow-brick buildings. Goods station closed 1969 and goods shed demolished.

Hollin Grove Mill SD 686234. East

India cotton mill with Venetian-style chimney, Darwen, 1970

of Blackburn Road. Earlier stone-built north-light weaving shed and three-storey preparation block at north, later brick-built shed and two-storey mill at south. Opposite west of Blackburn Road is site of **Dob Meadow Works** in valley of Sunnyhurst brook where James Greenway started calico printing in 1808 and took into partnership his son-in-law, John Potter, whose son, Charles, carried out his early experiments in wallpaper printing before moving to Belgrave Mills.

Hollins Paper Works SD 688238. Former bleach works taken over by Potter's *c*. 1844 and rebuilt 1859. Mostly recent buildings, but traces of earlier stone-built sheds. In use by Reed Paper & Board (UK). To west is **Anaglypta Paper Works**, built by Potter's in 1894 for the Anaglypta wall-covering process acquired from Storey's of Lancaster: the four-storey building has been modernised and extended. North of Hollins Lane are the former **Cobden and Peel Mills**, weaving sheds taken over by Walpamur and now used by Crown Decorative Products for paint and wall-covering manufacture.

Bog Height Road SD 680246. Two rows of stone-built early 19C cottages with traces of former ground-floor weavers' workshops, including triple windows. There is another example farther west at Peake.

EAST: HODDLESDEN

Vale Rock Mill SD 718224. Four storeys, stone-built, internal structure of cast iron pillars and timber beams, square stone chimney, large stone-built north-light weaving shed.

Hoddlesden Colliery SD 718222. Traces of spoil heaps of one of later collieries in area, still working in late 1950s with about 150 employees. Tramroad south-east to another pit at SD 734214. Also mined fireclay which was used by adjoining works to make pipes, chimney pots and tiles. To north is site of Hoddlesden Goods Station, terminus of branch from main line at Hollins, opened 1876, closed 1950. The line can be traced as an earth work for much of its length.

DOLPHINHOLME See *Ellel*.

DOWNHAM
Downham Mill SD 790451. Former water-powered corn mill on Ings beck, L plan, stone-built with stone-flag roof, cottage attached. Loading opening with inscription 'WA 1818' above. Overgrown mill pond to east, weir 200 yd (183 m) upstream. Of early origin: a water mill worth 26*s* 8*d* yearly is recorded in *inquisitio post mortem* of Henry de Lacy, 1311.

Lime kiln SD 789445. Good example of local kiln built into bank with loading at top, arched opening for access to grate for removing lime at bottom, quarry behind.

EARBY
Small Yorkshire cotton town transferred to Lancashire in local government reorganisation with half a dozen late 19C weaving mills, now mainly used for other purposes.

Kellbrook Mill SD 903464. Earlier than most of the mills, two storeys, stone-built, two-aisled roof, squat square stone chimney, derelict stone-built engine house with cast iron water tank on top, weaving shed to north.

ECCLESHILL/YATE AND PICKUP BANK
East of Darwen, with former collieries and brickworks. Traces of workings of Brocklehead, Close's and Harwood's Collieries west of **Glazed Brick Works** SD 712233, still working, white-tiled office building of 1927, clear traces of former tramroad and incline east to drift mine at Waterside.

Waterside Paper Mill SD 708242. Modern buildings of New Waterside Paper Mills on site of former Grimshaw

Iron tension water wheel, Corliss corn mill, Dolphinholme, Ellel, 1966.
Photograph W. J. Smith

Bridge Cotton Mill. There were a number of other cotton mills along the line of Waterside brook to the east: three and a bobbin mill marked on OS 6-inch map of 1848.

ELLEL

Galgate Silk Mills SD 485557. Just east of A6, west of M6, one of the most interesting groups of mill buildings in the North West. Started 1792 on site of water-powered corn mill by William Thompson, John Noble and John Armstrong; later Armstrong's only. Limited company 1869, later taken over by Paton Baldwin & Co. First mill west of road, three storeys, rough-stone walls, small rectangular windows, many with small panes, wooden beams and floors with cast iron pillars inserted later, projecting staircase tower at south-west, millpond to north. Second mill adjoins, early 19C, three storeys, irregular plan, stone-built, seven-aisled roof, windows with rustic stone sills and lintels, internal structure of cast iron pillars, wooden beams and floors. Third mill east of road, 1851, five storeys, brick-built, three-aisled roof, corner pilasters, rectangular windows with stone sills and lintels, small panes, internal structure of five rows of cast iron pillars, wooden beams, joists and floors, internal beam-engine house. Associated community along road.

Galgate viaduct SD 483554. Six-arch viaduct over river Conder on Lancaster & Preston Junction Railway, opened 1840. Galgate Station was closed 1939. To south is Galgate Basin on Lancaster Canal.

Corless Mill SD 517528. Water-powered corn mill on river Wyre south of Dolphinholme. Two storeys, stone-built, Gothic windows in gable walls, former drying kiln on south with two ventilators. Iron-tension waterwheel, breast-shot, 17 ft 6 in (5·3 m) diameter, 5 ft (1·5 m) wide, eight main square-section iron spokes with two tension bars crossing between each pair, penstock with iron sluice and grille in front. Dried up race from weir immediately upstream.

Dolphinholme Mill SD 519534. Former worsted spinning mill south of bridge over river Wyre. Started 1784 by Thomas Edmondson, Lancaster ironmonger, with two partners, using Arkwright water frames. Taken over 1795 by Hinde & Patchett, who built new mill with very large waterwheel, cottages for workers, church and school. Raw wool from Bradford and Norfolk. Steam engine installed in early 1820s. After 1850 used for cotton spinning and weaving. Ceased 1867. Traces of long curving mill race across bend in river, site of millpond, remains of wheel pit and of circular brick chimney on hill above, ruins of mill building. Two rows of workers' cottages (Corless Cottages), two and three-storey. Three-storey warehouse in village north of Wyre bridge. There is a very good account with excellent photographs in P. P. Hall, *Dolphinholme: a History of the Dolphinholme Worsted Mill, 1784-1867* (Fylde Historical Society), 1969.

FARINGTON
Mill Street SD 547232. Cotton mill started by Bashall & Boardman, 1835. Brick-built north-light weaving shed with two-storey preparation and warehouse block. Adjoining community with long rows of brick-built workers' cottages in Mill Street and East Street. To west across railway is large British Leyland works.

FLEETWOOD
New 19C railway port at mouth of river Wyre developed by local landowner, Sir Peter Hesketh-Fleetwood of Rossall Hall, and Preston & Wyre Railway Dock & Harbour Co. Line from Preston opened 1840, town planned and laid out on grand scale by Decimus Burton with streets radiating from the Mount. There were schemes for steamer services to Furness linking railway travellers from London with a new railway along Cumberland coast to Scotland. Money ran out in 1840s and plans were never completed. There was, however, a considerable cargo traffic with Europe, America and West Indies, coastal trade, and passenger services to Ireland, Scotland and Isle of Man. Later 19C development was mainly carried out by Lancashire & Yorkshire Railway, with a new dock, opened 1878, new passenger station and a trawler fishing fleet.

North Euston Hotel SD 338485. Built 1841 as part of original plan with fine curved frontage and porch with Doric columns. Used as barracks and school of musketry after 1859, but is now again a hotel. Travellers were intended to stay here en route between London and Scotland, hence the name.

Lighthouses. Two by Decimus Bur-ton, one in Pharos Street, tall circular stone tower with narrow circular gallery and outside reflector at top, the other on the front, now used as promenade shelter.

Queens Terrace. Also by Burton, facing railway station, long row of stone-built residences with three pediments and iron balconies.

Fleetwood Dock SD 337473. Earlier there was a wooden pier and iron wharf built as part of original development. The new dock was built by the LYR, 1869-78. Large rectangular dock 1,000 ft by 400 ft (310 m by 120 m), ten acres, walls of large stone blocks with Cornish granite coping. Entrance lock at north-east with hydraulically operated gates. Irregularly shaped fifteen-acre timber pond to south.

FOULRIDGE
Industrial village north of Colne with three weaving sheds, mainly associated with building of Leeds & Liverpool Canal.

Foulridge tunnel SD 888424 (entrance). Longest canal tunnel in Lancashire, built by Robert Whitworth 1792-96, 1,640 yd (1,500 m) long, 17 ft (5·2 m) wide at water level, 8 ft (2·4 m) high, no towpath. Considerable difficulties in construction: there were later collapses in 1824 and 1843. To north-east is **Foulridge Wharf**, with stone quay, two-storey, three-bay, stone-built warehouse, central arched opening with loading openings above, three-light mullioned windows, metal base of crane at north end. To north-east, steel-girder railway bridge on timber piers.

Foulridge Reservoirs. Built in 1790s to supply summit level of canal, later enlarged and deepened. Now form an attractive feature of the landscape and an amenity area.

Foulridge Station SD 887425. On Midland Railway's Skipton–Colne line, opened 1848. Closed 1959. Track removed but line walkable in both directions. Platforms, late 19C single-storey

Wyre aqueduct, Lancaster Canal, Garstang, 1964. *Photograph W. J. Smith*

stone station building with gables and semi-circular arched windows. Site of goods station in use.

FRECKLETON

Ship Inn SD 434287. Main survival of late 18C/19C port and shipbuilding community which developed along a pool on the north side of the Ribble at the mouth of Dow brook. Coal trade from Douglas Navigation and Leeds & Liverpool Canal. Coasting vessels repaired until late 19C. Associated industry of sail-making: six sail-makers or sailcloth workers in Baines's *Directory*, 1825. In 1827 there was a scheme to link the Leeds & Liverpool and Lancaster canals by means of wooden beams across the Ribble and a canal from Freckleton to the Lancaster Canal at Salwick, and via Kirkham and Poulton

to river Wyre at Thornton.

GALGATE See *Ellel*

GARSTANG

Wyre aqueduct SD 491448. Fine single-arch stone-built aqueduct on Lancaster Canal, 34 ft (10·4 m) span, deeply bowed in plan, shallow segmental arch, projecting string course at spring of arch, rustic masonry, elaborate projecting cornice below parapet. To north is Garstang Canal basin on east side of canal with boathouse and brick-built warehouse.

Moss Lane bridge SD 487432. Good example of Lancaster Canal stone-built accommodation bridge, single arch, humped, bowed in plan, parapet of larger stones with projecting string course below, buttresses each side of arch.

Garstang Mill SD 493448. Former water-powered corn mill on river Wyre just north of Garstang bridge. Three storeys and attic, stone-built, pitched slate roof, rectangular windows, some blocked. Weir removed and mill race filled in. Mill converted to residence. Formerly had internal iron waterwheel 12 ft (3·7 m) diameter, 12 ft wide, breast shot, rim gearing. A mill is marked on Yates's map of Lancashire, 1787.

Garstang Town Station SD 491456. Former terminus and headquarters of Garstang & Knott End Railway, which ran west across the plain to Pilling (opened 1870) and thence to Knott End at mouth of Wyre (opened 1908). Closed to passengers 1930, goods 1965. Island passenger platform and goods platform with remains of goods shed survive. There was a signal box on the passenger platform adjoining the waiting room. The line was extended east to join LNWR at **Garstang & Catterall Station** SD 509439, using west side of LNWR down platform. Stone bridge over road to south widened with steel-girder span. Station buildings on east, built on embankment, two storeys, stationmaster's house at south with living rooms at platform level, bedrooms below. Closed 1969.

GISBURN
Gisburn tunnel SD 826489. On LYR line from Chatburn to Midland at Hellifield, opened 1880. Not really a tunnel, but a covered way under Gisburn Park 500 ft (152 m) long, castellated stone portals each end. To west is Gisburn Station. Closed 1962, with surviving stationmaster's house.

GLASSON
Glasson Dock SD 444561. A site of great interest in relation to both port and canal history. A dock was built 1783-91 at the mouth of the Lune by the Lancaster Port Commissioners as the passage up to Lancaster became increasingly difficult. Linked with Lancaster Canal by Glasson branch, opened 1826, with lock connection between the dock and a large basin at the end of the canal branch. Important trade links developed with Kendal and with east Lancashire via Preston: cargoes were mostly transhipped at Glasson, but there was some through traffic. LNWR built a railway branch from Lancaster in 1883 with idea of developing traffic to Ireland: closed to passengers 1930 and station now demolished, goods traffic until 1964, line can be followed along edge of marsh to east. Most active period of dock was in mid-19C before development of Fleetwood and Morecambe, but it is still used. It is 500 ft by 200 ft (152 m by 61 m), masonry side walls, heavy wooden entrance gates at river end, small stone-built office and lighthouse on east pier, dry dock on west side filled in. The lock between the dock and the canal basin has masonry side walls, iron gates at dock end, wooden at canal end, swing bridge between gates, winch by Phoenix Foundry, Lancaster, to operate gates. Canal basin some 400 yd by 300 yd (365 m by 275 m), overflow with iron grille at west, stone wharf on north where there was formerly a warehouse. East of dock is Victoria Hotel, c. 1840, three storeys, stone-built, bay windows.

GREAT HARWOOD
Small cotton-weaving town developed largely in late 19C following opening of LYR line from Blackburn to Padiham, opened 1877, closed 1957-64, line landscaped south of town. Mixture of stone-built cottages and large brick-built weaving sheds of which good examples are **Record Mill** SD 740329 and **Premier Nos. 1 and 2 Mills** SD 737326 in north; **Deveron Mill**, 1899, and **Palatine Mill**, 1913, SD 730318, south of former railway; **Premier No. 3**

Mill and **Waveridge Mill** SD 730318, on west. Now used for variety of industries, but only two for textile weaving. Some were built by property companies and leased to textile firms. (Cf. *Accrington*.) There is a detailed survey in Michael Rothwell, *Industrial Heritage: a Guide to the Industrial Archaeology of Great Harwood*, (Hyndburn Local History Society), 1980.

GREAT MITTON
Mitton bridge SD 716387. Early 19C three-arch stone bridge over river Ribble, replacing former ferry. The old road down to the ferry is traceable east of Mitton Church. The Aspinall Arms on the south side of the river was formerly called the Mitton Boat.

GRIMSARGH
Grimsargh Station SD 585344. On Preston & Longridge Railway, track removed, single-storey stone station building with stone-flag roof and four chimneys, platform. Goods yard to east. Whittington Junction for line to hospital to north.

HASLINGDEN
Most westerly of the Rossendale townships crossed north–south by the Bury–Whalley road, turnpiked under an Act of 1789, and by the East Lancashire Railway's line from Stubbins to Accrington, opened 1848. Water-powered mill sites, later stone-built mills and associated housing along valleys of Swinnel brook and Ogden brook, west of town centre.

Haslingden Station SD 783239. Closed 1960-64, site being cleared. Single entrance to short tunnel on south, line visible to north at Hud Hey Road, with overgrown cutting, and at Rising Bridge, Baxenden.

Higher Mill, Helmshore SD 777217. Important textile museum maintained by Lancashire County Council on site of woollen finishing mill built 1789 by William Turner, who had two other woollen mills in Helmshore. Three storeys, stone-built, stone-flag roof. On ground floor is fulling shop preserved as it was being worked by L. & W. Whittaker in early 1960s: four sets of fulling stocks, one dated 1820, two milling machines, small carriage for distribution of urine used as cleansing agent. High-breast waterwheel 17ft (5·2 m) diameter, 9 ft (2·7 m) wide, iron axle, hubs and rims, wooden spokes and buckets, rim gearing with drive to cam wheels on shaft to raise and lower fulling hammers, and drive to floor above formerly used for raising machines. To north is millpond and race 300 yd (275 m) to weir on Ogden brook. Upper floors of mill are used for collection of early textile machinery, mostly moved from TMM Research (now Platt-Saco-Lowell) farther down the road at Hollies Bank Mill: collection includes reconstruction of Hargreaves's original spinning jenny, a later jenny from Dobcross, Saddleworth, an Arkwright water frame from Cromford, Derbyshire, early carding engines, spinning wheels, power looms. The museum also has a simple rotative beam engine built by Peel Williams & Peel of Soho Foundry, Ancoats, Manchester, for a Stockport cotton mill. The mill to the west has been used for mule spinning: there is a square stone chimney on the hillside opposite with a flue under the road.

Helmshore Station SD 782211. On East Lancashire Railway line to Accrington, closed 1966. Single-storey stone buildings survive on each platform with semi-circular headed doorways and windows in pairs. Particularly attractive building on south with wooden canopy over platform, worthy of preservation. The viaducts in the valley to the north are also worthy of notice.

Laneside Foundry SD 789226. West side of Manchester Road, engineering works of S. S. Stott & Co., who built many steam engines for cotton mills in the area, including a tandem compound for **Syke Mill** to the south and a cross-compound horizontal engine for **Grane Manufacturing Co**, SD 790228, with 18 in. and 36 in. (46 cm by 92 cm) cyliners, 500 h.p., drove large weaving shed with Lancashire looms by overhead shafting until end of 1978.

Two mills at Baxenden on northern boundary: **Rising Bridge Mill** SD 782256, started as woollen mill in 1790s, later cotton-waste spinning and weaving, stopped c. 1930, now used for poultry food manufacture; **Hope Mill** SD 779256, three storeys, stone-built, single-storey weaving shed, square stone chimney. Started c. 1870. Spinning and weaving until 1880, weaving only until 1934. Now used by bakery firm.

HELMSHORE See *Haslingden*

HEYSHAM See *Morecambe and Heysham*

HOGHTON
Hoghton Bottoms. Very interesting former water-powered textile site below Hoghton Tower, where in early 19C there were two cotton mills and a shuttle-making works between them. **Higher Mill** SD 628265, three storeys, stone-built, four-storey section at west, internal structure of cast iron pillars, timber beams, joists and floors. Last used for weaving, with Lancashire looms driven from overhead shafting. Wheel house on west with penstock and traces of gearing for former 40 ft (12·2 m) diameter waterwheel, head race 350 yd (320 m) south to fine curved, stone-built weir on river Darwen. Tail race runs north via site of shuttle works half a mile (800 m) to **Lower Mill** SD 627272, now demolished, ponds on south, partly driven by water turbine until it closed. Stone-built cottages associated with both mills. South of

Higher Mill the river Darwen is crossed by **Hoghton Tower viaduct**, built 1844-46 by Blackburn & Preston Railway, three high semi-circular stone arches.

Tollhouse SD 635251. Two storeys, pyramidical slate roof, at junction of Preston Old Road from Blackburn (A674) and road via Wheelton to Chorley (A6061).

HURST GREEN (AIGHTON, BAILEY AND CHAIGLEY)
Site of three former water-powered **bobbin mills** on Dean brook, SD 683380, two north, one south of B6243. Top and bottom mill have been converted to residences: at middle mill foundation only. Baines's *Directory of Lancashire*, 1825, lists five bobbin turners in Hurst Green. It was a significant industry in the area: there were mills at Billington, Ribchester, Dutton, Dilworth and Chipping.

KIRKHAM
Well known centre of linen and sailcloth manufacture in 18C and 19C, associated with Hornby and Birley families. Flax imported through port of Wardleys at mouth of river Wyre in 18C. Former Hornby warehouse, converted to dwelling houses, 22-24 Poulton Street; Thomas Hornby's house 28-30 Poulton Street.

Kirkham Linen Mill SD 424323. Built by John Birley and John Langton in late 18C and gradually extended in 19C with ranges of buildings around square with reservoir in middle. 1,600 employees in 1876. Taken over for cotton-waste spinning, 1917. Closed and sold, 1972: site developed for housing.

Kirkham & Wesham Station SD 420327. On Preston & Wyre Railway (LYR–LNWR joint), opened from Preston to Fleetwood 1840. West of station is junction with Lytham branch, opened 1846, same year as branch from

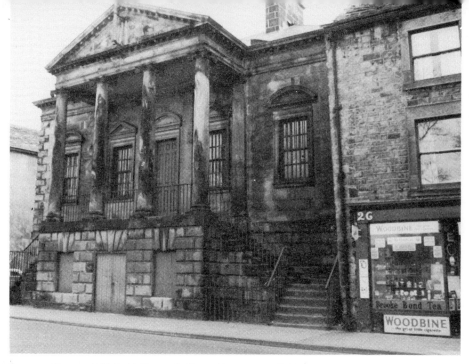

Customs House of 1764, St George's Quay, Lancaster, 1966

Poulton to Blackpool. Late 19C and early 20C buildings: yellow and blue-brick booking office in Poulton Road, yellow-brick and timber stairways to island platform with three single-storey yellow and red-brick waiting rooms and offices. Wide bridge over tracks at west: single blue-brick arch with two steel-girder spans on north, one on south.

Windmill SD 432319. On hill east of town centre, brick-built tower, now completely restored, re-roofed and incorporated in modern residence. Built late 18C/early 19C to replace older wooden post mill: Yates's map of Lancashire, 1786, shows two mills, old and new. Reported as 'ruined' by Allan Clarke in *Story of Blackpool*, 1923. Photograph showing damaged cap and remains of sails in Bennett and Elton, *History of Corn Milling*, vol. 2, 1899, p. 317.

LANCASTER

Historic town with castle, Priory Church and site of Roman fort on top of a hill above the Lune crossing. Became an important port in 18C, trading with northern Europe, West Indies and the American colonies, importing sugar, tobacco and, later, cotton. Ancillary industries of shipbuilding, rope-making, sail-making, block-making and anchor-making developed. Imports formed basis of industrial development in sugar refining, cotton, linen and silk manufacture, furniture making and, later, linoleum manufacture. Decline in later 19C owing to difficulty of navigating the river, lack of railway connection to the quays and growth of new ports, e.g. Fleetwood and Barrow.

St George's Quay SD 474623. The place to capture the atmosphere of the old port. Developed in mid-18C. Line of four and five-storey stone-built warehouses with narrow fronts and gables to quay, wooden and later iron hoists, projecting corbels below loading openings to support planks. Customs house by Richard Gillow 1764 with classical portico: now electricity substation. To west are Carlisle viaduct, carrying Lancaster & Carlisle Railway over river Lune, and **Lune Mills** SD 463617, oilcloth and linoleum works started by James Williamson from 1839 onwards: his son became Lord Ashton, whose

Dry dock, Leeds & Liverpool Canal, Lathom, 1979

memorial in Williamson Park is a dominant feature of the town.

Penny Street Station SD 479611. A railway station which is now the nurses' home of Lancaster Infirmary. Original terminus of Lancaster & Preston Junction Railway, opened 1840. Closed after opening of line to Carlisle in 1846 and sold in 1853. A new station with Tudor-style station buildings was opened at Lancaster Castle. Penny Street at junction of roads to Preston and Cockerham has two-storey classical stone building, and to south line of original track to junction with later line to Carlisle.

Lune aqueduct SD 483639. The finest canal aqueduct in the North West, carrying the Lancaster Canal over the river Lune. Built 1794–97 to John Rennie's design by Archibald Miller and William Cartwright, with Alexander Stevens & Son of Edinburgh as contractors. 600 ft (183 m) long, five 70 ft (21 m) span semi-circular arches, 60 ft (18 m) high, stone-built, buttresses between arches, concave abutments, entablature above arches, balustraded parapet, inscription in Latin over central arch. Cost £48,000.

LATHOM

Canal Junction SD 451115. Site of great interest at junction of main line of Leeds & Liverpool Canal, opened to Wigan 1779, and Rufford branch (Lower Douglas Navigation), opened 1781. Two locks on Rufford branch, masonry side walls, double wooden gates top and bottom, iron bollards, stone balance-arm treads, wooden lock-end bridges. At first lock two-storey brick-built lock keeper's house, single-storey stone-built tollhouse. Ship Inn near by. Single-arch humped stone bridge with cobbled roadway carrying towpath of main line over Rufford branch. On east side dry dock, stone sides, floor of stone setts, blocks to support boats under repair. Near by is row of two-storey brick-built cottages. All form a canal community with features maintained in good condition by British Waterways Board.

LEYLAND

British Leyland works SD 544221. Fine 20C office building and extensive range of engineering shops of the bus and lorry works which developed from a smithy taken over by James Sumner, 1892. Joined by George and Henry Spurrier to form Lancashire Steam Motor Co., producing steam lorries for sale from 1897 to 1926. Produced first petrol lorry 1904, first double-decker bus 1905. Supplied thousands of bus chassis to all parts of the world: equally well known as 'Leyland Motors'.

LIVESEY

Star Paper Mill SD 644250. On river Roddlesworth, started 1875. In 1890 had about 300 workers producing 200 tons of paper weekly. Equipment included chopping machines, keirs for bleaching rags, 26 beaters for making pulp, four paper-making machines, seven reeling machines. Still working, as is Sun Paper Mill to north.

Preston Road viaduct SD 650259. Three-arch, high, stone-built viaduct on Lancashire Union Railway's line from Blackburn to Chorley, opened 1969. Canal viaduct to south.

LONGRIDGE

Famous for its stone: line of quarries north-east of town along Longridge Fell, now being landscaped. Widely used for buildings in the North West in 19C.

Longridge Station SD 603374. Terminus of single-track Preston & Longridge Railway, opened 1840, closed 1930 for passengers, 1967 for goods. Single-storey, 19-bay stone station building, platform, small projecting canopy at north end. Level crossing on Berry Lane removed, site of goods station north of road. The line formerly continued to Lords Quarry.

LYTHAM ST ANNES

Lytham windmill SD 371270. Long a familiar feature on the green on Lytham front, brick-built tower mill with restored boat-shaped wooden cap and replaced sails. Mill on site built 1805 by Richard Cookson, destroyed by fire 1918: on evidence of postcard in 1916 had shutter sails (information from J. H. Norris of Wilmslow). Reported as ruined by Allan Clarke in 1923, later restored and became café. Now an electricity substation. At an earlier period there were two post mills farther inland between St Cuthbert's Church and Lytham Hall.

Lytham Dock SD 383280. Built 1840–42 by Ribble Navigation Co. in agreement with Thomas Clifton of Lytham Hall at mouth of main drain from Lytham Moss, for vessels waiting to go out to sea or up river to Preston. Timber wharf on west, branch line from Preston & Wyre Railway 1846, with cranes and turntable. Traces of railway and former iron sluice gates at entrance from main drain survive. To south in Dock Road a shipbuilding industry developed, making, among other things, river steamers for Africa between the two world wars. Now site of **Lytham Motive Power Museum**, with locomotives, model railway and road vehicles, open May to October.

MELLING WITH WRAYTON

Melling tunnel SD 606707. On Midland/Furness joint line from Wennington to Carnforth, opened 1867, providing direct link from Furness to the Midland's Leeds–Morecambe line, at time of development of Barrow as a port. 1,200 yd (1,097 m) long from north of river Wenning to Melling. Melling Station was closed to passengers 1952, to goods 1960.

MELLOR

Former hand-loom weaving community north of Blackburn. Good examples of stone-built cottages with traces of ground-floor workshops (double or triple windows, some blocked) at **Long Row** off Barker Lane, and **Saccary** SD 664315. Timmins also notes a number of examples in Mellor Lane in the central area of the township.

MORECAMBE AND HEYSHAM

Morecambe Quay SD 426645. The stone jetty is the main survival of Morecambe's period of development from *c*. 1850 as a railway port, connected with the building of the 'little' North Western Railway through the Lune and Wenning valleys, linking Lancaster and Morecambe with the Midland Railway's Leeds–Carlisle line opened 1849 and taken over by the Midland 1858. The port had a coastal trade, steamer services to Barrow, Fleetwood, Glasgow and Belfast. Decline after the development of Barrow and opening of railway between Carnforth and Wennington. The link with the Midland, however, meant that Morecambe's holiday-makers came to a great extent from the West Riding towns, contrasting with Blackpool's, who came more predominantly from east Lancashire.

Morecambe Promenade Station SD 428643. Fine early 20C stone-built Gothic-cum-Tudor frontage with prominent chimneys, large circulation area with iron and glass roof. Replaced earlier station at terminus of North Western Railway. The line from Lancaster was electrified by the Midland Railway 1908 with overhead 6·6 kV a.c. supply, closed 1966. LNWR built a line from Hest Bank on the Lancaster–Carlisle line 1864: the terminus is now a bus station and the line goes through to the Promenade Station. Earlier there was a station at Morecambe Harbour, closed to passengers 1904 when the line to Heysham was built. The Midland Hotel near Promenade Station is a late example of railway hotel building, 1932-33 by Oliver Hill with curved frontage to the sea.

Heysham harbour. New 36-acre harbour built by Midland Railway 1897-1904 with electric railway connection from Lancaster–Morecambe line. Two breakwaters built from Near Naze on north, Red Nab on south, enclosing 100 acres of foreshore; 3,000 ft (914 m) of quay walls, concrete with coping of Shap granite, lattice tower with leading light on Near Naze, lighthouse on south wall. During construction there were a maximum of 2,000 workers living in specially built villages known as Klondyke and Dawson City, 16 miles (22 km) of works railway, six steam navvies. First ship sailed on day excursion to Douglas, Isle of Man, 13 August 1904. See F. Whewell Hogarth, *A History of Heysham*, 1904.

NELSON

A 'new' cotton town created in the second half of 19C out of the old townships of Great and Little Marsden, which were centres of domestic woollen manufacture. Only four mills were built before 1850, but by 1900 there were over 20 and by 1914 some 35. The emphasis was on weaving and the characteristic buildings are single-storey, stone-built, north-light weaving sheds, two or three-storey preparation and warehouse blocks, separate engine and boiler houses, and tall stone or brick chimneys. From the hills to the south there is a fine view of this late Victorian landscape of mills, rows of stone-built workers' cottages, churches, chapels and public buildings. Nelson was well known for the 'room and power system', where companies built mills with steam engines and shafting and rented them out to manufacturers at so much per loom. For the background see W. Bennett, *The History of Marsden and Nelson* (Nelson Corporation), 1957.

CENTRAL AREA

Victoria Mills SD 861379. Three-storey stone building is surviving remnant of mill built by a room & power company in 1857. There were four or five mills in this central area, either side of Leeds Road. Nelson Baths in Bradley Road to north are on site of mill pond of old Bradley corn mill, which worked as cotton mill 1812-54.

Nelson Station SD 860376. On East Lancashire Railway's Burnley–Colne line, opened 1849, in use. Track carried over Railway Street by twin bridges with cast iron beams. Island platform with attractive wood and glass canopy supported on two rows of cast iron pillars, each with four decorated brackets. Station Hotel opposite entrance with red-roofed towers and dormer windows, 1893, described by Pevsner as 'Elizabethan to Stuart style'.

Walverden Mill SD 862376. South of Netherfield Road, built by B. & J. Smith of Colne, 1849, with 25 h.p. steam engine, and subsequently bought by Walverden Room & Power Co. Good example with stone-built weaving shed, three-storey mill, separate engine house, boiler house with open cast iron water tank on top.

Vale Street Shed SD 866375. Built by Nelson Room & Power Co. in late 1880s with 500 h.p. steam engine. Long range of two-storey buildings with large weaving shed south-west. Still partly used for weaving.

SOUTH

Valley Mills SD 868372. Built in 1890s: one of best examples in north-east Lancashire. Nos. 1 and 2 mills west of Southfield Street, two and three-storey stone buildings, 29 bays long, engine house on north with open cast iron water tank on top. Housing, recreation ground and sports club on hill to east. All in use by Courtauld's Northern Weaving Division. On opposite side of Walverden valley are two other large weaving mills: **Clover Mill** and **Marsden Mill**, occupied by furniture and carpet manufacturers.

SOUTH-EAST

Remains of former collieries and stone quarries on hills above town. **Catlow Quarry** SD 884368, extensive workings each side of Catlow Lane, now planted with trees. Provided stone for many towns in area: carried by carts and waggons to wharf on Leeds & Liverpool Canal.

Clough Head Pits SD 873373. Coal mining in 18C, two shafts in use in early 19C, two coke ovens. At **Castercliffe** SD 884383, an early hill fort site, are numerous traces of surface workings for coal.

NORTH-EAST

Group of **six cotton-weaving mills** SD 870382, all with single-storey north-light sheds, two and three-storey preparation buildings, separate engine and boiler houses, at least two still weaving: **Oak Bank Mill**, built in 1890s; **Hendon Mill**, also 1890s but on evidence of date stone rebuilt 1913; **Malvern Mill** with date stone 1912; **Glenfield Mill**; **Dale Shed**; **Manor Mill**, south of Hallam Road.

WEST

Lomeshay Mill SD 851377. On east side of Pendle Water, one of Nelson's older mills, built 1780 by Ecroyd's of Edge End, prominent 18C clothiers, as wool-spinning mill supplying hand-loom weavers. Small steam engine by 1836. New power-loom shed 1851. Worked by Ecroyd's until 1900: two-storey stone-built cottages with stone-flag roofs in Sun Street, Water Street and Ecroyd Street. Had its own gas works and water supply to houses.

Lomeshay Bridge Mill SD 853377. Built 1841: date stone with initials S.H. Another date stone inscribed 'TBE 1899' suggests restoration or extension. Four storeys stone-built, pitched stone-flag roof, ten by four bays. Probably oldest surviving textile mill building in Nelson. Near by bridge over Leeds & Liverpool Canal, single arch, stone-built, humped, bowed in plan, is typical of those in the area.

There are two later weaving mills

along canal in Lomeshay: **Spring Bank Mill** SD 852375, built in 1890s, long three-storey stone building with two iron dog-leg fire escapes, weaving shed with traces of square bearing boxes for shafting in outside wall, engine house on canal side; **Whitefield Mill**, built in 1880s by Whitefield Room & Power Co. to hold 2,000 looms. North-west towards Reedyford is another line of canalside weaving mills: **Laurel Bank Mill**, *c*. 1880, and **Seed Hill Mill**, earlier, in George Street, SD 857381; **Albert Mills** SD 859383, built 1863 for worsted and cotton, now partly demolished; on west side of canal, **Reedyford Mill** and **Pendle Street Shed**, with plaque on engine house: 'Pendle Street Room & Power Co. Ltd 1855'.

Clifton windmill, Newton with Clifton, 1964. *Photograph W. J. Smith*

NETHER KELLET
Limestone quarrying township on north side of Lune valley, just east of M6. **High Roads Quarry** SD 515687, north of road to Over Kellet, disused; **Ash Grove Quarries** SD 510684 **Long Dales Quarry** SD 514678. 'Central' village of limestone cottages and Limeburners' Arms Inn.

NETHER WYRESDALE
Cleveley Mill SD 500504. Former water-powered corn mill on river Wyre with long race from weir three-quarters of a mile (1,200 m) north, large pond immediately north of mill. May have had two waterwheels, later water turbine fed by iron pipe. Three storeys, stone-built, two filled-in stone arches, stone-flag roof. Looks as if mill was extended when turbine was installed. Vertical shaft drive to gearwheel on horizontal shaft, from which drive was taken to different parts of mill. Marked on Yates's map of Lancashire, 1786, OS 6-inch map of 1848.

Bobbin Mill SD 521511. On Lords House brook, tributary of river Wyre. House with two-storey stone-built mill at right angles, small-paned windows, stone-flag roof. Formerly had an external waterwheel at south-west and two lines of machinery on each of two floors. Pond in front of mill is now part of garden, there was another pond higher upstream.

NEWTON WITH CLIFTON
Clifton Windmill SD 464313. Brick-built tower mill with boat-shaped wooden cap built by Ralph Slater in late 18C. Iron cross, on which common sails were mounted, and staging for fantail to turn cap with the wind survive. Restored and used, along with adjoining single-storey building, as a club. Formerly had wooden staging around tower to give access to sails. Ceased working in 1920s.

Private turnpike. South of A584

Preston–Lytham road are traces of a private toll road built across Lea Marsh and Newton Marsh by local landowners, Thomas Clifton and Sir Henry Hoghton, from 1781 onwards. Runs from SD 458294 to Old Toll House at SD 443294. There was another toll gate at Lea near the present Lea Gate Hotel: both are marked on OS 6-inch map of 1844.

ORMSKIRK
Waterworks Works of former Southport Birkdale & West Lancashire Water Board. At Scarth Hill, SD 430067, recent concrete bowl-shaped tank on circular support, with older three-bay brick-built pumping house, on site of former windmill. East of town centre at SD 433085 is covered cast iron tank on triple sandstone piers, with pumping station to north at Bath Farm.

OSWALDTWISTLE
Between Accrington and Blackburn with built-up area in north around 19C cotton-spinning and weaving mills, scattered traditional stone-built farmhouses and numerous former domestic workshops on higher ground to south and west, many remains of coal workings. Famous for its connection with the Peel family and the beginnings of calico printing in Lancashire and with James Hargreaves, inventor of the spinning jenny. There is a detailed published survey: M. Rothwell, *Industrial Archaeology of Oswaldtwistle*, (Lancashire County Council Library and Leisure Committee), 1978.

CENTRAL AND NORTHERN AREA
Aspen Colliery SD 737285. Sunk 1869 by Thomas Simpson & Co., pillar-and-stall working, closed 1922. Well preserved bank of beehive coke ovens near overgrown canal basin, unusual and important survival. To north is Aspen embankment on East Lancashire Railway, built in early 20C to enclose former 33-span single-track timber viaduct.

Holland Bank Chemical Works SD 740286. Started 1845 by William Blythe from Kirkcaldy, Scotland, who studied chemistry at Manchester, and then worked at Church Bank Printworks. Manufactured variety of chemicals for textile industry. Still chemical works with mainly recent buildings, 19C office in Holland Bank House.

Moscow Mills SD 744280. Parts of stone-built spinning and weaving mill started by Walmsley Bros in 1820s. 60,000 mule spindles and over 1,100 looms in 1880. Workers' cottages in near-by streets. Paddock House, convent school to south-east, was built by Benjamin Walmsley *c.* 1830.

Foxhill Bank Printworks SD 741282. Reservoirs and remains of buildings in valley of Tinker brook, west of Union Road. Started as printworks *c.* 1780, operated by Peel's in 1790s, Simpson's from 1813. 14 printing machines and 273 hand-block tables in 1846. Sold to Steiner's of Church Bank 1892, stopped printing 1931. There is a line of mid- and late 19C cotton mills along the west side of Tinker brook.

WEST
Stanhill Ring Spinning Mill SD 730282. Large four-storey brick-built cotton-spinning mill with stone decoration, built by Stanhill Spinning Co. 1906-07; 72,000 ring spindles in 1910. Large engine house and water tower at north-west. Still working.

Stanhill Post Office SD 729277. This is the cottage where James Hargreaves lived when he was working on the spinning jenny *c.* 1764. Hargreaves was associated at this time with Robert Peel of Brookside.

Vine Mills SD 732272. Built by Vine Spinning Co. Interesting and unusual contrast of four-storey, stone-built mill of 1875 with later brick-built extension, and typical large brick-built mill of 1905-07 with ornamental tower and extension of 1913-14. Engine house between two mills. Had over 190,000 mule spindles in 1914. Now industrial estate.

Brookside Printworks SD 722272. Reservoirs and remains of buildings where Robert Peel (1723-95) started hand-block calico printing in early 1760s, when the industry first developed in Lancashire. Start of the great Peel textile empire. Later operated by John Reddish of Brinscall. Four printing machines in 1846. Printing ceased 1862: paper-making in later 19C. Robert Peel lived at Peel Fold, SD 717280, 17C farmhouse north of Stanhill Road.

Cabin End Mill SD 711279. Two-storey preparation building and walls of former weaving shed survive from spinning and weaving mill built c. 1835, closed 1955. Workers' houses on Stanhill Road at Cabin End, SD 712262, row of 24, two storeys, stone-built, some three-storeyed at rear.

Mount St James SD 715277. Rows of cottages each side of Stanhill Road with evidence of former triple windows of ground-floor domestic workshops.

SOUTH

Fern Mill SD 721266. Highest mill site in Oswaldtwistle. Small stone-built weaving shed, engine and boiler houses, square chimney. Built 1860, ceased production 1968.

Sough Lane Colliery SD 718261. Good example of mid-19C workings, started in 1840s, two shafts. Embankment and cutting of tramroad clearly visible running north-west to coke ovens at Knuzden, with remains of tunnel lower down. To west is Collier's Row, nine two-storey cottages, modernised. There are other coal-mining remains to south either side of Sough Lane: **Clough Pits**, traces of bell pits at SD 718254, **Bellthorn Colliery** SD 723246, worked until 1884.

Tollhouses Surviving two-storey tollhouses on Bury Haslingden Blackburn & Whalley Trust's Blackburn–Haslingden road (A677), built 1790-91: Sough Lane Ends, SD 716270; Whams brook, SD 734255; Jumble Holes SD 767252.

OVER KELLET
Capernwray Mill SD 530719. Former water-powered corn mill on river Keer. Three storeys, stone-built, external breast-shot wheel, with direct bevel-gear drive to two pairs of stones. Drying kiln with remains of perforated-tile floor at south. Near by are old humped stone packhorse bridge over the river and ten-arch stone-built railway viaduct on Furness/Midland joint line from Wennington to Carnforth, opened 1867.

OVERTON
Sunderland Point SD 426560. At south end of headland on west side of Lune estuary. Busy trading centre in early 18C with warehouses built by Robert Lawson, a Quaker merchant from Lancaster. Declined after building of Glasson Dock and for a time became a seaside resort, described by Baines in 1825 as '. . . rapidly advancing in reputation as a sea-bathing place'.

PADIHAM
Small cotton-weaving town in Calder valley west of Burnley.

Thompson Street SD 796334. Good examples of stone-built weaving sheds with two-storey preparation buildings.

Jubilee Mill SD 797333. 22-aisle stone-built single-storey weaving shed, two and three-storey preparation and warehouse buildings. Engine house with plaque inscribed 'Padiham Room & Power Co. 1887'. Second shed added 1906. Originally driven by cross-compound, horizontal steam engine by Yates of Blackburn.

Albion Mill (Perseverance Mill). South of Jubilee Mill. Large stone-built weaving shed with two-storey preparation buildings and tall, circular, brick, banded chimney. Partly occupied by dyeing firm, partly by cotton manufacturers running power looms driven by overhead shafting from horizontal steam engine by Yates of Blackburn. One of the few steam-powered sheds still working (cf. Queen Street Mill, *Briercliffe*).

Britannia Mill SD 796339. Stone-built mill and weaving shed north of river Calder, with tall engine house and water tower with name of mill and date 1866. In use by cotton-waste firm.

PARBOLD

Parbold Wharf SD 491105. On Leeds & Liverpool Canal. West of bridge on road to Rufford are five-storey stone-built tower of windmill now converted to residence and two-storey stone-built canal office, east of road former stone-built warehouse with loading openings on canal side now in use as farm shop. On north bank of canal is later brick-built, steam-powered corn mill, also with loading openings on canal front. A little farther east is opening in bank which marks the start of the original route planned under the first Canal Act of 1770, going via Mawdesley, Eccleston, Leyland, Walton le Dale and the Ribble and Calder valleys to Foulridge.

PILLING

Mossland township of north Fylde, known for production of salt by evaporation of brine in 16C and 17C, many references to salt cotes in inventories and other documents.

Pilling Mill SD 407487. Five-storey brick-built tower windmill converted to residence. Windmill marked on Yates's map of Lancashire, 1786, and OS 6-inch map, 1848. Had twin drive to stones on different floors. Steam power introduced 1870. Working until early 1920s. There was also a water-powered mill, probably a tide mill on the Broad Fleet, of which there are plans in Lancashire Record Office, DDX/24.

Pilling Station SD 413478. Terminus of Garstang & Knott End Railway from its opening in 1870 until the extension to Knott End in 1908. Closed to passengers 1930, goods 1963. Level crossing overgrown line, station house, goods siding which had considerable agricultural traffic and warehouses of Preston Farmers' Association.

PLEASINGTON

Alum Crag SD 635281. South of Woodfold Park to west of Blackburn. Site of alum mines operated in 17C and visited by James I in 1617. References to alum workers in area in 18C. Alum was widely used as a mordant in the dyeing industry.

POULTON LE FYLDE

Old market town with fine 18C church, now on outskirts of Blackpool.

Skippool SD 357407. Creek at mouth of river Wyre used by shipping in 17C and 18C and even as late as 1870. Poulton had a customs house in 18C and early 19C, prior to development of Fleetwood.

Poulton Station SD 350396. The original Preston & Wyre station on line to Fleetwood, opened 1840, was northeast of the town near the A588, and later became a goods station. The branch to Blackpool, originally single track, was opened in 1846. With the increase in traffic in late 19C a deviation to the west was made at Poulton and a new connection to the Blackpool branch, allowing direct Blackpool–Fleetwood traffic. The new Poulton station on the present site was opened in 1896.

PREESALL
WITH HACKENSALL

Preesall Salt Works SD 347463. On area of salt marshes on Ann Hill peninsula on east side of Wyre estuary. Built by Fleetwood Salt Co. c. 1902 and later taken over by United Alkali Co. and

ICI. Closed in 1920s but brine continued to be supplied by pipeline under river to works at Burn Naze until 1930s. There was a branch from the Garstang & Knott End Railway, operated by four industrial locomotives.

Preesall Mill SD 368468. Brick-built, tower windmill without cap or sails. Built 1839 to replace post mill. Working in early 1920s.

Preesall Station SD 365476. The road bridge is a good point from which to see the line of the Garstang & Knott End Railway as an earthwork, running east to west. Platform, station building reconstructed for industrial use. Opened 1908, closed to passengers 1930, goods 1950. The terminus at Knott End has been demolished and the site used for a car park.

PRESTON

One of Lancashire's four medieval royal boroughs; market town and administrative centre which was transformed by development of cotton industry from 1791, when John Horrocks built his first mill in area of Stanley Street, east of the parish church. Preston's cotton mills are examined in detail in an important pioneering piece of industrial archaeology of the 1950s: N. K. Scott, 'Preston Textile Mills', unpublished MA thesis in Liverpool University library. Scott showed that the majority of mills in the town before the late 19C were built with cast iron pillars supporting timber beams, joists and floors, rather than with cast iron beams and brick arches, as in many other towns. A number survive, characteristically of four or five storeys, brick-built, plain in style, rectangular windows with stone sills and lintels, often with internal engine houses.

CENTRE AND SOUTH

Preston Station SD 534290. Preston's railway history involves at least eight companies and at one time as many stations. The present Central Station, with late 19C yellow-brick buildings and three-aisle train shed, marks the site where the North Union Railway from Wigan terminated after its opening in 1838. The Lancaster & Preston Railway, opened 1840, and the Bolton & Preston Railway, opened 1843, originally shared Maxwell House Station, north of Fishergate, before moving into the North Union station.

To east is former goods station now used as car park, with five-storey, brick-built LYR warehouse with four projecting timber-covered loading openings. To south is Park Hotel of 1882, formerly connected with station by a covered footbridge, now used as offices by Lancashire County Council. The station is approached across the river Ribble by two fine viaducts: at east on Preston & Blackburn line four-span steel-girder bridge on brick and sandstone piers, brick approach arches on south, sandstone on north, footbridge on east side; to west on North Union line (LNWR–LYR joint) five stone-built, segmental arches on stone piers, with stone parapets, steel lattice-girder extension on west.

Old tram bridge SD 542286. New bridge, but with original stone abutments, across river Ribble on the route of the **Preston & Walton plateway**, built in place of the originally planned aqueduct to connect northern and southern arms of Lancaster Canal. Built by William Cartwright, opened 1803, closed 1864, four and a half miles (7·3 km) to Walton summit (see *Walton le Dale*), L section cast iron rails, 4 ft 1 in. (1·24 m) gauge, laid on stone blocks, double track. To south of bridge is tree-lined embankment. To north was incline (now in Avenham Park) operated by stationary steam engine at top: oil painting in Harris Art Gallery, *c.* 1862, shows four waggons drawn by two horses crossing the bridge and the engine house, demolished 1868. The line passed east of the later main-line railway, through a tunnel under Fishergate to Preston Wharf at the end of the northern arm. A stone wall in Garden Street, SD 537290, marks the line. The site of the wharf is now occupied by Preston Polytechnic.

Penwortham bridges The old bridge is just west of the railway viaducts at SD 530283, 18C, stone, humped, five segmental arches, four piers in river bed, triangular openings in parapet walls, roadway of stone setts. Downstream is the new bridge, fine sandstone structure with three wide, segmental arches, rectangular openings in parapet wall.

Pitt Street Mill SD 534294. *Circa* 1826, five storeys plus basement and attic, five rows of cast iron pillars, timber beams.

NORTH/NORTH-WEST

Maudland Goods Station SD 532298. Original terminus of Preston & Wyre Railway, opened to Fleetwood 1840, to Lytham and Blackpool 1846. Two-storey brick-built goods shed survives.

Hanover Mill SD 533299. Built 1796 by Horrocks, probably oldest surviving mill building in Preston, four storeys and basement, 11 bays long, rectangular windows with stone sills and lintels, three-bay central pediment with stone quoins.

Fylde Road Mill SD 530300. *Circa* 1860, five storeys and basement, corner pilasters, lower two floors with cast iron beams, upper floors with timber beams, all with rows of cast iron pillars.

Arkwright Mill SD 532302. First mentioned 1854, five storeys, corner pilasters, rectangular windows with stone sills and lintels, internal structure of cast iron pillars and timber beams (cast iron beams in mixing room).

Aqueduct Street Mill SD 529304. Two ten-bay five-storey buildings, cast iron pillars and timber beams in older part, cast iron beams in later, original internal engine house, added later engine house on north, square ornamental water tower. Just west of Aqueduct Street the northern arm of the Lancaster Canal now terminates.

Shelley Road Mill SD 525303. Four-storey 'fireproof' mill of 1864, with late 19C three-storey building on Shelley Road, with flat-topped six-storey water tower, weaving shed to north.

Tulketh Mill SD 524309. On the north ring road, built 1905 by Tulketh

Hanover cotton mill, Preston, south front, 1979

Spinning Co., 140,000 spindles in 1952. Four storeys, machine brick with yellow-brick decoration, 42 by 13 bays, maximum window area, internal structure of cast iron pillars, steel beams, concrete floors. Six-bay engine house at south-east, ornamental water tower, tall circular brick chimneys. Occupied by switchgear manufacturers.

Embroidery Mill. Opposite Tulketh Mill, built 1910-13 for cotton weaving with buildings arranged round courtyard from the yarn warehouse through warping and winding departments to main weaving shed and on to cloth warehouse. Another weaving shed to south, **Stocksbridge Mill** SD 525306, built 1904, second shed added 1911, 1,000 looms in 1952, engine house with ornamental facings on south.

NORTH-EAST/EAST

Brookfield Mill SD 538305. East of Lancaster Road, three and four-storey buildings of 1840s, internal structure of cast iron pillars and timber beams, later weaving sheds, partly demolished. Opposite is **St George's Road Mill** SD 539306: opened 1869, three storeys, 16 bays long, structure of cast iron pillars and timber beams, occupied by firm of corn millers.

Deepdale Station SD 546300. Now a coal yard, was the terminus of the single-track Preston & Lonridge Railway, opened 1840, closed to passengers 1930, goods 1968. Along the track to north-east are level crossings over Deepdale Mill Road, with crossing keeper's house, and Skeffington Road, with signal box. The Preston & Longridge Railway was linked in 1850 with the Preston & Wyre at Maudland Road by the mile-long Fleetwood Preston & West Riding Junction Railway, the plans for the extension into Yorkshire never being carried out.

Centenary Mill SD 551297. In New Hall Lane, built by Horrocks in 1895, four storeys, 25 by 9 bays, large windows, ornamental frontage with pro-

jecting towers, carding extension on north, internal structure of cast iron pillars, steel beams and concrete floors.

Hartford Mill SD 551298. 1860, four storeys, 18 by 6 bays, corner pilasters, internal structure of cast iron pillars and timber beams.

Ribbleton Station SD 567320. Two-storey stone station building on west occupied as residence, platform used as part of garden, single-arch, humped and bowed bridge at north end. On Preston–Longridge line.

Cliff Mill SD 557297. In Fishwick View overlooking the Ribble, 1904, four storeys, Accrington brick, terracotta decoration with Doric columns between top-storey windows, flat roof, internal structure of cast iron pillars, steel beams and concrete floors.

WEST

Fishergate Station SD 530289. Former terminus of West Lancashire Railway to Southport, opened 1882, closed 1965. Building demolished except for buttressed, stone side walls and approach road of stone setts. To south is embankment and curving brick viaduct. The bridge over the Ribble has been removed except for four sandstone piers now carrying pipes.

Preston docks. The Ribble was navigated up to Preston by small vessels from the 17C with an anchorage below Penwortham Hill. The main development of the port came in 19C, following the creation of the Ribble Navigation Co., the deepening of the approach channel and the draining of the marshes along both banks of the river.

Victoria Quay and Warehouse SD 527294. Built by Preston Corporation 1839-45, with a railway branch from the North Union station. Goods traffic developed to and from the Mediterranean, northern Europe and North America, passenger services to Liverpool and Scotland. The warehouse of 1844 is four storeys, brick-built on stone foundations, windows with vertical iron bars, some now blocked, stone quoins and parapet, ball finials on gables, four loading slots on road front. Internal structure of five rows of cast iron pillars, cast iron beams, brick arches, three internal dividing walls, four-aisled roof with iron trusses, gravity wheel hoists in roof structure.

To west is the **New Dock** SD 515296. Built 1883-92, involving diversion of the river to the south (the old river bed is visible north of the dock) and building of 1,500 ft (457 m) long quay wall. Dock 3,000 ft by 600 ft (914 m by 183 m) with walls of Longridge stone, approached by lock with two compartments from a basin north of the river. Hydraulic power system for gates, cranes, hoists and capstans.

QUERNMORE

Castle Mill SD 520609. On river Conder north of St Peter's Church. Mill marked on Yates's map of Lancashire, 1786, and on OS 6-inch map of 1848. Present mill built 1818. Overshot, external waterwheel, 36 ft (11 m) diameter, fed from wooden trough, rim gearing, pond to east and weir 500 yd (460 m) upstream. There is description of the mill in *Lancashire Evening Post*, 5 December 1961. There was another water-powered corn mill lower down the river at Conder bridge, and east of that **Narr Lodge** SD 515594 is a former horse mill, brick building with circle where horse walked round to turn central timber shaft with horizontal wheel giving drive to farm machinery.

RAMSBOTTOM

Only the northern area is in Lancashire: for the south see under *Greater Manchester*.

Cheesden valley. A classic waterpower area along the valley of the Cheesden brook, which runs down from the moors between Ramsbottom and Rochdale. There were 14 mills working by 1840s, some of 18C origin. All were later abandoned, except Simpson Clough at the bottom of the valley, but their ruins remain, with weirs and millponds stepped down the valley from the 1,000 ft (305 m) contour to the Rochdale–Bury road. The valley is accessible by foot from the A627 Edenfield–Rochdale road. The mills are

Stone-flag bleaching tanks, Lee Hill bleachworks, Shuttleworth, Ramsbottom, 1965

...isted from the highest site down.

Four Acre Mill SD 828175. Highest mill site in the Cheesden valley, on or near 1,000 ft contour. Remains of stone building with waterwheel pit, pond and race to north. Marked on tithe map of 1838. There are remains of coal workings in the area and an old coal-pit road runs along the side of Turf Moor above the valley.

Cheesden Lumb Mills SD 824162. At Higher Mill, embanked pond above foundations, marked on OS 6-inch map of 1848. Lower Mill is one of most interesting in the valley, at junction of Kill Gate and Cheesden Brooks. Started as woollen finishing mill, later carding also: advertised for sale in the *Manchester Mercury*, 29 August 1789, with waterwheel, fulling stocks, teazler for raising nap on cloth, carding engine and billy for preparing rovings. Changed over to cotton in early 19C. Ruins of three-storey, stone-built mill with extension across stream, stone-sided wheel pit with square iron axle, hubs and brackets for timber spokes of high-breast or overshot waterwheel. Recent investigation shows possible traces of another, possibly earlier, mill to west. Line of the access road down the valley side is clearly visible.

Croston Close Upper Mill SD 824158. Stone-built weir, mill pond with overflow, foundations of mill below pond with wheel pit, partly overgrown. Foundations of two rows of cottages to south. Marked as cotton mill on tithe map of 1838. At the Lower Mill there are remains of the pond, but little of the mill itself. It was a woollen mill in 1838.

Longland Mill SD 823153. Large reservoir with traces of buildings and site of wheel pit below. It was a cotton mill in 1850. There is a school at the north-western corner of the reservoir.

Deeply Vale SD 823148. There were two cotton mills in this area in 1838, one known as Cobhurst Nab Mill, with cottages adjoining. By 1851 Deeply Vale Printworks, which may have started as early as 1815. In 1846 two printing machines, 100 hand-block tables, making rainbow prints, and three, four or five-coloured cloths. Long reservoir, foundations of mill buildings and cottages. Used at one time for paper-making.

Lower Wheel Mill SD 829142. Printworks marked on OS 6-inch map of 1851. Mill pond, foundations and chimney: there were coal workings on the valley side above the mill.

For Birtle Dean and Kershaw Bridge Mills, lower down the valley, see **Heywood**, under **Greater Manchester**.

Lee Hill Bleach Works SD 805175. On Cross Bank Brook in Shuttleworth, east of Bury–Whalley turnpike road. Foundations of buildings, site of waterwheel, with a number of rectangular bleaching tanks with sides of flagstone from local quarries.

RAWTENSTALL

New 19C industrial town created out of medieval cattle ranches, enclosed piecemeal from 16C onwards. Old farms on hillsides above valleys of Whitewell brook, Limy Water and river Irwell along which industrial growth of 18C and 19C is marked by stone-built mills and weaving sheds, interspersed with rows of workers' cottages. Like Bacup, prominent in late 19C and early 20C development of felt, slipper and shoe manufacture.

CENTRAL AREA

Rawtenstall Lower Mill SD 811228. Five-storey, stone-built cotton mill with fine single-storey, north-light weaving shed to north. Started by Whitehead brothers in early 19C and associated with adjoining community of Hollymount, described in glowing terms by W. Cooke Taylor in his *Notes of a Tour in the Manufacturing Districts of Lancashire*, 1841:'. . . handsome houses consisting of four to six rooms, provided with every comfort necessary . . .' and occupied by 'healthy, happy and contented' villagers. A memorial tablet in Old Fold Garden records the site of Hollymount School, built 1839, where Cooke Taylor was impressed both by the elegance of the school and the intelligence of the children. There is an interesting account of the early days in *David Whitehead of Rawtenstall, 1790-1865*, 1956, an autobiography of the manufacturer.

Rawtenstall Station SD 809225. Originally terminus of East Lancashire Railway's line from Clifton Junction, opened 1846, extended to Newchurch 1848, to Bacup 1852. Line to Bacup closed 1966, station closed 1972. Platforms and overgrown track remain with stone-built goods shed and engine shed to south. The bridge over the river Irwell has been removed.

VALLEY OF LIMY WATER

Three mills at **Reeds Holme**: **Holmes Mill** SD 808244 on west side of Burnley Road, three storeys, stone-built, two-aisled roof, weaving shed at north, partly built over stream; **Holmes Shed**, east of Burnley Road, three-storey mill with weaving shed to north, occupied by Newchurch Boot Co.; **Reedsholme Mill**, sizable three-storey mill with date stone 1864, stone-built engine house, octagonal brick chimney,

occupied by leathercloth manufac turers.

Sunnyside Printworks SD 811249 Overgrown foundations of works o: Butterworth & Brooks, started *c.* 1803 In 1844 three printing machines, two steam engines, 220 hand-block tables. Crawshaw Hall on the opposite side of the valley was built by John Brooks in 1831, Sunnyside House to north was bought by John's son, Thomas, who also built the church of St John the Evangelist at Crawshawbooth.

Love Clough Printworks SD 810272. Still working. Started as block-printing works in late 18C. Firm of Cook & Unsworth in 1846: seven printing machines, two steam engines. Taken over by Lee family in later 19C: Lennox B. Lee became director and later chairman of the Calico Printers' Association, who took over the works in 1899. Bad fire in 1906 led to migration of many workers to Birch Vale in Derbyshire. Rows of workers' cottages either side of Commercial Road, leading from Burnley Road to the works.

IRWELL VALLEY

Hall Carr Mill SD 817226. Substantial stone-built cotton mill on south side of Irwell, marked on OS 6-inch map of 1848. Went over to shoe manufacture in 20C: sole cutting in 1943. Still in use in this industry. Ilex Mill on north side of

Waterfoot tunnels, Lancashire & Yorkshire Railway (East Lancashire Railway), Waterfoot, Rawtenstall, 1979

river also became a shoe works.

Waterfoot became the main centre of the growing felt, slipper and shoe industry in the late 19C and early 20C: for an account see Phyllis Cronshaw, 'An industrial romance of the Rossendale valley: the development of the shoe and slipper industries', *Trans. Lancs. & Ches. Antiq. Soc.*, vol. 60, 1948, pp. 29-46. By 1900 there were 13 slipper firms, and the industry also stimulated the growth of ancillary trades, such as cardboard box making, rubber processing, quilting and leathercloth making.

Baltic Mill SD 833219. Woollen mill taken over for felt making by Henry Rothwell. Taken over by Mitchell Ashworth & Stamfield, whose name appears on the present office. Richard Ashworth started at Shawclough Mill, the Mitchell brothers had the Albert Works at Whitewell Bottom (now demolished), where they developed the manufacture of printed felt carpets. There were also felt mills at Myrtle Grove, started by Edward Rostron 1854, Holt Mill, and Bridge End Mill.

Gaghills Mill SD 836221. Large three-storey, stone-built cotton mill, bought in 1899 for slipper manufacture by H. W. Trickett, whose name appears on the two-storey office with date 1900, by when he was employing about 1,000 people. Trickett started life as an apprentice block printer, became a traveller for a slipper firm and started on his own in 1882. Developed large export trade. Trickett's Memorial Ground is on opposite side of Burnley Road.

Waterfoot Station SD 835217. Formerly named Newchurch, to which line was opened in 1848. Closed 1966, buildings demolished, site of goods yard visible. To east where river Irwell runs through a narrow gorge are the two **Newchurch tunnels**, 162 yd and 290 yd (148 m and 265 m), built when the line was extended to Bacup, 1851-52. Impressive twin openings of No. 1 tunnel,

with track removed, and south tunnel blocked.

At **Newchurch** is a line of stone-built mills on east side of Burnley Road, at least two associated with shoe manufacture. The four-storey **Globe Mill** SD 827225 is occupied by Newchurch Boot Co. At **Dale Mills** and **Clark Holme Mill** (1854) to north are traces of former water-power systems with dried-up race, millpond, and arched opening in mill walls. Dale Mills are occupied by waste spinners, Clark Holme Mill by shoe manufacturers.

Shawclough Mill SD 841233. Former water-powered site on Shaw Clough brook, marked as fulling mill on OS 6-inch map of 1848. Taken over for felt-making in 1869 by Richard Ashworth, who later moved to Bridge End Mill, Waterfoot. Down the valley is **Shawclough Lower Mill**, cotton mill in 1848, three storeys, stone-built, later became rubber works and has 'Bowmans Mineral Waters and Confectionery' on west wall.

Whitewell Bottom. Another line of mills along the valley. The main survival at Whitewell Bottoms Mill itself is a square stone chimney on the hillside above.

Osborne Mill SD 835238 is a modernised, single-storey weaving shed occupied by slipper manufacturers. There are only two and three-storey buildings and a hillside chimney at **Sagar Holme Mill** to north, mill used for cotton manufacture. At **Water** at the top of the valley there are two three-storey mills with weaving sheds: **Isle of Man Mill**, used by quilting manufacturers; **Forest Mill**, with date stone 1861.

RIBCHESTER

Famous as site of Roman fort, which includes area of St Wilfrid's Church. In 19C there were a number of bobbin mills on the local streams— Duddon brook, Cowley brook, Boyce's brook—

and two or three cotton mills.

Ribchester bridge SD 662357. Fine stone bridge over river Ribble with three segmental arches on stone piers, rising to centre, parapet walls curving towards road. Built 1774, before when there was no bridge between Edisford (Clitheroe) and Preston but a series of ferries, e.g. at Mitton, Hacking, Dinckley, Salesbury, Osbaldeston, Balderstone and Samlesbury.

RISHTON

Small cotton-weaving town south of Great Harwood, but differing from its neighbour in being crossed by the Leeds & Liverpool Canal, leading to earlier mill development. There is a line of stone-built mills and weaving sheds on the west side of the canal: from the north, **Unity Mill** 1894-95 SD 727308; **Britannia Mill** 1887; **Bridgefield Mill** 1879-85, with stone-built engine house; **Albert Mill** SD 727301, with engine house, boiler house, size house and cloth warehouse of 1912, equipped by Ashton Frost & Co. of Blackburn; **York Mill** SD 726305, 1910.

For a detailed survey see Michael Rothwell and Kathleen Broderick *A Guide to the Industrial Archaeology of Rishton*, Hyndburn Local History Society, 1981.

RUFFORD

Tollhouse SD 459168. At junction of Liverpool–Preston road (A59) and Rufford–Chorley road (A581). Single-storey, rendered, central chimney, windows projecting along two roads.

SABDEN

Sabden Printworks SD 772370. Started before 1792 by Taylor Fort & Bury, who also had Oakenshaw Printworks in Clayton le Moors. Taken over by Bury when partnership was dissolved in 1811. In 1846 nine printing machines, three steam engines, 135 block-printing tables. Foundations in valley of Sabden brook. There were also two cotton-weaving mills in the village: Victoria Mill and Cobden Mill, south of Whalley Road.

SAMLESBURY

Samlesbury Bottoms Mill SD 619289. Water-powered cotton-spinning mill started 1784 by William Slater; near corn mill. Two factories and 14 cottages in 1821. Worked as cotton mill until *c*. 1873 and taken over as paper mill by Isherwood's in 1879.

Roach Bridge Mill SD 596288. Another water-powered cotton mill on the river Darwen started in late 18C by John Watson, who built a gallery for his apprentices in Salmesbury Church. Worked until 1870s: some thirty workers' cottages in 1867. Taken over for paper-making by Roach Bridge Paper Co. before 1880 and still in use for this. Three-storey, stone-built mill, seven by three bays, dressed quoins, impressive weir at side.

SINGLETON

Singleton Hall Farm SD 377391. Horse mill in brick roundhouse attached to farm buildings: opening through wall for drive to machinery. Roundhouse is seven-sided structure with timber roof truss radiating from central post, originally brick pillars with rectangular openings, now blocked, in outside walls. Remains of metal bearings on wooden beams to hold shafting.

Shard bridge SD 369411. Iron toll bridge over river Wyre, 500 yd (457 m) long, replacing ferry in 1864.

STALMINE WITH STAYNALL

Wardleys SD 365429. Former anchorage in creek on east side of Wyre estuary, used by ships from late 16C. Import of flax from the Baltic to Kirkham linen industry in 18C and early 19C. Used by ships from North America bringing timber and from Russia bringing flax and tallow in period prior to the growth of Fleetwood. Remains of wharf built of large stone blocks, brick-built warehouse unfortunately demolished.

TARLETON

Former 'canal port' at north end of Douglas Navigation and Rufford branch of Leeds & Liverpool Canal, near junction with river Ribble.

Sollom lock SD 458188. Masonry side walls and lock keeper's house at junction of Rufford branch of Leeds & Liverpool from Lathom (opened 1781) and tidal river Douglas. Abandoned 1805 when a new cut was made to Tarleton.

Tarleton lock SD 454215. At junction of new canal cut of 1805 and river Douglas, masonry side walls, double wooden gates. A basin was built to the east to accommodate coastal traffic, including coal from Wigan for transhipment to Preston, Freckleton, Lytham, Liverpool, Barrow and Ireland, slate from Wales, gunpowder from Ulverston, iron from Cumberland. Large volume of traffic until mid-1850s; now filled in. Associated rope-making and sail-making industries developed. When the West Lancashire Railway was built from Preston to Southport, 1878–82, a branch was made along the west bank of the river Douglas to Tarleton Basin.

THORNTON CLEVELEYS

Marsh Mill SD 335425. The best-preserved Fylde windmill, built 1794 by Ralph Slater, stopping working in 1920s. Five-storey, brick-built, white-washed tower, wooden staging for access to sails at second-floor level, wooden boat-shaped cap, originally common sails, now roller shutter type, mounted on iron cross. Fantail at rear of cap on wooden staging connected by gearing to rack and kerb on top of the tower. Machinery survives: cast iron

windshaft behind sails, on which is brake wheel driving horizontal crown wheel on wooden main upright shaft. Drive from spur wheels to stones on third floor and to auxiliary machinery on second floor. Grain lifted by sack hoist through trapdoors to top floor and emptied down chutes to stones. Storage on bottom two floors. Now in custody of Lancashire County Council. There is a description by R. B. Butler, K. B. Ellwood and J. A. Tillotson in *Architecture North West*, April–May 1964.

Burn Naze Salt Works SD 342442. Like works at Preesall, started by Fleetwood Salt Co. with pipeline across the river Wyre. Became part of United Alkali Co. and later ICI.

THURNHAM

Conder Mill SD 461554. East of Lancaster–Cockerham road. Water-powered corn mill on river Conder, bought by Lancaster Canal Co. in 1824, when they were building Glasson branch, and rebuilt. Water taken from river to canal, through mill, and by tail race to canal below lock to south of mill. Water turbine by Gilkes of Kendal 1924, replacing waterwheel. Mill three-storeys, stone-built, pitched slate roof, central loading openings. Drying kilns at west with complete floor of square perforated tiles and hearth below, row of ventilators in roof. In use.

TRAWDEN

Agricultural and industrial community stretched out along the valley of Trawden brook from Lower Hall in south to Winewall in north. Early water-powered mill sites, later weaving mills of which three or four survive. An oustanding feature is the long rows of two-storey, stone-built cottages, with stone-flag roofs and small windows along each side of Lanehouse Lane.

Black Carr Mills SD 912390. Three three-storey, stone-built preparation and storage blocks with weaving sheds between. There is another weaving mill, **Forest Shed**, on the opposite side of the road.

TURTON

The northern part of the old township is in Lancashire, for the southern part see *Greater Manchester*.

Armygreaves House SD 728168. House and loomshop built by James Brandwood 1809. Ground floor loomshop lit by six-light mullioned windows front and rear.

Turton Corn Mill SD 738158. Foundations of stone-built mill with waterwheel pit on Bradshaw brook at Turton Bottoms, tail race under road to south. Marked on OS six-inch map of 1850. Iron breast-shot waterwheel removed, restored and preserved at Turton Tower, SD 731152: 14 ft (4·3 m) diameter, 5 ft (1·5 m) wide, cruciform-section axle, eight circular-section

Armygreaves house, domestic workshop, Turton, Lancashire

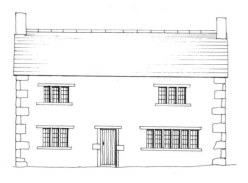

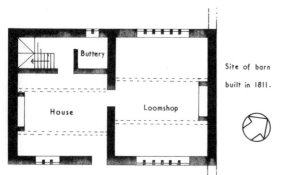

spokes, curved buckets, mountings for rim gearing, iron penstock.

Belmont SD 674162. Good example of early 19C industrial community with rows of stone-built cottages along High Street (A675 Bolton–Preston road) and streets to east and west, including South View (houses with stone-flag roofs), Ward Street and Manor Square (row of fourteen cottages with date stone 1804 on corner house). To south is Belmont Bleach & Dyeworks, still working, group of older stone and later brick buildings with reservoirs north and west.

Turton & Egerton Station SD 731157. On line from Bolton to Blackburn. Closed 1961. Remains of platforms and single-storey stone building. Single track in use.

UP HOLLAND/DALTON

Stone quarries, Ashurst Beacon SD 504075. Extensive flagstone quarries and underground workings developed from early 19C. Tramroad east along line of footpath to Rockville Quarry, SD 513075, along line of Farley Lane to Roby Mill, SD 518074, then on line of footpath north of Walthew Green and on north side of Ayrefield brook as earthwork to basin on river Douglas and later on Leeds & Liverpool Canal at Gathurst, SD 533075. The track was mounted on stone blocks and the tramroad worked until *c.* 1860.

WADDINGTON

Waddow Hall SD 734427. On north bank of river Ribble. J. & J. Parker leased water rights for Low Moor Mill, Clitheroe, from Thomas Weddall of Waddow Hall. The Garnetts, who owned Low Moor Mill after 1799, later leased and then bought the Hall and it became the residence of James Garnett and his family in the mid- and late 19C. It is now a residential training centre of the Girl Guides' Association.

WALTON LE DALE

Formerly known for cotton hand-loom weaving. Scott in his thesis on 'Preston Textile Mills' refers to weaving rooms in cottages at Coupe Green in Higher Walton and in Victoria Road (basement workshop). Also in Victoria Road was the house of Joseph Livesley, who remembered his grandfather working three looms in the basement and taking the pieces to Horrocks's warehouse in Preston.

Bamber Bridge Mill SD 566255. Large cotton-spinning mill of 1907, four storeys and basement, large window area, ornamental water tower with stone decoration and name 'Bamber Bridge Spinning Co.'.

Higher Walton Mill SD 554284. Two earlier buildings with cast iron pillars and beams on ground floor, cast iron pillars and timber beams on upper floors, early 20C extension, weaving shed for 2,000 looms.

Penwortham Mill SD 540273. Originally water-powered site on river Lostock, running by 1810. Mid-19C buildings with later additions, including engine house, boiler house and chimney.

Preston & Walton Plateway. See *Preston.* The terminus of the southern arm of the Lancaster Canal at Walton summit, SD 583246, and the approach line are lost in new housing development. The line of the tramroad is identifiable at the Bamber Bridge crossing, SD 565256, but is built on both sides. Main surviving feature is 1,200 yd (1097 m)-long Penwortham embankment from Carr Wood, SD 541274, to Old Tram Bridge over the Ribble: originally planned as line of canal approach to Ribble aqueduct.

WARTON

Millhead SD 497714. Community built for workers of Carnforth Haematite Co. in 1860s. Row of two-storey cottages with lines of slate-roofed double privies between some of the rows.

Copper mines, Warton Crag. Sites of numerous shafts and square chimney of engine house at Crag Foot, SD 481738, where there were three roasting kilns. Worked from 1750s to 1818, reopened briefly in late 1830s and again between 1881 and 1918.

Tewitfield locks. Only locks on northern arm of Lancaster Canal between Preston and Kendal, built 1817–19. Eight locks with rise of 76 ft (23 m) from Tewitfield Basin SD 518736, to Saltermine, SD 519748. Masonry side walls, wooden gates, examples of rack-and-pinion gate-paddle gear, where paddle is moved from side to side. Tewitfield bridge on A670 south of the locks is a good example of a skewed, single-arch structure.

WENNINGTON See *Melling with Wrayton*

WHALLEY

Abbey Mills SD 733360. Formerly water-powered corn mill on or near site of the mill of the famous Cistercian abbey nearby. Built 1837 by J. Taylor of Moreton Hall. Four storeys, stone-built, central loading openings and line of four windows each side, two-storey extensions west and east. Internal structure of cast iron pillars, timber beams, joists and floors. Once had six pairs of millstones. Stone-built wheelhouse on north, with grille and iron sluice worked by counterweights. Waterwheel 15 ft 6 in. (4·7 m) diameter, 9 ft (2·7 m) wide, iron axle, hubs and rims, buckets, wooden spokes, stopped 1961 but still *in situ*. Mill race 200 yd (61 m) under King Street to fine shallow V-shaped stone-built weir on river Calder. Sluice at entrance to race with rack-and-pinion gear operating two wooden paddles.

Whalley viaduct SD 727361. Major

engineering work on Bolton Blackburn Clitheroe & West Yorkshire Railway, built 1847–50. Brick, 48 arches, stone parapet, 680 yd (622 m) long, 70 ft (21 m) above river Calder. Seven million bricks, mostly made near by, used in construction, during which two of the arches collapsed in October 1849, killing three men. There is an interesting account of the construction in Stephen Clarke, *Clitheroe in its Railway Days*, 1900. Whalley Station at the northern end of the viaduct was closed in 1962: two-storey stone building remains.

WHITTE LE WOODS

Johnson's Hillocks. Flight of seven locks raising Leeds & Liverpool Canal 60 ft (18·3 m) from junction with southern arm of the Lancaster Canal at SD 591207 to Top Lock, SD 596213. Masonry side walls, double gates top and bottom, mostly renewed, iron bollards, wooden lock-end bridges, stone treads for balance arms. Small two-storey, stone-built tollhouse by bridge at fourth lock, two-storey stone-built lock keeper's house with stone-flag roof and Anchor Inn at Top Lock. South of Bottom Lock is Moss Lane bridge, stone, single arch, humped, slightly bowed in plan, stone parapet with rounded top, projecting string course below parapet.

WHITWORTH

Cotton and quarrying township north of Rochdale with settlements strung out along line of the Spodden valley and the road to Bacup. Contrast of earlier stone-built and later brick-built spinning mills, with many good examples of rows of stone-built workers' cottages. The LYR line from Rochdale to Bacup, opened to Facit 1870, throughout 1881, closed 1947, also follows the valley: traceable as earthwork but much of it now built upon.

Orama Mill SD 883178. Late spinning mill at Hall Fold by the railway near the site of former Whitworth Station. Four storeys and basement, brick-built, long rectangular windows in threes, corner pilasters, yellow-brick decoration, tall circular brick chimney with name 'Orama', water tower at south-west, engine house with tall semi-circular arched windows on east, occupied by firm of kitchen furniture manufacturers.

Bridge Mills SD 884182. Group of mid-19C stone-built mills and weaving sheds, including **Brookside Mill**, four storeys, 16 by 4 bays, rectangular win-

Workers' cottages, Bolton Road, Abbey Village, Withnell, 1979

dows with stone sills and lintels, internal engine house at north for beam engine, projecting latrine tower on west front, occupied by engineering firm. On opposite side of Bacup Road are **Dora Mills**, stone-built, similar in style to Brookside, row of ten early two-storey, stone-built cottages with stone-flag roofs in front, row of five later two-storey stone-built cottages in Mill Street above. In use for cotton doubling.

Facit Mill SD 889190. Large late four-storey, brick-built spinning mill, large window area, south-western corner tower with dome and wrought iron railings, base of chimney and boiler house to east. Occupied by leather merchants. By contrast on opposite side of Bacup Road at **Mill Fold**, stone mill buildings, some very early, with small, rectangular windows and possible trace of arched opening for water power.

Facit and Britannia quarries On the west side of the valley between Facit and Bacup, among the largest in east Lancashire, supplying building stone for many of the cotton towns in 19C. Remains include stone chimneys for winding-engine houses and inclines connecting the quarries with the LYR. See B. Roberts, *Railways and Mineral Tramways of Rossendale*, 1974.

Shawforth Station SD 891205. The tiled subway under the line survives, though the station buildings have gone.

WILPSHIRE

Wilpshire Station SD 687320. On Bolton Blackburn Clitheroe & West Yorkshire Railway's line from Blackburn to Chatburn, opened 1850. Named 'Ribchester' until 1874, closed 1962. Single-storey, six-bay, brick platform building, two-storey station house, brick-and-timber signal box at south. Line still used for goods traffic and occasionally as deviation. To north is a long cutting and the 325 yd (297 m) long Wilpshire tunnel.

WITHNELL

Township between Blackburn and Chorley, with two outstanding examples of industrial communities.

Abbey Mill and village SD 640225. Four-storey, stone-built early Victorian cotton mill with aisled roof, windows of former internal engine house at east, later brick additions, including separate engine and boiler houses, square brick chimney on stone plinth. Stone-built north-light weaving shed to west. Rows of two-storey stone-built cottages with slate roofs, yards and privies at back, among Bolton Road; over 60 houses of earlier date, and several rows of late 19C houses. At least two styles: one with semi-circular arched doorways, the other with stone-framed doorways and projecting lintels. School and church near the mill, row of cottages in Garden Street near by.

Withnell Fold Paper Mills SD 612232. Built 1840–44 by T. B. Parke on banks of Leeds & Liverpool Canal, making tissue paper, writing paper, cartridge paper and newsprint. Amalgamated with Wiggins Teape & Co., 1890. Closed 1966: now industrial estate. Long two-storey, stone buildings along canal north and south of Withnell Fold bridge, with later brick additions. East of the mills is the community with five rows of two-storey, stone-built workers' cottages with stone-framed windows and doorways, yards at rear with privies and ashpit openings with wooden covers, some 29 cottages in all. School of 1897.

Withnell Station SD 639228. On Lancashire Union Railway's line from Blackburn to Chorley, opened 1869. Closed 1960, tracks removed, but earthwork clearly visible north and south of Bolton Road. Two platforms with masonry edging, two-storey, stone-built station house with single-storey extensions north and south.

Brinscall village SD 625214. Early 19C cottages in School Lane associated with former **Brinscall Hall Printworks** SD 623205, built *c.* 1800, employing over 300 in 1890s, closed 1930. Now little trace of buildings. There was also a bleach works to the north and a water-powered logwood mill to the west on Brinscall brook, probably older than the print works and on site of earlier corn mill.

WRIGHTINGTON

Appley Locks SD 517096. First set on line of Leeds & Liverpool Canal from Liverpool. Three locks, one still in use on channel to south, two out of use and derelict on channel to north. Double wooden gates top and bottom, masonry side walls, gate paddles top and bottom, ground paddles in addition at top. All the locks up to Wigan were doubled as traffic increased.

Appley Bridge SD 523093. Former canal wharf linked in 1820s by tramroad with stone quarries to north: Central Quarry, Appley Road Quarry, Dawber Delph. Wharfside cottages still inhabited. On north bank, works of West Lancs Floor Cloth & Linoleum Co.

Appley Bridge Station on LYR Wigan–Southport line, opened 1855, has cottage-style stone building with bays and gables.

YATE AND PICKUP BANK
See *Eccleshill*

YEALAND REDMAYNE

Leighton Furnace SD 485778. Charcoal-iron blast furnace built by Backbarrow Co., 1713. Charcoal from Leighton Wood, iron ore brought across Leven and Cartmel sands by cart from Dalton in Furness. Water power for bellows and forge hammers from Leighton beck. Production of cast iron ware from 1721. In use until late 18C. Site of furnace and slag heaps, containing much clinker and vitrified material.

Select bibliography

Works relating to particular places or individual sites are listed at the appropriate point in the gazetteer.

Owen Ashmore, *The Industrial Archaeology of Lancashire*, David & Charles, Newton Abbot, 1969.

Christopher Aspin, *Lancashire, the First Industrial Society*, Helmshore Local History Society, 1969.

J. J. Bagley, *A History of Lancashire*, Phillimore, Chichester, 1976.

T. W. Freeman, H. B. Rodgers and R. H. Kinvig, *Lancashire, Cheshire and the Isle of Man*, Nelson, London, 1966.

A. D. George, *Introduction to the Industrial Archaeology of Manchester and South Lancashire*, Manchester Polytechnic, Faculty of Community Studies, 1977.

Sidney Horrocks ed, *Lancashire Business Histories*, Joint Committee on Lancashire Bibliography, Manchester, 1971.

R. Millward, *Lancashire: an Illustrated Essay on the History of the Landscape*, Hodder & Stoughton, London, 1955.

N. Pevsner, *The Buildings of England, Cheshire*, Penguin, 1971; *The Buildings of England, Lancashire*, 2 volumes, Penguin, 1969.

J. H. Smith ed, *The Great Human Exploit: Historic Industries of the North West*, Phillimore, Chichester, 1973.

D. Sylvester and G. Nulty ed, *Historical Atlas of Cheshire*, Cheshire Community Council, Chester, 1958.

Various, *A Guide to the Industrial Archaeology of Merseyside*, North Western Society for Industrial Archaeology and History, second edition, 1978.

P. D. Burdett, *A Survey of the County Palatine of Chester, 1777*, reprinted with introduction by J. B. Harley and P. Laxton, Lund Humphries, London, 1974.

J. B. Harley, *A Map of the County of Lancashire, 1786, by William Yates*, Hist. Soc. Lancs & Ches, 1968.

J. Aikin, *A Description of the Country from Thirty to Forty Miles round Manchester*, London, 1795.

E. Baines, *History, Directory and Gazetteer of the County of Lancaster*, 2 volumes, 1824–25, reprinted David & Charles, Newton Abbot, 1968.

TEXTILES

C. Aspin and S. D. Chapman, *James Hargreaves and the Spinning Jenny*, Helmshore Local History Society, 1964.

Duncan Bythell, *The Handloom Weavers*, Cambridge University Press, 1969.

Harold Catling, *The Spinning Mule*, David & Charles, Newton Abbot, 1970.

Frances Collier, *The Family Economy of the Working Classes in the Cotton Industry, 1783–1833*, Manchester University Press, 1964.

G. W. Daniels, *The Early English Cotton Industry*, Manchester University Press, 1920.

William Fairbairn, *Mills and Mill Work*, 1861; *Report on the Construction of Fireproof Buildings*, 1844.

D. A. Farnie, *The English Cotton Industry and the World Market, 1815–1896*, Clarendon Press, Oxford, 1979.

John Graham, *History of Print Works in Manchester and District, 1760–1846*, 1846. (MS in Manchester Central Library bound with *Chemistry of Calico Printing, 1790–1835*).

S. H. Higgins, *A History of Bleaching*, Longmans Green & Co., London, 1924.

Richard L. Hills, *Power in the Industrial Revolution*, Manchester University Press, 1970; 'Hargreaves, Arkwright and Crompton. Why three inventors?', *Textile History*, volume 10, 1979, pp 114–27.

J. and F. Nasmith, *Recent Cotton Mill Construction and Engineering*, Manchester, 1909.

W. J. Smith, 'The cost of building Lancashire loomhouses and weavers' workshops: the Account Book of James Brandwood of Turton, 1794–1814', *Textile History*, volume 8, 1977, pp 56–76.

Sir Alan J. Sykes, *Concerning the Bleaching Industry*, Bleachers' Association, Manchester, 1925.

J. G. Timmins, *Handloom Weavers' Cottages in Central Lancashire*, Occasional Paper No. 3, Centre for North-west Regional Studies, University of Lancaster, 1977.

L. C. H. Tippett, *A Portrait of the Lancashire Textile Industry*, Oxford University Press, London, 1969.

G. H. Tupling, *Economic History of Rossendale*, Manchester University Press, 1927.

G. Turnbull, *A History of the Calico-printing Industry of Great Britain*, John Sheratt & Sons, Altrincham, 1951.

George Unwin and others, *Samuel Oldknow and the Arkwrights*, 1924, reprinted Manchester University Press, 1968.

A. P. Wadsworth and J. de L. Mann, *The Cotton Trade and Industrial Lancashire, 1600–1780*, 1931, reprinted Manchester University Press 1965.

Sir Frank Warner, *The Silk Industry of the United Kingdom: its Origins and Development*, London, 1921.

George Watkins, *The Textile Mill Engine*, 2 volumes, David & Charles, Newton Abbot, 1970–71.

METALS AND ENGINEERING

T. S. Ashton, *An Eighteenth-century Industrialist: Peter Stubs of Warrington, 1756–1806*, Manchester University Press, 1939; 'The domestic system in the early Lancashire tool trades', *Economic Journal, Economic History Supplement*, volume 1, January 1926, pp. 131–40.

B. G. Awty, 'Charcoal ironmasters of Cheshire and Lancashire, 1600–1785', *Trans. Hist. Soc. Lancs & Chesh.*, volume 109, 1958, pp. 71–124.

F. A. Bailey and T. C. Barker, 'The seventeenth century origins of watch-making in south-west Lancashire', chapter 1 in J. R. Harris (ed.), *Liverpool and Merseyside*, Frank Cass & Co., London, 1969.

Chris Carlon, *The Alderley Edge Mines*, John Sherratt & Sons, Altrincham, 1979.

Alfred Fell, *The Early Iron Industry of Furness and District*, 1908, reprinted Cass, London, 1968.

William Fairbairn, *The Life of Sir William Fairbairn, partly written by himself*, edited and completed by William Pole, 1877, reprinted with introduction by A. E. Musson, David & Charles, Newton Abbot, 1970.

Alan Smith and others, *The Lancashire Watch Company, Prescot, Lancashire, England, 1889–1921*, Ken Roberts Publishing Co., Fitzwilliam, New Hampshire, U.S.A., 1973.

W. M. Lord, 'Development of the Bessemer process in Lancashire', *Trans. Newcomen Soc.*, volume 25, 1950, pp. 163–80.

A. E. Musson, 'James Nasmyth and the early growth of mechanical engineering', *Economic History Review*, Second Series, volume 10, No. 1, August 1957, pp. 121–8.

A. E. Musson and E. H. Robinson, 'The origins of engineering in Lancashire', *Journal of Economic History*, June 1960, pp. 209–33.; 'The early growth of steam power', *Economic History Review*, Second Series, volume 11, No. 3, April 1959, pp. 418–39.

G. H. Tupling, 'The early metal trades and beginnings of engineering in Lancashire', *Trans. Lancs. & Ches. Antiq. Soc.*, volume 61, 1949, pp. 1–34.

COALMINING

Donald Anderson, *The Orrell Coalfield, Lancashire, 1740–1850*, Moorland Publishing Co., Ashbourne, 1975; 'Blundells' Collieries', *Trans. Hist. Soc. Lancs. & Ches.*, volume 116, 1966, pp. 69–116; volume 117, 1967, pp. 109–44; volume 118, 1968, pp 113–80.

A. G. Banks and R. B. Schofield, *Brindley at Wet Earth Colliery: an Engineering Study*, David & Charles, Newton Abbot, 1968.

T. C. Barker, 'Lancashire coal, Cheshire salt and the rise of Liverpool', *Trans. Hist. Soc. Lancs. & Ches.*, volume 103, 1952, pp. 83–101.

Ken Howarth, *Dark Days: Memories of the Lancashire and Cheshire Coalmining Industry*, Radcliffe, 1978.

F. Mullineux, 'The Duke of Bridgewater's underground canals at Worsley', *Trans. Lancs. & Ches. Antiq. Soc.*, volume 71, 1961, pp. 152–9.

F. M. Trotter, 'The Lancashire coalfield', chapter 10 in A. E. Trueman (ed.), *The Coalfields of Great Britain*, Edward

Arnold, London, 1954, pp. 199–21.

Wigan Metropolitan Borough Museums Service, *The History and Development of the Wigan Coalfield*, n.d.

GLASS

T. C. Barker, *The Glassmakers. Pilkingtons: the Rise of an International Company, 1826–1976*, Weidenfeld & Nicolson, 1977.

T. C. Barker and J. R. Harris, *A Merseyside Town in the Industrial Revolution: St. Helens, 1750–1900*, Liverpool University Press, 1954.

J. R. Harris, 'Origins of the St Helens glass industry', *Northern History*, volume 3, 1968, pp. 105–17.

SALT

A. F. Calvert, *Salt in Cheshire*, 2 volumes, London, 1915.

W. H. Chaloner, 'Salt in Cheshire, 1600–1780', *Trans. Lancs. & Ches. Antiq. Soc.*, volume 71, 1961, pp. 58–74.

Cheshire County Council, *Salt: a Policy for Extraction*, 1969.

ICI Ltd, *The Story of Salt*, ICI Mond Division.

Mary Rochester, *Salt in Cheshire: Part 1, Salt Making; Part 2, Salt Mining; Part 3, Transport*, resource unit with slides, Cheshire Libraries and Museums, 1975.

Robert Taylor, 'The coastal salt industry of Amounderness', *Trans. Lancs. & Ches. Antiq. Soc.*, volume 78, 1975, pp. 14–21.

K. L. Wallwork, 'The mid-Cheshire salt industry', *Geography*, volume 44, July 1959, pp. 171–86.

SOAP AND CHEMICALS

D. W. F. Hardie, *A History of the Chemical Industry in Widnes*, ICI Ltd, General Chemicals division, 1950.

A. E. Musson, *Enterprise in Soap and Chemicals* (history of Joseph Crosfield & Sons of Warrington), Manchester University Press, 1965.

W. J. Reader, *Imperial Chemical Industries: a History*, 2 volumes, Oxford University Press, London, 1970–5.

Charles Wilson, *The History of Unilever: a Study in Economic Growth and Social Change*, 2 volumes, Cassell, London, 1954.

PAPER

D. C. Coleman, *The British Paper Industry, 1495–1860*, Clarendon Press, Oxford, 1958.

R. Sharpe France, 'Early paper mills in Lancashire', *Paper Making and Paper Selling*, volume 66, 1943.

B. P. Hindle, 'The paper-making industry of Bury and Radcliffe', *The Paper Maker*, July and August 1969.

A. H. Shorter, *Paper Mills and Paper Makers in England, 1495–1800*, Paper Publishing Society, Holland, 1957; *Paper Making in the British Isles*, David & Charles, Newton Abbot, 1971.

A. V. Sugden and E. A. Entwistle, *Potters of Darwen, 1839–1939*, 1939.

Martin Tillmans, *Bridge Hall Mills: Three Centuries of Paper and Cellulose Film Manufacture*, Crompton Press, Salisbury, 1978.

HAT-MAKING

Phyllis M. Giles, 'The felt-hatting industry, c. 1560–1850, with particular reference to Lancashire and Cheshire', *Trans. Lancs. & Ches. Antiq. Soc.*, volume 69, 1959, pp. 104–32.

J. H. Smith, 'Felt hatting', in J. H. Smith (ed.), *The Great Human Exploit*, Phillimore, Chichester, 1973.

CORN MILLING

E. Mitford Abraham, 'The old flour mills of Wirral', *Trans. Hist. Soc. Lancs. & Ches.*, volume 55, 1903, pp. 133–149.

R. Bennett and J. Elton, *History of Corn Milling*, 4 volumes, 1898–1904. (Volume 2 on windmills and watermills reprinted by E.P. Publishing Co., Wakefield, 1973.)

Allen Clarke, *Windmill Land*, 1932.

J. H. Norris, 'The water-powered corn mills of Cheshire', *Trans. Lancs. & Ches. Antiq. Soc.*, volume 75/76, 1966, pp. 33–71.

Rex Wailes, *The English Windmill*, Routledge & Kegan Paul, London, 1954.

Hazel Williams and John Crompton, 'The windmills of Wirral', *Journal of North Western Society for Industrial Archaeology and History*, 1976, pp. 12–18.

ROADS

F. A. Bailey, 'The Minutes of the Trustees of the Turnpike Roads from Liverpool to Prescot, St Helens, Warrington and Ashton-in-Makerfield', *Trans. Hist. Soc. Lancs. & Ches.*, volume 88, pp. 159–200; volume 89, pp. 31–90.

Bernard Barnes, *Passage through Time*, 1980.

W. B. Crump, 'Saltways from the Cheshire wiches', *Trans. Lancs. & Ches. Antiq. Soc.*, volume 54, 1939, pp. 84–142.

William Harrison, 'Pre-turnpike highways in Lancashire and Cheshire', *Trans. Lancs. & Ches. Antiq. Soc.*, volume 9, 1891, pp. 101–34; 'The development of the turnpike system in Lancashire and Cheshire', *Trans. Lancs. & Ches. Antiq. Soc.*, volume 4, 1886, pp. 80–92 (list of turnpikes in volume 10, 1892, pp. 237–48); 'Ancient fords, ferries and bridges in Lancashire', *Trans. Lancs. & Ches. Antiq. Soc.*, volume 12, 1894, pp. 1–29; volume 13, 1895, pp. 74–102.

G. H. Tupling, 'The turnpike trusts of Lancashire', *Memoirs and Proceedings of Manchester Lit. and Phil. Soc.*, volume 94, 1952–53, pp. 1–23.

RIVERS AND CANALS

T. C. Barker, 'The Sankey Canal', *Trans. Hist. Soc. Lancs. & Ches.*, volume 100, 1948, pp. 121–35.

Gordon Biddle, *Pennine Waterway* (Leeds & Liverpool Canal), Dalesman Books, Clapham, Lancs., 1979.

H. Clegg, 'The third Duke of Bridgewater's canal works in Manchester', *Trans. Lancs. & Ches. Antiq. Soc.*, volume 65, 1955, pp. 91–103.

J. Corbett, *The River Irwell*, 1907, reprinted E. J. Morten, idsbury, Manchester, 1974.

D. A. Farnie, *The Manchester Ship Canal and the Rise of the Port of Manchester, 1894–1975*, Manchester University Press, 1980.

Charles Hadfield, *The Canals of the West Midlands*, David & Charles, Newton Abbot, 1960.

Charles Hadfield and Gordon Biddle, *The Canals of North West England*, 2 volumes, David & Charles, Newton Abbot, 1970.

Peter Lead, *The Trent and Mersey Canal*, Moorland Publishing Co., Ashbourne, 1979.

Sir Bosdin Leech, *History of the Manchester Ship Canal*, 2 volumes, Sherratt & Hughes, Manchester, 1907.

Hugh Malet, *Bridgewater: the Canal Duke, 1736–1803*, Manchester University Press, 1977.

Frank Mullineux, *The Duke of Bridgewater's Canal*, Eccles & District History Society, 1959.

D. E. Owen, *Canals to Manchester*, Manchester University Press, 1977.

V. I. Tomlinson, 'Early warehouses on Manchester waterways', *Trans. Lancs. & Ches. Antiq. Soc.*, volume 71, 1961, pp. 129–51; 'The Manchester Bolton & Bury Canal, Navigation and Railway Company, part 1, The canal', *Trans. Lancs. & Ches. Antiq. Soc.*, volume 75/76, 1969, pp. 231–99.

T. S. Willan, *River Navigation in England, 1600–1750*, Oxford University Press, London, 1936, reprinted Cass, London, 1964; *The Navigation of the River Weaver in the Eighteenth Century*, Chetham Society, Third Series, volume 3, Manchester, 1951.

RAILWAYS

Lois Basnett, 'The history of the Bolton & Leigh Railway, based on the Hulton papers, 1824–8', *Trans. Lancs. & Ches. Antiq. Soc., volume 62, 1952, pp. 157–76*.

C. O. Box, *The Liverpool Overhead Railway, 1893–1956*, Railway World, London, 1962.

Robert E. Carlson, *The Liverpool and Manchester Railway Project, 1821–31*, David & Charles, Newton Abbot, 1969.

W. H. Chaloner, *The Social and Economic Development of Crewe, 1780–1923*, Manchester University Press, 1950, reprinted 1973.

F. Dixon, *The Manchester, South Junction & Altrincham Railway*, Oakwood Press, Blandford Forum, 1973.

G. Dow, *Great Central*, 3 volumes, Locomotive Publishing Co., Shepperton, 1960–66.

R. S. Fitzgerald, *Liverpool Road Station, Manchester: an Historical and Architectural Survey*, Royal Commission on Historical Monuments, Manchester University Press, 1980.

M. D. Greville, *Chronological List of the Railways of Lancashire; Chronological List of the Railways of Cheshire*, Railway and Canal Historical Society, 1973.

M. D. Greville and G. O. Holt, *The Lancaster & Preston Junction Railway*, David & Charles, Dawlish, 1961.

William Harrison, *History of the Manchester Railways*, 1882, reprinted with introduction by W. H. Chaloner, Lancs. & Ches.

Antiq. Soc., 1967.

R. P. Griffiths, *The Cheshire Lines Railway*, Oakwood Press, Blandford Forum, 1947, reprinted 1958.

H. J. Hewitt, *The Building of the Railways in Cheshire down to 1860*, E. J. Morten, Didsbury, Manchester, 1972.

G. O. Holt, *A Regional History of the Railways of Great Britain*, volume 10, *The North West*, David & Charles, Newton Abbot, 1978; *A Short History of the Liverpool & Manchester Railway*, Railway & Canal Historical Society, 1955.

John R. Kellett, *Railways and Victorian Cities*, Routledge & Kegan Paul, London, 1979.

John Marshall, *The Lancashire & Yorkshire Railway*, 3 volumes, David & Charles, Newton Abbot, 1969–72.

A. J. Pacey, 'Technical innovations in some late nineteenth century railway warehouses', *Industrial Archaeology*, volume 5, No. 4, November 1968, pp. 364–72.

Norman Parker, *The Preston & Longridge Railway*, Oakwood Press, Blandford Forum, 1972.

G. W. Parkin, *The Mersey Railway*, Oakwood Press, Blandford Forum, 1966.

B. Roberts, *Railways and Mineral Tramways of Rossendale*, Oakwood Press, Blandford Forum, 1974.

R. W. Rush and M. R. Connor Price, *The Garstang & Knott End Railway*, Oak-wood Press, Blandford Forum, 1964.

David Singleton, *The Liverpool & Manchester Railway*, Dalesman Books, Clapham, Lancs., 1975.

W. D. Tattersall, *The Bolton, Blackburn, Clitheroe & West Yorkshire Railway*, Oakwood Press, Blandford Forum, 1973.

R. H. G. Thomas, *The Liverpool & Manchester Railway*, Batsford, London, 1979.

PORTS AND HARBOURS

James Barron, *A History of the Ribble Navigation from Preston to the Sea*, Corporation of Preston, 1938.

J. Q. Hughes, *Seaport: Architecture and Townscape in Liverpool*, Lund Humphries, London, 1964; 'Dock warehouses at Liverpool', *Architectural History*, volume 4, 1961, pp. 106–16.

F. M. Jones, 'Liverpool dock buildings as historical evidence', *Trans. Hist. Soc. Lancs. & Ches.*, volume 118, 1967, pp. 87–104.

C. N. Parkinson, *Rise of the Port of Liverpool*, Liverpool University Press, 1952.

J. Picton, *Memorials of Liverpool*, 2 volumes, London, 1875. (Valuable account of Dock Estate.)

J. Porter, *History of the Fylde in Lancashire*, Fleetwood and Blackpool, 1876.

M. M. Schofield, *Outlines of an Economic History of Lancaster from 1680 to 1860*, Lancaster, 1951.

Subject index